THE COMPLETE BOOK OF YACHT CARE

— SECOND EDITION —

Michael Verney

Adlard Coles Nautical
London

This edition published in 1993 by
Adlard Coles Nautical
an imprint of A & C Black (Publishers) Ltd
35 Bedford Row, London WC1R 4JH

First edition published by
Adlard Coles Ltd 1986

Second edition published by
Adlard Coles Nautical 1993

ISBN 0–7136–3773–0

A CIP Catalogue record for this book is
available from the British Library.

Typeset in 9 on 11pt Century Schoolbook by August
Fiimsetting, Haydock, St Helens

Printed and bound in Great Britain by
The Bath Press

By the same author
Complete Amateur Boat Building (4th edition),
Adlard Coles Nautical

Contents

Tables

Preface

This book is dedicated to that grand breed of people of all ages who find pleasure, relaxation and fascination in going afloat – on sea, lake or river – in almost any type of vessel from a sailing dinghy to an ocean racer.

Only a small proportion of these happy people are boat owners. Crews and guests are more likely to be invited aboard if they know something about yacht care. This applies equally to the many families who take an annual bare-boat charter in some yachting paradise.

Yacht care means more than just cleaning, painting and oiling. It starts with choosing the right type of boat. Then, everyone afloat needs to know enough about seamanship, dinghy work, etiquette, mooring and engines to ensure safety, avoid breakdowns, minimize wear and tear, and to show consideration to others. Professional craftsmen are not usually to be found at sea, or up a quiet creek.

What everything costs when it comes to boat maintenance is detailed here for the first time. Established owners thinking of changing boat need this information, as do all newcomers.

Costs are given for both sides of the Atlantic Ocean. They are actual costs and bear little relationship to the official rates of exchange. Annual inflation figures are widely published, and are easy to apply to bring these 1993 costs up to date as time goes by. All dimensions here are given in both metric and American units.

The great differences in cost revealed between amateur and professional work will give encouragement to all do-it-yourself boating enthusiasts!

Michael Verney

1
Practical Ownership

Depending on the family situation, most people start boating with a sailboard, dinghy or small powerboat. Before buying a sailing dinghy, it pays to join a yacht club and choose one of the class boats they have adopted, as this will enable racing to be enjoyed to the full. Popular small powerboats include scooters, hovercraft, and runabouts, but remember that these are designed for high speed, rendering them unsuitable for most inland waters where a speed limit is imposed. Generally, water skis can only be used safely a good distance offshore, or within allotted areas of certain lakes and bays.

The right cruiser

Not all families enjoy big-boat cruising, so test this by arranging crewing sessions with others before embarking on ownership. You need to be very tough to cope with ocean racing in all weathers, while many people find discomfort in the heeling of a sailing cruiser or in the pounding and rolling of a powerboat. When there are at least twenty basic styles of cruiser to choose from, these crewing test sessions help to steer you towards the right choice.

Choices
The wind is free, so a high performance sailboat solves the fuel cost problem as well as the noise problem. A catamaran, or trimaran, additionally solves the heeling problem. It is normally only the largest power cruisers that have stabilizers. Many of the smaller ones are equipped for fishing; this adds

an extra dimension to powerboat cruising. The motorsailer or 50/50 (see later in this chapter) tries its best to combine the advantages of both sail and power. It forms the most popular configuration for family use today.

Moorings
Vast numbers of cruising boats are used as holiday homes and rarely leave their moorings. Unless trailable, a newly acquired boat must be assured of a mooring, and in some locations this is far from easy to arrange. A marina, although costly, is often the best bet. At many of these the smaller boats are stored on shore and launched when needed by a mobile hoist (see Plate 1).

The cheapest moorings in tidal waters dry out at low tide. To make use of these, you need the shoal draft of a beamy powerboat, or a sailing cruiser of catamaran, bilge-keel or drop-keel form.

Syndicates
By forming a partnership, all boating costs drop dramatically. This works fine with partners who sail together and share the chores, but difficulties often arise when two families each allot themselves certain periods afloat throughout the season. Also, if one partner wishes to sell his or her share, it may be impossible to find a replacement.

Old and cheap
Owners and crew who undertake all maintenance work themselves gain greatly increased satisfaction from boating compared with their unpractical

1

Plate 1 Drott Travelift shifting an outdrive cruiser on dockside.

counterparts. A new boat may need little maintenance work for several years, but the enthusiast who is not afraid of work will often be able to enjoy his hobby with an older boat obtained at less than half the initial outlay.

Character

Among the rows of modern bathtubs, an old yacht with character often stands out attractively. Practical owners become very attached to such relics. However, before sealing the bargain, get the old-timer surveyed and make sure you are going to have sufficient leisure to handle the upkeep work. An old class racing yacht converted for cruising has tremendous character and can produce exciting sailing at low cost with infrequent need for the help of an engine.

Choice of engine

An outboard motor makes a passable auxiliary engine for converted racing yachts or for trailer-sailers and similar small cruisers. An inboard engine is far more convenient, and raises the value of such a boat. However, it does occupy valuable space on board. Inboards using gasoline or petrol are frowned upon nowadays as fire hazards, and diesel-engined boats command a higher price. An engineering-minded owner can make sure there is no risk, and take advantage of the price differential.

Small diesels
Although a diesel engine is the cheapest type to run, fuel cost is not a critical consideration for auxiliary use. Outboard motors are often the thirstiest of all, using up to twice the fuel of an equivalent diesel. Those who are allergic to noisy boats generally avoid diesels – especially the air-cooled variety.

Power economy
With cruising powerboats the situation changes somewhat, as fuel costs become the main consideration. For racing powerboats, the light weight of gasoline motors is often preferred, but such craft are generally sponsored by companies, or owned by wealthy individuals or syndicates.

Extra speed

Each extra knot of speed on the water is dearly paid for. As a result of escalating fuel costs since 1975, the vogue for high-speed power cruisers (Plate 2) has diminished greatly and there is a lot more sail about. However, deep-sea fishing cruisers (Plate 3) still need a good turn of speed in many localities in order to reach distant fishing grounds and get back in time for dinner. The type of cruiser shown in Plate 4 often has one-quarter the value of the type shown in Plate 2.

Plate 2 Big twin-screw diesel yacht of modern design.

Plate 3 Sea fishing cruiser. The flying bridge provides the helmsman with a good view.

Plate 4 Old style motor yacht. Low value with plenty of character.

Less draft

Although most modern powerboats have shoal draft and can make use of half-tide moorings, remember that many of them have twin propellers which are vulnerable to damage if the boat should settle on hard ground. Craft with single or twin stern-drive (outdrive) propulsion, as seen in Plate 5, have a big advantage here, as the drive units can be tilted up. Furthermore, such boats have no rudders. Although outboard-engined cruisers have the same advantage, they are not normally diesels, and when left in position at isolated moorings they are vulnerable to theft.

Motorsailers

Because of propeller drag and a compromise in draft, a motorsailer (Plate 6) cannot be expected to match the sailing performance of an ocean racer. She can rival a medium speed motor yacht under power, especially in lengths above 33 ft (10 m), and will be more comfortable, with the steadying influence of sail. Examples built prior to around 1960 tend to be under-canvased and under-engined. Family owners often use more motor than sail, but a combination of the two can produce attractive fuel economy.

Plate 5 Twin outdrives. One leg tilted clear of water.

Plate 6 Motorsailers lying to swinging moorings.

Racing types

Beware of certain features on modern sailing cruisers which have been copied from ocean racers. Such craft are fast and point high, but they can be uncomfortable, especially if overloaded. Some have retroussé sterns (Plate 7) which prove expensive and dangerous if damaged, and narrow foredecks with minimal sunbathing space.

Multihulls

Large catamarans (Plate 8) make good, stable cruising boats but the extra weight associated with luxury living tends to dull their sailing performance considerably.

Weight is an even more critical factor with trimarans. Their extreme beam creates mooring problems, though the swing/wing type (Plate 9) has side floats which retract close to the main hull.

Capsize

Stories about multihulls capsizing 180° do not help the cruising owner to sleep soundly! The Henderson masthead flotation pod (Plate 10) and various self-righting devices have been developed to cope with such an emergency, and some boats have escape hatches through the bottom of each hull. However, only the most extreme weather conditions would normally cause a well-proven cruising catamaran to capsize.

Plate 7 A retroussé stern. Developed to reduce after deck weight in racing yachts. Restricts space in a cruiser and is vulnerable to expensive damage.

Plate 8 A cruising catamaran is fast without heeling uncomfortably in strong winds.

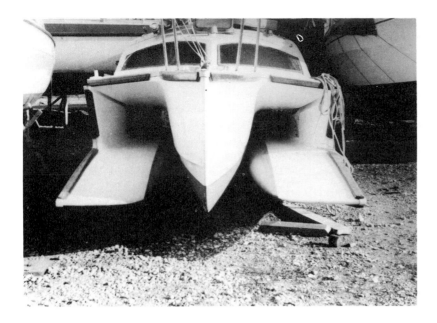

Plate 9 The 'swing-wing' trimaran has folding outrigger beams for convenience when moored or transported.

Plate 10 Mast flotation pod prevents a capsized multihull from floating upside down.

What materials?

Not only do the size, type and age of a boat affect the value and the maintenance costs, but the sorts of materials used for hull and superstructure also confuse the issue.

Popular trend

The largest yachts are usually built of steel, and always have been. In the medium sizes, plastics, light alloy, and ferrocement are rivals. Wood predominates in the older boats and is also used for modern one-off designs (especially ocean racers) utilizing the cold moulded or WEST systems.

Due to the increasing use of exotic materials instead of glass strands, the ever-popular fibreglass is now called FRP – fibre reinforced plastic. This is the easiest hull material to maintain, particularly inside. Keeping older topsides smart is always a problem and you need to watch out for the dreaded boat pox, osmosis blisters.

Small fry

Although plywood and hot or cold moulded dinghies still abound, you would have a job to buy a new one in any material other than plastics nowadays. The same conditions governing value and maintenance as mentioned above apply for popular cruisers. In all classes, light alloy masts and spars are always easier to maintain than the older types of varnished wood.

Specials
Hulls of cupro-nickel alloy, stainless steel, Kevlar or carbon fibre laminates are superbly durable, but generally command high prices. Large craft of considerable age are often of *composite* construction, with hardwood planking on steel frames. Many are already past their intended life span, but repair is not usually too difficult. A ferrocement hull which is still perfect (i.e. no core rust) when ten years old is likely to remain that way indefinitely if kept properly painted.

Finish

Combined with the above variations in the type, value and maintenance requirements for different sorts of craft, the matter of surface finish quality adds a further dimension to your choice of yacht.

Categories
Finish quality falls basically into three categories:

A   Absolute perfection. The boat appears virtually like brand new at all times.
B   Well-cared-for. All parts well preserved. Smart appearance early in the season.
C   Workboat fashion. Paint instead of varnish. Often kept in commission all year round.

Most yachts fall into category B. As long as the preservation jobs are not ignored, there is little point in the impecunious amateur trying to upgrade his boat from B to A. Some maintenance enthusiasts (who do little sailing) derive great satisfaction from doing just that, or even upgrading from C to B.

Worries
Owning a boat in category A is not always good for the nervous system. Unless you are sufficiently wealthy to ignore large insurance premiums and the cost of a safe berth in tideless water with a watchman constantly on duty, much agony can be created by watching a jewel of a ship being battered by beginners in hired boats, or suffering from the stains of oil-polluted waters.

Minimum
The category C owner avoids such cares. He is perhaps the happiest fellow afloat. She may not

sparkle, but his ship might still be fast, weatherly, and reliable. The only time the owner's joy may be stifled is when coming alongside a category A yacht for a well-earned night in a strange port!

Comparison
On shore, cars fit into similar categories. The owner of an expensive new car lives in fear of the first mysterious dent in a parking lot. His carefree pal with a ten-year-old model probably pays one-third as much in insurance premiums, but the older car could well be sound, smooth and reliable.

Boat care economy

The main purposes of annual fitting-out are to ensure that every item of gear is reliable, that all materials liable to deteriorate are preserved for the ensuing year, and that a well-cared-for appearance is given to the whole ship.

Performance
Irrespective of damage, few materials are permanent. Fibreglass can develop disastrous osmosis blisters (see page 247), ferrocement can spall and reveal its armature, while light alloy is subject to galvanic action (see Chapter 10). In all cases, painting and varnishing are sure to be necessary unless a yacht is allowed to drift from category A to B, or from B to C. Underwater maintenance is similar for nearly all types of construction.

Expense
The effort of maintaining a category C boat is minimal, but numerous owners would like to know how to keep a category B appearance with the same low expenditure of time and money. The first obstacle to this goal is, perhaps, adherence to the traditional idea (in Britain, Canada and large parts of the USA) of commencing fitting-out work as soon as spring comes around.

Seasons
The in-commission period for most yacht insurance policies runs from April to September inclusive, though extensions or variations are easily arranged. Conditions are rarely suitable for working out of doors in the above climates before the middle of March, which leaves little time in which to get all the painting and varnishing done. This means that many owners are forced to use hired help in order to get afloat in reasonable time.

Do-it-yourself

The most important rule for cutting costs is to restrict all the routine fitting-out work to owner, family and friends. To give yourself time, complete most of the painting and varnishing in October or November, when the weather is usually far more suitable than in February and March. However, should the bilges need painting, this must be done in late winter and spring to ensure complete drying out. Try to get engine overhauls and similar mechanical work done during the winter.

Autumn start

Even if you need to apply a final coat in the spring, the donkey work of scraping and sanding can still be done in the autumn. With a boat under cover or well protected outside, little deterioration of a final gloss should occur. Remember that newly applied paint is soon marred by the contact of fenders and ropes, while cheap deck paint needs several weeks of hardening to avoid permanent dirty footprints.

Smells below

You may be able to find effective paint additives to reduce the lingering smell which so often pervades newly painted cabins and makes some people feel ill. Another good reason for completing such work in the autumn. However, some owners like to leave a certain amount of inside paintwork to do while on moorings during inclement summer weather. Certainly, there might then be less condensation than at any other time of year.

Cover chafe

Dust sheets in a boatshed save hours of work when sanding is going on. Tarpaulins in the open air (see page 251) can cause chafing if not tended diligently. Fibreglass is especially prone to damage in this way.

Antifouling cost

Bottom treatment for salt water may cost more than any other fitting-out process – see page 58. An owner able to afford a marina berth can drive the boat into a floating bag in which a tiny dose of chemical keeps all fouling at bay. Most yacht fouling occurs while docked. Because weed growth is slower early in the season, cheap antifouling paint applied in June will often last through the major sailing months.

Boottop time

Nearly all category A yachts have a brightly painted boottop stripe around the waterline. Category C vessels eliminate this expense by expanding the antifouling to upper boottop level. There is no reason why the category B boat should not copy this idea. Red antifouling often looks best in this position. It requires little more frequent wiping than a normal boottop to keep it looking bright.

Worst weed

As weed grows most prolifically close to the waterline where the light is strongest and the water is warmest, scrubbing off the worst of it is simple if you heel the boat over a few degrees by using a halyard from the masthead as a tackle, made fast to a suitable anchorage on shore. When working from the dinghy, you need a *guest warp* (see page 253) to hold her close to the hull. If the exposed strip is antifouled after scrubbing and rinsing, this could postpone considerably the need for complete bottom treatment.

Smartness

Some short cuts to economy can actually make a boat look smarter. For instance, blemished wood on varnished masts and spars not only looks better coated with pale grey or buff paint, but this also proves cheaper than planing down to fresh wood and applying numerous coats of varnish. Note that, if the planing process has been undertaken several times previously, a spar could become seriously weakened.

Weathered

Much the same applies to coamings and other brightwork. Teak can nearly always be brought back like new by hard sanding after stripping the varnish. However, any type of mahogany (often used for its cheapness compared with teak) stains indelibly should dampness get underneath the varnish for a few months. An expert restorer can hide this by bleaching and then staining the whole area to a darker shade, but when the defects are extensive, the amateur is best advised to resort to a painted finish.

Relief

Never dispense with all varnishwork except on a category C boat. It breaks the monotony of large expanses of paintwork, whose effect is all too apparent on certain small fibreglass boats which are nicknamed floating bathtubs! Hatches, handrails, and small areas of trim are easy to keep in good condition when varnished, so these should be retained.

Freeboard

To make the interior spacious, many a yacht has excessive freeboard, or an unusually high deck superstructure. The unsightly appearance of such expanses can be greatly improved by adding bands of contrasting paint at top and bottom. A high boottop and a varnished rubbing strake just below the sheer (Plate 11) will assist topsides in this respect. To mask high varnished cabin trunk coamings, use deck and cabin top paint of a contrasting shade, and let these lap over the coamings, as in Plate 12.

Gold leaf

Cutting costs is all very well, but a pretty boat deserves some decoration. If she has a coved (hollow) line just below the sheer, this is intended to house a stripe of gold leaf (see Chapter 4), though bright paint may be used instead. Proper gold leaf is a colossal price, but relatively cheap self-adhesive gold tape is stocked by the larger marine stores, and this looks pretty good from a distance. Scrolls and nameboards use very little gold leaf in comparison with coved lines, and provide an easy method of adding decoration. Psychedelic stripes all over the topsides may suit certain types of craft!

Cutting coves

Without a cove to protect it, gold leaf or tape soon gets damaged. On a planked hull a cove line may be added by lightly nailing a temporary batten in the desired position, and then running a moulding plane

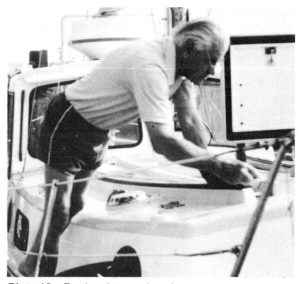

Plate 12 Deck paint overlapping a high cabin trunk reduces the apparent height.

along it. This cannot be done on a fibreglass, metal or ferrocement hull, so a painted line is used instead, applied between two strips of masking tape. To avoid waviness, take frequent measurements from the deck edge or sheer with a pair of dividers. Peel off masking tape as soon as possible, otherwise it could disturb recently applied topside enamel.

Ragged edges

Smartness is easily marred by ragged edges left when striking-in deck paint along varnish parts (or where any contrasting shades meet), but the worst defects are readily rectified by using a small artist's brush. Paint to match any shade of varnishwork is easily mixed, as described on page 57.

Plate 11 Bands of contrasting paint lessen the unsightliness of high freeboard.

Paint shield

Anyone with a shaky hand or in too much of a hurry is recommended to use one of those handyman sheet metal shields (see also page 37), as this avoids the need for care when cutting in along an edge (see Plate 13). However, for best results, you must wipe the shield's tip with a piece of rag each time you shift it along. If inexperienced helpers are mustered to help out with the deck painting, it pays to run masking tape along the edges instead of issuing painting shields!

Galvanized parts

Most category C boats (and some of the older breed in category B) will have galvanized deck and mast fittings. To add smartness, pick these out in bright aluminium paint – particularly such items as guard-rail stanchions, pulpit, tabernacle, rigging screws (turnbuckles), windlass, ventilators and fairleads. If you dislike the look of this, any desired gloss paint will do; white often looks pleasing. If any rust streaks appear later (especially noticeable with white paint) just go over the offending parts again.

Touching up

This is where the 'Stitch in Time' proverb pays off. If any small areas of surface damage to wood are rapidly touched up with the appropriate paint or varnish, moisture will not cause stains and jeopardize the adhesion of larger areas. The same applies to rust stains on a steel boat, or below the chain plates on a hull of any material.

Summer moments

Boat work is so much more pleasant in summer than when the snow is falling, that it seems a pity that more owners do not forgo a bit of sailing to keep their dream ships in good trim. Chances arise when one cannot find a suitable crew, or when a strong blow is forecast. In this way a yacht can be made to look her best at mid-season (perhaps ready for the annual vacations), while at laying-up time she will be little shabbier than when launched.

Accommodation

It would be simple to classify the interiors of most cruising boats as of A, B or C quality. Some mass-produced cruisers have very poor plywood joinerwork below decks. The handyman who enjoys a bit of furniture-making can happily renew the whole of this, piece by piece, producing a category A effect throughout the accommodation, which is always a great pleasure to live with.

Plate 13 A paint shield prevents ragged lines and eliminates the need for masking tape.

What will it cost?

At the onset of the fibreglass era, boat buyers were led to believe that this new material would need no maintenance except for an occasional wash down. If appearance is unimportant and the high cost of treating osmosis blisters can be avoided, the original prophecy is largely correct. However, the usual need for antifouling, and smart topsides, plus a fair amount of varnished teak, brings the maintenance costs closer to those for traditional hulls.

Useful figures

Table 1 gives a summary of the annual cost of owning seventeen different craft between 13 ft (4 m) and 60 ft (18 m) in length. Costs vary greatly from boatyard to boatyard and from coast to coast, but the prices shown were average ones in Britain and the USA in 1993. As mentioned in the Preface, the comparisons between pounds sterling and dollars in this context often do not tally with the official rate of exchange.

Repairs

The costs in Table 1 do not include for any repair work. With a little luck this can be avoided, and accident damage should mainly be covered by insurance. To hire skilled craftsmen is often very expensive and the handy amateur can reduce his boat repair costs greatly by following the instructions given in *Boat Repairs and Conversions*.

Equipment

The cost of complete electronic equipment below decks, coupled with that of sails, rigging and fittings, can easily exceed the cost of the basic hull on a cruising yacht or ocean racer. Old-fashioned equipment often suits the impecunious owner better, though perhaps demanding the expenditure of more time over maintenance. Below 33 ft (10 m) one can cut these costs by 30% with galvanized steel, commercial blocks, no winches or GPS, tiller steering, hand starting, trailing log and no batteries.

Capital cost

When taking into consideration the interest charges on the high capital costs of modern yachts, the owners of equivalent old-fashioned boats can still be in pocket even when any additional maintenance work is carried out by professionals.

Etiquette

It seems a pity that many more newcomers to cruising do not sail for a few seasons with experienced owners before forsaking racing dinghies for decked craft. Unlike the dinghy owner (who often pulls her ashore and departs with the burgee still flying) the cruiser owner who wishes to receive the approval of the local pundits should carry out a careful routine before leaving his ship.

Training

Most of the traditional etiquette concerning boats is coupled with common sense, safety, and the preservation of your own and other boats. When learning, it pays to make notes, and to refer to these until the routine, both under way and at moorings, becomes automatic. An important safety precaution is to train all crew members, however temporary, so that things do not fall apart should the skipper become incapacitated. Seamanship is a subject of its own which is closely tied to safety and etiquette, and ranges from keeping all ropes neatly coiled ready to run (and away from the walking areas on deck), to stowing everything in its rightful place or lashing it down to prevent loss.

Shipshape

When disembarking hurriedly, at least lower the ensign and burgee, adjust all mooring lines properly, lock the tiller or wheel amidships, fit the boom scissors or crutch when appropriate, tighten the mainsheet and slacken both topping lift and backstay tensioner.

Full treatment

When in no hurry, it can take up to one hour to leave a cruiser in shipshape order, especially when deck washing and cabin sole sweeping is indicated. There may be hatch, cockpit and sail covers to rig. There is sure to be much gear to take ashore (perhaps needing several trips in a dinghy), while in some locations a lightning conductor from the mast has to be coupled to a ground rod on shore (see page 209).

Noise

Frap your running rigging to the mast by winding a halyard fall around everything, or use gilguys of shockcord to the shrouds as in Plate 56. If you neglect this with a tinkling metal mast, do not be surprised if you find that it has been done for you by some guy in pyjamas trying to get to sleep on a nearby yacht! The rattles from internal halyards or wiring cannot be dealt with once a mast is stepped (see Chapter 6).

Seabirds

Having lowered the burgee, always hoist a short staff of dowelling or bamboo in its place to prevent seagulls from roosting on the masthead and fouling the deck. If they get on the spreaders, stretch a length of the thinnest shockcord from shroud to shroud about 4 in (100 mm) above the spreaders, passing for'ard of the mast.

All boats

A simpler mooring routine applies to powerboats and dinghies. In tidal waters, craft are normally moored with their bows facing upstream. In any case, orientate your own boat to conform with the local custom. When rafted alongside other boats, always run your own bow and stern lines direct to the quay, piles or buoys.

See Figs. 1 and 2 for the worst and best ways of going about it all.

Table 1

Typical annual upkeep costs in Britain and the USA (excluding tax)

Length and type of boat		Annual insurance (For 10-year-old boat)		Mooring (including port charges)							
				6 months		12 months obligatory					
				Ashore (including 20 launchings)		Half tide		Deep water		Marina	
		£	$	£	$	£	$	£	$	£	$
13 ft (4 m)	Runabout	40	100	150	200	100	250	—	—	—	—
14 ft (4·3 m)	Sailing dinghy	28	70	160	220	100	250	—	—	—	—
17 ft (5·2 m)	Launch	36	90	220	360	200	300	300	850	1200	1500
18 ft (5·5 m)	Sail dayboat	45	100	250	380	200	300	300	900	1200	1500
20 ft (6 m)	Outboard cruise	70	200	300	400	220	300	340	950	1500	1600
23 ft (7 m)	Aux. sloop	130	350	400	600	260	350	390	1000	1700	1800
25 ft (7.6 m)	Powerboat	200	500	600	900	280	400	430	1100	1900	2200
27 ft (8·2 m)	Catamaran	250	550	900	1200	400	900	550	1500	3000	3000
28 ft (8.5 m)	Family sloop	200	500	—	—	300	500	460	1200	2200	2400
30 ft (9·2 m)	Fast motoryacht	300	650	—	—	330	550	500	1300	2300	2600
32 ft (9·7 m)	Family sloop	260	600	—	—	350	600	550	1400	2500	2800
36 ft (11 m)	Motorsailer	330	700	—	—	400	700	600	1600	2700	3200
38 ft (11·6 m)	Trimaran	480	900	—	—	500	1200	700	2400	4000	4000
40 ft (12 m)	Sportfisher	500	1000	—	—	400	750	600	1800	3000	3600
45 ft (13·7 m)	Ocean racer	900	1600	—	—	—	—	700	2000	3400	4400
50 ft (15 m)	Schooner	700	1200	—	—	—	—	800	2200	3800	5000
60 ft (18 m)	Motoryacht	1100	2000	—	—	—	—	900	2400	4500	6000

Table 1

| Afloat | Six months' lay-up (Including hauling or cranage and mast storage) | | | | | | | | Amateur refit (Beached for antifouling) | | Boatyard refit (Hauled out for antifouling) | |
| | Under cover | | Open air | | Mud berth | | At home | | Minimum clean, wax, varnish. Prepare engine and rig (see also Tables 3 and 8) | | | |
	£	$	£	$	£	$	£	$	£	$	£	$
	250	500	100	200	—	—	20	30	30	60	200	500
	250	600	100	240	—	—	30	30	40	80	250	700
	400	1200	150	300	50	100	80	100	100	190	500	1300
	400	1800	160	350	50	100	80	120	100	190	600	1500
	700	2500	200	400	70	120	100	150	120	200	700	1600
	800	3500	300	450	80	150	200	300	160	300	1000	2300
	900	4000	400	550	100	200	200	300	160	300	1000	2300
	2000	9000	600	1800	200	400	—	—	250	450	1500	3500
	1000	5000	500	900	100	200	300	400	200	350	1200	2800
	1300	6000	550	1000	100	200	400	500	200	350	1200	2800
	1600	7000	600	1200	150	300	450	600	250	450	1500	3500
	2000	9000	700	1400	180	400	600	750	300	500	1800	4000
	4000	15,000	1000	3000	400	800	—	—	400	750	3000	6700
	3000	11,000	750	1700	250	500	600	800	350	600	2000	4500
	3600	12,000	800	2500	300	600	—	—	450	850	2800	6500
	4400	13,000	1000	3000	400	800	—	—	500	950	3000	7500
	5000	15,000	1200	4000	500	1000	—	—	600	1100	3500	8500

Included in charges for 12 months moorings afloat

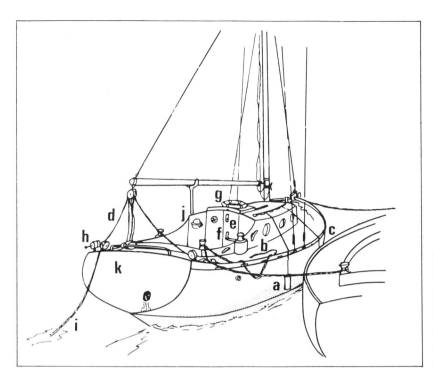

Fig. 1 Neglected boat. **a** fender too low and too small. **b** lines not coiled. **c** no springs rigged. **d** mainsheet slack. **e** hatch unlocked. **f** winch handle shipped. **g** lifebuoy left out. **h** taffrail log shipped. **i** stray line in water. **j** compass left out. **k** no nameplate.

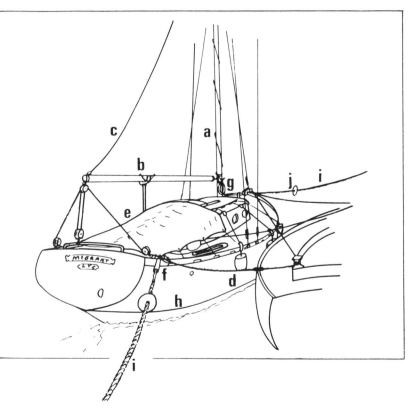

Fig. 2 Well kept boat. **a** halyards frapped. **b** boom crutch lashed. **c** topping lift slackened. **d** fenders big and high up. **e** cockpit cover rigged. **f** chafe pads on all lines. **g** rope tails coiled. **h** boottop clean. **i** shore lines rigged. **j** rat stoppers in place.

Springs

Diagonal lines (see Chapter 12) are essential under the above conditions to relieve the strain on the breast ropes, to ease the pressure on fenders and to keep the boat straight. Plastic tubing (Plate 14) makes ideal anti-chafe sleeving for all lines. Failing this, strips of old deck chair canvas wound around the rope and tied with twine at each end will suffice. Springs do not always pass through fairleads (chocks) and can easily chafe against rigging, guardrail stanchions and footrails.

Fendering

Keep a bow fender (Plate 111) on board for use when at anchor or when on a swinging mooring with chain bridle. This prevents the chain from scraping the topsides at slack tides or during wind-against-tide conditions. Ordinary hanging fenders must be cylindrical and of large diameter. (Tying three small ones together makes an emergency big one.) Square fenders (or old tyres wrapped with canvas) cannot roll with the movement of the ship and soon roughen glossy paint or fibreglass. Snatching all fenders inboard the moment you get under way is definitely the 'done thing'.

Loose gear

Only when actually in use should any item of deck gear be unlashed or unclipped. The chief culprits are boathook, mop, anchors, boarding ladder, lifebuoys, whisker poles, winch handles, and coiled ropes. Always make sure that no rope end trails overboard when you move off under power.

Rolling

The wash from inconsiderate passing craft can cause breakages below deck when proper stowage is not provided or used. Damage to spreaders and masthead equipment is not uncommon when two sailing

Plate 14 Plastic hose forms ideal anti-chafe protection around mooring lines.

craft are moored together, so leave adequate fore-and-aft drift when adjusting your springs.

Protection

Properly rigged cockpit, hatch, and skylight covers (Plate 15) show care for a vessel. They deter thieves, keep the boat dry, and protect the varnish. To ensure drainage, a cockpit cover needs a padded central ridge pole (or strongback) unless the for'ard end fixes high up on a pilothouse roof. Covers are easy to make (see Chapter 8) and their use can be extended with advantage to pilothouse, outboard motor, radar scanner and winches.

Remember that an inflated rubber dinghy on deck could be flipped overboard by a gust of wind if not properly tied down. Lifebuoys and winch handles are best stowed down below when a craft is left unattended.

Plate 15 Hatch covers deter thieves, reduce leaks and increase varnish life.

Flags

The somewhat complicated etiquette of flag flying is detailed in most of the nautical almanacs which cruising folk should carry on board. Doing the right thing is especially important when in foreign waters, but you cannot go far wrong if you avoid flying any flag at night, or when nobody is on board for most of the day. Few small craft carry all forty international code flags, but you will need them if you intend to dress a big boat overall for special occasions. Flag halyards must be kept taut to look shipshape. Flag material for deep sea cruising must be heavyweight nylon, not bunting. Stow flags rolled. Wash them after heavy use. Finally rinse in dilute phenol.

Cleaning

Any cruising boat needs a wash down (Plate 16) after being in sea spray. The old hands will tell you that wooden boat decks should be washed with sea water, not fresh. Fresh water leaks create rot below; sea water is a mild fungicide. However, fresh water is best for varnishwork, windows and portlights.

The chemicals made for house and car window cleaning work well on large wheelhouse windows. Note that most shore water supplies contain impurities which leave spots on topsides or brightwork when dried in the sun. To eliminate this, owners of large, category A yachts install a water softener (de-ionizer) on the dockside.

Jetsam

With so much overcrowding the traditional disposal of cooking waste overboard while at sea is now frowned upon. All rubbish should be taken ashore for disposal. If jars and bottles must be jettisoned at

Plate 16 'Start 'em young' is a good policy for deck swabbing.

sea, always fill them first to ensure that they sink. Never jettison plastic wrappers and similar items that float for ever.

Dinghy covers

Racing dinghy owners often fit their waterproof covers wrongly, allowing pools of rainwater to collect, as seen in Plate 17. This causes discoloration and puts a great strain on the eyelets. When using the boom as a ridge pole, always insert a sponge or other padding underneath where it rests on the deck, coamings, transom, or mainsheet track. (See also page 226.) Remember to lower the masthead flag when ashore, if only for the sake of its preservation.

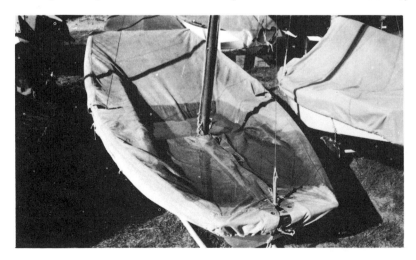

Plate 17 This is what happens when a dinghy cover has no ridge pole or halyard support.

Knock-down

When a gale blows, the windage on a dinghy's mast can roll her over and damage nearby boats. Old car tyres (tires) under the chine or the turn of the bilge will sometimes prevent this, but the only certain method is to lash the gunwales to driven stakes or heavy sandbags.

Tender sense

The care and etiquette of dinghies and tenders is covered in Chapter 11, including fendering, ensuring dry thwarts, safety equipment, and preventing theft of oars and rowlocks.

Identification

Having no name or other identification on a small boat may cause somebody unnecessary bother one day and therefore lacks etiquette. Runabouts are the worst culprits – often done purposely to avoid detection when breaking speed limits! Racing dinghy enthusiasts tend to rely on their sail numbers, but these are of little benefit in the case of theft or when a boat goes adrift and the sails are stored at home. Though useful to the coastguard, names in big letters on guardrail dodgers (see Plate 18) ruin the appearance of many a smart boat. Such dodgers were originally intended only for temporary use in rough weather. They limit visibility from a cockpit,

Plate 18   At one time rigged only in foul weather, permanent cockpit dodgers are now used as name boards. The reduced visibility is a hazard.

constituting a safety hazard. Transparent panels in them make any lettering undecipherable at certain angles. Making name-boards is described in Chapter 4.

Steps

A boarding ladder is essential for a high-sided vessel, and is traditionally rigged to starboard. Permanent emergency steps of some sort are a great safety feature. These are easy to contrive on most transom sterns, and folding ones are sold by chandlery stores. Even a simple notch cut into a transom-mounted rudder, as in Plate 19, may prove invaluable one day.

Thought

There is so much noise on shore that most boating people try to avoid taking it afloat with them. How about rowing the tender at night instead of using an outboard motor? Keep radio volume low when in port. Operate the generating plant when nearby crews are ashore, and eliminate the rattling of metal masts. If you are not equipped with proper deck shoes, slip off your shoes when stepping aboard a smart boat. When crossing the decks of boats rafted together, always steer yourself via each foredeck – stepping across the cockpit or via the after deck (especially when a boat is occupied) is considered bad manners.

Plate 19   A climbing step is simply devised on a transom hung rudder. It could save a life.

2
Tools and Materials

Although do-it-yourself house painting and repairs are commonly tackled by amateurs, the household tool-kit is often a disaster. It frequently includes saws red with rust, screwdrivers mangled by years of opening crates and cans of paint, pliers that have been kept out in the rain, a wire brush with bristles crumbling into dust, and congealed paint on brushes left in jam jars from which the water or solvent has long since evaporated.

Time out

Rarely used tools often need more attention than those in regular use. It pays to allow a little time after the completion of any job to clean, sharpen, oil and stow away all tools you have used. Few expensive tools are needed for routine boat maintenance, but additions to the range make excellent anniversary gifts for the practical owner, who can keep adding to the kit year after year.

Basic tools

A primary kit usually includes the following items:

(1) Good quality paint brushes of widths ½ in (12 mm), 1½ in (38 mm), and 2½ in (63 mm).
(2) A 1 lb (450 g) claw hammer.
(3) A wallet containing a few punches (nail sets) and a small cold chisel.
(4) A pair of pliers with wire cutting jaws.

(5) Cabinet screwdriver with ¼ in (6 mm) wide tip.
(6) An 8 in (200 mm) smooth flat file with handle.
(7) A 6 ft (2 m) tape rule.
(8) A small hacksaw.
(9) A replaceable hook scraper, bradawl, pair of scissors, putty knife, long-handled scrubber, and a cork sanding block.
(10) For a steel hull, a chipping hammer and wire brushes.

Augmenting
If you intend to burn off paint, caulk seams, or carry out alterations or additions to the joinerwork (or to the deck and rigging fittings), you will need a decent carpentry tool-kit which includes a plane or shaper, panel saw, hand drill, ratchet brace, back saw, sets of chisels and drills, a mallet, toolbag, clamps, pincers, oilstone, oilcan, marking gauge, try-square, spirit level, caulking irons, a blow-torch and a stripping knife.

For engines
Some new marine engines arrive with a useful selection of tools to cater for normal running adjustments and minor repairs. In any case, the minimum contents of an engine tool-kit should consist of:

(1) Wrenches of open-ended and box type to fit all nuts and bolts on the engine, including spark plugs.

(2) One small and one large adjustable crescent wrench.

(3) Three screwdrivers – 3/16 in (4 mm) tip, 5/16 in (7 mm) tip, medium Phillips.

(4) A 1½ lb (680 g) ball-pein hammer.

(5) A few pin punches, a centre punch, and some bits of brass bar to act as drifts.

(6) Feeler gauges and all small tools to deal with electrics, carburettors, and instruments.

(7) Long-nose pliers, as well as a standard pair.

(8) A full oilcan, some graphite grease, jointing compound and an old dentist's mirror.

Plate 20 shows a tool-kit such as this, as used by the author for many years.

(9) One or two bearing scrapers. Small and large Phillips screwdrivers.

(10) Equipment for soft and silver soldering.

(11) A 12 in (300 mm) steel rule, to serve also as a straight-edge.

(12) A valve lifter, a valve rotating tool, and a supply of coarse and fine grinding paste.

(13) To extend your drilling range, a 2-speed breast drill with a full set of twist drills, and a small can of cutting compound.

(14) A small roll of 1 in (25 mm) wide emery tape, fine grade.

(15) If not already in the bosun's locker, two wire brushes, one 2-row and one 4-row.

(16) A 10 in (250 mm) hacksaw with several coarse

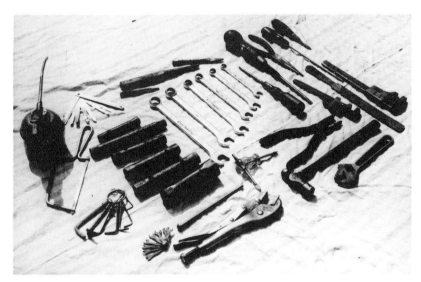

Plate 20 The usual wrenches, screwdrivers and pliers need augmenting with other small hand tools to make a basic engine tool kit.

Serious work

When it comes to top overhauls, oil pan removal and pipework, the following items should be added:

(1) An appropriate socket set. A torque wrench to fit can probably be borrowed when required.

(2) A set of repeating ring wrenches to cover the above range.

(3) A 10 in (250 mm) snap-shut pipe grip.

(4) Two Stillson-type pipe wrenches: one 8 in (200 mm), and one 18 in (450 mm).

(5) Sets of Allen keys for socket-head screws, both A/F (across flats) and metric.

(6) A hammer with one copper face and one hard rubber face.

(7) A long cold chisel with ½ in (12 mm) tip.

(8) An assortment of hand, warding, and Swiss needle files with the necessary handles.

and fine blades.

(17) A pair of sheet metal shears (tin-snips), also internal and external circlip (retainer clip) pliers.

(18) Some sort of bench with fitter's vice (vise) having removable soft jaws.

(19) Without electricity, a 4 in (100 mm) hand-operated grinder will suffice to sharpen drills, chisels and scrapers.

(20) A chunk of cast steel to use as an anvil. The balance weight off a big diesel engine crankshaft will serve quite well.

Bosun's store

Unless all of the above tools are kept on board, any cruising boat needs some sort of tool-kit in the bosun's store, to serve all duties while under way, from unscrewing shackles and touching-up paintwork to clearing away a broken mast or sealing a leak below the waterline.

Small cruiser

The minimum bosun's tools for a 30 ft (9 m) cruiser would be approximately as follows:

(1) Carpentry tools including a hammer, saw, screwdrivers, a small hand drill with wallet of suitable bits, a 4 in (100 mm) clamp, a wood rasp and a rule.
(2) In case the proper engine tool-kit gets left at home, metalworking tools always on board should include a small hacksaw, oilcan, pipe wrench, club hammer and cold chisel, plus an assortment of files and a portable vice. The latter may clamp on top of a sheet winch, or fix to a plank across the cockpit.
(3) Miscellaneous items generally include a knife, shackle key, funnels, marline spike, electrical tape, sail repair kit (see Chapter 8) plus, for deep sea, a collision mat, some underwater epoxy compound, an axe, bolt croppers and nut splitter.

Carpentry

For each of the above categories of tools, you will need various materials and spare parts. With the carpentry tools should be small cans containing a wide variety of nonferrous screws, nails, tacks, screw eyes and hooks. Even a fibreglass or steel boat should carry oddments of wood, including offcuts of marine plywood large enough to cover broken windows, some pine batten, hardwood chocks and wedges, and a range of tapered wooden plugs to seal a broken through-hull fitting.

Metalwork

Again, stored in clearly marked cans, you need for mechanical jobs a wide range of stainless steel and fibre washers, nuts, bolts, setscrews, split pins, hose clamps, plus gland packing for propeller shaft, pumps and cocks. It also pays to keep some pieces of sheet copper, shim stock, thin gasket material, sheet cork, some copper wire, emery tape, lagging rope, and a lot of rag.

Sundries

The bigger the craft, the fuller your bosun's store will grow. The practical owner always stows on board such items as sandpaper, shockcord, some old canvas and sailcloth, paint and varnish for touching-up work, some leather, corks, spare ropes, wire rope clips, rigging wire, shackles, turnbuckles, whipping twine, marline, sail thread, codline, Vaseline, paint thinner, body filler, and perhaps a spare propane cylinder, jet prickers, bulbs and fuses, or a fender inflator. Flat, wooden lolly or popsicle sticks make ideal spatulas for resin and filler mixing.

Spares

Naturally the above items are in addition to distilled water for batteries, oils and greases for engine and sterntube and the makers' recommended spare parts appertaining to engine, pumps, electrical and radio equipment, stoves, refrigerator, and any other complicated apparatus which needs to be kept running at all times. Do not forget some old clothing, overalls, dungarees, or denims, for unexpected dirty jobs.

In the workshop

Especially when fitting-out, precious time is easily wasted if you run out of paint thinner, fuel for the blow-torch, or detergent. In any case, stores are often closed at the critical time, so it pays to keep at home a good supply of all the commonly used fluids.

Stock

Although old lemonade or wine bottles hold a fair quantity, it proves wise to keep these topped up from something like ½-gallon (2½-litre) cans of ever-useful fluids including (as well as the above ones) gasoline or petrol, paint remover, denatured alcohol or methylated spirit, cellulose thinner, kerosene, and wood preservative.

Rare items

Many amateurs underrate the value of cellulose (car paint) thinner. It makes an excellent brush cleaner for use with most types of paint. Acetone and styrene are similar, and are essential for dissolving ordinary polyester resins. Xylene is the solvent for epoxy materials. Amyl acetate is useful to keep most types of plastic wood and rapid hardening fillers in soft condition. The steel boat owner may need to keep phosphoric acid (Jenolite or Naval Jelly) and similar rust removers and inhibitors. Other unusual but useful fluids include toluene or trichlorethylene for degreasing.

Paint choice
Also in the liquid department comes the question of paint. To minimize the range held, it pays to stick to one make as far as possible and also to keep rigidly to either the cheaper alkyd marine paints or the more expensive, but longer-lasting catalyst materials (see Chapter 4). Much the same applies to varnishes.

Early order
To avoid hunting around for the required shade, make or type of paint needed, always buy these well before the customary fitting-out rush. This also applies to antifouling paint, varnish, primer, fillers and stoppers. Antifouling paint takes a long time to stir after storage. It helps if you store each can on its side and shift its position every few weeks.

Knotting
Owners of old wooden boats need to keep a little shellac varnish (knotting) to seal off all the knots on bare wood prior to priming. Similarly, rust spots on bare steel need two coats of zinc-rich paint (or the equivalent), while light alloy needs a special self-etching primer to ensure good adhesion (see page 30).

Suitable antifouling
Good yacht chandlers will advise on the best choice of antifouling paint to suit the local waters and the best choice for your hull material, or to cover existing paint. For instance, they will know that preparations containing metallic copper (and some mercurial compounds) must not be used on light alloy hulls, or in the presence of galvanized underwater fittings.

Skinning
Except for some polyurethanes and acrylics, buying in bulk is not always economic, as, once a large can has been opened most paints and varnishes tend to deteriorate and form a surface skin. Always cut around any skin with a knife and lift out the skin before stirring or using. Especially with varnish, straining through nylon stocking is advisable before use. Never store cans upside down. This seals the lid, but a skin forms anyway and cannot readily be removed intact.

No air
To eliminate most of the air from a large, partly used can, and therefore prevent a skin from forming, drop in some clean pebbles (to raise the level almost to brimfull) or decant into a smaller can, with minimum air space left inside. When washed and dried, empty, airtight cans as used for syrup and molasses are ideal. Avoid the use of glass jars which can break and cause a terrible mess. A vacuum pump tool is marketed to withdraw all the air from any size of can, but few amateurs are likely to possess one. This pierces a small hole through the lid and seals it again after evacuation.

Labels
Keep a thick roll of masking tape in the workshop. This makes good labels for all bottles and cans. A strip should be passed right around each container (overlapping itself a little) until you are sure it will not peel off when damp. Print boldly on the tape with a ball-point pen or felt-tipped pen. Avoid using queer codes that might be confusing to other people. As well as for your future convenience, good labels are an essential safety measure.

Extras
The list of materials that different owners hoard goes on indefinitely. You may need gold leaf and goldsize, also aluminium paint for galvanized fittings, and caulking materials for a laid teak deck. Even with a false teak deck, a stock of Teak-Brite is useful to keep it looking smart. Teak oil is useful for treating bare teak below decks. There are also wax polishes for joinerwork and for fibreglass topsides.

Sealer
When you have canvas- or vinyl-covered decks, a tube or cartridge of mastic sealer is useful in case of damage or to fill leaks along coamings or around deck fittings. Your chandlery store will advise on the best type for the job, whether butyl, polysulphide or silicone. Some matching non-slip deck paint should be kept at home, if not also on board.

Plastics
For fibreglass decks and hulls, keep a small amount of matching gel-coat resin for instant damage repair and general touching-up. Owners of fibreglass boats often keep a complete repair kit, with some epoxy stopping, and a Stanley Shaper or Surform Plane for cutting down flush prior to sanding a repair job.

Deck coverings
If your deck is ever re-covered with a modern vinyl material, always keep the offcuts and some adhesive

to use for future repairs. Good liquid plastic coatings (such as Dekaplex) are available for use on canvas, plywood, and old planked decks. Where this has been used, keep a small amount on board in case of anchor fluke damage, staining, or blistering.

Sandpaper

Whenever abrasive paper is kept on board, it must always be of the wet-or-dry type (w.o.d.); the cheaper varieties absorb moisture and disintegrate when used. Grade or grit numbers of about 180 and 250 will cover most needs in w.o.d. paper. Do not discard used sheets of 250 grade paper, as these will act like 400 grade for very fine sanding. However, 600 or 1000 grade is used by dinghy racing enthusiasts for burnishing graphite bottom paint. It also serves on polyurethane paint or fibreglass gel coat before polishing a blemish or repair job.

Reminders

For the beginner, accumulating all the tools and equipment needed for boat maintenance usually takes at least one year. Although a dinghy requires almost the same list of equipment for annual painting and varnishing as a medium size cruising yacht, the latter may demand a longer list to cater for work below decks, on heavier rigging and sails, for caulking, bilge cleaning, ballast and deck treatment. Avoid going mad over expensive power tools until you have all those small but essential items enumerated earlier in this chapter, some of which may be available at zero cost.

Straining

Old nylon stockings or tights are ideal for straining paint and varnish – a process which is well worth while when a can has been opened more than once, or whenever a skin (however thin) has formed on the surface. Keep with the stockings a few large rubber bands to secure a piece of stocking over the top of the clean empty can or paint kettle (pail) when straining.

Cans

Few amateurs bother to buy a proper galvanized paint kettle with a nice handle, but this is unlikely to get kicked over and hangs neatly on a ladder by means of an S-hook made from 10-gauge wire. Empty food cans are disposable, however, and serve well for most purposes. It pays to keep a cardboard box full of clean, empty food cans of varying sizes.

Plastic ice cream tubs make excellent rattle-free containers for spare parts.

Danger

Some people using a can opener do not complete the cut, so preventing the lid from falling onto the contents. The lid is then twisted off, leaving a small piece of sharp metal inside the rim. Hammer this down before use, or get a modern can opener that cuts round the outside.

Big brush

Although any can or paint kettle must be considerably wider than the brush to avoid bristle damage, too wide a can allows the paint to congeal rapidly in warm weather. It also causes rapid cooling in winter when the material has been warmed to improve its flow characteristics.

Rag

Another free essential is an ample supply of old rags. Non-absorbent materials such as nylon and rayon are absolutely useless, so one needs to be quite choosy. Well-worn cotton bed sheets are best, while a few pieces of old towel should always be kept for mopping down after wet sanding.

Overalls

Talking about rags, protective clothing for boat maintenance is worth a mention. Overalls of the one-piece boiler suit variety are best, but they can be hot unless you wear next to nothing underneath. Three outfits are ideal, graded according to the dirtiness of the job in hand.

General tasks

The no. 1 outfit can be a new track suit for general tinkering about. A woolly ski hat is comfortable in cold weather, while a white cotton sailing hat will keep the sun off a bald head efficiently, provided the wind is not strong enough to blow it overboard!

Soiled clothing

An older outfit is sensible when soiling with paint or grease is inevitable. Old slacks and shirts, plus sweaters and slightly soiled hats will not look too disreputable for fitting-out work, on either boy or girl. Choose things you enjoy wearing and wash them before they get smelly!

Grubby work

Your no. 3 rig may not be fit to be seen, but should be kept for cleaning bilges, working in mud, applying antifouling paint, or cleaning down the engine. Naturally, no. 1 clothes can be relegated to no. 2 when old, eventually winding up as no. 3.

Shoes

Rubber-soled canvas shoes are ideal for most jobs around a boat. However, when laid up in a shed with an earth floor (or in a mudberth), keep a clean pair on board, within reach of the boarding ladder, and change into these whenever you step onto the boat. Well-worn deck shoes have the advantage of not holding dirt in the non-slip soles.

Never wear old slacks with turn-ups or cuffs at the bottom, as these catch on cleats unexpectedly and are positively dangerous.

Skin protection

Filthy hands are easier to clean if you have smeared them with barrier cream before starting work. Work it well into the finger-nails and cuticles. Its presence cannot be felt after a few minutes. Special barrier creams are available for working with fibreglass resins. They prevent dermatitis and itching on sensitive skin. Before washing dirty hands, treat the skin thoroughly with Swarfega (in Britain), or Amway L.O.C. or Sta-lub Formula 2 (in the USA). Dunking in warm water after this makes a fair job, but the addition of soap (even a bar of sea water soap) makes the hands smell better and helps replace the natural oiliness of the skin.

Soft bucket

When shopping, working aloft, or generally holding small tools, a canvas bucket (see Chapter 8) is ideal. A heavy duty, household plastic bucket is nice to handle on board – for carrying tools as well as for washing down – but a galvanized steel bucket has its uses.

Steel bucket

With a rope attached, a steel bucket is ideal for deck washing, for when filling from overboard it capsizes easily on hitting the water. Also, at fitting-out time, you can play a blow-torch on the outside for heating water, when galley facilities are not available.

Miscellanies

Of the countless items sometimes needed in workshop or on board, the following are sometimes forgotten:

(1) A piece of 22-gauge (0.77 mm) sheet steel or tin plate for making protective shields when burning off paint close to varnishwork.

(2) Two or three funnels of varying size to assist in decanting liquids.

(3) Various aerosol cans containing such items as touch-up paint, rust inhibitor, lacquer for brass and chromed fittings, moisture inhibitor for engine systems, releasing or penetrating oil, and ether for starting obstinate engines in cold weather.

(4) Eye shield and nose filter to wear when using a power sander or when spraying paint.

(5) A small metal shield to hold when cutting-in an awkward paint line.

(6) Industrial gloves for handling pigs of ballast or when applying antifouling paint.

(7) Tack-rags for dusting-off before varnishing.

(8) Oxalic acid for bleaching stains from bare wood and sails.

(9) Neatsfoot oil for treating leather.

(10) Caustic soda for boiling out exhaust systems or fouled crankcase breather pipes.

(11) Naphtha for cleaning brushes if you use bitumastic paint.

(12) Small quantities of resin glue and epoxy filler.

Care of tools

Most of us are guilty at times of neglecting to keep all tools sharp or clean, and the quality of the work we do is bound to suffer under these conditions. Luckily, for the most part, tool maintenance is readily accomplished at home, thus avoiding wastage of time when fitting-out the boat.

Expendability

When two-part paint or varnish is being used, you must clean brushes every hour or less (according to the air temperature) if irreversible hardening is to be avoided. Half-hourly cleaning is expedient in hot weather. To obviate this inconvenience some people use cheap brushes and dump them after use. Dealing with paint rollers or pads is almost exactly the same. However, remember that a high-class finish is difficult to achieve when using cheap brushes or rollers.

Dried paint

When using air-drying materials, brush cleaning is not so urgent. During a short lull (or when taking brushes home to be cleaned) wrap the brushes concerned tightly around with rag to check evaporation. If accidently left in this condition overnight, you will need to use one of the special brush cleaners marketed, or try paint stripper.

Suspended brushes

Provided a brush is going to be used again within a few days (using similar material) you need not clean it right out. Instead, suspend it in a can of the appropriate thinner with the bristle tips about ½ in (12 mm) above the can bottom. First, wipe all surplus paint from the bristles with a rag. To suspend it, either drill a hole through the handle and poke a short length of stiff wire through this, or use a small clamp resting on the can rim. Most of the paint will drop from the bristles to the bottom of the can, so take care when decanting the thinner. Lay a piece of rag around the handle on top of the can to prevent rapid evaporation.

Dry cleaning

To get a brush clean and dry ready for immediate use, pour about 1 in (25 mm) of thinner into an empty can and press the bristles firmly into this many times in different directions. Wipe the bristles well with a rag, pour the thinner into a bottle for later use, then repeat the process with fresh thinner as many times as necessary to remove all signs of paint.

Old newspaper

When thinner is in short supply, use this method: Open an old newspaper containing about twenty sheets on the floor. Holding the bristles flat on the paper, pour a little thinner over them, and work the brush firmly as though painting all over the top sheet. Discard the wetted sheet and repeat the process with fresh thinner several times until no more paint stains appear. Slapping the brush onto the newspaper helps to clean paint from the roots of the bristles.

Rinse

Having complied with the above suggestions, always wash a good brush in warm water and detergent before putting it away. A big brush will need working thoroughly in three separate lots of water and detergent, rinsing well in clean water each time. Finally, flick surplus water away and leave the brush in a warm room until dry.

Bristle cover

New brushes should arrive with a cellophane wrapper over the bristles, held on with a rubber band. It pays to keep this and replace it once the bristles are completely dry. Try to keep brushes for varnish separate from those for paint, and label them accordingly. A cardboard shoe box provides good storage for brushes.

New brushes

Even the best quality brushes tend to lose a few bristles when first used. In this respect, well-cared-for old brushes are better than new. Also, until used a few times, the bristles of new brushes are often too long and too limp. Some experts bind around the roots of the bristles with a whipping of string extending about ½ in (12 mm) beyond the metal ferrule. This should be removed after use to prevent permanent bristle damage. The extra stiffness prevents runmarks when using enamel on a cold day. A binding also prevents paint from lodging deep in the roots, and cleaning out is thus made easier.

Curdled varnish

Although a lot of polyurethane varnish is used nowadays, traditional spar (or yacht) varnish is still popular. Its use requires one warning: although ordinary paint thinner (genuine turpentine, mineral spirit, or white spirit) may be added to thin such varnish, it must *never* be used for the first brush cleaning bath after a varnishing session. If you do this, for some strange reason, the varnish within the bristles congeals into myriad tiny particles, some of which emerge onto the next surface you varnish as minute, hard nibs, however thoroughly you clean the brush. To avoid this, always use a 50/50 mixture of raw linseed oil and thinner for the first cleaning bath; all subsequent cleaning can then be carried out with straight thinner. Eggshell varnish needs stirring before use.

Special brushes

Most of us stick to conventional flat paint brushes for all purposes, but several other types are available, including flitches, round, oval, throwaway and wall brushes. Long-handled tar brushes are sometimes used for bottom painting on large vessels, while a striker (see Fig. 3(g)) is useful for painting underneath a keel, or inside the deep bilge keels on some small cruisers.

Thinner economy

Never skimp on the quantity of thinners you keep (which should be compatible with all the paints and varnishes to be used). Great economy is possible by storing used thinners in separate containers for future use. In time, paint particles form a sludge at the bottom, and so relatively clean fluid can be decanted repeatedly, the old bottles being discarded perhaps once a year. Further bottles containing the dirtiest thinners are useful for the initial cleansing of brushes used for dark paints or bitumastics.

Rollers

Although cheap throwaway rollers are convenient, the expensive mohair or moquette rollers generally work best. Lambswool rollers tend to trap air bubbles under a paint film.

The patient handyman will not mind the awful chore of cleaning out good quality rollers after use. The cleaning process is similar to that described above for brushes, using the proper sloping tray (repeatedly cleaned with rag) instead of old cans. Roller widths vary from 2 in (50 mm) to 12 in (300 mm), but 7 in (175 mm) is best for boatwork. (See also Chapter 4.)

Pads

Painting pads are preferred to rollers by many amateur painters, being easier to clean, and eliminating the need for laying off with a brush. A 6 in (150 mm) width is ideal for topsides. Small bevel-edged pads are made for striking in edges.

Rust

Little maintenance is required for the majority of the tools listed earlier in this chapter, but care is needed to keep them clean and free from rust. In a dry climate, this is no problem. During moist winters, steel tools need to be lightly oiled or stored in closed boxes containing sheets of rust-inhibition (VPI) paper. Remember to renew this at least once a year.

Blades

Tools with cutting edges such as planes, knives and chisels must always be kept correctly ground, sharpened and honed ready for immediate use. Special plastic caps are made to fit over the tips of wood chisels. If you wrap each one in rag, it proves difficult to find the one you want. However, planes and saws are best wrapped in old canvas, to prevent damage to the delicate blades or teeth, as well as one's fingers.

Honing

If the grinding angle on blades is maintained correctly on a grinding wheel, only a few strokes on the oilstone are necessary to produce perfect tips. A honing gauge which fixes rapidly to any type of blade will ensure that the correct angle is always maintained on the oilstone. If you were not taught these arts at school, ask a shipwright or joiner.

Scrapers

Interchangeable-blade scrapers (Plate 21) need to be kept razor-sharp to the original bevel using a very fine file, or the coarse surface of a combination Carborundum stone. Remember to keep a few spare hooks. The triangular and pear-shaped scrapers used by painters must be kept well sharpened, and the same applies to scrapers made blacksmith-style from old files (see under section headed *Home-made tools*). Any scraper can cause serious injury if not kept wrapped when out of use, or in a special box.

Plate 21   Use a very fine file when sharpening a hook scraper.

Home-made tools

Many useful tools can be made at zero cost, and some handymen become quite enthusiastic about this branch of their hobby. Items such as scrapers, knives, screwdrivers, chisels, punches and scribers must be made from tool steel, as found in old files, lawnmower blades and car parts like valves, gearbox shafts and kingpins. Tools such as marline spikes, bradawls, shackle keys and calipers may be fabricated from mild steel, as used in bolts and angle

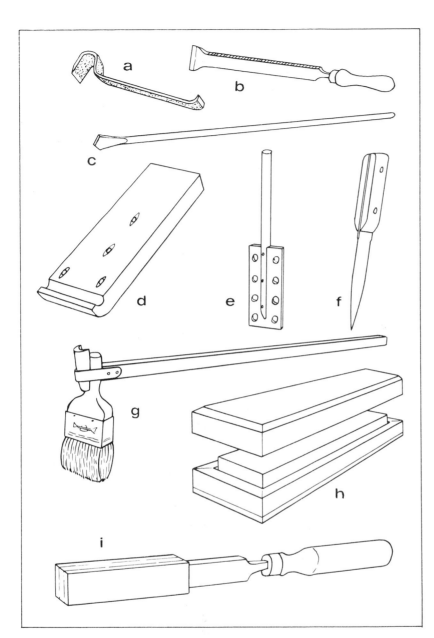

Fig. 3 Home-made tools. **a** and **b** scrapers from discarded files. **c** long drill bit. **d** serving board. **e** mixing paddle for hand or power drill. **f** sheath knife. **g** striker. **h** oilstone box. **i** chisel scabbard.

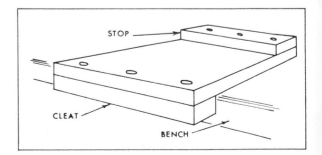

Fig. 4 Home-made bench hook.

fencing stakes. Offcuts of solid hardwood are ideal for making a multitude of useful boating and workshop tools as described below.

File scraper

A typical exercise in forming an edged tool is using old, flat files to make scrapers, as seen in Fig. 3(a) and (b). First, grind the teeth off one side for about 2 in (50 mm) back from the end, to come on the inside of the hook. Heat this end bright red and hammer at right angles into the required hook. After cooling slowly the tip will be soft, making it easy to file or grind a 15° bevel on the outside.

Temperature

Next make the tip glass-hard by heating slowly to bright red, holding in that state for ten minutes, then plunging into water. Tempering follows to remove the brittleness. Make a bright patch at the tip by rubbing with emery cloth. Heat the file very slowly, well back from the tip, watching the bright patch carefully. It will take on an amber shade, then turn through dark straw to purple and dark blue. On reaching dark straw, immediately quench in cold water and agitate for a few seconds.

Try again

If the shade was wrong or uneven, return the metal to the dead hard condition and try again with a cooler flame. The process may be repeated any number of times. If you have difficulty in drilling or cutting some hard steel, soften it first as mentioned above.

Long bits

Extra-long drill bits are sometimes needed in boat maintenance work. Wire wheel spokes, brake rods, or the silver steel bars (often called *drill rod*) stocked by tool stores are suitable. Heat the tip red hot and hammer this into a spade shape. File to a 120° angle as shown in Fig. 3(c), grind as necessary, harden and temper. A standard Morse or twist drill may be extended by brazing on a mild steel shaft of any length.

Strip stuff

Old lawnmower blades are fine for making a draw-knife or the business ends of triangular and oval scrapers. Old egg spoons make excellent scrapers for cove lines if their tips are sharpened by grinding or filing. Sheath knives and leather skiving knives (see page 224) are easily fashioned from power hacksaw blades with pieces of shaped hardwood riveted on

either side to make the handle (see Fig. 3(f)).

With wood

Tool-making enthusiasts often keep any pieces of good hardwood they find and convert these into such items as a bosun's chair, mallet, serving board (Fig. 3(d)), tool handles, clamps, mitre box, fid, paint stirrers or a bench hook. This last named is shown in Fig. 4 and fits on the edge of a bench to support strips of wood when sawing them.

With canvas

If you keep a modest sail repair kit, such useful items as canvas buckets, fenders and tool bags can be made using the offcuts of canvas easily available from sailmakers, upholsterers and awning makers, as explained in Chapter 8.

Other ideas

Making your own equipment is a continuing process. For instance, a useful item is a paint or resin mixing paddle (see Fig. 3(e)) to fit into an electric drill. Another is an engine stand (Fig. 5) for use when an

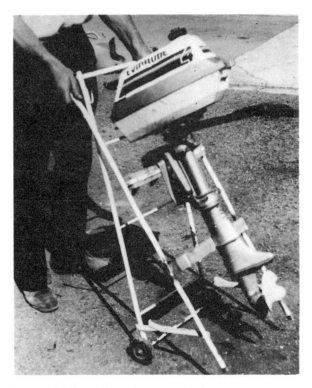

Plate 22 An outboard motor stand is even more useful when fitted with wheels.

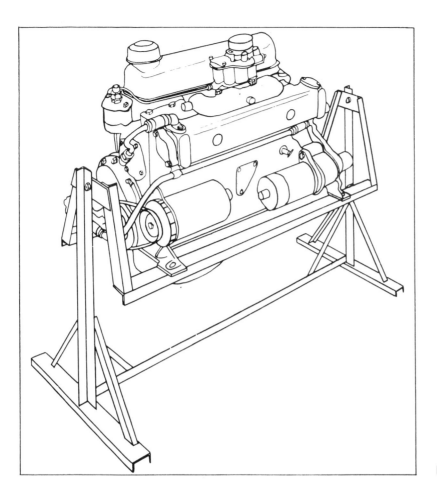

Fig. 5 Inboard engine repair stand.

engine is to be stripped down at home. This and an outboard motor stand (Plate 22) can be fabricated in wood or angle steel. You might need to make jigs for supporting handsaws (and circular saw blades) close to the teeth when being sharpened; perhaps an oilstone box (see Fig. 3(h)) or a chisel scabbard as in Fig. 3(i). Less practical sailors can often borrow rarely used tools such as a file scraper, serving mallet, sledge hammer, bearing puller, eyelet closing tools, sash cramp (bar clamp), or crowbar. To tackle electronic equipment or electrical wiring faults, you will need to borrow an AVO (amps/volts/ohms) meter, or a small multimeter. To find a leakage to ground you may need a Megger.

Power tools

Electricity is not always available at fitting-out time, but when you are lucky enough to have it, the facility for good lighting and the use of a vacuum cleaner are paramount. Cordless, rechargeable power tools are especially useful for intermittent drilling, grinding and sawing work on boats. However, where finance is limited, it certainly pays to invest in a good range of hand tools before acquiring rarely needed power tools.

Variable speed
An electric drill of ⅜ in (9 mm) capacity is useful for polishing fibreglass, and it will handle a wide range of attachments. However, for some of these (and certainly for drills larger than about ⅛ in (3 mm) diameter) a power drill must have infinitely variable speed control – either built into the trigger switch, or as a separate thyristor unit linked into the supply cable. Always keep your chuck key attached to the drill end of the cable by means of a short length of thin chain. Without this, the key is sure to go missing at a critical moment.

Scouring

For cleaning metal (and especially engine decarbonization), small wire brushes and burrs are ideal attachments for the electric drill. A large diameter wire brush is useful for de-rusting ballast and steelwork, but few electric drills have enough power to drive this effectively.

Sanding

Disc sanders have limited uses for boat maintenance as they dig whorl marks into the surface. Orbital sanders are kinder but slow (see Chapter 3). Belt sanders are superb, but are heavy to handle.

Gel coat peeling

When an FRP hull has advanced osmosis or boat pox, the entire affected gel coat will have to be taken off. Instead of grit blasting, most professionals now use a *gel coat peeler*, like a mobile milling machine which cuts swathes about $1\frac{1}{2}$ in (38 mm) wide, right down to the matrix. Most are supported on robotic arms, but some are hand held.

Powering is by compressed air, vacuum or water, each medium helping to clear away the swarf. A light sandblasting may follow, to open up the waterlogged cells in the matrix. An angle grinder is the best tool for the awkward corners. A clever amateur can use this to grind off an entire gel coat, but it takes a vast amount of time and is difficult to do well. Grinding is ideal for cutting out a small number of blisters on minor pox repairs. Without power, a cordless drill with a few burrs and endmills works well. See also pages 65 and 247.

Drying out

It could take three months to dry out the matrix after gel coat peeling. To hasten this, specialists use either dehumidifiers or infra red lamps, sometimes under a skirt around the hull. Hiring the lamps could prove difficult. As you might need six 1500 watt quartz infra red lamps, this means a load of 80 amps (on 110 volts) for a continuous period of about ten days. Watch that a matrix never gets too warm to touch with the back of your hand. You may be able to borrow an electronic moisture meter to check the progress of drying out – but it really needs an expert to interpret the readings. As a crude indicator, if a cellophane patch is taped on all night (with no heat in use), beads of moisture will form on the inside if the matrix is damp.

Hiring

In most sizeable towns you can find tool hire firms holding the more expensive power tools that few boating enthusiasts keep at home. Most have daily or weekly hire charges plus a deposit. The most frequently hired items are portable generators, belt sanders, paint sprayers, gas and electric welding equipment, space heaters, electric paint strippers, ladders and scaffolding. When hiring shot-blasting equipment, it will nearly always be necessary to hire the operator also.

Voltage

Especially in Britain, many boatyards use electricity at half the normal voltage for safety reasons. If this means borrowing compatible power tools and lights owned by the yard, remember to obtain permission beforehand, and return everything (duly cleaned) as promptly as possible.

3
Stripping, Priming and Caulking

Whether you are painting over wood, plastics, metal or ferrocement, unless surface preparation is thorough, not only will the final finish be poor, but the adhesion could be weak, leading to peeling or blistering within a year. Much the same applies to varnishwork.

Prime it quick

All types of surface preparation take a long time and a lot of energy. Putting on the paint is a much quicker job. To relieve the monotony of a big stripping job, clean and prime the surface as work progresses. This also ensures good adhesion.

Warm is good
If there is any hint of moisture about, waft a blowtorch over the surface before priming – but never make it too hot to touch. Materials other than wood benefit from this treatment. On a cold day, apparently dry steel or ferrocement will sweat as soon as heat is applied.

Why strip?

If you buy a yacht in fair condition and own her for five years, you should never need to strip any paint or varnish. After five to ten years, small areas of paintwork (and perhaps all exterior brightwork) will probably need stripping. At fifteen years old, a fibreglass hull will already have been painted for many years and could be starting to flake. Be suspicious of any paint build-up after twenty years. If small, chipped-off test areas (especially important on steel) prove that all is well, do not strip completely, unless the finish is hopelessly uneven.

Partial stripping
Simple dry scraping will normally remove an area of loose paint rapidly. For very thick paint, an old wood chisel and mallet used lightly at right angles to the surface works well. Body filler soon fills the gap and patient sanding should remove all trace of a subsequent scar. Patching up varnishwork is far more laborious, needing numerous coats of varnish plus stain, with occasional sanding to prevent an unwanted build-up on the adjacent sound surfaces.

Adhesion
If bare wood shows over a patch area, dope this with the chosen primer and let it dry before applying body filler. To ensure good adhesion for a rusty steel patch, kill the rust with phosphoric acid or Naval Jelly before priming. When paint flakes from fibreglass, the original adhesion was poor, warranting the further use of dry abrasive paper and a special fibreglass primer. Adhesion to ferrocement can be improved by etching with hydrochloric acid, which should be brushed on for one minute, then rinsed off.

Testing steel
On the topsides of fibreglass and ferrocement hulls, some poor adhesion is not usually detrimental, provided the external finish remains fair. On steel, any adhesion failure could mean serious rusting. Look for surface blistering to detect trouble, but chip off a few small areas every year (particularly below the waterline) to make sure.

Testing timber
Adhesion failures over any type of wood could lead to rot. Thick paintwork may show no blisters. If suspicious, tap lightly with a mallet and listen for a dull sound.

Sun damage
Too many coats of varnish create a dark tint, absorbing more heat from the sun, which leads to bond failure. Touching-up is easier on thin varnish-work, and complete stripping after about five years is quite common on exposed parts. In contrast, paintwork can still be satisfactory when forty or fifty coats thick.

Stripping methods

There are three main methods in use for stripping paint completely:

(1) Burning off with a blow-torch and scraper, or with an electrically heated tool.
(2) With the aid of a chemical stripper and scraper.
(3) Dry scraping, power sanding, or using a chipping hammer on steel.

Burning off
An ancient method, with several advantages. The idea is to only just melt the paint in small panels about 6 in (150 mm) by 3 in (75 mm) and then peel this off rapidly with a scraper (see Plate 23). With practice, it can be done quickly without charring the underlying wood.

Heat damage
Burning off is normally limited to solid timber and ferrocement. On thin metal it can blister interior paintwork. It can damage plywood by affecting the glue, and it should never be used on fibreglass. Otherwise the use of heat is advantageous, drying the surface and helping to get rid of harmful fauna, such as woodworm.

Plate 23 On solid wood, burning off is not only quick, but it dries the surface ready for priming.

Traditional method
The kerosene blowlamp (Plate 24) is still sometimes used for burning off. Preheating is done by igniting a little fuel poured into a recess on top of the tank. A tankful of fuel normally burns for about one hour. Jet blockages are normally easy to clear with a pricker, but a jet removal key is useful for more serious trouble.

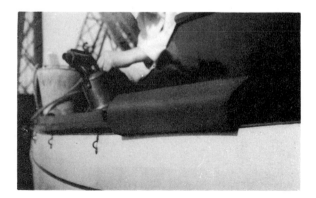

Plate 24 A simple tin shield protects the rub-rail when stripping topside paint.

Plate 25 This type of propane torch is light to hold with a stable flame in windy weather.

Modern burners

The bottled gas blowtorch (Plate 25) is a fine tool for burning off paintwork. The detachable canister type proves more expensive to run and is heavier to hold than the type illustrated, which is fed from a large cylinder. Easy to hire for the odd occasion.

Wind effects

A breeze is useful to disperse fumes when burning off. Some sort of canvas shelter or screen is sometimes needed in a strong wind to prevent the flame blowing out. Kerosene burners generally blow out more readily than those fired with bottled gas. The latter rarely suffer from blockages, but in the event, the gauze filter behind the jet is easily cleared with an artist's brush once the burner head is screwed off.

Shielding brightwork

Where varnished wood adjoins a paintwork area to be burnt off, bend up a tinplate shield (as shown in Plate 24) to prevent scorching the varnish. If a shield cannot be rigged, strip the final 3 in (75 mm) of paintwork with the aid of a chemical stripper, or by dry scraping.

Flame guns

Although a somewhat dangerous method, the bottom of a big old boat can be burnt off in record time using a flame gun weed destroyer, or the largest size of bottled gas blowtorch. A second operator is required, wielding a long-handled scraper.

Caution

All burning off jobs demand fire precautions, especially when a flame gun is used. If there is no mains water hose, fill a few buckets, or keep fire extinguishers handy. Tar and bitumen are the materials most likely to flare up, particularly when the weather is hot. Beware hot paint falling from overhead surfaces, avoid breathing the fumes, and remember that a flame is invisible in sunlight.

Direction of working

Most people prefer to work from right to left when burning off, using the left hand for the blowtorch and the right hand for the scraper. Should the wind be blowing from the left, a change of direction may be advisable.

Choosing scrapers

A wallpaper stripping knife (Fig. 6(a)) makes a good tool for scraping away molten paint. Some professionals prefer to use a sharp triangular scraper (Fig. 6(b)); others prefer one made from an old file, as shown in Fig. 3(b). A pear-shaped or oval scraper (Fig. 6(c)) is occasionally useful, while old spoons are handy, as mentioned on page 27.

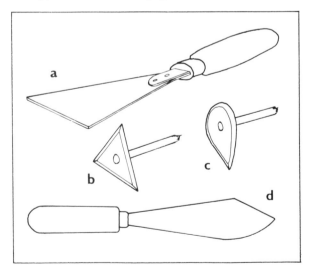

Fig. 6 Useful paint stripping tools. **a** wallpaper stripping knife. **b** triangular scraper. **c** oval scraper. **d** putty knife.

Electric Heater

Although marketed for over thirty years, electric paint removers never proved very popular until the advent of the modern types which deliver a red hot blast of air. These are used in the same manner as a blowtorch, but have the advantage that a slit-nozzle may be fitted for working into corners and against varnished trim.

Chemical stripping

Strong caustic soda solution (applied to the surface with a brush made from a bunch of old hemp rope ends bound together) will strip paint and varnish well, but can be harmful to the user. More expensive, less harmful, but equally effective chemicals in jelly form are available everywhere. Note that special chemicals are made for use on fibreglass: the common type can seriously damage a gel coat. The glue securing Cascover nylon sheathing to a hull can also be affected by chemical strippers, but they are suitable on most other hull materials.

Layer by layer

New types are appearing, but some chemicals will only remove about four layers of paint at each application. Removing thick old paint can be tedious and expensive.

Work in large panels. Brush on the stripper generously, leave for about ten minutes, then scrape away all soft material using a sharp triangular scraper, or the hook type illustrated in Plate 21. Repeat this process as many times as necessary.

Neutralizers

On completion, make sure that all chemical action is killed by washing down with the recommended neutralizer. This is normally either water or white spirit (mineral spirits). If water is used on woodwork, make sure this dries off completely before starting to paint.

Caution

Keep some neutralizer handy at all times in case any stripper splashes onto your skin. Use masking tape and paper to prevent chemical from getting onto parts which are not to be stripped, or from varnishwork onto fibreglass. Work in a breeze to avoid breathing the fumes.

Dry scraping

An interchangeable hook scraper (see Plate 21) as made by Skarsten in Britain and Warner and Red Devil in the USA, proves the best tool for dry scraping. Much energy is required and an inexperienced operator can produce damaging score marks. Sharpen frequently with the maker's special file (or a Carborundum stone) and slip in a new blade when sharpening fails to produce good results. Fast-action serrated blades are available, but their use is best avoided on varnishwork for fear of scoring the surface.

Main uses

Dry scraping works best on narrow surfaces such as rails, beadings, cleats and spars, or for loose paint on fibreglass. Although the Plate 21 type of scraper with 2½ in (62 mm) blade, will tackle big flat areas, the 1½ in (38 mm) size is generally better for narrow parts and spars. (Not recommended, but one ancient method used for scraping masts and spars was a broken piece of thick glass! This was held somewhat as shown in Fig. 18.)

Coarse sanding

With suitable power tools, any thickness of paint can be ground away. The tools are noisy, heavy, and produce a lot of dust. Do not attempt boat stripping with handyman drill attachments – hire or borrow the correct heavy-duty commercial power tools.

Big discs

A 7 in (175 mm) high-speed angle grinder, or a disc sander with a 40-grit abrasive disc, will handle any thickness of paint. This type of disc can make deep score marks. For topside stripping you need a soft-backed pad with special stick-on/peel-off abrasive discs. Remember to blow dust out of the motor occasionally on any power sander.

Relieving the weight

For single-handed topside work, try to suspend a heavy sander from above, preferably utilizing a spring to eliminate the need for constantly adjusting a lanyard. Bottom stripping calls for two people, taking it in turns.

Disc clogging

Friction heat causes even the coarsest abrasive disc to clog with paint. After changing discs, a clogged one can be partly cleared using a chisel-pein hammer and a power wire brush.

Health hazards

Failing the use of a space suit, you will need good protection for eyes, ears, nose, mouth and hair when using big sanders and grinders for more than a few minutes, especially where poisonous antifouling is concerned. This proves uncomfortable in warm weather, but at least use goggles and a nose filter. If you are having to work singlehanded, have some alternative job lined up. Fast angle grinder wheels can break and cause injury unless properly guarded.

Belt sanders
Slower in action than the above tools (but producing a much better finish) is the 4 in (100 mm) wide belt sander. It has the same weight problem, but makes less noise, and normally has a built-in extractor fan with dust bag. Best suited to stripping relatively thin paint, particularly on fibreglass. Buying many belts (to overcome clogging) can prove expensive.

Handyman tools
There are drill attachments for stripping, including a drum with metal cutters around it, and one with sharp steel flails, but the average home electric drill is too weak for the large-scale stripping of thick materials. Even a commercial vibrating sander is suitable only for taking away three or four coats of paint. Its freedom from scoring makes it ideal for use on fibreglass. Note that paint on fibreglass is best made a different shade from the gel coat to distinguish it and thus prevent damaging the latter when stripping.

Metal surfaces
If a steel hull has been zinc sprayed or galvanized, use only a chemical stripper with gentle scraping to avoid scratching the zinc. Burning off without blistering internal paint is possible on zinc coated steel thicker than ¼ in (6 mm).

Blast cleaning
Firms with portable equipment can be hired in most regions to strip an untreated steel hull using a stream of high pressure air mixed with sand or grit. Other firms use a water jet so powerful that it can bore holes in concrete. (Fine ways to clean pigs of rusty ballast.) Both methods leave an ideal surface for painting, though the water process may call for hot air drying, or the use of an epoxy primer intended for application on damp steel.

Chipping it off
Steel plate thicker than about ⅛ in (3 mm) may be stripped with a chipping hammer (Plate 26) using light but rapid strokes. The tool has chisel-like tips, one turned at right angles to the other. It works best on thick paint which has not bonded too well.

Plate 26 Widely used on commercial steel boats, chipping hammers could dent the thin skins of small yachts.

Cold chisel
For chipping small areas, a fairly heavy cold chisel held with one hand will do the same job. Electric and air operated vibrating chisels are normally too vicious for yacht work. A power wire brush is useful to remove the last remnants, plus any surface rust. Chipping can dent light alloy, which is best treated in a similar way to zinc sprayed steel.

Needle gun
This air tool looks like a short piece of steel pipe squashed into a slot at the open end. From this end protrude numerous pointed steel rods which rattle up and down in use. The action is noisy but most effective for de-scaling, de-rusting and stripping.

Working in comfort

Major tasks like stripping or painting a hull deserve the making of special efforts to improve the comfort (and hence the speed) of working.

At home
Most dinghy owners manage to work on their boats under cover at home. Owners with sufficient space

Plate 27 Snug in a mudberth. Shore lines need to be vandal-proof and well protected against chafe.

can trail boats smaller than 26 ft (8 m) to their backyard for overhaul. With space alongside (and with tanks and engine oil drained off) some small craft are easy to roll onto beam ends for convenient bottom stripping and painting. Twin bilge keels – and, to a lesser extent, a fin keel – make this operation difficult and risky.

Mudberth problems

Boats wintered in mudberths (Plate 27) must be hauled out (or moved to a grid or scrubbing piles) for bottom work. For topsides work, lay duckboards on the mud and use ladders. Duckboards need lanyards to stop them from floating away on the tide. Ladders should be lashed at the top to prevent them from slipping.

Using a raft

When afloat, try to hire or borrow a proper boatyard painter's raft (Plate 28) to deal with topsides. This should have fendering just below the waterline. With secure ropes fore and aft, a ladder will stand quite firmly on a raft.

Scaffolding

Hauled out ashore, most external parts can be reached by ladder. For boats longer than 36 ft (11 m) it usually pays to erect some scaffolding for topsides work, such as the typical boatyard trestles and planks shown in Plate 29. For bigger boats, a similar form of staging may be suspended from toerail or bulwarks and slid along as necessary. When modern catalyst paints are used (see Chapter 4), trestles should be positioned ready to permit a painting session without interruption.

Plate 28 A well-padded painting raft is often available at marinas and boatyards.

Plate 29 When laid up ashore, trestles and planks speed topside painting greatly.

Marking the waterline

Many wooden craft have the antifouling line scored permanently into the planking. This saves a lot of bother after stripping, but note that the marked line may not be correct on an old boat which has been subjected to ballasting alterations over the years. Some metal boats have marks made with intermittent weld runs. Few fibreglass hulls have waterline grooves moulded in, and ferrocement hulls should never have them. Dinghies and runabouts without contrasting bottom paint do not need waterlines.

Permanent grooves

A good time to locate the waterline is while laying-up, when a well-defined weed mark is visible. On solid wood, frequent indentations made with marline

spike and mallet sometimes suffice as permanent markers, but a continuous groove is better. Tack a thin batten in position (when the planking is thick enough), then scribe along this with the corner of a sharp chisel. Remove the batten, then form a V-shaped groove all the way along with chisel and mallet.

To obtain the same results more quickly, borrow a *granny's tooth* type moulding plane (or electric router) with correctly shaped cutter. Fix the batten the requisite distance below the waterline, then slide the plane along the batten. With care, a shallow groove can be cut using a handsaw, or back saw.

Possible error

Bottom weed marks could be inaccurate if the boat has had a permanent list all summer. To check this, set the boat dead upright, get a length of see-through hosepipe long enough to pass under the keel and up to the waterline on both sides at once. With some helpers, fill the tube with water and adjust its height so that when the fluid is level with the waterline at one side, any discrepancy may be observed at the other side. A length of rubber garden hose will do, if you push a short piece of transparent pipe into each end.

Sight rails

Provided you can agree waterline marks at stem and stern, setting out between is easy, using the rig shown in Fig. 7. The sight rails need to be at least half the beam of the boat in length and dead level. Stretch a piece of thin cord from rail to rail with minimal sag. When this touches the hull amidships, get someone to hold it there (or use tape), then slide the cord across each rail in turn, holding the cord against the hull (and marking its position there) as it wraps around. Although the boat must be upright during the above procedure, she does not have to be level fore and aft.

Other methods

Having set out one side as above, the transparent hose method will do to locate the waterline on the opposite side. If the boat is correctly trimmed fore and aft, set up pairs of sight rails each side of the boat. With someone sighting across these, a helper can adjust a piece of white cardboard to align at all necessary points.

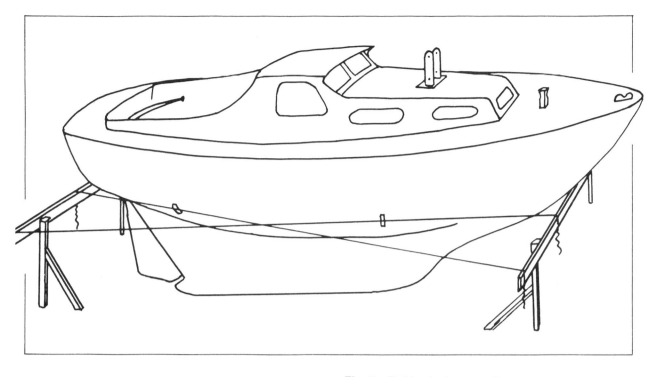

Fig. 7 Striking in the waterline.

Boottop position

Antifouling paint should continue above the true waterline by about 1 in (25 mm) on boats up to 30 ft (9 m) in length, and 2 in (50 mm) for boats around 45 ft (14 m). This is the line to mark permanently, as above. Most yachts have a boottop band of contrasting shade above the antifouling. This looks smart, camouflages scum, and is easy to re-paint when necessary. The upper line should be a curve, rising towards bow and stern. For boats around 30 ft (9 m), the width of the boottop band should be about 1 in (25 mm) at a point three-fifths of the waterline length from the stem, rising gradually to 2 in (50 mm) at the stern, and to 3 in (75 mm) at the stem. For a 45 ft (14 m) boat, these widths should be 2 in (50 mm), 3 in (75 mm), and 4 in respectively.

Cutting-in

With scored lines at top and bottom of the boottop, a small brush is all you need. Without scores, use a sheet metal shield – 6 in (150 mm) of flexy venetian blind slat works well. Wipe this frequently. If you mask the line (Plate 30) you need the best tape (such as 3M Fineline 218) to prevent paint seeping underneath. If tape sticks on too hard, moisten it before removal.

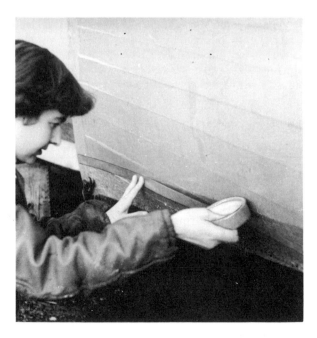

Plate 30 Especially for waterlines and boottops, masking tape ensures fair lines without runmarks.

Priming

After stripping old paint from wood, sand with 100-grit paper, apply two coats of shellac (patent knotting) to any knots which could ooze resin, and brush on a coat of primer. Two thin coats cling better than one thick coat.

Ancient and modern

The age-old pink primer containing white and red lead is still available and serves well under the common alkyd paints. The more modern metallic primers claim better adhesion and dry more quickly. Most of these wood primers require thinning for effective penetration. Special primer/fillers are made for plywood.

Without a primer

The role of priming paint (as well as undercoats) is taken over by thinned top coat material in the case of most varnishes and two-can paints used on wood. However, some varnish makers supply a special primer for oily hardwoods like teak. The use of an appropriate primer under two-can paints is advisable on metal and fibreglass.

On bare steel

There is a bewildering array of primers suitable for bare steel, from the reliable old red oxide, red lead, and calcium plumbate, to Rustoleum and various zinc-rich formulations. Without special knowledge, the amateur is best advised to adopt the recommendations of any noted marine paint maker.

Making good

Primers must enter all open cracks, seams, and nail holes. Your marine store should be able to provide all necessary stoppers and fillers; the range is enormous. Fully hardening fillers are generally used for topside seams, for all nail holes, and for small defects. Soft fillers are for underwater seams and for cracks in spars. Fillers (such as trowel or brushing cement) for shallow depressions always set hard. Exterior grades of Spackle or Polyfilla are often used used by boat owners.

Tools for stopping

A broad-bladed stripping knife (see Fig. 6(a)) makes the best tool for pressing stopping into seams, or for smearing on a filler. A glazier's putty knife (see Fig. 6(d)) or the tip of an old table knife works fine for stopping holes.

Foam sandwich finish

When fibreglass surfaces with no moulded gel coat are to be painted, epoxy putty (sometimes containing tiny air cells called micro-balloons or micro-spheres) makes a good filler to smear all over. This material sets even harder than trowel cement. After power sanding (or using 100-grit w.o.d. paper) a further thin skim of putty is sure to be necessary, followed by 180-grit sanding. To reveal the presence of hollows, work in semi-darkness, shining a light sideways across the surface.

Brushing cement

To complete the process of filling a poor surface prior to painting, creamy fillers are available, for application by brush. These readily flatten off using 220-grit wet paper.

Quick stoppers

Being able to sand down small, filled blemishes in less than quarter of an hour *and* get a coat of paint on, is often advantageous. Materials such as Brummer, Woodtex, and Plastic Wood will do this, but keep the lid on the can every possible moment. A few drops of the recommended thinner (usually amyl acetate) can be added occasionally to prevent premature hardening. These stoppers hardly shrink at all on hardening.

Deep holes

Some air-drying putties can take weeks to harden (and leave contraction cracks) when used in a deep hole. Building up in layers, and allowing each to dry, makes for the soundest job. Avoid stuffing bits of newspaper into a deep hole before stopping, as practised by house decorators. With a single pass of thick filler, leave a slight hump on the surface, to be sanded flush later. On big category C vessels, bolt countersinks are often filled with rich cement mortar.

Compatible stoppers

When sheathing a hull with fibreglass or nylon, all stopping must be of a compatible type recommended by the sheathing makers. The same thing applies under polyurethane paints. Polyester and epoxy putties are compatible with most materials, and may be levelled off with a Surform plane initially, as for car body repair work.

Matching brightwork

When wood is varnished, a big change in coloration occurs, and the effect on stopping can be even more dramatic. Priming the wood with thinned varnish before stopping gives an approximation of the final shade. Smears of filler on small pieces of cardboard, duly varnished, can be held over various parts of the brightwork to compare the match. Mixing light and dark fillers is often necessary.

Fine sanding

Sanding between coats is quite different from coarse sanding. A small trial panel will check whether the paint is yet hard enough to sand. If a category A finish is not necessary, overcoating adheres well enough to most modern paints and varnishes without sanding, provided you do this before the previous coat gets rock hard. International Paints make a brush-on liquid sander to soften and flatten hard enamels.

Dry preparation
Sand dry on bare timber (or over thin priming) to eliminate moisture and prevent the grain from swelling. Dry sanding also provides a better bond for reliable paint adhesion on fibreglass. If you prefer, first sand wet, leave a while, then finish off with dry paper.

Wet-or-dry paper
Waterproof abrasive paper is expensive. It can be used wet or dry. It clogs rapidly when used dry, but can be rejuvenated by scrubbing with warm water and detergent, then leaving to dry.

Sandpaper
The cheapest carpentry sandpaper or glasspaper will disintegrate when damp. It needs dry storage and is best not left on board. Always rub two sheets together before use to get rid of erratic grit which can leave score marks on delicate paintwork.

Garnet paper
Free second-hand belts from factory or boatyard sanding machines will still do useful work for hand sanding. The garnet paper normally used for 6 in (150 mm) wide belts has a rather stiff backing but it will wrap around a cork block. Although superior to common sandpaper, it must also be stored in the dry.

Non-clog paper
New products are always appearing. Non-clog silicon carbide paper (such as Tri-M-Ite Fre-Cut) has been in use for a long time by car body repairers, and is

now on the handyman market. This is the best choice for dry sanding and it also works well in orbital (vibrating) sanders. Though costly, diamond-coated sanding blocks can outlast hundreds of sheets of the best paper.

Stripper blocks
Generally too vicious on tender new paint, the soda block or pumice block (Plate 31) is a cheap and efficient tool for sanding. Three grades are available: fine, medium, and coarse. Always used wet, they level off high spots rapidly, but they can be troublesome on concave surfaces such as the flared bow sections of some powerboats. One block would normally complete one side of a 30 ft (9 m) boat above the waterline before wearing too thin to hold. A similar but superior tool is the 3M Flexible Sanding Sponge.

Plate 31 Provided surfaces are not wavy, a soda block sands perfectly at minimal cost.

Finger protection
Wearing gloves is a good idea when sanding. With a stripper block, finger protection is essential – unless you want to lose your fingerprints! A pad of thick cloth (see Plate 31) will do, renewed or rinsed out occasionally. Proceed as with wet abrasive paper (see later) but dunk a block every thirty seconds and the 3M Sponge every two minutes.

Table 2

Abrasive paper comparisons

Grit numbers (Silicon carbide, Al. oxide) Wet-or-dry	Sandpaper (for dry, bare wood)	Garnet paper (for dry, bare wood)	Emery paper, cloth and tape (for metal)	Appearance or feel
600				Silky
400		10/0		Egg shell
320		9/0		White flour
280		8/0	000	Clinging
240		7/0		Visible grit
220	00	6/0	00	Fine file
180	0	5/0	0	Table salt
150	1	4/0	FF	Fine-sawn wood
120	1½	3/0	F	Nail file
100	F2	2/0	1	Silver sand
80	M2	0	1½	White sugar
60	S2	½	2	Coarse file
50	2½	1	2½	Velcro
40	3	1½	3	Builder's sand
36		2		Rasp

Choosing the grade

Various methods are used for grading the coarseness of sanding materials. Table 2 gives an approximate comparison of the most common ones. Using wet-or-dry paper, a grade between 100 and 180 is generally best for sanding last year's paint or varnish – used wet, and with heavy pressure. For sanding between fresh coats, use a grade between 240 and 320, also wet, but with light pressure. Well worn, coarse grades work quite well for fine work. When sanding dry, choose a finer grade than for wet.

Cork block

Patent holders with rubber or felt pads are made for abrasive paper, but nothing is simpler or better than the standard painter's cork block, which generally measures 4¼ in (108 mm) × 2¾ in (70 mm) × 1⅛ in (28 mm). A block ensures that surface high-spots are cut down more vigorously than the depressions, but only fingers are capable of getting the paper into corners and around mouldings.

Shaped block

For sanding a long spar, gouge out a small pine block with a hollow to fit snugly onto the spar. For a pear-shaped spar, make two or more blocks. A convex shape is useful when sanding a coved topside band or stripe line.

Sanding wet

Crease and tear a sheet in half. Fold once and wrap this around the cork block. Turn the folded paper over occasionally during use. Also, turn it at right angles (and even diagonally), so that every part comes into use.

Soapy water

Keep a pail of *soapy* water near you and dunk the paper about once a minute when sanding. A muddy liquid forms on the surface and this will clog the paper without frequent dunking. Dampen the work surface to add lubrication when starting a panel.

Panel limits

Treat topsides in panels about 2 ft (600 mm) × 1 ft (300 mm), gradually getting an even lather over all. Use chalk or bits of masking tape near by to mark the ends of panels, thus avoiding needless overlaps.

Swabbing down

Having sanded about six panels, wipe down with a piece of damp towel, then wipe again with a clean towel which is frequently dunked in a pail of *fresh* water. Finally, dry off with a third piece of towel. After sanding for about a half-hour, discard the soapy water. Rinse the dirty towels in the fresh water, add detergent or soft soap, and fill the other pail with clean water. Warm water is more comfortable to work with than cold.

Surface quality

When dry, a matt frosted finish should appear. If many glossy indentations still show, use a piece of dry paper (without the cork block) to roughen them. To obtain an equally fine finish when sanding entirely dry, you may need to finish off with a finer grade of paper.

Interior work

Unless you have a good extractor fan, avoid burning off or using chemical stripper below decks. Dry sanding makes a lot of dust, but the drips from wet sanding are easily absorbed by sheets of newspaper or rag laid over any joinery work (or the cabin sole) immediately beneath.

Rough plastics

The rough interior surface of a fibreglass hull is impossible to sand. All you need do is remove any flaky paint with a wire brush or coarse abrasive paper, then wash away dirt and grit with a warm washing-soda (sal soda) solution, finally rinsing and drying.

Damp bilges

Boats of timber and steel generally have painted bilges which need re-coating at least once every five years. Complete stripping is rarely necessary, but you must scrape away loose material, clear the limber holes (waterways) under frames and bulkheads, gather up grit, and get rid of all oil and moisture. When laying-up ashore (see Chapter 12), wash out the bilges immediately (using degreaser or detergent and water) for they may take months to dry thoroughly. An old vacuum cleaner is ideal for pulling debris out of corners and crevices; otherwise dab with Scotch tape to collect the grit.

Fumes and dust

If your boat is housed in a small shed or garage, make every effort to get her outside for burning off, chemical stripping, or power sanding. Fumes and dust can be troublesome to other workers in a large shed. Under these conditions, you can still remain popular by doing such objectionable tasks early in the morning and avoiding weekends.

Caulking and paying

There are still plenty of boats around with planked hulls and caulked decks. Soft white cotton yarn is driven into the narrow seams found in yacht work, while oakum (hemp yarn impregnated with Stockholm tar) is often used on big old boats. All caulking is sealed in with a thin layer of stopping called *paying*.

Traditional pitch

For a rough old boat, you can still pay with cheap, old-fashioned pitch poured from a ladle for decks, and brushed on to hull seams, then scraped off flush when cold and brittle. Another ancient recipe for hull seams is tar putty, made by beating coal tar and whiting into a dough, sometimes with the addition of common Portland cement powder.

Synthetic compositions

Though they are expensive, most boatyards now use one of the air-curing or catalyst rubber compositions for deck seams – either as paying, or to fill the seams completely. Rubber is not easily sanded to a fine finish, but a white version suitable for topsides is available (see later). For the underwater seams of category C yachts, cheaper alternatives containing bitumastic putty and asbestos fibres are available, similar to the mastics used for repairing flat roofs.

Caulking tightness

Do not forget that correctly driven caulking adds strength to planked hulls and decks. This bonus is lost when seams are filled entirely with resilient compositions. However, caulking driven too hard can cause distortion, especially when fastenings are weak.

Caulking irons

Various shaped tools are needed to caulk seams of different widths, for working close to the keel, or for expanding seams which are too narrow. A few caulking irons, and the traditional mallet used, are sketched in Fig. 8. For a minor job you can get by with various stubby screwdrivers, a blunted cold chisel, and a hammer. Further information on the use of caulking tools is given in *Boat Repairs and Conversions*.

Rotten cotton

To re-caulk a leaky seam, run a saw along the paying and break it all out. A tool to rake out old caulking is shown in Fig. 8(e), or it can be formed on the tang end of a file, as described in Chapter 2. If a short sample of old cotton or oakum crumbles between the fingers, you must renew it all. If it resists pulling apart, harden down with a caulking iron and re-pay the seam.

Seam priming

Paint any bare wood found within the *Vee* of a seam before caulking, using a narrow seam brush (Fig. 8(g)) on thick planking, or an old toothbrush for shallow seams. Try to use a primer which is compatible with the paying.

Number of strands

Caulking cotton is sold in 1 lb (½ kg) balls, and the loose rope usually contains eight continuous strands. Separate the strands and carry out a few trials to see how many strands you need to drive neatly into a seam.

Twisting cotton

Having chosen the number of strands, twist these tightly into a rope by securing one end, tying the other end to a bent nail in the chuck of an electric drill or hand drill, and winding away for a few seconds. Lengths of 20 ft (6 m) are convenient when there are long seams to caulk.

Driving cotton

With a narrow tipped iron, pinch the cotton into the seam at intervals of about 6 in (150 mm), then go back and do likewise every 1 in (25 mm) as seen in Plate 32, finally driving continuously to an even depth of about ⅛ in (3 mm) below the surface. As the cotton beds down, use caulking irons of increasing thickness (which almost fill the seam width) and increase the force of the mallet blows. Professionals often dip their caulking iron in tallow to prevent it jamming. To join cotton, overlap the ends by about 2 in (50 mm) and twist them together.

Wide seams and butts

To deal with a short length of extra wide seam, bunch the cotton into closely-spaced loops. Use off-cuts of cotton to caulk the vertical butt seams between plank ends. Oakum proves much cheaper than cotton for the wide seams found in some old vessels. Take care to avoid driving right through such seams. In bad cases, first carry out the special

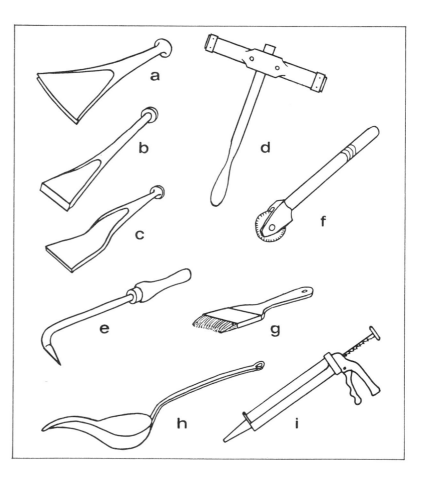

Fig. 8 A selection of caulking tools.
a single crease iron. **b** blunt iron. **c** bent iron. **d** traditional mallet. **e** home-made raker. **f** caulking wheel. **g** seam brush. **h** glue ladle. **i** caulking gun.

Plate 32 Holding a caulking iron this way means minimum injury should the mallet miss its mark.

43

repair work detailed in *Boat Repairs and Conversions*.

Rolling oakum

If your marine store cannot order oakum, try a boatyard that repairs fishing vessels. Transforming a bale of hairy, compressed oakum into a loose rope suitable for caulking takes a little time, but the knack is soon acquired. Pull a large wad from the bale, and tease this out between the fingers, aiming to form a sausage about 2 in (50 mm) in diameter and 3 ft (1 m) long. To reduce this to about ½ in (12 mm) diameter for driving into seams, twist it as tightly as possible by rolling it between thigh and palm of hand.

Heavy mallet

Shipwrights use a massive hardwood mallet (see Fig. 8(d) and Plate 33) with metal ferrules around the business ends. This tool is not easy for the amateur to wield. For brief repair work, a heavy carpenter's mallet will do on thin planking, and a 3 lb (1.5 kg) club hammer for big boats.

Holding the iron

To minimize injury should the mallet miss its mark, support a caulking iron on the palm of the hand, knuckles downwards (as shown in Plate 32). If you have never watched a shipwright caulking, a few words with such a person can save a lot of experimentation.

Deck seams

Caulking deck seams is easier than hull seams, because of the more restful working position. The seams of bare scrubbed decks are not normally primed, for fear of staining the surface. Otherwise, prime with paint or varnish compatible with the surface coating, or with the type of paying used. If thin priming paint drips right through, lay sheets of newspaper down below and wipe the deckhead (overhead) before the paint hardens.

Marine glue

Much superior to pitch is the more resilient hot-poured deck paying composition called *marine glue*. Being cheap and quick, the process is still widely used. Always get the best quality yacht glue, available in repair sticks as well as 56 lb (25 kg) kegs.

The ladle

The narrow-spouted ladle (see Fig. 8(h)) and Plate 34) must be of thick metal to retain the heat. Whether or not you leave a large central gluepot simmering, one operator needs two ladles, in order to keep one of them hot while the other is in use. A small gas burner resting on a metal plate supported by battens across the deck is generally more convenient than a wood fire on shore. For paying the miles of deck seams on big ships, electrically-heated ladles mounted on wheels are used, having guide blades to align them, and an offset spout for working close to bulwarks and deckhouses.

Single or double pass

Avoid stewing marine glue for too long, and do not let it boil. Insufficient heating leads to air bubbles, poor adhesion, and over-filling. An expert can pour marine glue flush with the surface in one run. Learners find it easier to make two passes. This gives good results provided no more than six hours elapses between pours, and the weather is dry.

Scraping flush

Marine glue or pitch scrape best when brittle, on a cold day or early in the morning. A heavy bent file scraper (see Fig. 3(a)) works fine and is less likely to damage a wooden deck than thin-bladed types. Wetting the deck is beneficial.

Modern paying

Whether you have a traditional solid teak deck, or an imitation one with thin teak strips glued over plywood, fibreglass, or ferrocement, the seams may be filled with one of the polysulphide rubber compositions (which have proved themselves for thirty years) instead of the old-style caulking and paying. These materials are so expensive that many people prefer to drive a few strands of cotton underneath!

Wide choice

You have to decide whether to use one of the cheaper single-pack compounds, supplied in cartridges fitting straight into a caulking gun (see Fig. 8(i)), or whether to use the more reliable, quick-setting catalyst type. Of the many makes, Life-Calk at present has worldwide popularity and is available in both types. Most makes recommend their special wood primer to ensure a perfect bond. This is especially important with oily timbers like teak. The wood must be clean and dry before priming.

Two-pack work

Do not mix too much catalyst composition at one time, for it may go stiff before you can get it into the seam. The knife shown in Fig. 6(a) makes the soundest job, though Life-Calk is available in a Type P, which can be poured.

Surplus composition

Removing surplus material is troublesome and can only be done by sanding when fully cured. Until you become proficient, masking tape both sides of each seam is not a bad idea. Luckily, most of these materials shrink slightly on curing.

Plate 33 When caulking decks, the working position is more restful than for topsides or bottom.

Plate 34 Traditional glue ladle being used to pay deck seams.

4
Painting and Varnishing

This chapter may be of little interest to the lucky few who buy a new boat every year or two. For the rest of us, however, painting and varnishing becomes the single most time-consuming task in annual maintenance. Varnish weathers rapidly on a deck or hatch top. Deks Olje is more practical for the busy sailor.

Seasonal damage

Few cruising boats escape at least some damage during a season. The culprits include anchor flukes, mooring chains, chafing at docks and alongside when unattended, racing dinghy bombardment, and the friendly tiro who comes alongside with a dinghy minus any form of fendering. Oil pollution plays havoc with topsides and boottops, while ugly stains form below scuppers and chainplates, and salty crystals left on varnishwork magnify ultraviolet light damage.

Abrasion resistance
Steel boats resist damage the best, followed by ferrocement, solid wood, fibreglass, light alloy, cold moulded wood, and plywood, in that order. Some fibreglass and plywood hulls can easily chafe right through during a single rough night at moorings when a critical fender carries away. On certain neglected canals, boats scrape along the thick silt, losing their bottom paint. Steel hulls are best for coping with this sort of treatment.

Paint formulations

To combat the various knocks and discolorations, most topsides need an annual repaint. This makes the adoption of expensive, long-life catalyst paints somewhat questionable. All catalyst enamels and varnishes (such as two-can polyurethane) are exceptionally durable, provided they stick on well. They are popular for coating fibreglass, and for any rarely-damaged part of a boat which, like a car, can be polished each season for several years.

Adhesion
Long-life materials need perfect adhesion to make them worth while. Most two-can (catalyst) types demand a warm, dry atmosphere (plus thorough surface preparation) for reliable adhesion. Varnish appears more susceptible to poor adhesion than enamel because teak and some other popular brightwork woods are oily and do not bond well. Furthermore, dark varnishwork becomes hotter under the sun than pale shades of enamel, and bond failures show up readily as yellowish patches under a transparent coating.

One-can enamels
The cheapest alkyd paints are still widely used for houses and boats, but they now have more durable rivals, including the one-can polyurethanes and acrylics. For spraying, car paint is good on FRP or metal. However, spraying can be a health hazard, especially with antifouling paints.

Eggshell finishes

For interior surfaces that do not need to be glossy, silk vinyl, matt vinyl, and eggshell varnishes can prove attractive. Externally, most deck paints and antifoulings are eggshell, as are epoxy and chlorinated rubber paints for steel. To help obliterate the topside waviness often found on ferrocement, metal, and fibreglass hulls, you can change a catalyst gloss finish to eggshell (after curing for three weeks) by sanding lightly with wet 400-grit paper, followed by bronze wool.

Added phenol

Make sure that any matt domestic paint used below decks is guaranteed to inhibit the growth of mildew and mould. Few makes have an effective fungicide additive, and the same applies to silk vinyl (eggshell finish) paint. Although phenol may be added to any water-based emulsion paint at the rate of 1 oz per gallon (24 ml per 5 litres), many of these paints are now of the non-drip variety which should not be stirred.

Bottom paint

Unless sheathed with copper or cupro-nickel (or fitted with special internal sonic vibrators), yachts left almost permanently afloat need poisonous bottom paint to minimize marine growths. When such craft are of fibreglass (especially in fresh water), there should be a thick coating of suitable epoxy paint beneath the antifouling to prevent osmosis or wicking damage. Copper-free paints must be used over marine alloy (including engine drive legs) or galvanized parts. For other surfaces, the soft antifoulings (which must be kept submerged) are cheapest. Middle-priced ones include hard racing types, often based on copper compounds. These may be allowed to dry and can be burnished. At the top of the price range come the co-polymers (no longer containing tin compounds) which dissolve gradually to reject all fouling. Teflon coatings remain slippery and inhibit growths. Cheap low-friction graphited paints (used on shore-based racing boats) are not true antifoulings.

Choosing enamels

Most boating enthusiasts are proud of their shiny topsides. When deciding what sort of gloss paint to use, consider the following facts.

(1) The cheapest alkyd enamels brush effortlessly to a fine finish, adhere well, but tend to lose their sparkle after one year.

(2) Alkyds are handy for repairs and touch-up work. Catalysts are troublesome to mix in small quantities, and any surplus must be thrown away. Brushes should be cleaned out regularly during a long session (see Chapter 2).

(3) Without the addition of a retarder, catalyst materials set so rapidly in warm weather that joining one panel of brushwork to the next, invisibly, proves impossible.

(4) On plywood and cold moulded hulls, polyurethanes and epoxies applied inside and out can stop the wood from absorbing water. This is important for racing craft and all multihulls.

(5) Most catalysts permit the application of two coats in one day, eliminating the need to sand between coats. Alkyds form surface skin during storage (see Chapter 2), creating wastage and the need for straining. Wastage occurs with catalysts only when too much is mixed for the job in hand.

(6) Special primers and undercoats are not always needed with catalyst paints – a simplification which also reduces wastage.

(7) Although perfect brushwork is difficult to achieve on wide surfaces with catalysts, if you have sufficient time, defects can be rubbed down and then polished, as with car bodywork.

What paint was used before?

When you buy a second-hand boat, finding out what type of paint or varnish was last used on her is not always easy. Rub a small area with wire wool, rub vigorously with metal polish, then buff with rag. Polyurethane will shine, while alkyd paint (and traditional boat varnish) will go dull. Rubbing with cellulose thinner will dissolve most car-type paints, while pouring on boiling water will soften most acrylic finishes.

Mixing

Most paints form sediment, especially after prolonged storage. New cans rarely form a skin inside and may be rolled about occasionally for several days prior to use. Antifouling needs this most of all. Once opened, pour off one-third of the liquid, mix the remainder with a smooth wooden stick or a power drill attachment (see Fig. 3(e)), then replace the liquid and mix again.

What to avoid

There could be failure if you apply catalyst or car

paint over existing alkyd finishes. No paint takes properly over anodized light alloy spars or fittings. Any type of varnish is best stripped before changing to a painted finish, and you cannot apply varnish reliably over hardwoods that have been treated with teak oil or wax.

Comparative costs

To compare the economics of using alkyd and catalyst material, four schedules are listed in Table 3, showing the total annual cost for amateur and professional work during the normal repainting of a sailing or motor cruiser about 30 ft (9 m) in length. Fibreglass hulls are covered in Part 1, bare steel in Part 2, marine alloy and zinc coated steel in Part 3, and wood in Part 4. The schedules include typical annual treatments during cycles of between six and ten years' duration, including one complete stripping job.

Fibreglass economics
Starting with a new boat which does not require topside painting until the fifth year, fibreglass maintenance works out the cheapest. The other craft could be much older, and thus save money on their lower capital values. Stripping paint off fibreglass is difficult and can damage the gel coat. Allowance has been made in that schedule for sanding thoroughly when repainting fibreglass, in an attempt to eliminate the need for any future stripping.

Paint specification
In the schedules, alkyd costs are not very different from catalyst, because the latter are made to last for two years, receiving a quick polish for the second season. Using this method, an alkyd finish is likely to be smarter than a catalyst during the second season. A drastic change from, say, red to white, will demand extra coats. The antifouling paints allowed for in the schedules are best quality with the catalyst specification, and medium-priced with the alkyds. No costs are included for the maintenance of masts, spars, rigging, sails, engine, ballast, dinghy, or plumbing equipment, as these items need similar attention regardless of hull construction.

Steel boat decks
In these schedules, the metal craft are presumed to

have decks clad with teak, and thus little deck maintenance expenditure is necessary. Steel decks coated with resilient composition, embossed vinyl, or fibreglass, may need painting when old.

Rust check
Sometimes, boatyard costs for the external painting of steel increase steadily each year as larger and larger areas start to corrode and need extra treatment. Rust can occur under a perfect film of paint without being detected, so stripping after five years ensures that the hull surface is checked, as well as ensuring that maintenance costs are reduced in subsequent re-fits.

The range of marine coatings available for steel is bewildering. Having decided to adopt one-can or two-can materials, stick to the recommendations given in a certain paint maker's data sheets.

Zinc sprayed steel
Provided a steel hull has been correctly metallized with zinc from new, maintenance requirements should cost no more than for a marine alloy hull during the first fifteen years or so. To ensure this, the metallizing thickness must be at least 0.01 in (0.3 mm) below the waterline, and 0.005 in (0.15 mm) for topsides and internal bilges.

No undercoat
The schedules in Table 3 are not intended to represent category A perfection. In any case, it may be necessary to touch up some paint and varnish during the season to maintain a smart appearance. Many variations to the conventional painting specifications shown are possible, especially when using alkyds. A matt undercoat need not be used at all; two gloss coats are more durable than one. In some cases a single coat of enamel or varnish may suffice. Should this fail to produce the required quality, it might pay to apply a second coat mid-season.

Catalyst costs
Two-can polyurethane enamel has been allowed for in the catalyst costing. One-can polyurethane would be cheaper, though quite a bit dearer than alkyd. Epoxy resin enamel is the most expensive of all catalysts, but also the most durable. Professional workers raise their rates when using two-can materials as weather conditions are more critical, while time must be allowed for mixing and regular brush cleaning.

Clean bilges

The craft in the schedules are presumed to be of modern design with very little inside ballast. Thorough bilge cleaning has been costed every few years, but some attention to bilges is wise every year to obviate foul smells and to keep the bilge pump intake clear.

Sprayed fibreglass

Schedule 1 assumes topside gel coat coloration; white fibreglass could well remain smart for eight years before needing paint. Do not be fooled by those new boats which are spray-painted at the factory – maintenance levels could be the same as for a wooden hull.

Fibreglass bottoms

Make sure that a new fibreglass hull arrives with the bottom already prepared to receive antifouling paint. This is not always the case, and much work is then involved in removing release agent and sanding a glossy gel coat. Although costly, anti-osmosis epoxy treatment (see page 65) is good insurance. Mostly on topsides, silicone is anathema to paint. Use the latest remover from your chandlery, or straight xylene.

Brushing technique

There is quite a difference between the brushing action for applying traditional boat varnish (or alkyd enamel) and the whole range of two-can materials. Although modern undercoats are intended to be self-levelling, some care is needed to apply them evenly without brushmarks. The topcoat should then produce a fine finish. Using a single material for two coats of catalyst paint, sand as necessary to prevent defects on the first coat from showing through the topcoat.

Alkyd brushwork

There is no need to hurry when applying alkyd paint. After skin removal and thorough mixing, pour a small quantity of paint into a proper paint pail, or a clean fruit can. Dip only one-third of the bristle length, and press the brush on the inside wall of the pail to remove surplus paint. Spread the paint rapidly into a small panel using your most comfortable arm and wrist movements (see Fig. 9(a)). Follow this with further strokes at right angles to the first ones (Fig. 9(b)) and, for best results, brush again diagonally (Fig. 9(c)), finishing with strokes in the original direction. On planking this should be parallel to the grain.

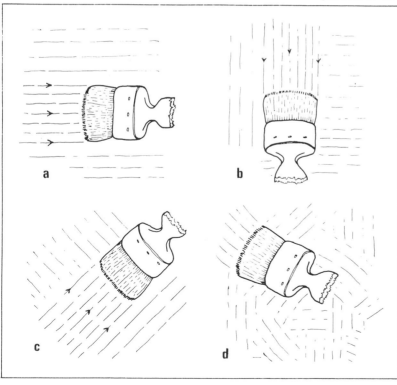

Fig. 9 Brush strokes. **a** starting and finishing direction. **b** second distribution strokes for alkyds. **c** third distribution strokes for alkyds. **d** random strokes for polyurethanes and epoxies prior to laying off.

Table 3

Typical maintenance schedules for fibreglass, metal and wood for a 30 ft (9 m) sailing cruiser

NOTES: Cost are in £ (UK). For $ (USA), multiply Amateur cost by 1.8 Boatyard cost by 2.5. Taxes and slipping costs are excluded.

A = Alkyd paint specification
B = Catalyst paint specification.

PART 1: FIBREGLASS

Some varnished trim and joinerwork. Pigmented gel coat. No boottop. Boat 5 years old at start.

Year	Task	Amateur cost		Boatyard cost	
		A	B	A	B
1st	Topsides – wash, fix surface damage, polish	10	10	240	240
	Bottom – scrub, sand, fill, two coats	90	160	390	460
	Deckworks – wash and polish	5	5	90	90
	Brightwork – sand, touch up, two coats	7	13	140	150
	Total	112	188	860	940
2nd	Topsides, bottom, deckworks and brightwork – as for 1st year	112	188	860	940
	Fo'c'sle – wash, paint and varnish } Bilges – scrub with detergent }	8	18	300	315
	Total	120	206	1160	1255
3rd	Topsides, bottom, deckworks and brightwork – as for 1st year	112	188	860	940
	Saloon – wash, paint and varnish	10	20	290	305
	Total	122	208	1150	1245
4th	Topsides, bottom, deckworks and brightwork – as for 1st year	112	188	860	940
	Galley – wash, paint and varnish } Bilges – as for 2nd year }	8	18	300	315
	Total	120	206	1160	1255
5th	Topsides – sand, touch up, two coats	40	80	510	600
	Bottom – strip, sand, two coats	105	175	645	715
	Deckworks – wash, fix surface damage, burnish	18	18	180	180
	Brightwork – strip, fill, three coats	20	35	260	295
	Total	206	363	1535	1715

Table 3

Year	Task		Amateur cost		Boatyard cost	
			A	B	A	B
6th	Topsides – touch up. A: sand and one coat. B: polish		30	12	330	240
	Bottom, deckworks, brightwork – as for 1st year		102	178	620	700
	Cabins and bilges – as for 2nd year		8	18	300	315
		Total	140	208	1250	1255
7th	Topsides – as for 5th year		75	150	510	600
	Bottom and brightwork – as for 1st year		97	173	530	610
	Deckworks – sand, fill, two coats		25	45	330	360
	Cabins – as for 3rd year		10.	20	320	335
		Total	207	388	1690	1905
8th	Topsides, bottom, deckworks, brightwork – as for 6th year		132	190	950	940
	Cabins and bilges – as for 4th year		10	20	320	335
		Total	142	210	1270	1275
9th	Topsides, bottom, brightwork – as for 7th year		172	323	1040	1210
	Deckworks – wash, touch up. A: sand and one coat. B: polish		15	6	180	90
		Total	187	329	1220	1300
10th	As for 1st year	Total	112	188	860	940
		Totals over 10 years	1468	2494	12155	13085
		Average cost per year	**147**	**250**	**1216**	**1309**

Table 3

PART 2: STEEL
Ungalvanized mild steel. Teak clad decks. Varnished trim and joinerwork.
Boat 10 years old at start.

Year	Task	Amateur cost A	Amateur cost B	Boatyard cost A	Boatyard cost B
1st	Topsides – chip rust and damage Build up, sand and two coats.	50	100	650	760
	Bottom – scrub. Treat as for topsides	80	140	500	660
	Boottop – sand, two coats	8	14	170	190
	Deckworks – as for topsides	30	50	400	430
	Brightwork – sand, touch up, two coats	7	13	140	150
	Total	175	317	1860	2190
2nd	Repeat 1st year, but reduce Spec. B. to one coat on topsides, boottop, deckworks and brightwork	250	280	2010	1900
	Fo'c'sle – sand, paint and varnish	6	16	185	200
	Bilges – scrub, chip rust. Build up. Two coats.	30	60	700	740
	Total	286	356	2895	2840
3rd	Repeat 1st year, but reduce Spec. B. to touch up and burnish on topsides, boottop and brightwork	250	310	2010	1700
	Saloon – sand, paint and varnish	12	24	350	365
	Total	262	334	2360	2065
4th	Topsides, bottom, boottop, deckworks and brightwork – as for 2nd year	250	280	2010	1900
	Galley – sand, paint and varnish	6	16	225	240
	Total	256	296	2235	2140
5th	Strip all external steel surfaces Derust, prime twice, fill, three coats	190	300	1750	1860
	Brightwork – strip, fill, three coats	20	35	260	295
	Bilges – as for 2nd year	30	60	700	740
	Deck – renew seam paying where necessary	20	50	470	500
	Total	260	445	3180	3395
6th	As for 1st year	175	317	1860	2190
	Totals over 6 years	1414	2065	14,390	14,820
	Average cost per year	**235**	**344**	**2398**	**2470**

Table 3

PART 3: LIGHT ALLOY OR ZINC SPRAYED STEEL
Unpainted bilges. Teak clad decks. Varnished trim and joinerwork.
Boat 5 years old at start.

Year	Task	Amateur cost A	Amateur cost B	Boatyard cost A	Boatyard cost B
1st	Topsides – sand, stop, two coats	40	80	510	600
	Bottom – scrub, sand, fill, two coats	90	160	390	460
	Boottop – sand, two coats	8	14	170	190
	Deckworks – as for topsides	25	40	300	330
	Brightwork – sand, touch up, two coats	7	13	140	150
	Total	170	307	1510	1730
2nd	Topsides, deckworks and brightwork – touch up A: sand and one coat. B: polish	37	16	660	500
	Bottom – as for 1st year	90	160	390	460
	Boottop – sand, stop, one coat	4	7	90	100
	Fo'c'sle – sand, paint and varnish Bilges – scrub	10	20	400	415
	Total	141	203	1540	1475
3rd	Topsides, boottop, deckworks, brightwork – sand, touch up, one coat	42	75	580	620
	Bottom – as for 1st year	90	160	390	460
	Saloon – sand, paint and varnish	12	24	350	365
	Total	144	259	1320	1445
4th	As for 2nd year except accommodation and bilges	131	183	1140	1060
	Galley – sand, paint and varnish	6	16	225	240
	Total	137	199	1365	1300
5th to 8th	Repeat 1st to 4th years **Total**	592	968	5735	5950
9th	Strip all external metal surfaces Prime, fill, three coats	170	280	1400	1500
	Brightwork – strip, fill, three coats	20	35	260	295
	Deck – renew seam paying where necessary	20	50	470	500
	Total	210	365	2130	2295
10th	As for 1st year	170	307	1510	1730
	Total over 10 years	1570	2901	13,290	15,649
	Average cost per year	**157**	**290**	**1329**	**1565**

Table 3

PART 4: WOOD
Planked, plywood, or cold moulded. Painted deck. Boat 20 years old at start.

Year	Task	Amateur cost A	Amateur cost B	Boatyard cost A	Boatyard cost B
1st	Topsides, bottom, boottop and brightwork – as for Part 3, 1st year	145	267	1270	1400
	Deck – scrub, touch up, one coat	20	40	220	240
	Total	165	307	1490	1640
2nd	Topsides and brightwork – touch up. A: sand, one coat B: polish	24	9	410	300
	Bottom and deck – as for 1st year	110	200	390	460
	Boottop – sand, one coat	4	7	90	100
	Bilges – scrub, two coats	30	50	400	440
	Fo'c'sle – sand, paint and varnish	6	16	185	200
	Total	174	282	1475	1500
3rd	Topsides, bottom, boottop, deck and brightwork – as for 1st year	165	307	1490	1640
	Saloon – sand, paint and varnish	12	24	350	365
	Total	177	331	1840	2005
4th	Topsides, bottom, boottop, deck and brightwork – as for 2nd year	138	216	890	860
	Bilges – scrub	4	4	150	150
	Galley – sand, paint and varnish	6	16	225	240
	Total	148	236	1265	1250
5th to 8th	Repeat 1st to 4th years — Total	664	1156	6070	6395
9th	Topsides, bottom and deck – strip check caulking and paying Sand, prime, fill, three coats	160	300	1870	1900
	Brightwork – strip, fill, three coats	20	35	260	295
	Total	180	335	2130	2195
10th	As for 1st year — Total	165	307	1490	1640
	Total over 10 years	1673	2720	14,455	16,375
	Average cost per year	**167**	**272**	**1446**	**1638**

Table 3

SUMMARY OF AVERAGE ANNUAL COSTS

	Amateur cost		Boatyard cost	
	A	B	A	B
Fibreglass	147	250	1216	1309
Steel	235	344	2398	2470
Alloy	157	290	1329	1565
Wood	167	272	1446	1638

Laying off

Continue the above process until you have an arm's length panel, then eliminate all brushmarks and joins by *laying off*. This is done as shown in Plate 35, by holding the brush lightly between thumb and forefinger (sloping at 45° to the surface) and making slow, steady strokes parallel to the grain. Work from top to bottom of the panel, in one direction only, towards the finished work, overlapping each stroke by about one-half a brush width. Carry each stroke very slowly onto the previously painted panel for a distance of about 2 in (50 mm), releasing all pressure on the bristles to zero at the end.

Plate 35 To lay off enamel, stroke lightly in one direction, always towards the previous panel.

Runmarks

If you feel an uneven drag on the brush while laying off, this indicates insufficient foundation brushwork. Thick paint is liable to form runmarks (*curtains*) before it dries. In addition, a thick film can wrinkle on hardening. When a coat is too thin, the brush drags heavily when laying off. The finish will probably have poor gloss and poor durability. Keep looking back in case any runmarks have developed on parts laid off some time previously. Further laying off may still be possible by using very slow strokes – brushmarks are less offensive than runmarks.

Insects

Any insects which land on wet paint are best left alone. They leave insignificant marks if mopped off a few days later.

Slow hardening

Alkyd enamel reaches optimum hardness when a thumb nail is unable to mark the surface – usually about three months after application. Before this, fenders can spoil the gloss; one advantage of painting topsides at laying-up time. A delay of about four days is advisable before using dry sandpaper on alkyd gloss. Wet sanding is usually possible in half this time.

Varnish brushwork

Having no pigment, traditional air-drying synthetic boat varnish (such as Rylard in Britain or Awlspar in the USA) flows more easily than enamel. Runmarks occur more readily, while dust and other particles more often mar the finish. Brushing technique is the same as already described for alkyds. A good quality 2 in (50 mm) paint brush is convenient for all except narrow parts. A special varnish brush with shorter bristles does a better job – if you can find a stockist nowadays.

Foaming

After working for a short time, boat varnish may foam within the bristles and the tiny air bubbles can cause surface imperfections. If this worries you, press the bristles across the rim of a spare can periodically, and remove the surplus from each new brushful of varnish into that same can. After standing for thirty minutes, the air bubbles will disperse, enabling this varnish to be used perhaps on some less important part.

Catalyst brushwork

The brushing technique for two-can polyurethane and similar materials is unique. They dry rapidly in warm weather, prohibiting the laying off of sizeable panels. Professionals like to use a 3 in (75 mm) brush, with fewer bristles than a standard paint brush. A rapid crisscross action (see Fig. 9(d)) works best, as used for household wall paints. Catalysts are slightly thixotropic (i.e. they will not sag) and do not like being brushed repeatedly. For category B work, apply a second coat as soon as the first one has set, without sanding. Once rock hard, catalysts should be fine sanded before being over-coated. The great application speed of a painting pad eliminates most problems caused by rapid hardening on vast topside areas.

Brightwork problems

As already mentioned varnish has little body. For high-class results, special care must be taken over laying dust, straining the varnish, avoiding air bubbles, cleaning brushes (see page 24), and cleaning the surface.

Fighting dust

Little can be done to eliminate airborne dust in a big shed or out of doors. For the mirror finish sought by racing dinghy owners, get the boat into a garage where all openings can be sealed, unauthorized entry prohibited, and flooring dampened to lay the dust. Wear clean overalls and take all the precautions for every coat of varnish – not just the last one.

Straining varnish

The slightest skinning can load traditional boat varnish with small particles which pock-mark the finished job with hard nibs, often thought to be dust. To obviate this, strain through a double layer of nylon stocking – even when a new can is opened, to be on the safe side.

Surface grit

Varnishwork quality may be judged by the number of nibs (from whatever cause) visible on completion. Feel proud if you count only two per square inch (6 cm^2). Average results reveal about ten per square inch. With no precautions taken, the number can rise to as many as 100 per square inch. Only a tack rag will remove all surface dust before varnishing. A dry cloth is useless and a rag soaked in turpentine weakens the varnish adhesion. Polyurethane varnish can be fine sanded and polished to get rid of nibs, but this takes a lot of time.

Tack rag

Impregnated with sticky resin and sealed in a waterproof envelope to preserve this, a tack-rag can be re-folded to offer many working surfaces. Perfect paint- or varnishwork cannot be done without one. Discard only when the rag looks dirty or feels dry. Clean your sticky fingers with turpentine or mineral spirits.

Weather conditions

Category A work is difficult to achieve in the open air and precautions are necessary to guard against rain, dew, and frost. Early in the year, work should cease well before 2 p.m. (1400), otherwise the surface may become bloomed. This condition kills the gloss on paint or varnish. It does not normally mean stripping – abrasive paper followed by re-coating suffices. A much harder sanding is necessary to get rid of the marks left by raindrops. Lay rags along decks or stuffed into scuppers to prevent marks on topsides caused by dew seeping down.

Filling grain

On bare wood (and sometimes after stripping) the use of a grain filler can save four coats of varnish when striving for a mirror finish. Each varnish maker has his own pet brand of transparent or tinted grain filler. Smear this across the grain with a piece of coarse cloth. Wipe off surplus, and fine sand when hard enough. Most marine hardwoods (such as teak and mahogany) have pores which cry out for grain filler. The need is far less essential with finely sanded softwoods such as spruce or cedar. In the USA, most wood stains come already mixed with grain filler.

Staining

Except for teak and afrormosia, all woods benefit

from a certain amount of staining before varnishing. Keep to your varnish makers' specification, but the liquid naphtha stains kept by paint stores are compatible with most materials. Stain nearly always needs to be thinned. Three dilute applications go on more evenly than one strong brushing, and this helps maintain better control. Staining before grain filling generally works best, but it can be done afterwards, or both before and after. Although not recommended, stains are made to mix with varnish. This is a quick way to get the right tint, but subsequent damage becomes more noticeable. Even on mahogany, brownish shades look better than red for boatwork. Dilute cedar stain is fine on spruce and it also works well on mahogany and agba when a touch of red is added.

Discoloration

Where varnish has weathered off (Plate 36), great care is necessary to stain the bare wood correctly. Too pale is better than too dark. Resort to stained varnish if necessary to deepen the tint later. Small areas of discoloration around fittings and fastenings are easily camouflaged by painting them with an artist's brush. Small dabs of matching enamel are easy to mix using orange and brown for teak, red with brown and white for mahogany, and yellow with orange, brown and white for spruce.

Rollers and pads

In addition to the well-known advantages of rollers for applying matt wall paints, with correct technique they can produce excellent results for gloss finishes, while reducing the time taken by as much as fifty per cent. Air-drying materials work better than catalyst ones: painting pads are superior for two-pack material.

The team

As a roller leaves a stippled finish, you have to lay off each panel with a brush to produce a high-class finish. One person rolling keeps pace with a second person laying off with a 2½ in (63 mm) brush. Ideally, you need a third person with a 1 in (25 mm) brush and a small pot of paint to cut in the edges.

Film thickness

Distribution is generally more even with a roller than with a brush, leading to paint economy. Keep looking back for runmarks, and load the roller with less paint if these are tending to occur. The usual sloping paint tray allows a big variation in loading the roller, while the pressure applied at the work surface, together with the number of traverses made in different directions, gives adequate latitude for controlling film thickness. The stippled effect left by a roller is satisfactory for antifouling the bottom of most cruising boats. Burnished graphite, copper, or Hard Racing antifoulings for racing boat hulls need to be laid off as for enamels.

Plate 36 Once the varnish has been allowed to weather off, teak is much easier to revive than mahogany.

Plate 37 A long-handled roller speeds bottom painting on a big hull.

Limitations

Brushes work better than rollers on narrow panels, beadings, spars and grooved boarding. Rollers and trays are troublesome to clean after use, generally making them most beneficial on jobs of long duration. Throwaway foam rollers simplify cleaning, but they do not work very well. Foam is dissolved by some paints and varnishes, so a brief test is worth while.

Special rollers

Details of types and sizes of rollers are given in Chapter 2. Lengthening the handle (Plate 37) by as much as 3 ft (1 m) often speeds up bottom painting – and will enable you to reach the high topsides of certain category C craft from beach level. The use of special narrow rollers is rarely warranted – a brush is more convenient. Remember to put a drop of oil on a roller spindle to prevent squeaking and wear.

Antifouling

A familiar mid-winter sight is the boat hauled out ashore with dried barnacles and weed still in position. A lot of unpleasant work could have been saved by cleaning these off when tender, immediately after hauling out. At that time, a small piece of plywood will scrape off barnacles, while a household scrubbing brush will make short work of weed.

Smooth bottom

Category C boats often have rough below-water surfaces. These are cheap and quick to maintain, but a category A finish improves a boat's speed so markedly under sail or power that it often pays to improve an old boat in this way. A further improvement in performance is possible between a normal category A finish and a racing finish.

What to use

New antifouling products frequently come onto the market (see page 47) while proven ones lose popularity. The most expensive materials are not necessarily the longest lasting, and certain paints seem to suit one locality better than others. Pick the brains of the local pundits before deciding.

Last job

Antifouling is traditionally the last major job before launching (after the annual re-fit), largely for the following reasons: some antifoulings still need to be applied no more than one day before launching; a planked hull dries out to the maximum just before launching; antifouling paint makes a good sealer for small drying-out cracks.

To avoid getting plastered with poisonous paint, reverse the normal procedure if possible and work mainly from the keel upwards.

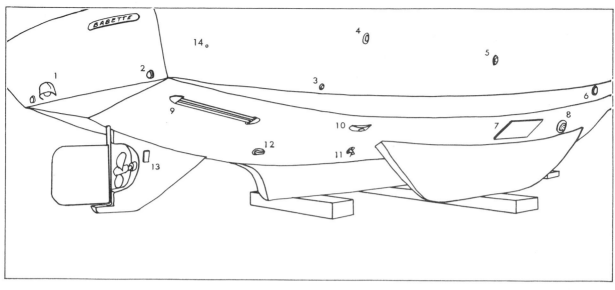

Fig. 10 Some hull fittings. **1** engine exhaust outlet. **2** cockpit drain. **3** cooling water telltale. **4** bilge pump discharge. **5** galley sink waste outlet. **6** toilet soil discharge. **7** radio ground plate. **8** toilet intake strainer. **9** engine keel cooler. **10** transducer for depth sounder. **11** log/speed impeller. **12** deckwash salt water intake. **13** sacrificial zinc anode. **14** drain from propane lazarette.

Plate 38 In tidal waters, a scrubbing grid saves the expense of hauling out.

Underwater fittings

Some owners never bother to paint the underside of the keel, and this is almost impossible when beached. On a grid (Plate 38) or chocked up ashore, movement over a tide or jacking up to shift the chocks is generally necessary to reach every part. Avoid painting a radio ground (earth) plate, zinc anode (see Fig. 10), or impeller, Pitot tube, or sensor for a speed/log instrument. Avoid clogging an intake strainer or cutless bearing feed pipe (Plate 39), but do paint over a depth sounder transducer, a keel cooler (see page 181) and the propeller of a boat which rarely moves under power. Poke antifouling well into any toilet outlet and clear out tiny anchor-well drains.

Plate 39 Barnacles sometimes block the water vent into a cutless rubber bearing.

Alligatoring

Category A and B owners should adhere to a certain paint maker's specification from the bare hull to antifouling coat. Category C owners often use black varnish (coal tar and naphtha) or bitumastic paint as both primer and undercoat. The fitting-out routine is then to scrape off any flaking or powdery antifouling, touch up bare places with black varnish, and apply one coat of it over all. *Alligatoring* (surface crazing) occurs to most antifoulings on top of tar or bitumen after a few months, so the system suits cheap antifouling which needs a further coat mid-season. If crazing occurs over fibreglass, the correct procedure is to sand off to the gel coat before repainting.

Sheathed hulls

Black rubber sheathing is available in some countries to put an elastic skin over a leaky hull. Some category C owners use car undersealing dope for this, while others swear by the sealants used for treating damp walls and leaky flat roofs! Fibreglass sheathing is painted in the same way as a fibreglass hull. Most antifouling paints are compatible with the vinyl coating used for Cascover nylon sheathing. Copper sheathing needs no antifouling. An annual fresh water scrub does it good, plus a check over for loose nails, damage and pitting.

Ballast keel

Cast iron ballast keels are remarkably resistant to rust. They are normally treated in the same way as the rest of the bottom, as are lead keels. Bare steel or galvanized bilge keels, rudders and skegs, need the same paint specification as hulls of similar material. Special paint for a concrete keel is not so readily available: most boatyards use epoxy or swimming pool paint, and antifoul over that.

Copper paint

Antifoulings containing large amounts of copper powder act in a similar way to copper sheathing, and can be burnished to a fair finish for racing. Avoid these (and paint containing mercury) on aluminium alloy hulls, for fear of galvanic corrosion.

Hard Racing

Like copper paints, the popular cellulose-based Hard Racing antifoulings will stand scrubbing, and can be applied at any time prior to launching. They do not inhibit growth as effectively as the latest copolymers (see page 47). With correct thinning, application by spray is possible.

Poisonous chemicals

Traditional soft antifoulings contain poisonous chemicals which leach out slowly. They are best applied within twelve hours of launching – certainly not more than twenty-four hours. Some owners like to slap on an additional coat along the waterline (and over the rudder) an hour or two before launching. This tends to prolong the protection of this region, which is subject to maximum sunlight and water temperature. Of thick consistency, this type normally covers about 300 sq ft per gallon (7 m^2 per litre), whereas Hard Racing and metallic copper antifoulings can cover up to 500 sq ft per gallon (11 m^2 per litre).

Between tides

Most antifoulings are formulated to permit application as a boat dries out on a falling tide (see Plate 40). To hasten drying, use fresh water if possible for scrubbing and rinsing off. Make sure that successive tides are getting bigger, or you may find your boat beneaped for a couple of weeks. Wear a wet suit or waders if necessary to enable scrubbing to start as the water recedes. Having painted around the waterline, start the keel as soon as possible in case the tide rises more quickly than you expect.

Useful strandings

Some owners like to carry a can of antifouling on board. Should they run aground on a falling tide, painting then commences, to make the stranding appear intentional! A little beach sand on the brush speeds weed scrubbing greatly.

Deck painting

With the exception of scrubbed teak, most deck surfaces require painting at some time. The full range of possible needs is rarely marketed by a single paint maker, but a good marine hardware store should stock all types of deck coating.

Slippery dangers

Although most fibreglass boats have anti-slip patches glued on where necessary, the remaining glossy areas can cause accidents when wet. A coat of anti-slip deck paint instead of enamel is a good idea when the gel coat becomes scratched and blotchy, if not sooner. Form accurate boundaries between coamings (and other glossy vertical surfaces) by the careful use of masking tape.

Plate 40 Plenty of help is necessary to scrub and paint the bottom of a large boat while the tide is out.

Over sheathing

Fibreglass sheathing (with an intrinsic roughness) is commonly found over decks of plywood, metal, and ferrocement. A layer of tinted gel coat resin will freshen this up, but too great a thickness could make it smooth and dangerous unless grit is added. Likewise, the special paint for reviving the appearance of embossed vinyl sheathing can eventually obliterate the pattern. However, its rubbery nature makes it fairly safe without added grit.

Liquid plastics

Instead of having to re-canvas a leaking deck (or cover it with embossed vinyl), much the same result is achieved by brushing or scraping on thick liquid plastics such as Dekaplex. The anti-slip properties are good and most of the common pastel shades for deckwork are available. All fittings need not be removed, but curing leaks is more certain when this is done. Study the makers' instructions to ensure correct application.

Sprinkled grit

Many paint and varnish firms produce a special anti-slip grit for sprinkling over ordinary gloss finishes (or gel coats) while still wet. After hardening, surplus grit is removed by brushing or hosing. Mixing grit with the paint or varnish makes for a better looking deck, but not such a safe one. Fine dry silver sand (available from pet-shops) is often used for this job.

Name boards

Nowadays, the identification of most cruising boats is simplified (even from a distance) either by a compulsory dock number at the bow (Plate 41), or by her name appearing in huge letters along permanent dodgers attached to the guardrails (see Plate 18) – efficient, though ugly. In contrast, vast numbers of trailer-mounted runabouts and dinghies bear no means of identification – a great lure to thieves.

Plate 41 Displaying a registration number at the bow is mandatory at some ports. Not a pretty sight.

Plate 42 Transom name boards can be made into attractive features.

Individual styles

The amateur is provided with plenty of aids in the form of decals, transfers, or rub-on poster letters, plus raised screw-on and stick-on letters of metal or plastics. Making individual nameplates (Plate 42) can be fun. Some category A owners insist on carved teak or genuine gold leaf, while the odd category C character may foil thieves by the use of a branding iron! New name boards can make a lot of difference to the appearance of a craft and a few winter evenings spent making new ones could pay dividends.

Lettering templates

Building contractors often keep sets of thin zinc stencils in various sizes. If you borrow these, remember to dab the paint on with stiff stubby bristles to ensure clean-cut lines. Fill in the gaps left by the metal bridge pieces using a small artist's brush. Lay out each word first with pencil marks scribed through the stencil. To get closely-spaced letters you may need to let the paint dry on every alternate letter before filling in the remainder.

Trade secret

To produce that professional signwriter finish, never set out capital letters with equal spacing between their extremities. This can result in a most uneven appearance. Study the top line in Fig. 11. Although all letters are equally spaced, the right-hand word

looks crowded – like a dark patch when viewed from a distance, or with half-closed eyes. The secret is to increase the spacing between letters with vertical sides, while reducing the space between letters with a lot of air space around them (particularly T, Y, A, O and the right-hand side of L) almost to zero.

Pricking through

To letter name boards (or direct on the hull) with an individual or fancy style, draw the word between ruled lines on a strip of paper, using a soft pencil. Not all sailors are good artists, so you may need to enlist the help of a draftsman or signwriter. Having secured the strip with masking tape, pricking through is possible on most freshly painted surfaces. On plastics (or where the paint is too hard to mark), hold the paper across the inside of a room window in sunlight and outline all lettering on the back of the paper heavily with soft pencil. Position the strip on the boat, then scribble across the lettering with a hard, flat carpenter's pencil (or similar tool), which will leave an outline once the strip is removed. As an alternative, lipstick, or wet paint, will do.

Real gold

Elegant yachts enhance their appearances with a gold coving line around the sheer, trailboards with inlaid gold carvings, and the ship's name picked out in gold. The most popular form of gold leaf is sintered (sprayed) onto thin paper. Beaten gold leaf

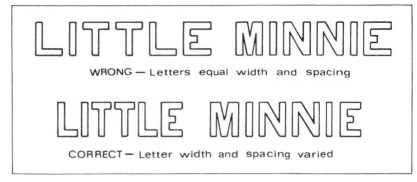

Fig. 11 Signwriting is not that simple. Equal spacing gives a slip-shod appearance.

costs twice as much, but makes a superior job. Most gold paint is unsatisfactory, turning dull when a coat of varnish is put over it. Aerosol gold paint is sometimes better.

Stick it on
Both types of gold come as leaves in a small book. Name boards need only six or seven leaves, sometimes available from a signwriter or building contractor. Gilding is the final job on a name board. Paint each letter accurately with thin yellow topcoat. When tacky, press on gold leaf (while holding the backing) until every bit is used. Press with dry rag for firm adhesion. Next day, brush away loose scraps. If in the future some gold gets scratched off, it will still look yellow until repaired with dabs of varnish and gold leaf. Varnish on top of gold leaf mars its brilliance.

Down below

The interior of a sailing dinghy or yacht's tender often receives more abuse than the outside. The inside is readily seen, and therefore needs careful maintenance. Except for the cockpit area, the interior of a cruising boat normally receives (and needs) less frequent beautification than the outside.

The easy way
The cabin decoration of a big boat takes an unexpectedly long time. The wise owner will plan this work so that only one compartment is tackled each year and the smell of new paint is minimized.

Bilge paint
Wooden boats of categories B and C usually have bilges painted with some form of bitumastic paint. For category A, eggshell white lead paint (or something similar to the topside specification) is common. Keep to the same type of material as used previously when re-painting. A white finish (as in most fibreglass bilges) helps to locate lost parts, and debris which could cause evil smells. Some wooden racing yachts use catalyst bilge paint, preventing the additional weight of bilge water soaking into the wood. Except when flaking occurs, bilge paint should last many years.

Pig paint
To prevent pigs of inside iron ballast from fouling the bilges with rust, apply a couple of coats of epoxy pitch when they are next unshipped. This should last up to 20 years. For concrete ballast, use swimming pool paint. Lead ballast needs no protection.

Steel bilges
The internal bilges of fibreglass, ferrocement and marine alloy boats are often left unpainted. Steel should be protected, even when zinc sprayed. Epoxy-pitch is popular for category A work, while bitumastic or red oxide may be found on a category C boat. Each paint maker has his own pet product for steel bilges. To test compatibility with existing paint, some makers will supply small sample quantities. Bubbling, crazing, or flaking indicates incompatibility. To make sure, apply the sample several months before complete re-painting.

Degreasing and drying are all-important factors when painting bilges. Even a domestic hair dryer can prove useful!

Cabin paint
Polyurethane enamels are ideal for cabin decoration: they are harder than alkyds, show less discoloration in the presence of stoves, and they can be rejuvenated by polishing. Eggshell and matt finishes help reduce condensation troubles – most persistent on hulls of fibreglass, ferrocement and metal. Household vinyl

paints are easy to apply and all such surfaces need little more than thorough washing before re-coating. Make sure these materials are guaranteed mildew-proof (see page 47).

Cabin varnish
Polyurethane varnish is popular below decks, though the appearance is often improved by flatting with steel wool. Special eggshell and matt varnishes are available; easier to clean than oiled teak, but of similar appearance. Some of them need stirring.

Which finish?
Telling the difference between traditional boat varnish and polyurethane is easy, as the latter will burnish and the former will not (see also page 47). French polishing is often found on the joinerwork of old yachts. This dissolves when rubbed with alcohol or methylated spirit. Teak oil is widely used on most hardwoods, giving a waxy, porous look; acetone and rag will clean the dirt off it. If you cannot stand the smell of acetone, use warm turpentine.

Dripping
The granular cork paint mixtures traditionally used inside steel hulls to stop condensation are comparatively cheap. Uncored fibreglass sweats badly and really needs panels of polyurethane foam bonded on – or sprayed on in liquid form – to provide better insulation. Matt or eggshell vinyls are simpler to apply than enamels on such surfaces.

Hot parts
To paint engines and stoves, you must obtain heat-resisting enamel. This is rarely stocked by marine stores, and is more a line for automobile factors and engine overhaul specialists. No marine engine looks right (or seems to *work* right) unless neatly painted! An engine room (especially the overhead) may with advantage be coated with fire-retardant paint. Some local factories can undertake stove enamelling suitable for space heaters, but the vitreous enamelling used on cooking ranges (and exhaust manifolds) is almost impossible to get done. You are supposed to buy brand new parts!

Tank paint
Fuel tanks are not normally painted inside. If the inspection cover is large enough to permit thorough internal cleaning and de-rusting, the life of steel water tanks may be greatly extended by correct internal painting (see page 207). Sandblasting makes the best preparation for epoxy where a tank is removable. Untreated galvanized drinking water tanks are believed to cause zinc poisoning.

Drop keel case

Painting problems occasionally arise – such as how to work underneath the engine, behind the stringers and beam shelves, or inside a centreboard trunk.

Dinghy slot
For a sailing dinghy, dry her out, plug the keel slot (using a batten sealed with canvas and mastic), then fill the trunk with wood preserver, linseed oil, or thin paint, and let this stand for at least a full day before draining off. Thick paint or varnish is not likely to stay intact everywhere, due to the scraping action of the drop keel.

Concealed case
On a cruising yacht, the situation is different. The trunk is likely to be accessible only from the keel slot upwards, perhaps with just a hoisting cable pipe inside leading to the deck. A cruiser needs to be high and dry to drop the board out. As the case must dry before treatment, the job is best done during a winter lay-up period. To paint inside, if a standard long-handled tar brush is too big, make a *striker*. Cut the handle off a 2 in (50 mm) paint brush and screw the brush at right angles to the end of a batten. (See Fig. 3(g).)

Metal trunk
Where a drop keel is of galvanized steel, the keel slot may be too narrow to insert a brush. In that case fill the trunk with preservative, as mentioned above for a dinghy, but fit a drain cock (or a wooden plug) into the slot sealing batten, to facilitate emptying the fluid. If a galvanized steel trunk has rusted inside, borrow a cylindrical wire boiler-tube brush to scour it. Alternate this action with soakings of phosphoric acid. Wipe out with rag on a stick, let dry, fill with bitumastic paint, then drain. Do not forget to paint the slot after removing the sealing batten. Even when no rust is visible inside, interior painting will double the life of a steel case.

The blade
Having chocked a boat up high (or dug a trench under the keel) to drop the centreboard, this makes a good opportunity to draw a few keel bolts for examination – or to get them X-rayed *in situ*. At the

same time, all necessary repair work must be done on the board, includings its fastenings, hoisting gear, pivot pin, ballast weights, friction pads, and edge protection bands. While laid up ashore, rest a drop keel on a pad, to allow the hoisting gear to be slackened.

Jammed solid
On certain drying moorings, pebbles get forced into the keel slot, proving difficult to dislodge. If the trunk sides are accessible, some owners install two or more inspection plates just above the water level.

Bottle brush
It takes patience to paint the hidden parts of a framed hull, such as behind clamps and stringers. This may never have been done since the original builder's primer. Use a bottle brush lightly charged with paint. Hardware stores and pharmacies keep bottle brushes in a range of about seven diameters. Watch for drips and wipe these away as they form. Two coats are sure to be necessary.

Experiments
Boatowners get bombarded with details of revolutionary new paint products. Those from well-known firms will normally have been subjected to rigorous testing, but not often do such products reduce boat maintenance costs drastically. Aqueous crack-seeking elastic sealers with compatible topcoats (including ultra-violet blocking varnishes) are getting familiar – so are paint additives that improve brushing and adhesion. Teflon-based antifoulings need to get cheaper.

Blisters and worse
Despite the adoption of improved resins and techniques by many builders, thousands of yachts are still susceptible to so-called osmosis damage. This occurs below the waterline when FRP craft are left afloat for long periods, especially in fresh water. The gel coat – often slightly porous – acts as a membrane, allowing soakage into minute defects in the matrix, or by wicking and capillary action along individual strands.

Funny smell
Unless found by moisture meter scanning, the first signs are tiny gel coat blisters – hence the popular

expression *boat pox*. Some liquid oozes out when a blister is pierced, often smelling of styrene, like a mixture of ammonia and pear oil (amyl acetate).

First aid
Caught soon enough, you can dig out a blister (see page 29), syringe out with warm fresh water, dry off and fill flush with epoxy underwater putty, which adheres well over moisture. All this could be an early warning sign to treat the whole bottom as follows.

Epoxy seal
To waterproof a suspect gel coat, fill and sand carefully before applying (under ideal conditions) a primer and two coats of two-can solvent-free epoxy paint, such as International Gelshield. With a really bad case of pox, after the gel coat has been removed (as described on page 29) the final operation usually consists of steam cleaning, then the special epoxy. The primer is brushed on thinly, then the gel coat is built back on with five thick coats applied by roller. To avoid leaving any holidays (gaps), every other coat is given a little contrasting pigment. Up to three coats a day is possible at 75°F (24°C).

Faulty laminate
If erratic gel coat peeling has damaged the laminate, the best repairers (before epoxy painting) apply a layer of fibreglass cloth set in epoxy resin. If the laminate reveals weak or spongy areas, they may decide to apply a layer of 18 oz (600 g) woven rovings sandwiched between two layers of 1½ oz (450 g) chopped strand mat.

Balsa breakdown
In some respects, getting water into an absorbent balsa wood core creates worse damage than boat pox. Being cheap and light, balsa sandwich decks have appeared on some 75% of all FRP yachts – both power and sail. A crack in the outer skin (or a leaky fitting) can destroy much of the deck, especially after severe frost. More danger lurks where topsides or bottom are balsa cored. In contrast, a Divinycell (PVC) core (properly bonded as described in *Complete Amateur Boat Building*) is impervious to water and will not delaminate.

5
Deckwork and Sheathing

Decks are important structural members of most boats. Careful maintenance is advisable to eliminate leaks and ensure safety, as well as to improve appearance. On wooden boats, rainwater causes rot far more readily than salt water, so deck leaks create more than just discomfort down below. For this reason (see also page 16), sea water is always better than fresh water for washing traditional wooden decks.

Types of decking

The majority of yachts nowadays have decks of fibreglass, ferrocement, or metal, which are all relatively free from leakage. However, where grabrails, stanchions, vents and deck fittings are bolted on, there is plenty of scope for leaks.

Smart teak
On good quality sailing craft and powerboats, narrow teak planking is still considered the smartest and safest deck surface. The same in appearance as the solid teak caulked decks of old, modern versions consist of thin wooden strips fixed to the basic deck.

Frequent scrubbing and hosing keeps a teak deck smart. Few owners have time to do this properly, so preparations such as *Teakbrite* are available to bleach the wood and remove stains. Doping teak or pine decks with the Danish product *Deks Olje* simplifies in-season maintenance greatly. (See page 44 for seam treatment.)

Canvased decks
Although laughed at nowadays, a tongue-and-groove or plywood deck covered with unproofed cotton canvas weighing at least 12 oz per sq yd (400 g per m²) can be highly satisfactory. Modern sailcloth is useless, but secondhand tent canvas is ideal for the impecunious. Past failures were caused in three ways – canvas too thin (like calico); gluing this down (it cracks if the wood shrinks), and bending it over a sharp edge, as in Fig.13a. Good canvasing needs little care except scrubbing and renewal of no-skid paint. Surface damage may be repaired with a smearing of epoxy putty, duly painted over.

Sheathed decks
Although far more expensive, fibreglass or embossed vinyl sheathing is now more popular than canvas for covering new and repaired light wooden decking. Of the embossed vinyl materials, *Trakmark* in Britain and *Nautolex* in the USA are typical. Woven nylon sheathing (described later in this chapter) relies on a paint covering, while various easy-to-apply rubbery liquid sheathings are also marketed (see page 78 and Table 5).

Launch decks
Sailing dinghies, runabouts, and similar small craft often have decks of varnished plywood, sometimes with teak veneer and simulated deck seams. Annual re-varnishing (see Chapter 4) keeps them in good condition. The appearance of mahogany-faced ply-

wood is ruined once the varnish is allowed to weather off. Gloss paint then makes the best future finish.

Metal surfaces

Well-built steel and alloy yachts have decks clad with teak strips, but these may terminate before the deck edge (see Fig. 12), leaving a region requiring similar paint maintenance to the boat's topsides. Some category B yachts have a screed of resilient composition (such as Semtex, marketed world-wide by Dunlop A.G., D-6450 Hanau, West Germany) covering a metal deck, often coated with standard anti-slip deck paint. Commercial craft with epoxy-treated bare steel or treadplate decks sometimes have removable teak gratings or duckboards over the frequently trodden parts.

Renewing canvas

Although requiring a lot of manhours, renewing deck canvas is a fairly simple job and constitutes a worthwhile amateur undertaking – as does changing to a more modern system.

Other benefits

Renewing a deck's covering not only prevents future leaks and rot, but it also offers a good opportunity to rejuvenate a boat where necessary, with new foot-rails (Plate 43), beadings, and the fastenings to deck fittings – also perhaps to get the chainplates regalvanized.

Common faults

Make sure that previous faults are not perpetuated. As well as those detailed on the previous page, see that the wood is planed dead fair, quadrant mould-ings are shaped to fit snugly (Figs 13(c) and (d)), and that you measure the exact locations of any plugged holes for bolts and screws.

Groundwork

First strip off all removable deck fittings, beadings, and footrails. Thin beadings are sure to break, especially if nailed, but new ones always make a better job, and should be obtainable (in teak, mahogany, or pine) from a good marine hardware store or moulding supplier. Small beadings certainly remove most easily if you split them longways with a chisel and withdraw the fastenings later.

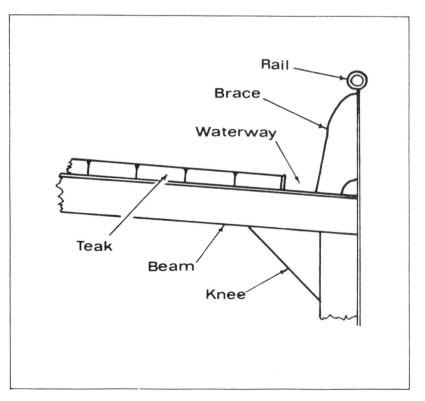

Fig. 12 A common scupper arrangement found on metal boats.

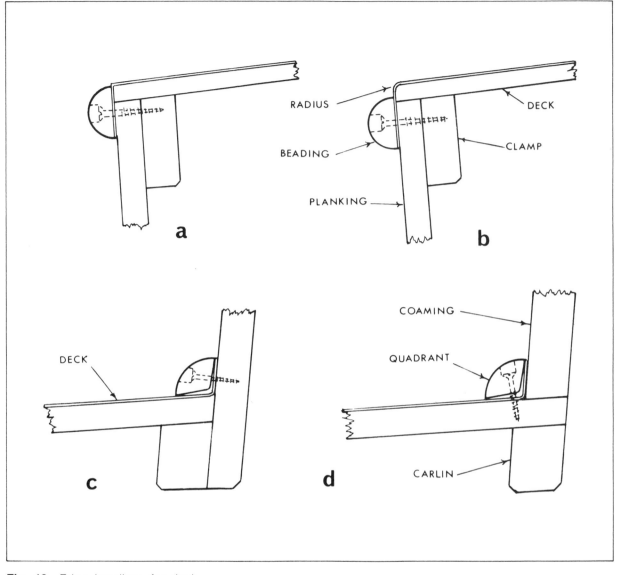

Fig. 13 Edge beadings for deck canvas or vinyl covering. **a** sharp arris leads to cracking. **b** a lower rub-rail permits rounded deck edge. **c** and **d** angle of screws depends on coaming construction.

Plate 43 Fitting new footrails after re-canvasing a deck.

Removing old canvas

When the canvas is firmly stuck down, burning off proves more successful than using a chemical stripper. Some parts usually pull off more easily than others, so it helps to divide the area into 1 ft (300 mm) squares, cutting through the paint and canvas with a razor knife or fine saw.

Planing down

Removing copper tacks is easy, by tapping under each head with an old wood chisel and mallet, followed by pincers. Decking nails should be punched down to enable the whole surface to be planed fair. The Stanley Surform plane is useful for this, as it will not be damaged when striking broken copper tacks.

Foundation

After soaking bare wood with a preservative, apply two coats of white lead exterior paint or undercoat. A popular alternative consists of mixing together all the paint remnants you can find lurking in old cans and giving two coats of that!

Old methods

Traditionally, canvas was laid onto wet paint and doused with water to shrink out any wrinkles before the paint dried. The amateur can avoid this messy job (except on concave surfaces, see later) by stretching his canvas over a dry foundation and then saturating it with thin paint. New canvas should be pre-stretched in the open air for about one week, repeatedly dousing it with water while stretched, if there is no rain.

Cutting

If you can obtain canvas up to 3 yd (or 3 m) wide this will often speed up the work, and it may eliminate the need for a central joint. A sailmaker will stitch such a joint for you, but you will find that stretching (Plate 44) is facilitated by securing all other seams with closely spaced ½ in (12 mm) copper tacks. If you cannot cut the cloth to bring the selvage along a tacked seam, fold the raw edge under by about ½ in (12 mm). A central seam simplifies the fitting of canvas around a mast, hatch, ventilator, or samson post (see Plate 44). For very wide decks it could prove better to run the cloth athwartships.

Tacked seams

For an exposed row of tacks, leave only about half a tack head width between each head, and the same distance back from the selvage or folded edge. For the underneath covered edge use ⅜ in (9 mm) tacks at about 2 in (50 mm) intervals (sufficient to hold the stretched edge until the upper cloth is tacked down) on a different line from the final tacks. When the lower cloth is to be stretched away from the seam before fixing the upper cloth, the hidden tacks will need to be at about ¾ in (18 mm) intervals. All seams should be bedded in mastic. Shift new seams away from the original lines of tack holes.

Plate 44 When singlehanded, a clamp and lanyard ensures that deck canvas is well stretched.

Concave surface

On some side decks having little or no camber, canvas tends to lift above the surface when stretched, so it must be glued down. Special canvas glue is made, but few marine supply stores keep it. Any non-hardening mastic (such as butyl) will do; even thick wet paint. Some stretching is possible if weights such as half-filled sandbags are laid all over.

Stretching

With sufficient helpers, hand stretching suffices. Failing this, light ropes with tackles or weights at the ends may be attached to the canvas by means of small clamps and pads of wood, as shown in Plate 44. Pull first in the direction of the major seam, and fix that properly (including beadings where necessary) before pulling in the opposite direction. Spread a band of sealer underneath all seams and corners. Note that the positions of notches around any obstacles on deck must be marked out while the canvas is stretched, or sizeable errors could occur on a long run.

Quadrant beadings

Fitting new fillet mouldings where deck canvas turns upwards along coamings and deck obstacles (see Fig. 13(c)) often improves the appearance of an old boat. Standard teak or mahogany quadrant usually needs planing along its back (Fig. 13(c)) to make a snug fit and retain a band of sealer. Cutting irregular corner mitres is speeded up if small cardboard templates are made, thus avoiding the need to hide your mistakes with stopping. Although mouldings under ½ in (12 mm) thick may suffice for dayboats, ⅝ in (16 mm) or ¾ in (18 mm) makes a better job on cruisers. Small woodscrews about 6 in (150 mm) apart are better than ring nails, facilitating the adjustment of mitres, as well as future removal. Lengths of quadrant are not normally scarf jointed – simple butts with a screw each side suffice. Screws are best driven nearly horizontal (see Fig. 13(c)) rather than at 45°, but nearly vertical if the coamings happen to be fixed on top of the deck, as in Fig. 13(d). Cut a small notch at the back to house a sewn or tacked canvas joint, ensuring a snug fit.

Half-round beadings

For a first-class job with varnished finish, gunwale rub-rails need glued scarf joints in preference to butts. Cut each scarf (with fine saw or plane) at an angle of about 5 to 1, by clamping the beadings back-to-back, as in Fig. 14(a). Traditionally, such a scarf has its aftermost point to the outside (see page 214). A lipped scarf (Fig. 14(b)) makes a superior job, but takes longer to cut. For a painted finish, dope the scarf faces with paint and secure with a couple of thin woodscrews. For varnished work, use resin glue

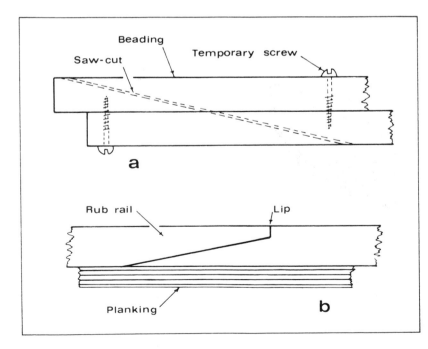

Fig. 14 Rub-rail scarf joints. **a** clamping back-to-back makes sawing easier. **b** a lip scarf is superior, but troublesome to cut.

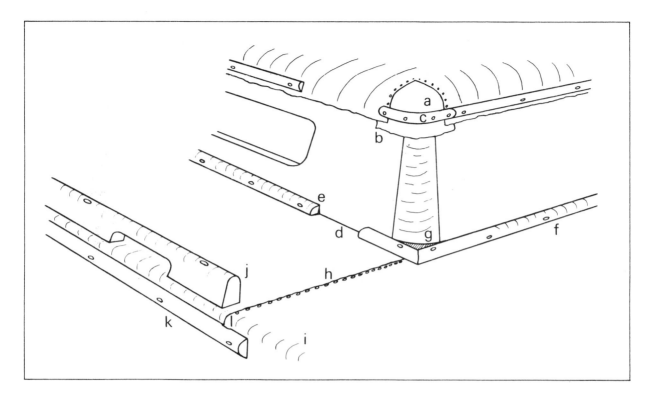

Fig. 15 The trickiest deck and cabin trunk covering jobs. **a** separate patch over rounded corner. **b** canvas yet to be trimmed off. **c** beading made from lead. **d** canvas bedded in mastic. **e** and **f** quadrant mouldings. **g** epoxy filler. **h** tacked canvas joint. **i** deck edge well-rounded. **j** footrail bolted over canvas. **k** rub-rail screwed over canvas. **l** notch in back of rub-rail to house canvas joint.

and brass pins. The hidden parts of all beadings must at least be primed before the final bedding in mastic. Surplus canvas is readily cut off by careful use of a razor-sharp knife. Clean excess mastic with a putty knife, followed by a rag soaked in paint thinner.

Curved corners

Particularly on old yachts, the vertical corners of cabin trunks and cockpit coamings are radiused at deck level. If you cannot get the lead alloy beadings which are made to form around these places, whittle them from solid wood, in short lengths to avoid weak

grain. For a corner of small radius (see Fig. 15), mitre the quadrant and fill the space behind with epoxy putty. Make cuts in the canvas to let it turn up behind a radiused beading.

Cabin top

For the compound curvature of an upper cabin trunk corner, fit a separate patch of canvas as in Fig. 15(a), slit as necessary and glue on with tacked seams each side. Lightweight canvas is acceptable on a cabin trunk roof, and its use simplifies stretching. Avoid joints if possible, but use stitching in preference to tacks, as the deck may be very thin.

Bedding fittings

Cleats, eyebolts, and other stressed deck fittings should sit on pads or chocks to prevent them cutting through the canvas. Marine plywood (well chamfered around the edges) makes ideal pads, though teak looks better when a varnished finish is required. You must put mastic over and under each pad. Almost any bedding compound will do, but so many different ones are available that it pays to enquire at your marine hardware store and read the labels on each carton. Details of repair work to canvas and the decking underneath it are given in the companion volume, *Boat Repairs and Conversions*.

Vinyl coverings

Instructions about canvasing decks, as above, are difficult to find. In contrast, the makers or suppliers of the more modern deck coverings (such as vinyls, fibreglass, and nylon cloth) usually provide step-by-step instructions. Embossed vinyl fabrics (such as Trakmark and Nautolex) are thicker and stiffer than canvas, but are tailored in the same way, and glued down with special adhesives. Cut pieces of these materials may be glued to shiny fibreglass decks to act as anti-slip patches, but thick cork/neoprene (such as *Treadmaster*) makes a better job. Antiquated houseboats sometimes adopt cheaper alternative deck coverings such as roofing felt, or even painted linoleum!

Jointing

Glued joints overlapping about 1 in (25 mm) are normally recommended for vinyls. Butt joints are neater (special vinyl tape is supplied to stick beneath the joints and form a seal) but the inevitable shrinkage eventually creates unsightly gaps. To hide these (or to prevent an overlapped edge from getting scuffed), thin rounded marine alloy strips, bedded in mastic and secured with a few small countersunk woodscrews of the same metal, make a sound job over a wooden deck. No tacks should be needed to secure the fabric prior to fitting these strips, or the rub-rails.

Sticking

Embossed deck coverings are supplied with the correct grade of contact glue, and full instructions. Some of these adhesives have a valuable property which allows the material to be shifted slightly after laying, just before full adhesion occurs. All these glues must be spread evenly on both surfaces, using the toothed applicator supplied. Panels of fabric should not be too large and a few willing hands are useful to get them placed quickly and accurately. Surplus contact glue is best cleaned off when dry by rubbing with a stiff ink eraser, but it pays to use masking tape where beadings will run, and around embossed patches on fibreglass decks.

Deck leaks

Do not rush into a big deck re-covering job when there are only a few weak places, or some leaks along the beadings. Patches of the same covering material glued on with contact adhesive could stay in place for years; or they may soon peel off. Anyway, they are worth trying. Smears of epoxy putty often seal small cracks effectively, while sealants (see below under *silicone rubber*) flow well along beadings when there is no time to strip these off and re-bed them in mastic.

Simulating rain

The entry points of deck leaks are notoriously difficult to locate. When a certain spot along a fillet or at a deck fitting is suspected, improvise a small trough made from Plasticine or window putty (Fig. 16(a)), to hold water (perhaps dyed) at the spot, and then check below for leaks. Larger and deeper troughs demand the use of bottomless cans (or strips of plywood) sealed down with putty (Fig. 16(b)). The deeper the trough, the quicker a leak can be forced to show up.

Silicone rubber

Although expensive, the fine-nozzled tubes of silicone rubber sealant (sold in black by autofactors and in white by marine and hardware stores) are often effective and long-lasting when used to cover cracks. Popular brands are made by Boatlife, Darworth and Dow Corning. Butyl sealants are cheaper but less durable. Leak-seeking epoxy resin sealants are now becoming available.

Leaky paying

Original caulking will not stay tight if the stopping (paying) was too thin, or if there has been severe wear. Short lengths of leaky marine glue paying can often be sealed again by running a hot soldering iron (with tip of suitable width) along it. Note that if the iron is too hot, the glue may become brittle on solidifying. Teak is resistant to scorching, but a pine deck could easily be blemished by this process. Do not moisten the wood, or the paying will not adhere properly.

Extensive caulking

When short repairs prove ineffectual, you may need to re-caulk whole seams, as described in Chapter 3. Changing to synthetic (polysulphide) rubber composition is a good idea on any deck which flexes slightly.

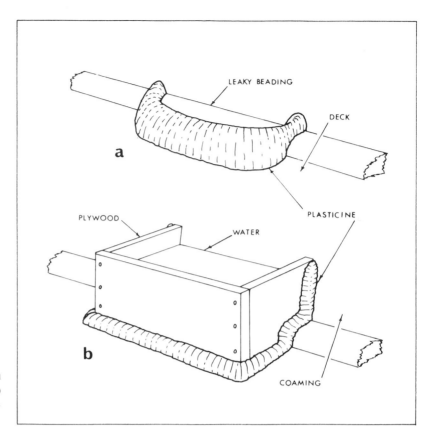

Fig. 16 Locating deck leaks. **a** Plasticine trough to hold water. **b** plywood trough sealed with Plasticine.

Wood sheathing

Should you wish to lavish loving care on an old boat (giving her decks a category A appearance by avoiding the use of painted canvas or fibreglass), decks of almost any material can be sheathed with strips of teak about ⅜ in (9 mm) thick, simulating genuine laid teak. Such strips are normally made 5 in (125 mm) wide with one false seam grooved down the middle.

Over an old, worn, pine deck, level up any hollows with resin putty, lay the strips on a waterproofing layer of mastic and fasten with thin bronze ring nails, countersunk and plugged. On a good wooden surface, belt sand, then use resorcinol glue and brass pins. On ferrocement or fibreglass, bond with epoxy glue, pressing down with numerous sand-filled plastic bags.

Using plywood
If a bad old deck is first covered with marine plywood, this makes a good foundation for teak sheathing. Plywood (such as Plydek) is available with teak strip veneers and simulated caulked seams, looking exactly like laid teak. This is fine for small decks, cockpit flooring, or cabin soles, but concealing the transverse joints between the sheets is difficult on a big expanse. Its use certainly saves a lot of tedious work. (See *Boat Repairs and Conversions* for further details of wood sheathing.)

Fibreglass sheathing

The following notes apply equally to hull sheathing and deck sheathing. Glassing over old decks is normally done to curb leakage and to reduce future maintenance. Hull bottom sheathing is used to combat teredo and other marine borers, to waterproof, to insulate against galvanic action, and to protect against damage – particularly over the thin veneers of marine plywood.

Limitations
Strengthening a weak hull is a different proposition. The sheathing must be fixed on by driving staples or

nails through the first two layers; from two to six layers are bonded over this. With epoxy resin, if the wood is pricked with $\frac{3}{16}$ in (5 mm) holes $\frac{3}{8}$ in (9 mm) deep spaced 4 in (100 mm) apart, this holds better than nails. Glass sheathing is a messy job. Try to get the hull rolled over to allow downhand working for most parts. This also helps filling and smoothing. The more layers applied, the more filler you will need to get a fair finish. Extra hands are useful to speed the job; make sure that you keep tools and fingers clean. Once fixed, the above heavy sheathing is laid up like a new hull, with alternate layers of CSM and WR.

Considerations

Wood must be cleaned free of paint, oil, or preservatives, to ensure a good resin bond. The materials are expensive, so think carefully before sheathing an old boat. Heads of fastenings may be too close to the surface to permit heavy planing or sanding. All stopping used must be compatible resin putty.

Resin choice

Although polyester resin is normally used for fibreglass work, the more expensive epoxy resin gives better results for sheathing old wood. Since many variations in materials and surfaces are possible, the amateur should seek advice from one of the firms advertising in practical boating magazines. For working on vertical surfaces, the resin must contain a thixotropic additive to prevent it from sagging. Slow-setting resin is useful in hot weather and when working short-handed.

The fabric

Chopped strand mat (CSM) makes the cheapest, densest, most waterproof laminate, but woven rovings (WR) or other types of cloth give the best finish and drape around curves more readily. Your supplier will know what material to use for any particular sheathing job. The coarse open weave cloth called *scrim* is often preferred for the top layer on deck sheathing as this, augmented by a sprinkling of grit on the wet resin, produces a good anti-slip surface. To avoid chafe on ropes, keep gritted resin clear of deck cleats.

Specifications

Table 4 shows approximate details of the weight, weave, and number of thicknesses of glass cloth required for sheathing boats of various sizes, on deck, topsides and bottom.

Priming resin

Good instructions for priming bare wood are usually supplied with sheathing materials. By using special priming resin (made by Bondaglass-Voss in Britain and Bradson in the USA), polyester adhesion can be as reliable as epoxy.

Having added the correct quantity of catalyst (hardener), plus any other recommended additives, activated resin needs to be used promptly. Only the area intended to be sheathed during the next few hours should be primed. For best results in all fibreglass work, the process should be continuous, never allowing any layer to cure completely before applying the next. Handle catalysts with great caution. Even a trace in the eyes can cause grave damage.

Tailoring

On cruising boats (Plate 45) the glass cloth is normally hung up and down like wallpaper. On small boats which can be turned over, laying fore-and-aft is simpler, especially if one roll width will cover one side of the hull. Make joints overlap about 1 in (25 mm) and keep subsequent joints well away from earlier ones. Cloth is flexible enough to follow most hull curves. Cut and form gussets when wrinkling cannot otherwise be avoided. Shaping glass cloth for deck sheathing is similar to tailoring deck canvas, see earlier in this chapter.

Wet lay-up

As soon as the priming resin has gelled, a thick coat of the moulding resin is brushed on quickly and a previously tailored sheet of glass cloth is pressed into the resin. Rolling with a washer-type or vane-type roller (augmented by stippling with a stiff brush) is necessary to get rid of all air bubbles from under the cloth. Brush on extra resin if any of the cloth appears dry after thorough rolling. Try to get all beadings back in place before the resin hardens completely (enabling a sharp knife to trim off the excess cloth), but place pieces of hardboard under foot before treading on a tender deck.

Over planking

Fibreglass sheathing over a carvel or clinker (lapstrake) hull needs to be twice as thick as for sheathing plywood, to resist any seasonal expansion and contraction. Avoid keeping such a boat out of the water for too long.

Feather edge

When a planked hull is to be sheathed from boottop

Table 4

Fibreglass sheathing specifications

Specification		Fine cloth	Woven rovings	Open weave scrim	1½ oz mat	Surface tissue
Weight of material	oz per sq yd	7	18	9	13.5	2
	(gm per m²)	(237)	(618)	(304)	(458)	(68)
Thickness of material	thou. (mils)	9	20	15	15	3
	(microns)	(228)	(508)	(380)	(380)	(76)
Resin for one layer (with primer and gel)	lb per sq yd	2	2.8	3	2	included
	(gm per m²)	(1080)	(1513)	(1621)	(1080)	(included)
Resin for two layers (with primer and gel)	lb per sq yd	2.5	4.5	5	3.3	included
	(gm per m²)	(1351)	(2431)	(2701)	(1782)	(included)

Boat length	Job					
Under 14 ft (4.3 m)	Whole hull	1 layer	—	—	—	—
14–20 ft (4.3–6 m) sound hull	Topsides	1 layer	—	—	—	—
	Bottom	1 layer	—	—	—	—
	Deck	—	—	1 layer	—	—
14–20 ft (4.3–6 m) weak hull	Topsides	1 layer	—	—	1 layer	—
	Bottom	—	1 layer	—	1 layer	—
	Deck	—	—	1 layer	1 layer	—
20–30 ft (6–9.2 m) sound hull	Topsides	1 layer	—	—	—	1 layer
	Bottom	1 layer	—	—	1 layer	—
	Deck	—	—	1 layer	—	—
20–30 ft (6–9.2 m) weak hull	Topsides	1 layer	1 layer	—	1 layer	1 layer
	Bottom	1 layer	1 layer	—	2 layers	—
	Deck	1 layer	—	1 layer	1 layer	—
30–50 ft (9.2–15 m) sound hull	Topsides	1 layer	—	—	1 layer	1 layer
	Bottom	—	2 layers	—	2 layers	1 layer
	Deck	1 layer	—	1 layer	—	—
30–50 ft (9.2–15 m) weak hull	Topsides	—	3 layers	—	2 layers	1 layer
	Bottom	—	3 layers	—	4 layers	1 layer
	Deck	—	1 layer	1 layer	2 layers	—

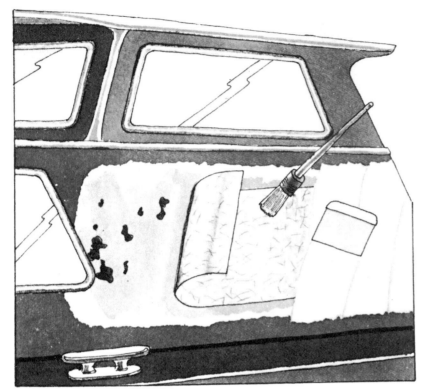

Plate 45 Typical fibreglass sheathing procedure. Super-bonding primer, polyester resin, impregnated cloth or mat, polyester filler. (*Picture by courtesy of Bondaglass-Voss Ltd, Beckenham, England.*)

to keel only, plane a shallow rabbet (see Fig. 17(a)) in way of the top edge to house the sheathing and make it flush with the topsides. To avoid this bother (and always on a plywood hull) sand off the sheathing to a feather edge as in Fig. 17(b). With two or more layers of glass, stagger the edges (Fig. 17(c)) to minimize the sanding.

Time factor
The amateur is rarely able to sheath continuously through to completion. Before laying cloth over previous resin which is fully cured, you will not get a reliable bond without resorting to coarse sanding or grinding. Even after only a few hours, stiff protruding whiskers and blobs of resin should be cut off or ground away before proceeding.

Gel coat
Note that most gel coat resins will only harden completely when a special wax is added, or a covering of cellophane is applied. Avoid adding too thick a pigmented gel coat – this may craze in time. It is better to achieve a good finish with compatible

filler, followed by two-can paint. Too thick a gel coat on deck sheathing will obliterate the anti-slip pattern. To reduce cost and weight, up to 15% by weight of filler (such as French chalk, talc, or titanium oxide) is often added to a pigmented gel coat on sheathing.

Nylon sheathing

The *Cascover* process (originated in England, by Borden (UK) Ltd) consists of sticking special nylon cloth to any wood surface with resorcinol glue, then finally doping the cloth with vinyl paint. Although more expensive than fibreglass, the process is less messy, more convenient on overhead surfaces, and better for clinker boats. The vinyl dope may be overcoated with deck paint, antifouling, or topside enamel. Cascover nylon is made in one thickness weighing 12½ oz per sq yd (430 g per m^2) but in two widths – 38 in (1000 mm) and 54 in (1370 mm). The similar *Dynel* process in the USA uses polyester cloth bedded in epoxy glue.

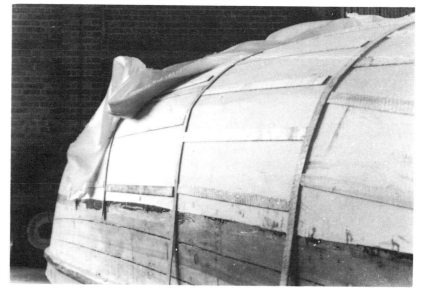

Plate 46 Thin stapled battens keep nylon sheathing in place while the glue is setting.

Close contact

Nylon sheathing has only one slight complication. To enable the cloth to be stretched well, and kept in close contact with the glue, thin strips of pine (see Plate 46) must be stapled on top until the glue hardens. Close-sawn wood about 7⁄8 in (22 mm) wide and a bare 1⁄8 in (3 mm) thick proves ideal, in lengths to suit the girth of the hull. Use 3⁄8 in (9 mm) staples fired by an industrial trigger stapler. As a rough guide, these battens need to be fitted at about 30 in (750 mm) intervals fore-and-aft, and at 18 in (450 mm) athwartships. You may need one every 2 in (50 mm) on sharp concave curves.

Obstacles

As with fibreglass sheathing, to make a sound job, remove any skin fittings and recess them a further $\frac{1}{32}$ in (0.5 mm), as shown in Fig. 17(d), to house the sheathing. Put each fitting back temporarily until the glue sets, or else use a few bare staples. Staples are easily prised out later without damaging the nylon. The holes are in any case completely filled when doping the cloth. Complex fittings such as rudder straps and metal bilge keels need not be removed, but do not glue the nylon *over* them; staple it neatly around them. Stem and keel bands are best removed. This is often a good opportunity to renew corroded or damaged parts.

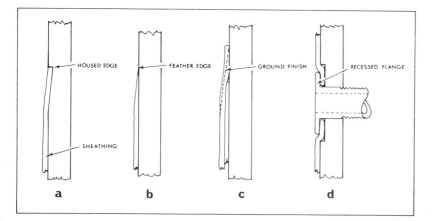

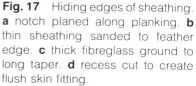

Fig. 17 Hiding edges of sheathing. **a** notch planed along planking. **b** thin sheathing sanded to feather edge. **c** thick fibreglass ground to long taper. **d** recess cut to create flush skin fitting.

Bare wood

Preparing an old hull can be the longest part of the job. Except for a few permissible blemishes, you must get it back to virgin clean wood. Having attended to stoppings (see page 38), sheath all the awkward small areas first, such as stem, keel, sternpost, wooden bilge keels and propeller shaft blisters. This is a good rehearsal for the main task, but also remember that by leaving rudder (or bilge keels) until last, you could utilize offcuts to best advantage.

Fore-and-aft cloth

Joints normally overlap by about 2 in (50 mm). For an amateur sheathing the bottom of a hull under 25 ft (8 m) in length, cloth is generally best laid longitudinally. Use a full-width roll with its selvage along the boottop, plus a cut roll tailored to close the gap towards the keel. A boottop recess $\frac{1}{32}$ in (0.05 mm) deep (Fig. 17(a)) is ideal, as Cascover cannot be ground down. Epoxy filler creates a neat feather edge.

Bonding

Having tailored a cloth roughly to shape at the ends, hold it to the boat with drawing pins (thumbtacks) and staple a pine strip across it amidships, stretching the cloth as you do so. Roll up the length from stem to strip, apply glue to the hull over a panel extending about 30 in (750 mm) from the strip, and bed the cloth into this, stretching and stapling on strips. Continue in similar fashion right to the stem, then prise off the amidships strip, roll up the cloth from aft, and proceed in that direction. For stretching the nylon, a small piece of hardboard, held and used as in Fig. 18, is ideal.

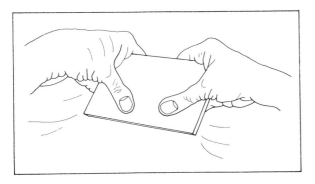

Fig. 18 Removing cloth sheathing wrinkles with hardboard pad.

Clean edges

A useful trick ensures that where sheathing ends along the boottop (whether recessed or not), an accurate clean cut line is left, with no glue starvation and no blemishes on the topside enamel. To accomplish this, a 2 in (50 mm) wide pine batten about ¼ in (6 mm) thick is tacked to the hull with its lower edge exactly where the sheathing is to end. Draw a pencil line on the hull at top and bottom of the batten, then take the batten off.

Masking

Run a continuous band of 2 in (50 mm) wide Scotch tape between the pencil lines. When sheathing, allow glue and cloth to spread up to half-way across the tape. When the glue has set (but before it gets rock hard) tack the batten back into its original position and draw a razor-sharp knife along the lower edge. Again remove the batten, then strip off the sticky tape, taking all surplus glue and nylon with it.

On decks

Using Cascover on decks involves the same procedure as for hulls, though tailoring is rather as previously described for a canvased deck.

Other sheathing systems

The approximate costs of some hull and deck sheathing processes are listed in Table 5. For thick wooden hulls, copper sheathing is the most successful, though zinc sheathing is more compatible with a boat having galvanized steel fastenings. Cupronickel foil (Mariner 706) bonds permanently to most hull materials. Its franchises operate in most countries. Thick paint-on sheathings such as Dekaplex, Rub-R-Cote, Multican X109, Limpetite and Liquid Seaprene are quick to apply and can last indefinitely.

Ahesion failure

Most modern sheathing methods rely on perfect adhesion for success. There is often no simple way to detect bond failure. When this does happen, water trapping and timber rot can develop. This problem does not arise with copper sheathing, which is not intended to be glued on: sound hull painting beneath the sheathing should never deteriorate. Further information on copper sheathing can be found in *Complete Amateur Boat Building*.

Table 5

Some sheathing cost comparisons

Process	Amateur cost		Boatyard cost		Remarks
	£ in UK	$ in USA	£ in UK	$ in USA	
	All costs per m², excluding sales tax				
Polyester resin and two layers of fibreglass cloth	16	26	70	120	one layer CSM, one layer fine cloth. For all wood surfaces.
Cascover*	20	35	75	140	Glued nylon cloth, vinyl doped. For all wood surfaces.
Limpetite**	48	70	120	200	Synthetic rubber composition. Cost for $\frac{1}{16}$ in (1.5 mm) build-up on bottom of steel or wood hull.
Dekaplex	15	24	65	105	Resilient composition applied at 1 litre per m². Types for all surfaces, including ferrocement.
Mariner 706	Professional only		100	180	Bonded cupro-nickel foil. Bottom only. Ideal on fibreglass.
Copper	18	30	76	140	Cost for 24-gauge sheet. Bottom only of planked hull.

* Worldwide mail order service by Wessex Resins & Adhesives Ltd, 11A Weston Grove Road, Southampton, England.
** Worldwide mail order service by Protective Rubber Coatings Ltd, Payne's Shipyard, Coronation Road, Bristol, England.

Anti-slip panels

Although only planked or plywood decks normally need sheathing, the maintenance of fibreglass decks includes renewing anti-slip panels and strips which are starting to peel off, and adding extra ones where the glossy deck could prove dangerous. For instance, people do inadvertently step on top of hatches; smart, glossy lids can cause accidents. Marine stores keep stick-on strips of suitable material and they will often arrange to have larger panels cut to paper templates of any shape. International Paints sell a transparent anti-slip coating intended for use on sailboards. Never use gritted panels on a sailboard if you want to avoid grazed knees!

Ventilation

Few cabin boats have adequate ventilation when left unoccupied. This gives condensation and deck leakage no chance to dry out. Improvements are easily made by adding extra ventilators and slatted panels (jalousies) in doors.

Condensation

True enough, wooden boats are vulnerable to rot caused by chronic internal moisture, but such craft (and those of foam sandwich construction) are much less likely to suffer from condensation than hulls of metal, ferrocement, and ordinary fibreglass.

Mushrooms

Some care is necessary in the choice of ventilators. The common, screw-down mushroom type is neat and not too expensive, but is by no means sprayproof, and is a snare for trapping ropes. Always keep the screw thread of metal vents lightly oiled. All vents need fly screens, which should be removable for cleaning.

Cowls

The traditional ship's cowl vent is neither spray- nor rainproof, but it directs an enormous quantity of air below – especially useful for engine compartments and bilges where occasional wetness may not be detrimental. Canvas covers with shockcord sewn into the hems are useful in bad weather. Rubber cowl vents possess the advantage of collapsing when snarled by ropes.

Shell vents

Among the least obstructive forms of above-deck ventilators are clam shell vents (Plate 47(a)) and half-cowl vents (Plate 47(b)). They are best fitted on the side of a wheelhouse or cabin top trunk, perhaps with ducting leading downwards.

Sprayproof domes

The traditional mushroom vent has been largely superseded by the Lo-Vent or Ventair type (Plate 47(c)) in stainless steel or plastics, with a spray trap built in. Some incorporate a circular decklight, or an extractor fan. Others have a built-in solar panel powering a small fan to help keep a cabin continuously aired.

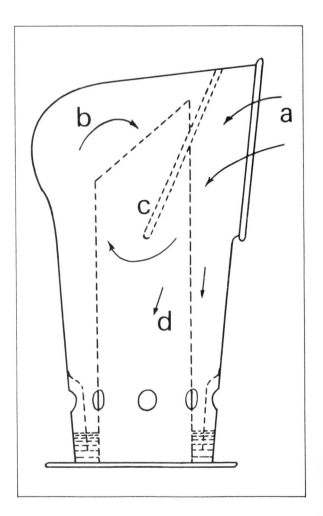

Fig. 19 How the Revon sprayproof cowl ventilator works. **a** air and spray entering. **b** dry air going below. **c** baffle. **d** water going to scuppers.

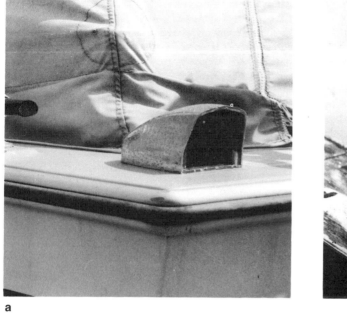

a

b

Plate 47 Popular ventilators. **a**
clam shell. **b** half cowl. **c** sprayproof
dome. **d** cowl on Dorade box.

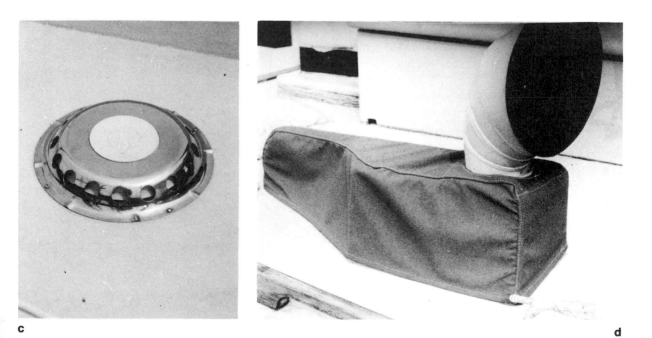

c

d

Sprayproof cowls

The finest cowl vents (such as the Revon, shown in Fig. 19) are capable of filtering out all water unless submerged by a green sea. Rotating a cowl away from the wind is often expedient.

More efficient extraction of air is possible with a *venturi* vent. Most of these are sprayproof when turned in the right direction. The latest vents incorporating a buoyant flap valve are intended to endure prolonged submersion without leaking. For other types, blanking plates are available for foul weather. Especially in the tropics, each extractor fan vent is powered by its own solar panel.

Dorade boxes

To filter air from spray, the handyman is readily able to fabricate (from wood, plastics, or metal) *Dorade* boxes with any type of vent on top. These may be tucked into an internal corner, under the deckhead as in Fig. 20, built into a boat's bow, or situated on deck as in Plate 47(d). In the tropics, fit external screens to prevent flying fish from getting into the boxes!

Mast vents

Especially for short alloy masts on powerboats, venting down from the truck is feasible, while the engine exhaust pipe goes the other way. Engine rooms need plenty of air. Cool air is better than hot. Avoid boring ventilation holes through any mast at a highly stressed location.

Fig. 21 Wind scoop to fit through open portlight.

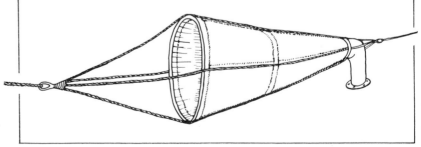

Fig. 20 Home-made Dorade box built into fibreglass cabin trunk.

Fig. 22 Improvised tropical wind-sail using a drogue or sea anchor.

Scoops

In the tropics, the word *ventilation* takes on a new meaning. Bell-mouthed canvas windsails fitted to open hatches and skylights are fine at moorings, while metal wind scoops (Fig. 21) through portholes are also suitable under way when not too stormy. An improvised windsail made by fitting a canvas sea anchor onto a cowl vent (Fig. 22) is occasionally seen! Most traditional forehatches are made to prop open a short way, resting on hinge-down cheek boards at each side.

Leaky hatches

The simplest way to cure leaky hatches and skylights is to have canvas covers for use when left unattended or in rough weather. These also preserve varnish-work most effectively. The Maurice Griffiths type forehatch has double coamings to filter off spray (see Fig. 23). The simplest way to convert single coamings to double is to increase the size of the lid, seating new outer coamings (with scuppers) on deck.

Wipers

Most pilothouse for'ard-facing windows are equipped with car-type or pantograph electric wipers. Failure can lead to danger, so it pays to keep one spare set on board. The motors have a limited life if not lubricated annually. The blade rubbers often go hard and the arm hinges need a touch of oil monthly to prevent stiffness. If your boat has rotating disc wipers, always carry a spare drive belt.

Deck fittings

Whether adding ventilators or any other sort of deck fitting, careful bedding in mastic, secure through-bolting, and good load-distributing pads above and below are the essentials.

Sandwich

Substantial fibreglass decks have two skins, with end-grain balsa or foamed PVC in between. The builders replace the core with plywood inserts where fittings are bolted. Without these pads, new fittings would crush the core. The problem can be overcome by boring larger holes and inserting thick tufnol spacer tubes of precise length in way of each bolt.

Stanchions

Replacing a broken guardrail stanchion is one of the trickiest jobs to face the amateur, and the original mounting system may not have been good enough. Bolts are usually poor of access behind an internal ceiling or trim, demanding the use of a knuckle-jointed socket wrench extension and a lot of patience. One thing to note: with stainless steel, what went in will usually come out again!

Slackness

Annual inspections for loose bolts on deck fitting are wise. At the same time, look for cracks and movement above deck, especially in stanchions. If nylon sleeves lining the cable holes are missing, release the terminals and wrap the wire at each chafe point with self-amalgamating tape.

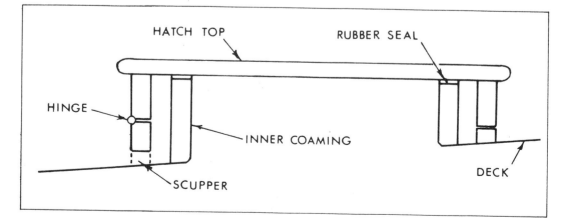

Fig. 23 Old-style forehatch converted to double coaming type.

6
Spars, Rigging and Anchors

The wind is free. With fuel getting scarcer and dearer, some sail area is generally preferred on all cruisers except high-speed powerboats and inland water craft. As well as the traditional masts, booms and bowsprits, many large sailing craft today possess certain additional spars in the shape of staysail and spinnaker booms, whisker and jockey poles, wishbones, twin running jib booms, or roller jib headfoils.

Costly equipment

A modern sailing rig with alloy spars and a full set of winches is likely to cost more than a main engine. Although often considered antiquated, gaff rig (Plate 48) works out at around one-third of the cost (see later) and is ideally suitable for eased-sheet conditions, for saving fuel, and for safeguarding against engine failure. Incidentally, a slender, hollow mast with spreaders and masthead electronic equipment is far more easily damaged when being hoisted aboard (or when yachts are rafted together) than is a stocky gaff mast.

Mast stepping
For a sailboat under 25 ft (8 m) in length, you can lower a tabernacle-stepped mast with two helpers and a tackle (pronounced *taykul* by seamen to distinguish it from fishing tackle and ground tackle) or winch, as in Fig. 24. Clap a guy to each back shroud and adjust throughout as necessary.

Plate 48 Gaff rig has a surprising number of advantages. Windward efficiency is not one of them.

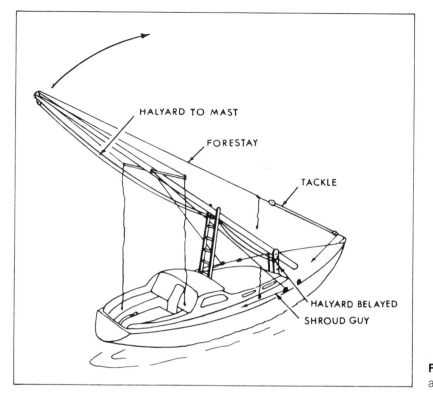

HALYARD TO MAST

FORESTAY

TACKLE

HALYARD BELAYED

SHROUD GUY

Fig. 24 Simple rig to raise or lower a light mast.

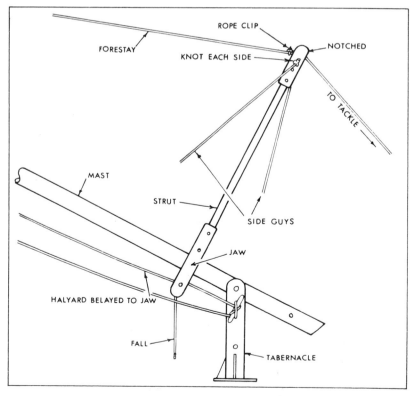

FORESTAY

ROPE CLIP

KNOT EACH SIDE

NOTCHED

TO TACKLE

MAST

STRUT

SIDE GUYS

JAW

HALYARD BELAYED TO JAW

FALL

TABERNACLE

Fig. 25 Single strut to give the forestay leverage.

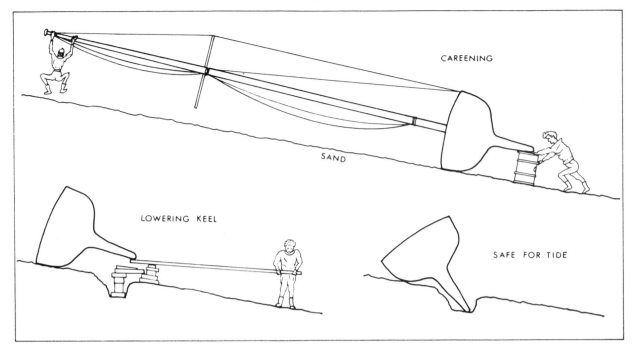

Fig. 26 Careening a dayboat to unship the mast.

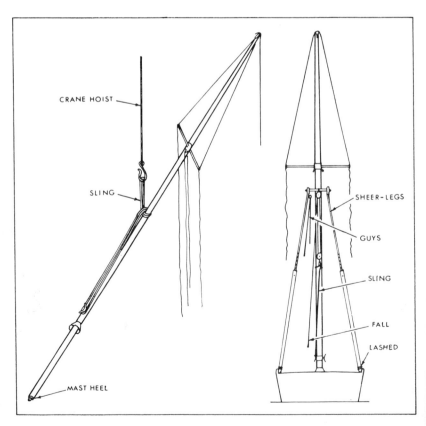

Left
Fig. 27 Sling rigged for easy removal after mast stepping.

Right
Fig. 28 Light alloy telescopic sheer-legs are not too difficult to erect.

Safety struts

Using the above method, danger arises when a heavy mast is almost down, unless some sort of strutting system (see Fig. 25) is adopted to keep an effective angle between forestay and mast. Craft which regularly 'shoot' bridges need to keep good strutting equipment on board. For a one-off occasion (when no crane is available) a guyed single strut can often be improvised, utilizing one of the boat's legs, the spinnaker pole, or even a launching trolley for the lighter mast. Side guys are most important with a single strut, to prevent it collapsing sideways. They may need to be slackened or taken up during the hoisting or lowering operation.

Careening

Many masts pass through the deck and need the services of a crane or sheer-legs for stepping and unstepping, unless the boat is careened onto her beam ends (Fig. 26): a simple procedure with dinghies and small dayboats.

Slinging

With most masts, a safe point to sling from is just above mid-height, including the piece below deck. If a suitable sling is not available on loan, a double part of sound, thick rope will do. Rig this as in Fig. 27, with a marling hitch at the top. Belay or lash the bottom end to a halyard cleat or winch. A marling hitch readily collapses when the load is taken off, but when unstepping a mast, the hitch will travel upwards more easily if tied with a bit of twine to form a slack eye.

Sheer-legs

Twin sheer-legs (Fig. 28) standing on deck with guy ropes to steady them are practical for small masts, but they become too heavy to manhandle in the larger sizes. When estimating the height required for unstepping, remember to allow for the sheave or tackle, and for the lift required to get the mast heel above deck. Without a crane, having lowered a mast to the deck, a way must be found to transfer it ashore, if that is where it has to go. With some help, planks, ropes and padding, almost any shifting is possible, but it takes time.

Derrick

When stepping or unstepping a mast in remote places, erecting a derrick is often the best solution. This makes a useful exercise for advanced Boy Scouts. Referring to Fig. 29, the pole can be a tree trunk, another mast, a telephone pole, or a length of steel water pipe. A hole in the ground is the simplest way to keep the pole heel under control, yet allowing the jib to slew when swinging the mast ashore. By lying alongside a bigger boat, her mast may be used to step or unstep your mast, using her halyards to hoist a temporary gaff (Fig. 30) with a handybilly (double over single block tackle) clapped to its outer end to act as the crane hoist.

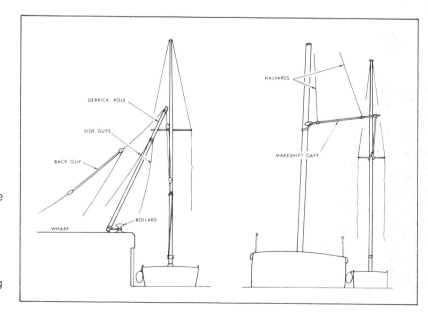

Left

Fig. 29 A crude derrick can cope with any size of mast.

Right

Fig. 30 Improvised gaff from a big sailing craft.

Preparing to step

In general, a lot more care is necessary when putting a mast *in* than when taking one out. Nothing must be damaged. Shackles, clevis pins and bolts must be moused with seizing wire, lock-nutted, or cotter-pinned; ropes must be rove through blocks in the correct direction; all lights and electrical wiring must be checked; threads and metal sheaves should be greased. Having dressed the mast with gear, frap standing and running rigging close to the mast, preferably by means of thin twine stops which can be broken by tugging the stays. Try to get the aftermost pair of shrouds and the forestay tied (perhaps temporarily) to their chainplates quickly once the mast is in position.

Electrocution

Although fortunately rare, serious accidents have occurred due to a metal mast touching overhead power cables. When manhandling a mast in an unfamiliar location, upward glances should not be forgotten.

Deck wedges

Where a mast passes through the deck, the requisite clearance around it is filled in various ways, ranging from shaped wooden wedges covered by sealant or a canvas coat, through stiff rubber liners, to a neoprene O-ring (which is rolled in as the mast drops into its step) sealed with a neoprene gaiter. If you need to make new wooden wedges, cut these from teak or iroko (which will not swell or shrink much) and form a lip on top (see Fig. 31(a)) to prevent them dropping downwards. For a round mast, numerous narrow, flat wedges serve almost as well as fewer curved ones. To press rubber liners in or out, adjust the rigging to pull the mast forward to free the after piece then reverse the procedure. Note that hardwood wedges can dent an alloy mast. Should the collar around a metal mast ever need renewal, contact the spar makers (nameplate usually to be found just above deck level) or, in the case of a standard fibreglass hull, her builders may be able to supply.

Mast apron

Old-type mast aprons are stitched up from canvas and doped with paint. The top is bedded in mastic and bound to the mast with codline (Fig. 31(b)) or a strip of lead held on with tacks or screws. The bottom is often secured by a screwed metal ring, or two half-rings. If using a complete ring, do not forget to stand the ring in its position on deck before stepping the mast!

Gaiter

You can repair a torn modern mast boot or gaiter temporarily with vinyl tape, but as with so much modern gear, loss or damage usually means ordering a new part. Many small craft step their alloy masts into a small socket on deck, or onto a bracket with a single bolt. This eliminates leakage and the mast is as short as possible. However, without a proper tabernacle you still need some sort of hoist to step or unstep such a mast.

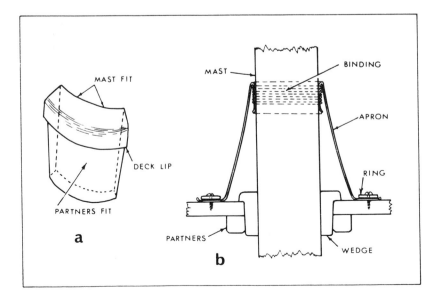

Fig. 31 Traditional through-deck mast system. **a** one of the wooden wedges. **b** canvas apron in place.

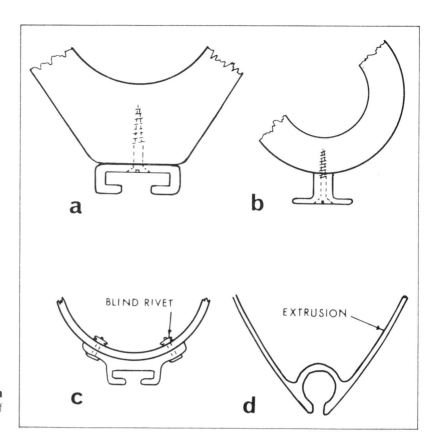

Fig. 32 Four types of mast track. **a** internal. **b** external. **c** flanged. **d** luff groove.

Spar check

A mast looks bare and simple when stripped of all its gear at laying-up time (see Chapter 12) and you then have a fine opportunity to check it for defects. Some masts are never taken ashore. In that case, an annual examination aloft must be arranged – see later. Booms, gaffs and whisker poles are more often at eye level and are constantly under observation.

Boxed sheaves
Both on sailing dinghies and on larger vessels, internal halyards through hollow masts require housed sheaves (at top and bottom) which are often neglected. Metal sheaves need annual oiling, but those of nylon or tufnol on stainless steel pins are meant to run dry. When removing a sheave, tie a piece of twine around its groove, to prevent it from falling out of reach as the pin comes out. (See also page 127.)

On small wooden masts, sheave boxes are a push fit, with pins passing right through the mast walls. On removal, treat any bare wood with varnish to prevent absorption of rain and spray. With alloy spars, most boxes are retained by set screws. Some have well-hidden internal anti-chafe rollers which need oiling. The present trend is to bring halyards out through slots at chin height, so eliminating bottom sheaves.

Metal fatigue
The safety of any mast normally depends on the strength of metal fittings. Cracks in eyes, cranes, tangs, straps, bands, and ball keyhole slots, need a magnifying glass, or spray-on tracer which shows up cracks in purple. Flaws can lurk under bosses or flanges. Faults such as shackle pin wear and corrosion are much easier to see. Dissimilar metals are found on most alloy spars. Although insulation against galvanic action is inserted where possible, this does not apply to the fastenings – so beware! The making and repairing of spar fittings is described in *Boat Repairs and Conversions*.

Sail track
Loose screw fastenings through both internal (Fig.

32(a)) and external track (Fig. 32(b)) can stop a sail from lowering, with disastrous results. The flanged variety (Fig. 32(c)), often seen riveted to alloy spars, avoids this danger, but a regular check for loose fastenings is still prudent.

Longer screws into wood hold well, provided the wall thickness is adequate. If you have no plastic wood, whittle a wooden peg to a snug fit, glue this in, cut flush, and re-bore for the original screw. Fitting a track screw in varnish will often prevent loosening. Loctite thread sealer will secure machine screws, and sometimes self-tapping screws. You can bore extra fastening holes through the track without having to remove a complete length.

Track damage

Buckled track lips are easy to straighten if you first cut and file a small, mild steel anvil to fit snugly under the rim and then use a light hammer to peen the track straight. If a short piece needs replacing, and matching track is unobtainable, try robbing a piece from the masthead end and replacing the damaged part with that. Chamfer all cut ends slightly to prevent slides jamming where alignment is not perfect.

Track lubrication

Few owners ever grease or oil metal track, as this is difficult to accomplish once a mast is stepped and sails could become stained. To avoid such problems, use a PTFE, Teflon or Fluon dry film lubricant. This lasts several months and does not attract grit. Where metal slugs run inside a mast groove, cut a piece of foam plastic to fit the groove, soak it in lubricant and pull it up and down while sandwiched between two slugs. Attach the lower slug to the halyard and the upper slug to a light downhaul. No lubrication is necessary when either track or slides are of plastics, or when the sail boat-rope fits direct into a luff groove (see Fig. 32(d)).

Glued spars

Glued joint failures are not uncommon, particularly on old sailing dinghy masts. If you can poke a 1 thou. (1 mil. or 25 microns) feeler gauge into a joint over a distance of 6 in (150 mm) or more, something should be done about it. The semi-concealed joint within a luff groove is the one generally needing most careful inspection.

Injecting glue

Clear dirt from the seam as well as possible, using feeler gauges. Inject one-shot resin glue with an old hypodermic syringe, if necessary boring tiny holes along the joint to enable the needle to be inserted. In bad cases, light clamping is advisable. To do this on a round or pear-shaped mast, cut some pine chocks (see Fig. 33) to fit the mast and clap G-clamps across these. Adding a few thin screw fastenings across the seam (neatly stopped over) is never a bad thing.

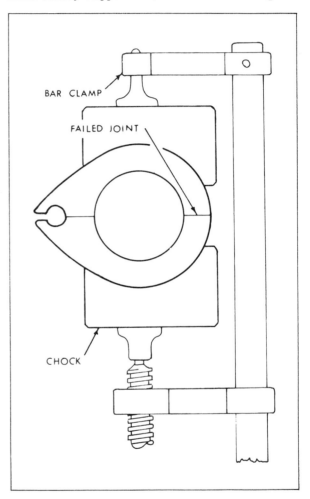

Fig. 33 Clamping a dinghy mast after injecting glue.

Loose fittings

Should any component fixed to a mast or spar work loose, the stress on its fastenings increases dramatically, and immediate action is essential. Alloy spar fastenings are mentioned on page 89. Most trouble is found on wooden spars, where screws are popular to avoid weakening the structure with through-bolts. Screwed belaying cleats are frequent offenders.

Boring them to accommodate thicker screws is often better than using longer screws of the original diameter.

Mast sheathing

Whether hollow or solid, a shaky wooden spar can be rejuvenated by complete or partial fibreglass sheathing. Unless Kevlar or carbon fibre is used instead of common glass, you might need at least four layers of open weave tape to do any good, applied spirally in alternate directions. A big mast could well need ten layers.

Give it thought

With pigmented resin or a painted finish, the results need not look too awful, but with the necessary modifications to metal fittings, the cost is often higher than for making a new spar. Remember also that additional weight aloft is usually undesirable. When sheathing a mast with luff groove, this part can be cut off and replaced by a screw-on groove extrusion. Alternatively, sheathe over the groove, then saw through and sand down neatly.

Further details of fibreglass sheathing are given in Chapter 5.

Sailboards

Fibreglass masts are popular on sailboards. Repair by wrapping is certain to affect the essential bendiness, especially high up. Breakage is most common at the wishbone mounting. The usual repair procedure is to lay-up (over a cardboard former) a 2 ft (600 mm) length of fibreglass tube which just pushes into the hollow mast. Having glued this into place and made good the break with resin putty, a three-layer well-tapered spiral wrap is laid-up outside.

Solid spar defects

Longitudinal cracks are often found in solid wood spars, especially when the varnish has been allowed to deteriorate at some time. Such cracks are not normally detrimental to strength, but if you find cracks at right angles to the grain, the spar could break without warning.

Spar putties

Either dope harmless cracks copiously with raw linseed oil during lay-up, or fill them with elastic stopping and varnish over. Stock products for this include Seamflex in Britain and Weldwood Blend-Stick in America. You may not be able to get the exact shade you want, but re-touching with paint should do the trick. White synthetic rubber (polysulphide) caulking composition (see Chapter 3), plus touch-up paint, is also suitable.

Graving pieces

Small but deep scars and dents on varnished spars – and on any other brightwork parts of a boat – are traditionally repaired by inlaying a diamond-shaped graving piece, as shown in Fig. 34. Except at corners, graving on a square mast is easy. Make the new diamond piece first, offer it up and scribe around it with a sharp knife, then chisel out the recess about ⅛ in (3 mm) deep, glue the patch in and plane down flush next day. On rounded surfaces, chisel the recess first, then make a cardboard template to fit, and shape the diamond piece from that. Pinning or gluing a short wooden peg to the template helps a lot when shaping it. Slightly

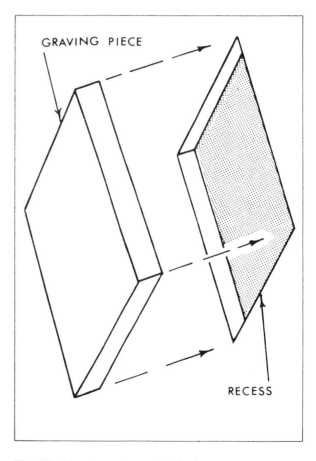

Fig. 34 How to repair small defects on a varnished spar.

tapered edges to the diamond ensure a snug fit. Stain applied with a small art brush should ensure a perfect match, even when you cannot find the precise species of wood.

Rot spots

Well-maintained hollow spruce spars are highly resistant to rot. Of solid masts, the gaff rigged types are the most susceptible, mainly behind the bolster cheeks at the hounds (see Plate 49) where the shrouds loop over. Rot can start at any place where rainwater lodges, such as behind the various battens

used to support tracks, to prevent chafe, and to enlarge the clew end of a roller reefing boom. The heel of a mast can rot if the mast step (Fig. 35) is not properly drained.

Core testing

The heart of any solid spar can rot even though the outside looks perfect. Tapping all the way along with a mallet often produces a dull sound if there is rot. Telephone poles are tested with a tool which bores a small hole into the heart and removes a complete core sample. Failing the loan of one of

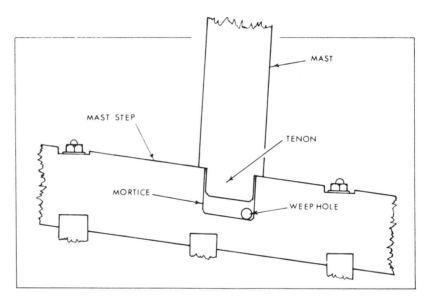

Fig. 35 A traditional mast step mortice must be drained.

Plate 49 Expensive stainless steel fittings are not necessary to secure the rigging on a gaff mast.

these, a $\frac{5}{16}$ in (7 mm) lengthened drill – followed by probing with a thin screwdriver – will soon show up a soft heart. Plug all holes with matching dowels (see page 215) on completion.

Protruding knots

A solid spar shaped from a tree normally has many more large visible knots than a similar glued spar. When knots form humps, this often means that the surrounding wood has been scraped clean many times and there could be a loss of strength. Spar renewal might then be prudent instead of bothering to plane down all the knots.

Eyebolts

Found mainly through solid spars, eyebolts tend to crush the wood and become slack (see Fig. 36(a)). The usual remedy is to remove the bolt, counterbore (by driving a temporary softwood plug into the hole if a wood auger is to be used) and insert a short tufnol bush each end, as in Fig. 36(b). Avoid boring right through for a single bush; this could seriously weaken the spar.

Mast bands

Marine supply stores carry plastic materials (such as Fix or Mendex) for building up repair defects in wood. This is useful where a loose mastband has crushed the soft wood of a spar. For a bad case, remove the band, fill flush with epoxy putty and bind all around with fibreglass tape and epoxy resin. Remember, this will not do much to increase the strength of a weakened spar.

Metal fittings

In round terms, popular mast fittings have a reliable life of about twenty-five years. After that, galvanizing tends to break down, while thin stainless steel may suffer from crevice corrosion or fatigue cracking. Bronze and light alloy should last longer, but cheap, cadmium-plated steel fittings are likely to need replacement after about ten years.

Regalvanizing

Most boatyards and marine stores can arrange to send away mast fittings and chainplates for regalvanizing. It may take two weeks for the parts to come back. A quicker service is likely if a local firm can shotblast and zinc spray to a thickness of 0.005 in (5 mil. or 125 microns). This, if correctly done, has about the same life as galvanizing.

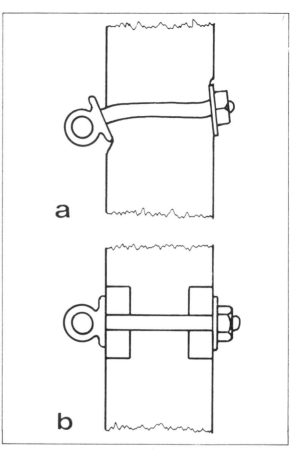

Fig. 36 Repairing strained eyebolt damage with bushes.

Fixing to wood

When replacing the fittings on masts and spars, renew any fastenings which are suspect. Boatyard advice is useful to help identify existing materials or when a change to different materials seems necessary. Galvanized woodscrews have been ousted by zinc-plated and sherardized ones in hardware stores, but these are useless at sea. Stainless steel screws are worth their extra cost. Especially in a salty atmosphere, electrolytic action can corrode adjacent parts when these are of different metals. The extent of activity between various combinations of metals can be assessed from Table 9 (Chapter 10).

Thread clearance

When galvanized bolts of a certain size cannot be obtained, one solution is to send standard black steel bolts to be metallized (zinc or aluminium sprayed) or hot dipped. However, before doing this, re-cut the threads with an adjustable die so that the nuts are a sloppy fit. The same applies when making bolts from standard lengths of continuously threaded bar (studding), or when cutting threads on plain steel bar. Buying galvanized or stainless steel nuts is easy at most ports or marinas.

Metal spar fastenings
One loose pop rivet (blind rivet) is not usually detrimental, but worse faults are generally best dealt with by the original makers. Monel pop rivets are easily replaced if you can borrow a commercial tool suitable for $\frac{3}{16}$ in (4 mm) or ¼ in (6 mm) rivets.

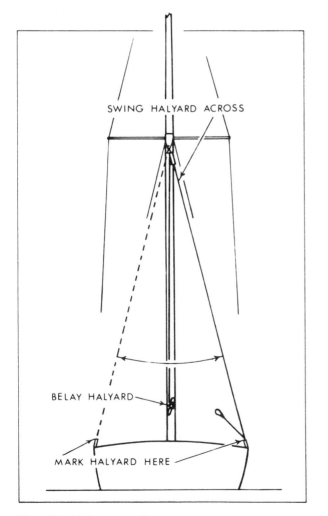

SWING HALYARD ACROSS

BELAY HALYARD

MARK HALYARD HERE

Fig. 37 Halyard used as tape to set a mast true athwartships.

Use a power drill to bore off old rivet heads, before punching the remains inwards. A method for drawing small bolts into a hollow spar for the attachment of extra fittings is described in *Boat Repairs and Conversions*.

Spreaders
Any slight defect found in a spreader (or its attachments) needs immediate rectification. This applies particularly to tubular metal spreaders – they lose their stiffness if slightly dented or buckled, and this could lead to a broken mast. See page 100 for spreader tip chafe problems.

Cleaning alloy
Anodized spars need an occasional wash down with soapy water, especially after storage on shore. If a spar has never been anodized, use soap-impregnated household bronze wool pads, with plenty of water. Finally, apply boat wax. Even better, spray on two coats of the transparent cellulose lacquer used to protect car chrome and bodywork.

When gold anodizing wears off in places, successful camouflaging is usually possible if you mix a little aluminium and gold cellulose paint (stocked by handicraft shops) and apply it with a small artist's brush. For similar work on varnished wooden spars, see page 57.

Black bands
The spars of many racing craft have black measurement bands at each end. These should be maintained, and scribed through to prevent obliteration when stripping paint or varnish off a wooden spar.

Tuning

Once a mast is stepped, tensioning the standing rigging correctly can then proceed. This tuning operation is normally finalized after the first sail, but initially you have to make sure of athwartships perpendicularity by using a low halyard as a tape measure (see Fig. 37), striking an equal chord from masthead to matching spots on the rail at port and starboard.

Turnbuckles
Wire rope tensioning is mainly effected by means of turnbuckles (also called rigging screws or bottlescrews) at deck level, though some jumper and diamond stays have strainers aloft. Open cage turnbuckles (Fig. 38(a)) are usually of stainless steel

nowadays. The bottle type (Fig. 38(b)) is made in stainless, bronze and galvanized. Beware electrolytic action – make sure you choose the correct type! Set all your rigging screws the same way up – right-handed people normally prefer the left-hand thread at the top – so that all barrels rotate like a screwdriver when viewed from above. Cheap commercial galvanized turnbuckles (Fig. 38(c)) are not normally used for highly stressed rigging.

Tightness

Some racing masts are meant to bend (or have a curved top section), but otherwise the tension of standing rigging is correct when just taut enough to keep the track or luff groove straight under hard sailing conditions. Upper shrouds are generally tighter than lower shrouds, and a masthead forestay tighter than a backstay. An inner forestay (baby stay) is usually tighter than a masthead forestay. Riggers use clamp-on instruments to compare stay tensions. Except on a gaff rig, if lee shrouds feel slack at sea, tuning is faulty and a ball-end aloft could jump out of its keyhole. To make a cheap backstay tensioner, split it into two legs, say 10 ft (3 m) long, with a tackle across them at shoulder height.

Deadeyes

Traditional gaff boats have deadeyes and lanyards (Plate 50) in place of turnbuckles, and the shrouds are pulled down as tightly as possible using this form of tackle. The same idea is used on gunter and lugsail dinghies, where codline lanyards are rove from thimbled eyes on the shroud ends to chainplates having broad flat eyes at the top.

Seizing wire

Having decided that all standing rigging is correctly tuned, secure the turnbuckles, not only with their own locknuts (when fitted) but also with a twist of seizing wire at each end, as shown in Figs. 38(a) and 38(b). If you parcel (bind) them with white or black vinyl sticky tape – to keep dirt and corrosion at bay (and to protect sails) – start at the bottom so that water is shed from the overlaps, like the shingles on a roof. This is less important with self-amalgamating tape, which is unaffected by the weather.

Antenna

Many craft utilize an insulated stay for radio reception. Other stays and guardrails are often insulated to improve the accuracy of radio direction finding. Although marine insulators need replacing when cracked or damaged, they contain an internal fail-safe interlock which eliminates any risk of sudden parting.

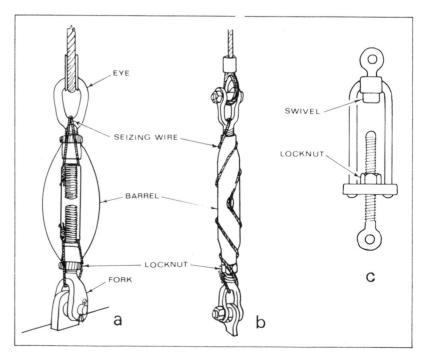

Fig. 38 Rigging screws. **a** turnbuckle. **b** bottlescrew. **c** cheap strainer not intended for boatwork.

Plate 50 Except in remote places, deadeyes are only used nowadays to give a boat period character.

Plate 51 A toggle between chain plate and turnbuckle forms a universal coupling to avert metal fatigue.

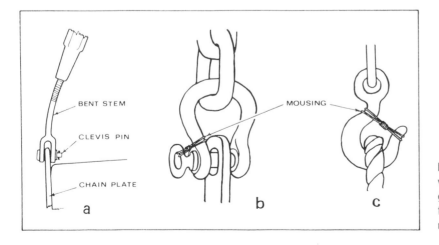

BENT STEM

CLEVIS PIN

CHAIN PLATE

a

MOUSING

b

c

Fig. 39 Rigging precautions. **a** without a toggle, something has to give. **b** shackle pins need mousing for security. **c** simple hook needs mousing even for temporary use.

Chainplates

It is quite common to see chainplate eyes which are not in line with the corresponding turnbuckles, or the fork ends are too tight a fit (see Fig. 39(a)). Something has to bend, especially if the rigging gets pressed inwards when lying alongside. The introduction of a toggle (see Plate 51) is always advantageous. Bending chainplates into line normally demands their complete removal from the ship. Cold bending is nearly always preferable to hot, especially with bronze and similar metals. Less frequently, the above problem may occur aloft, when tangs do not align with stays.

Shackles aloft

For every diameter of shackle pin, up to eight shackle shapes are available, in at least three different metals. Yet shackles are still to be found with insufficient freedom of movement to avoid jamming, especially aloft. Likely improvements include changing from galvanized to thinner stainless steel of equal strength; using a wide D-shackle (or bow shackle) in place of a narrow D; or substituting a single twisted shackle for a pair of interlocked D-shackles. Again, avoid mixing metals and causing galvanic action.

Mousing

Rigging vibration can loosen shackle pins. Mousing with seizing wire (see Fig. 39(b)) is simple when each pin has an eye. Loctite fluid will secure the threads of pins having screwdriver slots or key heads, but you will need an impact screwdriver or a wrench to undo these. The clevis pins used on some turnbuckle fork ends need no mousing, but they must be taped over to conceal the sharp ends of all cotter pins. An ordinary hook needs mousing as in Fig. 39(c). A safety hook has a spring-loaded gate like a snap hook or carbine clip, and needs no mousing.

Standing rigging

Good instruments (with the experts to use them) are available to check rigging for hairline cracks, broken strands, weak swages and T-ball ends. Little-used 1×19 stainless steel wire rope can last thirty years. The more flexible 7×7 rope lasts nearer ten years – the same as galvanized standing rigging. The galvanized type, which is vinyl impregnated and coated at the factory, often lasts fifteen years.

Extending the life

Galvanized shrouds start rusting first at the lower ends. If you have identical terminals at each end, a shroud can be reversed after a few years and its life prolonged greatly. Ropes composed of a few thick wires normally have a much longer life than the more flexible variety composed of numerous thin wires.

Wire care

In days gone by, the standing rigging of commercial gaff boats would last indefinitely, as it was doped with boiled linseed oil, coated with tar, then parcelled and served all over. Details of the latter processes are given in the next chapter. Galvanized wire rope enthusiasts now smear it every year with anhydrous lanoline – from a pharmacy or chandlery. Wear gloves. First check for broken strands by dragging tissue paper along. Use pliers to remove protruding strands by bending and breaking them; not cutting. A bandage of self-amalgamating tape is wise.

Terminals

Spliced ends suit gaff rig. The enthusiast can soon master them. Most ball-end fittings are factory-swaged, but the familiar turnbuckle and tang terminals (also soft and thimbled eyes) can be put on at home (see next chapter).

Traditional

Many a gaff boat looks incomplete without the traditional sheer pole (to prevent the deadeyes from twisting) and ratlines up the shrouds (see Plate 52). The latter make a useful ladder for obtaining a high lookout position, but you would need very narrow feet to climb as far as the crosstrees! Ratlines of cordage (see Chapter 7) look better than those made from wooden battens, and are less likely to cause chafe.

Going aloft

Few newcomers to sailing manage to escape from losing the end of a halyard up aloft at some time. An athletic person can shin up a mast under 6 in (150 mm) in diameter, with legs wrapped around it and hands grasping a halyard or two. Few yachts carry a bosun's chair on board (Plate 53) but some masts have step-irons (Plate 54) attached to each side. Roll-up ladders are marketed which hoist up the mast track or luff groove. On big gaff boats, the mast hoops form rungs for getting as far as the crosstrees. Other ways of reaching the masthead consist of careening on a beach in conjunction with a ladder, or heeling the boat slightly while alongside a high wharf or quay.

Bosun's chair

If you want to avoid buying a smart canvas-sided bosun's chair, it does not take long to make a wooden seat as sketched in Fig. 40. Round off the edges generously and chamfer the rope holes to avoid chafe. Although a man can hoist himself aloft on a halyard, this is dangerous, and it pays to have an assistant. Wearing a safety harness with a strop around the mast prevents the chair from swaying about and averts an accidental fall.

Chafe

With pads of baggywrinkle (see later) on topping lifts and backstay, the sails of old gaff boats suffered little chafe. Nowadays, with mainsails rubbing spreaders when squared off, and overlapping headsails arguing with guardrails and shrouds, the matter needs attention.

Plate 53 Working aloft from a bosun's chair. No picnic when the mast is swaying.

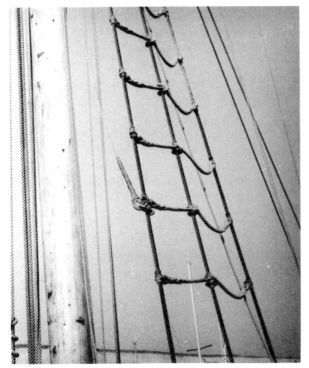

Plate 52 Ratlines are easy to climb when a boat is heeling. A high lookout position is important in some waters.

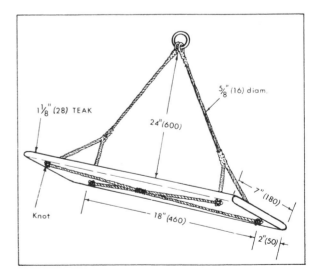

Fig. 40 Home-made bosun's chair. (Dimensions in mm. given in brackets.)

Plate 54 With a mainsail hoisted on slides, climbing steps may be fitted to the mast.

Jib clew snarling

When going about, jib sheets often catch on mast cleats and winches, while the jib clew may flog against these. A pair of preventer ropes rigged as shown in Fig. 41 (or a single central rope if there is a suitable fitting on deck to secure it) will generally cure the trouble – especially useful for single-handed sailing. To tame foredeck mooring cleats, fill them with turns of old rope, or make streamlined wooden chocks to slip under the horns, secured by shockcord.

Scotchmen

Shroud rollers of tufnol or white plastics (Plate 55) are standard fitments these days when making up new stays which could cause chafe. Split tube ones, and others in helical spring form (together with a bottom bearing collar to allow free rotation), are available to fit on existing rigging. Traditionally called scotchmen, split cane shroud rollers were in use seventy years ago.

Note that Dyform wire (the nearest in strength to rod rigging) tends to cut sails more than ordinary 1×19 wire.

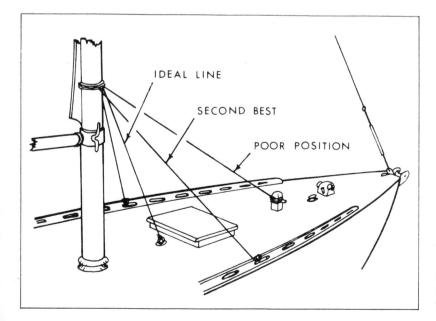

Fig. 41 Possible preventer line positions to avert jib sheet snarl-ups while tacking.

Plate 55 Shroud rollers are used mainly to lessen the chafe of overlapping jibs.

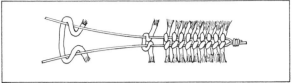

Fig. 42 Making baggywrinkle.

have swinging spreaders is fortunate – these hinge away from a squared-off mainsail, as the lee stay has less tension than the weather one.

Running backstays
Even when correctly tended while tacking, slack runners can flog against a sail. A shockcord preventer (gilguy) will keep the lee one quiet. When short handed, a piece of thin twine is better. This will break when setting up the stay in a hurry.

Shockcord
Some uses of shockcord have already been mentioned. Marine stores normally keep three diameters plus hook terminals for home assembly. Tension needs to be about right for each job. Halyards banging against a metal mast are a familiar nocturnal nuisance at moorings, and shockcord makes ideal gilguys to draw these slack ropes towards the shrouds, as in Plate 56.

Plate 56 Shockcord gilguys prevent the annoying rattle of halyards against the mast.

Baggywrinkle
Looking like coconut matting, baggywrinkle suits old-fashioned boats and effectively prevents ropes or stays from chafing and marking sails. To make it, unwind the strands of some stiff old $\frac{3}{4}$ in (18 mm) rope; cut these into 5 in (127 mm) *thrums* and twist each through a pair of tarred marline cords as shown in Fig. 42. Push the thrums close together as they go on. Wind this around the stay (woolly side outwards) and seize the ends tightly.

Spreader ends
A split tennis ball or a canvas bandage will prevent most spreader and jumper strut ends from chafing sails. Nowadays, special plastic wheels with locating collars are available, using the stay as an axle. To

Plate 57 With a mizzen mast, an octahedral radar reflector may be mounted permanently out of harm's way.

Plate 58 Smooth cylindrical radar reflectors are fine for avoiding sail damage.

Radar reflector

Finding a safe location for the common metal radar reflector is easy on a ketch (Plate 57) but difficult on a single-masted vessel (if sail chafe is to be avoided) except at the masthead, which is usually already cluttered. With a good crew, shift the reflector out of harm's way in accordance with sail changes. The windward spreader signal halyard makes a good hoist, but pass a bight of cord around the topmast stay to prevent losing the reflector should the signal halyard chafe through. Few reflectors are mounted in the most efficient catch-rain manner. If you wish to be recorded on big ship radar screens, use a reflector 18 in (450 mm) across. The much more expensive cylindrical reflectors (Plate 58) are not likely to cause chafe. At one-tenth the cost of a radar set, a radar *detector* signals the whereabouts of a vessel with radar – especially comforting in fog.

Uses of leather

Gaff, lug and gunter spars can chafe together unless protected by leather or something similar. Leather over steel gaff jaws is stitched crisscross at the edges (with a needle in each hand), well padded underneath. Over wood, copper tacks are positioned as shown for a pair of boom scissors in Fig. 43. Soaking in water makes leather supple and causes it to shrink on tightly when dry.

Fig. 43 Leathered jaws for boom scissors.

Leather treatment

If kept saturated with neatsfoot oil (widely used for horse tack) or tallow, leathering can last for twenty years or more. Leather for boatwork needs to be just under ⅛ in (3 mm) thick. If not obtainable through a boatyard or marine store, try a handicraft shop. Sailmakers' calf's hide may be too thin. Fitting oar leather is described in Chapter 11.

Rope chafe

Particularly when ocean voyaging, the chafe of running rigging presents a hazard. Sheaves are often too small, especially for main and headsail sheets, with no simple provision for shifting the position of habitual wear. Even halyards of flexible wire rope may need an occasional change of nip. The use of small chain in way of sheaves is not practicable on most yachts.

Uses of copper

Just as copper tingles are tacked onto wooden hulls to seal leaks, 22-gauge sheet copper works better than leather for certain anti-chafe duties around spars. Modern craft rarely need this, but where gaff jaws habitually ride, and under the shroud eyes shown in Plate 49, coppering is valuable. Spruce oar blades should be capped with 26-gauge copper, but failing this, tack a band of the same metal around the blade just inboard from the tip.

Running gear

Unless you sport a squaresail yard or have a junk rig, the running rigging of most sailing craft comprises halyards, sheets and topping lifts, plus a variety of cordage for boom and spinnaker guys, reefing, tack tackles, roller headsail control, and vangs. All-cordage suits small boats. On medium sizes, wire halyards with rope tails are common. As sizes increase, all-wire halyards are to be found, permanently stowed on reel winches.

Man-made fibres

Strength for strength, there is little difference in price between good hemp and synthetic lines. The latter do not rot, or shrink when wet, but often need to be several sizes too thick just to enable the human hand to grip them comfortably. Lightly tarred sisal or Manila suits a gaff boat with no winches – but remember to slacken halyards, topping lifts and mainsheet when you leave her, for fear of damage to lines and gear by shrinkage in rain or dew.

Choice of rope

Prestretched polyester or Kevlar (aramid) ropes are at present the best choices for halyards (see Chapter 7), while non-kink braided polyester is ideal for sheets. Nylon rope is too elastic for running rigging, except for such items as boom guys, topping lifts and downhauls. Nylon makes good mooring lines and, being heavier than water, is suitable for an anchor rode. The cheapest polypropylene and polythene ropes are commonly used for mooring.

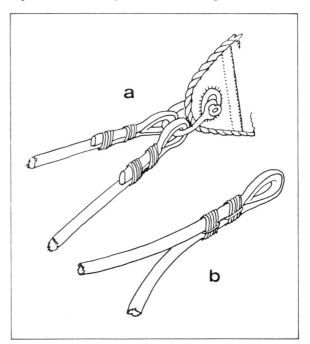

Fig. 44 Jib sheet eyes. **a** separate sheets can be shortened or reversed when chafed. **b** continuous sheet with seized eye can be ruined if chafed.

Rope wear

Running rigging life can be doubled by turning end-for-end or shortening occasionally at the eye splice to freshen the nips around sheaves and shift points of chafe. Note that the wire rope part of a flexible wire halyard with cordage tail has to be a precise length if the splice will not pass readily through the sheave. This may mean fitting a new wire also when the rope tail gets damaged.

Sheets

The nips through blocks and jam cleats in the close-hauled position cause the greatest jib sheet wear,

Plate 59 Lever-action rope stoppers eliminate the need for a multitude of winches.

but less seriously with a mainsheet. The latter normally has plenty of length to permit reversal, or occasional shortening at the terminal eye. The economical yachtsman makes his jib sheets separate port and starboard (see Fig. 44(a)). If continuous (Fig. 44(b)) you cannot get rid of the usual rope damage around the thimble. Stoppers or clutches (Plate 59) are kinder to cordage than jam cleats. They enable one winch to handle several lines – especially useful when jiffy reefing from the cockpit. To avoid cheek chafe, lead the most heavily-used ropes (e.g. main halyard and first luff pendant) fair to the winch drum.

Topping lift

When the mainsail is non-reefing (as on a racing dinghy), or when a rigid boom vang is fitted, no topping lift is required. Small family sloops get by with a clip-on pendant from backstay to boom end (Plate 60). This acts as a boom support, but limits reefing to exact head-to-wind conditions. On a long passage, a masthead topping lift is best unclipped to prevent it from beating against the sail. A single gaff topping lift must lead higher than the top peak halyard block to avoid hoisting snarl-ups. Twin topping lifts may lead to the spreaders, thus guiding the sail between them. With the windward one set up and the leeward one slack, reefing a gaff mainsail under way is possible without coming head to wind, and chafe is avoided.

Mast clutter

A topping lift belayed on the mast or tabernacle is normally convenient to swig up without winch or purchase, and it makes a reserve halyard or jury shroud in an emergency. With slab reefing and a loose-footed sail, a topping lift starting at the

masthead, passing over a block at the boom end (and adjusted with a tackle under the boom), will help lessen the confusion of ropes belayed to the mast at deck level. Some craft have a fixed topping lift from masthead to boom end, which slackens sufficiently when the mainsail is hoisted. Some roller headsails have a halyard which rotates with the sail, internally

Plate 60 A pendant topping lift keeps the boom level when in port without the hindrance of a crutch.

a

b

c

Plate 61 Boom supports. **a** scissors. **b** gallows. **c** crutch. **d** deckhouse chock.

d

rove through the luff spar. All these systems help reduce the clutter of cleats at the mast base.

Gallows

With a fixed topping lift, scissors (Plate 61(a)), gallows (Plate 61(b)), or boom crutch (Plate 61(c)) are not essential. Chocks on top of a deckhouse or pilothouse (Plate 61(d)) form a neat alternative to conventional gallows. Scissors must always be well lashed at top and bottom to avoid loss overboard should the mainsheet become slack and the topping lift shrink when wet.

Flexible wire

Stainless steel flexible wire rope is liable to failure without warning – especially when running over sheaves which are too small, or when subjected to the unforgivable crime of belaying it on a cleat. A wire halyard with no winch or purchase can have a thimbled eye at the end to slip over a hooked pin, a tack tackle (see page 139) being used to tension the luff.

Parrel line

An often neglected item of running gear is the parrel line which prevents a gaff saddle from jumping off the mast. Flexible wire rope works well on big craft, but where cordage is used, it pays to make knots between the parrel balls to prevent their loss should the line part.

Life lines

Flexible wire rope, usually plastic coated, is used for most guardrails and safety harness jackstays. Frequent inspection of wire terminals and fittings is advisable. Note that a Latchway roller enables harness lanyards to slide the full length of the boat without disconnection to get past support brackets. When renewing guardrail wires, make sure that any radio DF interference insulators are replaced as before. Guardrail netting is a wonderful safety precaution with small children on board.

Improvements

Few rigs exist which cannot be improved in one or more ways, and this, including experimentation, is all part of boat care. If you intend to keep the same boat for many years, it pays to keep a record of all running rigging renewal dates, with details of rope brands, lengths, sizes and terminal fittings.

Loose ends

Make a figure-eight knot at the bitter end of a jib sheet after reeving, so it will not disappear through the fairlead block or bullseye in an emergency. Although the falls of halyards are readily prevented from running aloft by knotting their ends to cleats or eyebolts, extreme care is necessary (when unshackling the head of a sail) to hang on to *that* end until you have secured it. Remember to check the condition of signal halyards occasionally. When afloat, to reeve a new one, sew it end-to-end to the old one. Such slightly-worn small cordage is always useful on board.

Ground tackle

Whether compelled by regulations or for common-sense safety reasons, most craft, from racing dinghies upwards carry anchoring equipment. However, in popular yachting areas, anchorages shrink, while marina facilities flourish. Numerous craft race or cruise for several years without needing to anchor. Many yachts have anchors which come nowhere near the required weight. Fortunately, anchors, chains and windlasses demand little maintenance time and should have a life of at least twenty years.

Small anchors

New designs and improvements to traditional types of anchor continue to appear. Some small anchors are modelled on the lines of their larger brethren, but those shown in Plate 62 are generally only available in small sizes.

Big anchors

The traditional anchor with folding stock (see Plate 62(c)) is now difficult to buy in big sizes, as modern anchors of half the weight (Plate 63) have the same holding power. Never use the type shown in Plate 62(c) without making sure that the stock retaining pin is securely lashed. Navy anchors (Plate 63(b)) work best when massive, and are commonly seen stowed neatly in the topside hawsepipes of big motor yachts and ocean liners.

Anchor chocks

Sets of fittings can be bought to support most types of anchor on deck, which include eyes for lashing down. Especially for an ancient or unusual type of anchor, such chocks are readily made at home from hardwood offcuts.

The kedge

Any boat too large to shove off a mudbank by hand

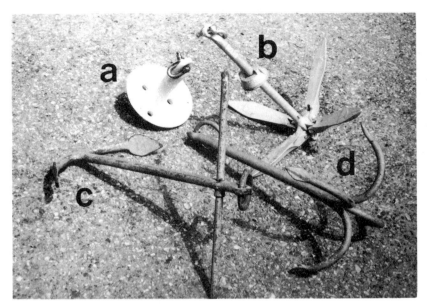

Plate 62 Some types of dinghy anchor. **a** mushroom or angler's. **b** folding. **c** fisherman or mariner's. **d** grapnel.

needs a kedge anchor at least half the weight of the bower (main) anchor. It forms a second bower and is used for *kedging* – repeatedly rowing the kedge out to full scope, to shift a yacht any distance.

Cat davit

Stowing an anchor as seen in Plate 63(c) is just as convenient as using a hawsepipe. Otherwise, to lift a heavy anchor on to the foredeck you need a cat-head or folding cat davit.

Rust

A couple of coats of aluminium paint per year will hide slight rusting on anchor or chain for a long time. New anchors are dear, so it pays to get a shipyard to straighten distorted ones and have them regalvanized when necessary. Chain generally rusts first at the anchor end. Swapping ends is expedient when that happens. Complete regalvanizing is rarely worth while – better to sell the old chain for moorings and buy new. Remember, new chain must fit perfectly over a windlass gipsy wheel, or wildcat.

Chain

The perfectionist unships anchor chain once a year to examine for worn or stretched links and shackles, repaints the length code and cleans out the cable locker, and sends the chain away to be tested every five years. For boats which rarely anchor, such intervals may be increased fourfold. Beware of thieves when cable is left unshipped.

Chain shackles

For matching strength, you need enlarged links at chain ends to take standard shackles. Proper chain shackles have oval pins to match the regular links. An eyebolt in the cable locker enables the inboard end of an anchor rode to be secured. A strong lashing of polyester rope is reckoned to be better than a shackle in this position, to permit rapid slipping of the cable in an emergency. When this must be done, try hard to buoy the cable – any long rope with an empty fuel can attached will do – to simplify retrieving your gear at a later date.

Split links

New cruising boats rarely have enough anchor chain for safety in all conditions, but adding extra is simple enough using galvanized connecting links (Fig. 45(b)) of correct size. When interlocked and riveted together these forged steel links are very strong. The same procedure is useful for replacing short lengths of rusty or damaged chain. Chain repair links (also called lap links, see Fig. 45(a)) may not match the full strength of a chain, but are useful for temporary repairs, or on calm waters. A lap link is bent open sufficiently to get the chain links on, then the laps are closed with a vice or clamp.

Length code

In tidal waters you should always know what length of anchor cable has been let out. A few links painted with different enamel every three fathoms (18 ft), or

a

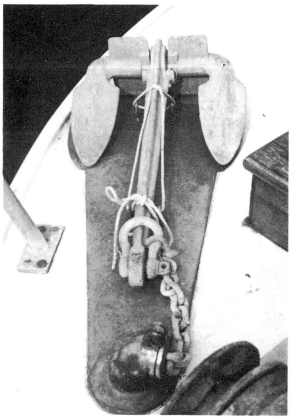

Plate 63 Common yacht anchors.
a Bruce. **b** stockless or navy. **c**
Danforth. **d** CQR or plow.

b

c

d

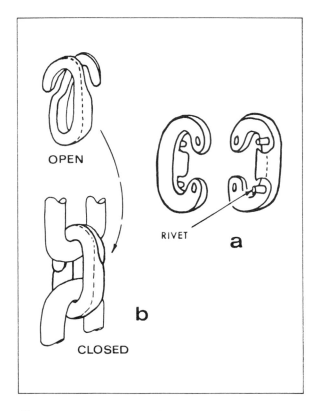

Fig. 45 Joining lengths of chain. **a** lap link. **b** connecting link.

five meters if you use metric charts, usually suffice, and last about three years. Red, white and blue are usually remembered in that order (as they are used in several national flags), so use one stripe for the first three marks, two for the second series and three for the third. Aerosol car paint is suitable, shown in use in Plate 64.

Shock load

The wash from fast powerboats careering through an anchorage can snub a cable violently enough to break it. Special spring buffers with devil's claw hooks to catch between two links are made with various tensions according to the size of chain. Rubber snubbers (see Chapter 12) are easier to buy, and are mainly used on mooring lines. Use two or more in parallel for light chain. In the absence of such equipment, improvise with multiple lengths of springy rope (such as coir or nylon) from the chain to the mast. Allow slack chain at the windlass to put full load on the spring. This system also stops the chain's rumbling noises which can be so disturbing at night. Remember to take adequate chafe precautions.

Angels

Another good form of snubber is the anchor rode weight, or angel. By means of a span shackle and a

Plate 64 A code mark even every five fathoms helps to judge how much cable is veered.

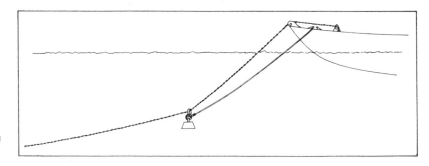

Fig. 46 Weight lowered down anchor rode prevents snatch.

length of cordage this is lowered a good distance down the cable catenary (as in Fig. 46) and the line made fast. Some marine stores sell special weights and shackles for this purpose. The heaviest weight that can be handled in this awkward position is about 56 lb (25 kg) – suitable for ½ in (12 mm) chain or larger. A 14 lb (6 kg) weight is normally adequate for ¼ in (6 mm) chain.

Nylon rode
Nylon rope sinks readily and is popular for anchoring. Flat braided nylon is less springy and chafes more easily. Rope rodes need plenty of chain next to the anchor, from 6 ft (2 m) for a 7 lb (3 kg) anchor up to 20 ft (6 m) for a 50 lb (22 kg) anchor. At the joint, weaving the nylon through eight links with four seizings is neat – but not so easy to scrub clear of mud as a hard eye and shackle.

Wire
For deep anchorages, wire rope (stowed captive on a special windlass drum) is often better than chain. As with nylon, take care to avoid kinks, and insert some chain next to the anchor.

Tripping line
Unless an anchorage is known to be clear of old chains and rocks, it pays to buoy the anchor. Do not choose too thin a buoy rope. Hitch this to the anchor crown or gravity ring so that the buoy rope (tripping line) can be used to pull the anchor free while the rode is slack. To prevent someone picking up your anchor buoy in mistake for a vacant mooring, lead the tripping line back on board, roughly parallel to the anchor rode. If floating rope (such as polypropylene) must be used, tie a weight to it about 20 ft (6 m) down from the stemhead to submerge the line clear of passing propellers.

Fairleads
A big roller fairlead at the stemhead (or a matching pair) assists anchor work considerably, especially on large craft. Owners often forget to lubricate these rollers. When they freeze solid, repeated doses of penetrating oil and the use of a large pipe wrench might work. If that fails, and the bolt will not drive out, prolonged heating with a blow-torch is certain to work, though it will not do the galvanizing much good. Even a Delrin roller in a stainless fitting can seize up and wear away. Fit a pin across the top to stop ropes leaping out.

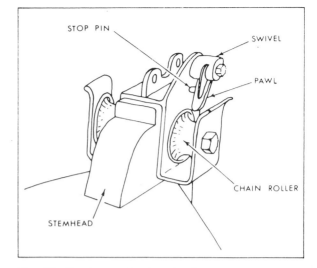

Fig. 47 Pawl over stemhead roller simplifies weighing anchor without a windlass.

Fairlead pawl
Until the strain becomes too much, many small boat sailors find it quicker to reeve in anchor cable by hand than to use a typical small yacht windlass. In such cases, if you do not have a Claude Worth pawl at the fairlead (Fig. 47), it pays to get one fitted. This stops the chain from running back out each time you take a fresh grip. A correctly mounted cam-type jamb cleat will do the same thing for a nylon rope. Do not let these devices take the full strain of anchoring.

Windlass
A good foredeck windlass with rope drum is handy for kedging and warping as well as normal anchor work. Make sure the gipsy wheel (wildcat) fits the chain exactly, and add a breaker claw if the chain fails to peel off neatly into the navel pipe. Seek out any oil holes and lubricators for monthly attention and at the same time rotate the mechanism briefly, whether ratchet, hand, or power operated. A useful addition available from good windlass makers is a meter which indicates the amount of cable run out. Oil leakage from an oil-bath windlass (Plate 65) is soon detected by the tell-tale stains and the frequent need for topping up. Sump cleaning every three years is prudent to remove moisture and to check for broken gearwheel teeth.

Sheet winches

It pays to follow makers' instructions closely to keep sheet and halyard winches in tip-top condition. All good ones strip apart readily and need the correct grease to prevent pawls from jamming, and salt water from starting corrosion damage. Once per year is the minimum period for stripping. Note that clamp-on self-tailing equipment is marketed for some older winches – especially useful for the singlehanded mariner.

Other winches

To eliminate the need for tackles, specialized winches are installed on certain shoal draft boats for operating lifting keels and leeboards. Most of these need frequent lubrication and careful attention to the detent pawls which prevent the load from running away unexpectedly. Worm gear types are less likely to fail, but they still need lubrication. Much the same applies to telescopic backstay and boom vang adjusters.

Plate 65 Checking the oil and internal condition of an enclosed windlass is often forgotten.

Like new

One essential when stripping down a winch is to scrub all gears and pawls with a toothbrush while submerged in paint thinner, kerosene, or similar solvent. Place on rag in a box to dry, then apply the maker's recommended grease sparingly as each part is replaced. Remember also that some jib furling gears need oiling every three months.

7
All About Ropes

The newcomer buying a brand new boat may feel little need to acquire the true seaman's knowledge of ropes and ropework, but even an incorrectly tied knot can mean danger, either by jamming or by working loose, while inability to splice can mean missing either an important race or a pleasant afternoon's cruise with the family. With a little know-how, the impecunious owner can prolong rope life and fabricate many otherwise expensive items of gear.

Dirty ropes

The water in some ports is constantly polluted with thick black oil which readily attaches itself to mooring lines. Laundries and cleaners are not too keen to tackle this, and good rope is costly. It usually ends up as a do-it-yourself job ashore, scrubbing in a tray of one of those super solvents mentioned in Chapter 2, followed by warm water and detergent.

Knot practice

Many amateur sailors become fascinated by ropework and delight in showing people how to tie a bowline blindfold with only one hand! It can be done. Learning to tie the much-used reef knot, sheet bend, clove hitch, fisherman's bend, rolling hitch and bowline with eyes closed is certainly satisfying for all who venture on the water. An accomplished Boy Scout comes in useful when learning, as demonstra-tion is better than puzzling through a book of knots. A few short lengths of rope around the home are handy for occasional knot practice. Less common knots, such as sheepshank, carrick bend and slippery hitch, have their uses, and are simple enough to master and remember.

Fancy work
The basic splices are described later, but if you have a yen to make Turk's-heads, monkey's fists and Matthew Walkers, it will be worth getting a book specializing in these arts.

Cordage cost

Uses in rigging for the various types of cordage and wire rope at present available were given in the previous chapter. Most people are cost conscious, and Table 6 gives comparison figures for the main current types of cordage in the popular ½ in (12 mm) diameter, together with their main uses on board.

Weights

The safe working load on cordage is best taken as about one-sixth of the breaking strength on a straight pull. Makers of modern ropes issue strength figures, but these are not readily available for hemp ropes. To get the safe working load of these in pounds, square the circumference (in inches) and multiply by 150 for Manila and European hemp, 120

Table 6

Popular modern and traditional ropes

Type of rope	Approximate cost per 10m length, all ½in (12mm) diameter. (excluding sales tax)		Breaking strength (kg)	Typical uses for various diameters
	£ in UK	$ in USA		
Kevlar core	48	140	5600	Winched halyards and sheets
Polyester double braid	16	55	3600	Sheets, signal halyards
Nylon (most sorts)	14	50	3000	Anchor rode, mooring, towing
Polyester 3-strand	13	45	2800	Halyards, tackles
Polypropylene	10	22	2000	Mooring, ski towing
Manila	7	18	1700	Gaff rig, most purposes
Sisal	5	14	1300	Kedging, mooring, small stuff
Coir	4	12	900	Fendering, mooring lines

for sisal, and 80 for coconut fibre (coir). For the load in kilograms, square the diameter (in millimetres) and multiply by 1.0, 0.8, and 0.5 respectively.

Choosing cordage

When strength is the consideration, the difference in cost between synthetics and hemps lessens. With life expectancy also taken into consideration, the difference lessens again. Thin rope is difficult to pull by hand. A diameter of 1 in (25 mm) is ideal: suitable for the halyards of a 100 ft (30 m) schooner! For ropes which lead direct to winches, the thin and strong materials are best. Rot, mildew, and chemicals can weaken hemp ropes invisibly and make them unsafe. Synthetics can break down and go stiff under bright sunlight, though some modern materials are treated to minimize this effect. Serious friction heat can melt them.

Constructions
Most ropes are either plain-laid (also known as hawser laid) as in Fig. 48, or plaited (braided) as in Fig. 49. The three strands of a plain-laid rope are nearly always twisted together (laid up) right-

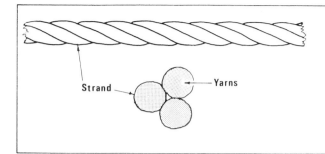

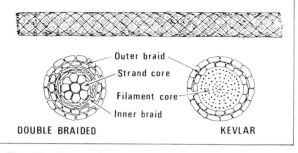

Fig. 48 Plain-laid rope with right-hand lay.

Fig. 49 Types of braided rope.

handed – clockwise when looking along the rope. Shroud-laid rope (rarely seen nowadays) has four strands. The biggest ropes are cable-laid, where three standard plain-laid ropes are twisted together left-handed. Sometimes, the three plain-laid ropes are plaited together, thus increasing elasticity. Limp braided ropes have a plaited core covered by a plaited sheath. With Kevlar and other non-stretch types, the core is of continuous parallel strands. The latter are intended for winches. Belaying on a cleat might buckle the core and weaken it.

Synthetic range

The main materials currently used for man-made ropes are listed in Table 6 (in approximate order of decreasing strength), with their popular uses. Nylon and plain-laid polyesters are generally white. Polyester braid can be purchased in red, black, blue, white and gold, to help identify complicated running rigging. Polypropylenes and polythenes (which float) are often dyed to avoid confusion with stronger materials, while others have a single dark yarn (called a *rogue's yarn* by seamen) running along the outside. Spectra and Vectran are cheaper rivals to Kevlar (aramid) which are less easily damaged when rendering around small sheaves.

Old range

At a modern marina holding two hundred boats, you may not find any traditional natural fibre ropes in use. However, they are still available, and generally keep more stable in cost than the synthetics, which are largely made from oil. The range mainly comprises hemps (Manila, European, and sisal), coconut fibre (coir) and cotton. Linen (flax) is used for traditional plain and waxed twines and threads.

Treatment

All marine hemps should be rot-treated or lightly tarred, giving them a nut-brown appearance. New hemp rope needs stretching before use, to remove stiffness and lessen kinking. To do this, take turns between two posts in the open air, for several days, taking up the slack occasionally, douching with water, or hanging weights in the middle of each span.

Ratlines

White rope looks queer for ratlines (see page 97), and tarred hemp is preferred. They must not be taut. If clove hitches are used, seize the bitter ends to the standing part, and also clap seizings around the shrouds and across each clove hitch to prevent the ratlines from slipping downwards.

Extra care

All natural ropes need to be stowed dry to prevent damaging rot, mildew and musty smells. Coir is, however, rot resistant. Especially at laying-up time, salty ropes need washing with fresh water before drying and storing. Hemp and cotton shrink when wet, demanding adjustments to halyards and other lines to avoid over-stressing.

Rope ends

Frayed and unravelling rope ends are annoying and wasteful. Small synthetic ropes are easily sealed by melting the end with a match or soldering iron, then rolling under foot or (after pause) between wetted thumb and forefinger. Telling the difference between man-made and hemp or cotton rope is not always easy when they are old. Burning the end will tell, as synthetics melt while naturals smoulder.

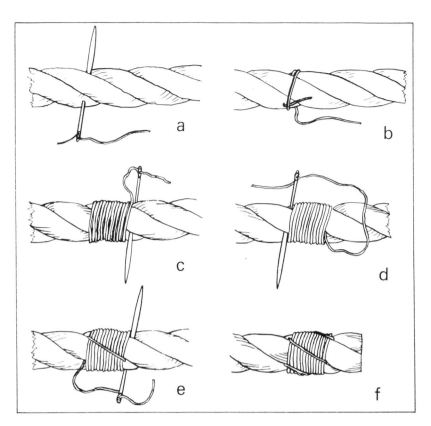

Fig. 50 Six stages in making a sailmaker's whipping.

Sleeves

Push-on rubber collars are often used to protect the ends of new ropes, but these are not intended to take the place of proper whippings. Permanent shrink-on plastic sleeves are available for all rope sizes. These are positioned, then dunked in boiling water (or rotated over a gentle flame) to shrink them on tightly. Always leave about one and one-half rope diameters from the bitter end before the start of any type of whipping.

Twine

Most marine stores sell waxed polyester thread in at least three thicknesses suitable for binding the ends of all except the largest ropes: thin codline or thick tarred marline is generally suitable for these. When in doubt, use cord too thin for the size of rope to be whipped – if the cord is too thick, the whipping is more likely to get pulled off.

Spliced end

A fast way to seal the end of any three- or four-strand rope is to make a back splice (see later in Fig. 59). The swelling limits reeving through blocks and

bullseyes, but is not normally detrimental on mooring lines.

Sailmaker's whipping

The needle-and-palm whipping in Fig. 50 – the strongest of all – is often preferred by sailmakers. It is made as follows:

(a) Push a threaded needle through the middle of a strand, about four diameters back from the rope end.

(b) Press a small cork on the needle point, to prevent injury as the whipping turns are wound on tightly towards the rope end. Bury the starting end of thread under at least the first three turns. Wind against the lay of the rope (as shown in Fig. 50(c)). This comes naturally to a right-handed person.

(c) Having wound on fourteen close and tight turns, or a whipping length of one and one-half rope diameters (whichever is the greater), bare the needle, and thrust it between two strands to emerge in the groove (*contline*) the other side.

(d) Following this groove along to the start of the whipping, push the needle through again to emerge in one of the other grooves. Pull the cord tight; follow that groove along to the far end.

(e)   Sink the needle to emerge at the remaining groove.

(f)   Sew twice through a strand and cut off the thread, producing the effect shown in Fig. 50(f). Trim the rope end if necessary.

Details of needles and palms are given in Chapter 8.

Braided ends

The sailmaker's whipping is applicable to braided rope, except that four outer stitched binding strands are better than three, parallel to the rope. Plaits are more supple than laid ropes, and a thinner grade of twine works best. Also, two shorter whippings (each about one rope diameter in length with a gap of similar size between them) is better than a single, longer one.

Plain whipping

There are at least five different ways to whip a rope end, just using twine and your fingers. The most popular method is shown in Fig. 51.

(a)   Start by burying the end under five turns, but leave about 6 in (150 mm) of spare cord hanging out.

(b)   Pull the spare piece gently to take up any slackness of the first turn. Form a loop with the spare cord (Fig. 51(b)), then continue winding while holding this loop in place with your thumb.

(c)   Continue winding over the top of the loop, tightly and against the lay. With sufficient turns, cut off surplus cord and pass the end through the loop as illustrated.

(d)   Holding the last turn from slackening, draw the loop back under about five turns, taking the bitter end with it. Trim off.

Wire ends

Most wire rope in yacht work ends with a hard eye or metal terminal (see later). Any bare ends are best whipped with copper wire and solidified by soldering. Shrink-on sleeves, or plain whippings of twine (both described above) are adequate for coils of wire rope in storage. Riggers stop unravelling by heating the tip to redness, then twisting tightly between two pairs of pliers.

Serving

Like an extended whipping, but with thicker cord, serving is now used mainly over wire rope splices and the strops for traditional wooden-shelled blocks, and also to prevent chafe. Sewn leather produces similar results, protecting one's hands from injury on sharp protruding wire ends, and keeping out the weather.

Parcelling

Sticky black linen insulation tape (or canvas in strip form) is generally used to seal a wire rope before serving. This *parcelling* should be wound on with the lay (see Fig. 52(a)), starting at the bottom of an upright stay to minimize moisture trapping. Vinyl tape will do to parcel a small splice. Smear galvan-

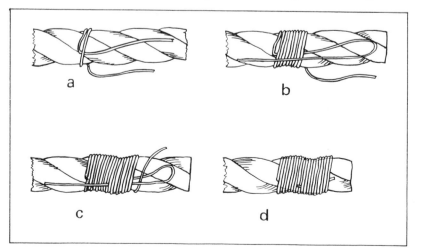

Fig. 51 A plain whipping needs no tools.

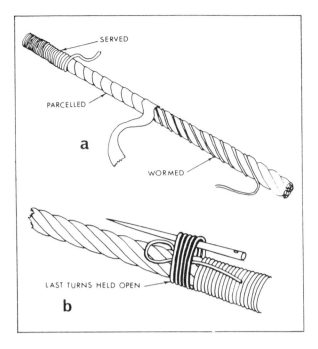

SERVED

PARCELLED

a

WORMED

LAST TURNS HELD OPEN

b

Fig. 52 Serving a wire rope. **a** serving follows worming and parcelling. **b** burying the end under final turns.

ized rope with anhydrous lanoline or underwater grease before parcelling. Fibreglass tape is not waterproof, but is better than nothing under a long serving.

Worming

Rarely needed by amateurs, *worming* consists of filling the dimples in a big rope with cordage (Fig. 52(a)) to produce a more even surface to receive the parcelling and serving. Tarred marline makes the best cord; perhaps two or three lengths twisted together to fill big grooves. Both worming and parcelling are wound on *with* the lay – clockwise when viewing along the rope from the starting point. Serving is wound on *against* the lay, as for whipping.

Marline

Although a serving resembles an extended whipping, the cord used is about three times thicker than whipping cord for a given rope. Small synthetic cordage (such as signal halyard stuff) works well for serving big ropes, but standard unproofed (and unvarnished) codline has a life of only about three years under bad weather conditions. Tarred marline is ideal for wire rope up to about ⅜ in (9 mm) diameter. See also the section headed *Finishing*.

Termination

As for a common whipping, start serving by burying the end under a few turns, leaving enough spare to enable the first turn to be pulled tight before proceeding further and cutting off the protruding piece. At the far end, proceed as in Fig. 52(b). With a marline spike (or even a pencil) under the last five turns, to keep them slack, pass the bitter end under these turns, withdraw the spike, pull the turns tight one by one (using pliers if necessary) and yank on the protruding end to tighten the final turn.

Covering splices

Start at the small end when covering an eye splice. To finish off, either use the above method, or poke the end three times through the usual gap at the tail of the thimble to form three half-hitches at one side. Seizing wire is used commercially to serve eye splices in heavy wire rope, though cord or sewn leather is better for yacht work. With seizing wire, the starting end is usually buried right along under the serving, enabling both ends (after twisting together) to be tucked out of sight under the thimble.

Serving mallet

Some amateur sailors – boys and girls – get involved with the maintenance of traditional craft of large tonnage, which could require long lengths of serving. To make sure this never works loose you need a serving mallet, or the simple block shown in Fig. 3(d) (see Chapter 2). If you cannot buy or borrow one, making it (from any hardwood) takes a maximum of two hours. Helping hands are useful to pass the ball or coil of cord around with each turn when the rope being served has no near-by free end. Trials soon show how many turns around a mallet handle (or through the holes seen in Fig. 3(d)) are needed to create the friction necessary to produce taut serving.

Serving board

The superior tool shown in Fig. 53 enables you to serve rapidly single-handed. The spool has an adjustable friction device. For prolonged work it pays to make up a mandrel to permit rapid spool winding with a hand-drill or low speed power drill. Spare spools save time when working aloft.

Fig. 53 Patent serving board simplifies single-handed work.

Support
When serving unrigged ropes or splices, much better work results if the workpiece is firmly supported between two taut lanyards.

Length
Running out of cord near the end of a longish serving is annoying, though the ends are readily twisted together and buried under the next few turns. To make sure you have enough cord, serve a couple of inches temporarily, measure the length of cord used, then calculate how much is needed for the whole length.

Finishing
Servings are normally meant to be stiff, and two or three coats of varnish (with another coat added each year) are then advantageous in every way. Varnish takes a long time to dry on tarred marline, so allow for this.

Seizings

When binding two ropes together – or two spars at any angle to each other – a seizing of cordage or wire is used. The amateur encounters this mainly when forming the clew eye for jib sheets (see Fig. 44(b))

using a single length of rope. On gaff rigged boats, lower shrouds are often seized together in pairs at the hounds (see Plate 49) and the strops for wooden blocks are secured by seizings at eye or becket.

On cordage
The same thickness of small stuff used for serving is generally applicable for seizings, though plain copper wire or seizing wire is often used on block strops. Waxed twine is popular for the special seizings securing slides and hanks to sails (see page 139).

On wire rope
The standard galvanized soft iron seizing wire kept by marine stores (usually composed of seven thin strands) is suitable for seizings on galvanized wire rope up to about ½ in (12 mm) diameter. Above that, plain galvanized fencing wire is better, and flexible wire rope for big wooden spars. Over small served wire ropes, seizings of marline or codline are kinder than wire. Monel seizing wire is sometimes available and is compatible with stainless steel.

Round seizing
Ideal for most purposes, the round seizing is formed as follows, illustrated in Fig. 54.

(a) Make a small eye splice (or a bowline if using marline), form a noose around both rope parts as shown, and yank up tight.
(b) Apply about twelve turns (or a length of at least three rope diameters) as tightly as possible.
(c) Half-hitch the last turn, then wind riding turns back to the starting point – not quite so tight as the first layer, and one fewer in number.
(d) Pass the working end through the small eye splice or bowline, then take two very tight frapping turns as shown, passing between the main rope parts.
(e) Finish on the reverse side with two half-hitches around both frapping turns. Raise these sufficiently with a screwdriver or spike to get the end underneath them. Before cutting off, make a figure-eight knot to secure the last hitch.

Flat seizing
For lighter loads, a flat seizing may suffice. This is similar to the above exept that the riding turns are omitted. A type of flat seizing across the gap is used for mousing hooks (see Fig. 39, Chapter 6), and for securing slides, slugs, mast hoops and hanks, to the luff eyelets of sails (see Chapter 8).

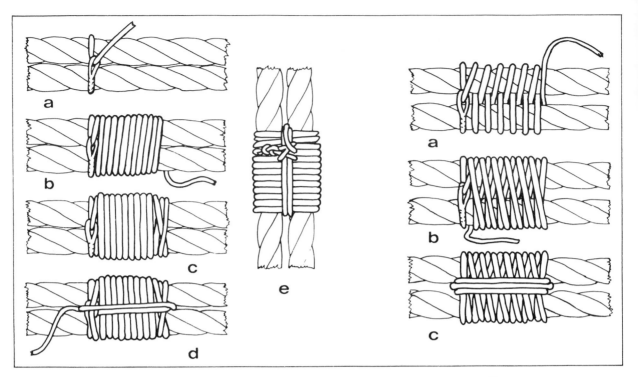

Fig. 54 A round seizing in five stages.

Fig. 55 Racking seizing will take high stresses.

A stopping

For a temporary seizing (perhaps to be broken intentionally by a sharp pull on one rope part) a stopping is used. This is often of thin twine and varies in strength from a single reef-knotted turn, to four or five turns without frapping, closed with a reef knot or slippery hitch. A headsail is said to be *in stops* when hoisted ready to break out by a sharp pull on the sheet.

Racking seizing

To resist high, uneven, or sideways loading on the rope parts (also to lash spars together), the racking seizing (Fig. 55) is best.

(a) Start as for the round seizing, but space the first row of turns one cord width apart, and thread them over and under as shown.

(b) Work along again, drawing each turn as tight as possible, then work back with round turns filling the gaps.

(c) Finish off with frapping turns, as for a round seizing. As the main ropes now have a small gap between them, there is usually room for a few extra frapping turns.

Bedding down

Most ropework benefits from dressing with a mallet. Some whippings, servings, and splices can be rolled underfoot. A leather or rubber faced lead hammer is best for cord seizings, while a copper or lead hammer suits seizing wire.

Splicing cordage

For leading to winches, the more costly braided ropes are nowadays used more than 3-strand. Makers issue data for eye-splicing their brands of braids, but most amateurs prefer to use seizings (as in Fig. 44(a)) or to sew the parts together using criss-crossed stitches right through. For neatness, taper down the bitter end and serve over the whole splice.

Eye splice

With either type of cordage, a hard eye (hard thimble inserted) is used at the working end of a halyard, anchor rode or sheet, to mate with a shackle. A soft eye (as in Fig. 56) is used on such items as mooring lines, rowlock lanyards, bucket ropes or dinghy painters. Eye splicing 3-strand rope is easy to master.

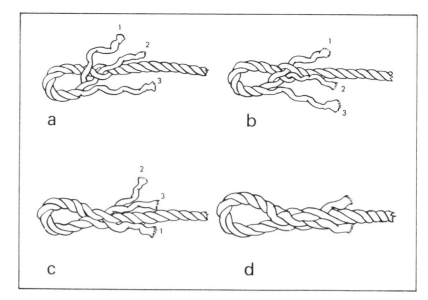

Fig. 56 Starting a soft eye splice.

It can be done on one's lap at odd moments (often using just fingers and knife) as follows:

(a) Having unwound the rope end for a distance of about twenty diameters, form the required size of eye with two strands on top of the standing part and one hanging underneath. Tuck strand no. 2 first, against the lay, under the strand which lies directly beneath it.

(b) Taking no. 1 over the strand just used to house no. 2, tuck it under the next strand away from you as shown.

(c) Turn the whole thing over to tuck no. 3. This goes under the remaining free strand, but remember to tuck *against* the lay. This seems awkward at first, though it looks better once all three parts have been drawn up tight.

(d) You have done all three first tucks, and now comes the second series. Take each part in turn (in any order) over the strand immediately underneath it, and tuck it under the next strand away from you.

Number of tucks
For maximum strength, make a third set of tucks for hemp ropes, but add a fourth set for synthetics. To give the splice an attractive tapered finish (especially prior to serving), tuck once more, having cut away one-third of the yarns in each strand, and then tuck again, having halved the remaining yarns. Do not cut off the yarns too close to the standing part – you can always trim the protruding stubs later with

scissors, or by singeing. Reduced strands tuck more easily if smeared with tallow or Vaseline.

Twisted eye
Referring to the above instructions for making the first set of tucks, there is a valid reason for starting with strand no. 2. If you start with no. 1, a soft eye will finish up twisted. This does not show when a thimble is inserted.

Thimbles
Professional riggers often make a hard eye by stretching a soft eye sufficiently (with the aid of a fid – see Fig. 58(a)) before driving the thimble in. The splice is then hammered to tighten things up. The amateur will find it simpler to insert his thimble after making the first set of tucks, pulling each strand in turn (outwards and towards the thimble) until there is no slack.

Securing ends
Particularly with large ropes, ends need binding with twine or sticky tape to stop the strands from unwinding while tucks are passed. When drawing up each set of tucks tightly, always apply a twisting motion *with* the lay. This reduces the strand diameter and stiffens it. If a thimble is slack after finishing a hard eye, serve the splice or whip both sides around the tail of the thimble, as in Fig. 57.

Tools
Under about ½ in (12 mm) diameter, most three-

Fig. 57 To secure a loose thimble, whip well away from the working surface.

strand ropes can be spliced using no tools except fingers and a knife. A backward twist of the main rope will open the lay, allowing your thumb to expose an aperture sufficient for passing the tuck. A useful adjunct is the shell spike illustrated in Fig. 58(b). Push this under the lay, feed the strand through the hollow shell, then withdraw the tool. A fid (Fig. 58(a)) is usually made of lignum vitae and is commonly about 1½ in (38 mm) in diameter at the big end. Better than a steel spike when splicing big ropes, its use for stretching eye splices when inserting thimbles has already been mentioned. For splicing codline, all you need is a 2 in (50 mm) wire nail to open the lay.

Back splice

Once started, by forming a crown knot (Fig. 59(c)), the back splice is tucked as for the second and third tucks of an eye splice. The number of full tucks is not important, as a back splice is never highly stressed. A crown knot and one series of tucks is sometimes used as a temporary whipping and takes only about two minutes to put on. Three tucks are shown in Fig. 59(d).

Crown knot

By folding the free strands in one direction you get a wall knot (Fig. 59(a)), the strands aiming upwards after tightening. Folded the other way (Fig. 59(b)), the ends hang downwards, as required to start a back splice. Proceed as follows, as shown in Figs. 59(b) and (c):

(b) Sit down with the rope clamped vertically between your knees. Holding strand no. 1 out at right angles to the rope, slip no. 2 over it, and hold the two parts at right angles to each other. Fold no. 3 over no. 2 and poke its end downwards through the awaiting hole under no. 1.

(c) Gently draw the strands up tight. Pulling too hard on any one strand can distort the crown knot. Looking along the rope, if the protruding strands are evenly spaced (at 120° to each other), all is well.

Over-one-under-one

To produce the result shown in Fig. 59(d), complete the series of tucks as described for an eye splice. This is the ritual with nearly all splicing. Once started, work against the lay, taking each loose part in turn over the strand directly beneath it, and tuck underneath the next strand. Any error will be apparent if the tails do not lie at 120° to each other. Continue the over-one-under-one routine until the splice looks right. A back splice is not normally tapered off or served over. On completion, always lay a back splice on the floor and roll it vigorously to and fro under your shoe.

Short splice

For joining ropes end to end with little loss of strength, the short splice is ideal. It takes no longer to make than two eye splices. A bulge is formed in the rope (see Plate 66) so a short splice has limited uses on running rigging.

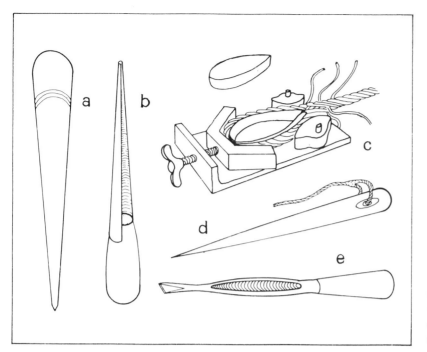

Fig. 58 Some ropework tools. **a** lignum vitae fid. **b** Swedish shell spike. **c** rigger's clamp. **d** marline spike. **e** wire rope spike.

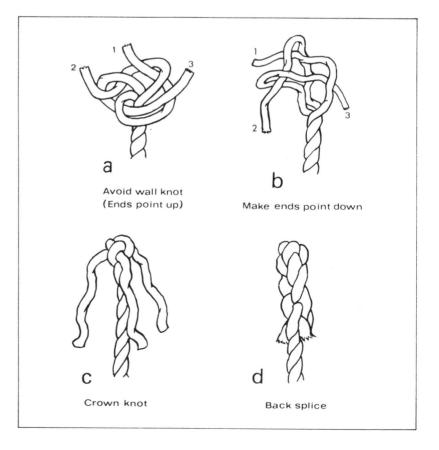

a Avoid wall knot (Ends point up)

b Make ends point down

c Crown knot

d Back splice

Fig. 59 Starting a back splice.

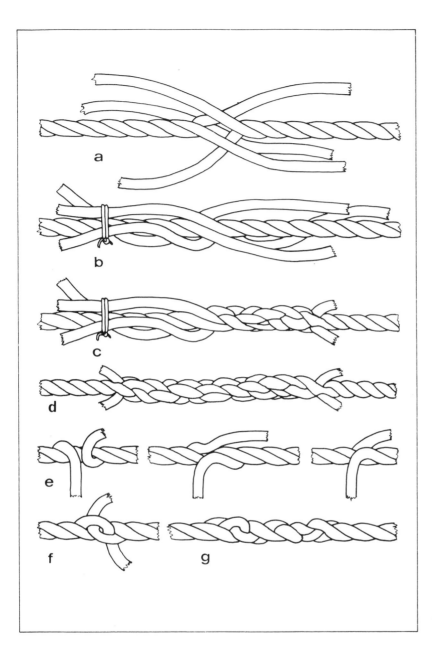

Fig. 60 Joining plain-laid ropes. **a** to **d** short splice, **e** to **g** long splice.

Unlay the same amount of each rope as for an eye splice. Proceed as in Fig. 60(a) to (d)).

(a) Mesh the two rope tails together so that the three strands of one alternate between those of the other.

(b) Secure the three loose strands to the left-hand rope with twine or sticky tape as shown.

(c) In any order, tuck the loose strands to the right over-one-under-one.

(d) Having made the same number of tucks as for an eye splice, turn the assembly around, cut the tape, and tuck exactly as for the first half.

Long splice

Except for three small humps, widely spaced apart, invisible rope joining is possible by means of the long splice. This wastes a lot of rope and is the weakest of all splices, but is particularly useful for

Plate 66 There is no limit to the length of a strop. The short splice bulge is rarely detrimental.

repairing sail boltropes. Start with alternating strands intermeshed as for a short splice, but unlay three times as much of each rope beforehand. Lash two strands to the main rope at the left side, leaving the third strand dangling. Unlay this strand to the right, replacing it with the corresponding free strand previously unlaid from the left side rope. Lash that temporarily, then do the same trick with a pair towards the left, having untied the original lashing. That leaves you with one long pair of strands hanging from the middle, plus one long and one short some distance away at left and right (see Fig. 60(e)).

Hiding the ends
It is the securing and hiding of the above ends that makes or mars a long splice. You have to make an overhand knot (or, more correctly, a half-knot) at each pair (Fig. 60(f)), then tuck the ends over-one-under-one (Fig. 60(g)) at least twice. Clearly, this might make too much of a bulge, so expert riggers shave the rope tails down just the right amount,

before tying and tucking. Some neat stitching helps to keep the tails in place. Hammering and rolling should then allow the splice to pass all except the tightest sheaves.

Splicing wire rope

There are still enthusiastic and impecunious owners (particularly in remote parts of the world) who need to splice wire rope. The job is satisfying and interesting, but modern press-on sleeves have largely taken over from hand splicing, the latter being suitable for only a limited range of rope constructions.

Possibilities
Hard and soft eyes are quite the most frequent form of splice likely to be needed. Working with flexible wire rope up to ³⁄₈ in (9 mm) diameter is not much more difficult than working with hemp. The stiffer 7 × 7 standing rigging is much more troublesome, and 1 × 19 construction is intended only for swage or compression type terminals.

Alternatives
Instead of using eye splices where gaff shrouds terminate in deadeyes (shown in Plate 50), seizings are often used with caps or tape over the bitter ends. This needs to be carefully done with strong seizing wire in four separate positions a few inches apart. The method can be used for any hard eye with thimble or solid heart insert. Where appearance does not matter, three wire rope clips (see Fig. 70) make an even better eye, especially if some later adjustment to length is likely.

Wrapping
Hard eye splices in wire rope are best served over or leather covered. To do this, serve the part around the thimble before splicing, or sew the leather on that part first, leaving enough leather hanging loose to sew over the splice on completion. Even thick vinyl tape is better than nothing. Failing a proper rigger's clamp (see Fig. 58(c)), always fit three secure whippings to hold the rope closely around the thimble – wire cannot be stretched to insert a thimble after splicing.

Setting up
Unlay at least 30 rope diameters for an eye splice, and tape the ends. Riggers often heat and twist as detailed on page 115. Clamp the thimble as shown in

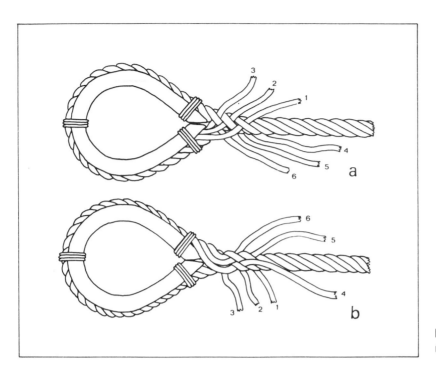

Fig. 61 Eye splice in flexible wire rope. **a** front face. **b** back face.

Fig. 61(a), with the standing part lashed horizontally to the right – if you are right-handed. Some people prefer to work with the splice vertical. Particularly with a soft eye, it pays to clap a temporary whipping at the point beyond which the strand must not be unlayed.

Useful gear
Screwdrivers (down to ⅛ in (3 mm) diameter) are more useful than marline spikes (see Fig. 58(d)), for parting the strands when splicing wire. The proper tool for this looks like a screwdriver at the tip (see Fig. 58(e)), thence merging into a tapered round spike with a half-round groove running along it. This enables tucks to be passed in similar fashion to the shell spike described on page 120 for splicing cordage. Side cutters are useful, but the best tools for cropping off strands are a sharp cold chisel and a club hammer, used over a heavy block of scrap metal (preferably brass) for the anvil. Pliers are always handy. A simple rigger's clamp (Fig. 58(c)) could be made in a good home workshop. To form a soft eye, the temporary heart-shaped metal blank shown is inserted.

First three
You need six free strands to tuck, so cut out any

seventh core strand of wire, hemp, or plastics. As shown in Fig. 61(a), divide the strands into two lots of three, lashing nos. 4, 5 and 6 out of the way behind the rope. Tuck nos. 1, 2 and 3 against the lay at the places where they fit naturally, much as previously described for an eye splice in cordage.

Stiffness
Opening the lay to pass a tuck without damaging the core strand is not always easy. Having forced the tool through, swing it counter-clockwise to lie at 90° to the rope, thus offering the largest possible opening for the tuck. Avoid the formation of any kinks, and use pliers if necessary to draw each strand outwards and backwards towards the thimble as tightly as possible.

Back three
Rotate the thimble 180° in the vice to tuck nos. 4, 5 and 6, as in Fig. 61(b). Just as with a hemp splice, this is the place where the splice gets ugly, as these strands must bend sharply to tuck against the lay. Various tricks are used to combat this problem, including crossing nos. 5 and 6 under one strand, one against the lay and one with the lay. The simplest device is to poke nos. 5 and 6 together under one strand, but let them emerge in their

rightful places, as seen in Fig. 61(b). Pull all tucks tight, remove from the vice, then dress the splice with a lead hammer before doing any more.

Further tucks
The over-one-under-one rule now applies. You need at least a further three tucks if using slippery stainless steel and two if using galvanized. To taper the splice neatly, cut off two strands and tuck the remaining four. Cut off two further strands, then tuck the last two.

Joining wire
A short splice in wire rope is made as described for cordage, but with six strands instead of three. This is rarely used for yacht work, but can be useful when lengthening cable for winter mooring purposes, and also for making wire rope strops (see below).

Making strops

Any continuous circle of rope (like a car fan belt) is known as a strop or strap, but those smaller than deck quoits are called grommets, normally pronounced *grummets*. Very small grommets are sewn into sails and canvas covers to form eyes for rope attachment (with or without swaged metal inserts), and are stronger than common punched eyelets. Large strops are made from cordage or wire rope for use as lifting slings, anchor rode buffers, and to form the eyes and beckets on wooden shelled blocks (see later).

Splice method
Most strops are made by short splicing the appropriate length of cordage or wire rope (Plate 66). The neatness of a long splice is usually limited to a total finished rope length of about 6 ft (2 m) or more, and is not possible with wire rope.

Grommet method
Take a single strand of cordage about four times as long as the circumference of the required grommet. Lay up this strand around itself (Plate 67) until a three stranded rope is formed, of the original diameter. Cut the ends to butt neatly together, then tape over, and clap on a whipping to cover the joint. For maximum strength, when a small bulge does not matter, finish off the two ends as for a long splice – shave down, half-knot and tuck twice.

Wire grommet
A single strand from a wire rope is laid up around

Plate 67 How to start making a rope grommet.

itself four times to make a wire grommet strop. This will then contain only five strands, but it proves impossible to get six strands back into place – you might only manage four. Parcelling and serving all over is standard practice, so butting the ends is no problem. Make due allowance for the fact that such a strop could be twenty per cent weaker than the original rope.

Selvagee strop
At least in the smaller sizes, a selvagee strop is easier for the amateur to make (in cordage or wire) than other types. It needs serving all over to look neat. Proceed as in Fig. 62:

(a) Tap a few nails into a board representing the desired internal strop diameter.
(b) Build up the thickness using at least ten turns of synthetic cord, seizing wire, plain wire, or flexible wire rope, neatly coiled around the nails.
(c) Clap on a few stopper seizings and withdraw the nails.

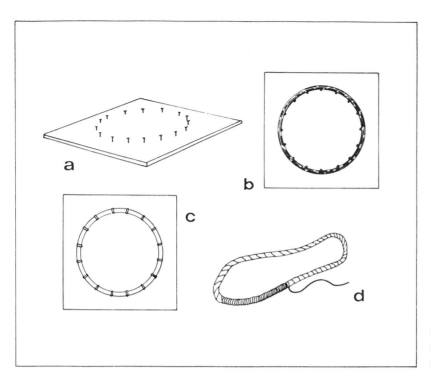

Fig. 62 Stages in winding, marling and serving a selvagee strop or strap.

(d)   Parcel with insulation tape and serve all over.

Sewn eyes
Use the selvagee method to make the tiny grommets for padding sewn canvas eyes, described further in Chapter 8. Make a coil of marline or thick twine around your finger tip. Slide this off and use sewing thread to tie the coil in place with about four stoppers.

Marling
For a big (or temporary) selvagee strop (which is not to be served), keep the strands in place by the process of marling (Fig. 63). This is similar to the lacing used to secure sails or awnings to spars (see Chapter 8) or to tie the bottom of a sail coat. Proceed as follows:

(a)   Take a ball (or neat coil) of strong cord. With the strop pulled taut, clove-hitch the cord around it.

(b)   Make a half-hitch every 3 in (75 mm) or so, pulling the cord tight at each one. Use a marked stick to get all the half-hitches equidistant.

(c)   At the end, make another clove hitch just beyond the first one, reef knot the two ends together and trim them off.

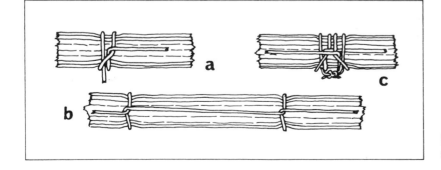

Fig. 63 Marling details, including starting and finishing.

Block strop

A wire selvagee makes a good strop to support a wooden shell block (Fig. 64), though not so easily moulded to the shape as single spliced flexible wire rope. Always offer up the strop to make sure it fits before parcelling and serving; a small correction is sometimes possible by changing the thimble size or shape. If the first seizing turns will not pull the strop parts together, rig a simple Spanish windlass or tourniquet (Fig. 65) and wind this up by means of a big nail. For a spliced wire strop, position the lumpy splice in the score (slot) at the base of the shell. When there is a becket (thimbled eye) at this end as well as an eye at the top, position the splice to one side of the shell.

Block maintenance

Before fitting strops, grease pins and sheaves using underwater or graphite grease. With the sheaves out, varnish the shell inside and out, and also varnish the strop serving. When assembled, varnish again all over to include the seizing. Not all wooden shell blocks need strops. The best quality ones are internally bound, with eye and becket fixed to a concealed metal frame. Except for annual washing, modern blocks of tufnol, nylon and stainless steel rarely get any maintenance attention. Oiling is not necessary, but spraying with silicone-based lubricant will often cure squeaking.

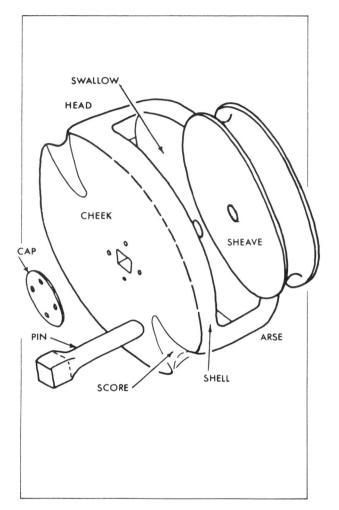

Fig. 64 Exploded view of a common wooden shell block.

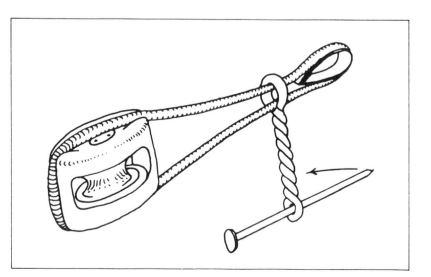

Fig. 65 Drawing up a block strop before seizing.

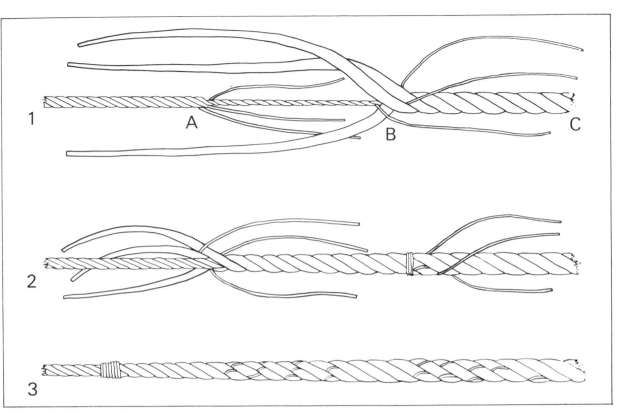

Fig. 66 Tail splices are most often used where wire halyards are joined to rope tails.

Tail splice

Most amateurs get a rigger to long-splice a wire halyard to its braided tail. Following makers' data sheets for this can take too long when needed once every three years. See page 248 for reeving a new halyard and page 89 for removing sheaves. Tail splicing with 3-strand rope is comparatively simple, as follows:

Beforehand
Unlay the wire rope for a distance of 120 diameters and tape all six ends. Cut out the heart cord, then lay up again three alternate strands (to form the three stranded rope shown from A to B in Fig. 66) for a distance of about 60 diameters, applying tape to secure both positions. Unlay the rope tail for a distance of about 1½ times A–B. Shave down the last one-third so that the tips are only one-quarter of the full diameter. Grease these to keep a good shape.

Into action
The three essential stages are shown in Fig. 66. This is not to scale. An actual splice would be about three times as long.

(1) Start as for a short splice, meshing the three rope strands with the wire ones at B. Tie these temporarily.

(2) Lay up the rope strands from B to A (concealing the wire) and tie them there. Start tucking the three wire strands from B to C, followed by the other three from A towards B.

(3) Do not use the over-one-under-one routine, but wind each wire strand around a rope strand six times (in an elongated spiral) and cut off any surplus. Sew the ends into the heart of the rope to ensure they never pop out. Lay up the tapered cordage strands to the left of A (on top of the wire rope) and clap on a whipping to secure the ends.

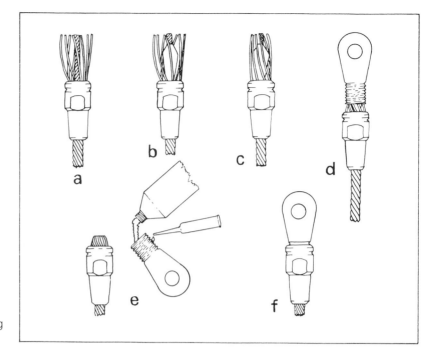

Fig. 67 Six stages involved in fitting a Norseman wire rope terminal.

Quick terminals

When time is more important than money, clamp-on or swaged terminals are generally preferred to eye splices. Fitting screw-on Norseman, Sta-Lok or Mate eyes and forks is within the capabilities of most amateurs, while marine stores often keep a press for swaging on the Talurit (pronounced *Tailor-it*) or Nicopress terminals used for making hard or soft eyes.

Two wrenches
The secret of screw-type terminals lies in the tapered plug which clamps the strands inside the fitting. A couple of wrenches is basically all you need to do the job. The Norseman plug is precisely engineered for each different class of standing rigging material. The Mate cone is universal and is also suitable for flexible wire rope, once the heart core is cut out sufficiently to clear the cone.

Norseman method
The series shown in Fig. 67 illustrates how a Norseman terminal is fitted to 1 × 19 wire. Originally British, Norseman products are now marketed in the USA by Norseman Marine Inc., Fort Lauderdale, Florida.

(a) Push the shrink-on plastic sleeve (if required) down the rope, followed by terminal body. Separate the outer twelve wires from the central bunch of seven.
(b) Press the hollow cone into position, the central bunch passing through this. Leave the wires protruding one rope diameter beyond the cone.
(c) Bend the twelve wires inwards over the cone.
(d) Screw the male part of the terminal into the body, tighten up, then unscrew again.
(e) Make sure the wires are evenly spaced and have completely closed over the cone. Fill with silicone rubber sealant supplied.
(f) Apply Loctite fluid to the thread and re-fit the male part. If used, shift the plastic sleeve to cover the body and rope equally, then shrink on with steam from a kettle spout.

Mixing metals
Stainless steel terminals should not be used with galvanized rope. Norseman make industrial terminals for this, and for their plastic-filled rope. Mate terminals (made in the USA) are similar to Norseman, but have sighting holes in the body to enable the rope end position to be checked before final tightening.

Resin plug

In America, the Castlock range of do-it-yourself terminals utilizes rapid-hardening resin instead of a metal plug to anchor the rope strands. These are suitable for flexible as well as stiff wire, but are not normally available above ¼ in (6 mm) rope diameter. With the strands fanned out for 1½ rope diameters from the end, the terminal body is pulled up flush, the resin poured in and the top fitting screwed on.

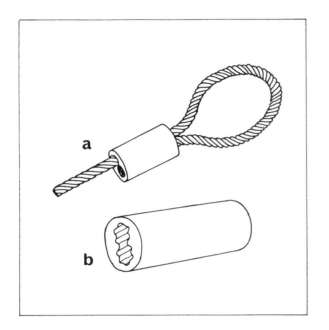

Fig. 68 Nicopress and Talurit sleeves are swaged on by a powerful press.

Swages

As shown in Plate 68, swaged terminals are the neatest of all. Putting them on is a factory job, so precise length details are necessary when ordering stays with these ends. Ball terminals are popular for small craft rigging. Hooked into hollow mast walls (or suitable tangs) these allow stays to deflect without damage. Like swages, the fitting of terminals to rod rigging does not come within the realms of do-it-yourself work.

Crimped sleeves

Many yacht clubs and individuals nowadays own Nicopress kits for attaching the sleeves or ferrules (Fig. 68) on five sizes of wire rope up to $\frac{3}{16}$ in (5 mm).

Separate dies are inserted in the pincer end of the long-handled compression tool for each size of sleeve. Make sure you use the right sleeve for the rope – usually 7 × 19 or 7 × 7. For 1 × 19, two sleeves in tandem are recommended. After looping through, leave the bitter end protruding about one diameter to allow for the usual draw-in during crimping. If too much is left sticking out, finish with a dollop of epoxy putty to prevent injuries. Crimp three or four times, starting nearest to the eye. Nicopress sleeves are of nickel-plated copper. Talurit use copper for stainless steel and light alloy for galvanized rope.

Piano wire

Single-strand stainless steel rigging (usually called *piano wire*) has been used successfully on sailing dinghies for half a century. A simple but effective hard eye is often made as shown in Fig. 69. The sleeve is made from $\frac{3}{16}$ in (4 mm) or ¼ in (6 mm) outside diameter thick-walled copper tube – offcuts usually available from a boatyard engine shop. Proceed as follows:

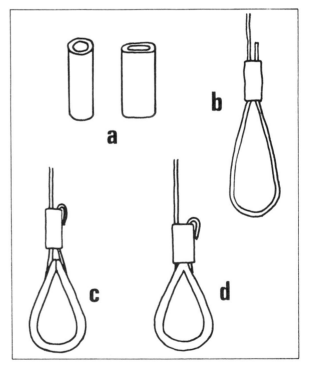

Fig. 69 Eye splicing piano wire for racing dinghy rigging is easily done with a bit of copper tube.

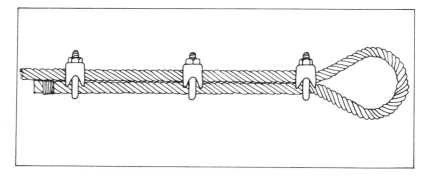

Fig. 70 The way wire rope clip saddles should sit to prevent crushing damage to the standing part.

(a) Flatten the sleeve slightly with hammer or vice.
(b) Thread wire through sleeve, loop and thread back through sleeve.
(c) Insert thimble, bend wire end back to tuck along sleeve as shown.
(d) Draw eye tight and flatten sleeve fully to pinch wire.

Soldered sleeve

A neater, stronger, but more laborious method is to use a seizing of copper wire in place of the flattened tube, and then solidify it with soft solder – pronounced *sodder* by engineers. Parcelling with vinyl tape is always a good idea to hide the sharp wire end, with either of the above methods.

Clips

Although ugly, galvanized wire rope clips (bulldog grips) make quick and sound hard and soft eyes – especially useful for mooring lines, temporary derrick stays, and slipway winch ropes. Use three clips, about ten rope diameters apart. Place the grooved saddles against the standing part and the U-bolts over the rope tail, as shown in Fig. 70. Make sure they match the rope size exactly. Keep a few spare clips on board for rigging a jury mast or for other emergencies.

Choosing wire rope

Table 7 lists the wire rope products of one firm in the sizes most commonly used for yacht work, with strengths and 1993 costs. Although stainless steel does not appear to be vastly stronger than galvanized, it pays to choose a size larger with the latter, to provide some allowance for possible future hidden corrosion.

Plastic coatings

A useful modern development is plastic filled galvanized wire rope; not to be confused with the plastic *sheathed* variety which has been used for guardrails for many years. With each wire embedded in plastics, long life is assured, provided the terminals are adequately sealed. Windage is greater compared with plain wire, but at half the cost of stainless steel, this rope makes an attractive proposition for cruising yacht rigging.

Advice

A full range of wire rope is not always available in every part of the world. If reliable advice is difficult to get locally, a direct approach to the rope makers concerned should yield the necessary information. Queries arise mainly when new or unusual materials are offered, such as any not mentioned earlier in this chapter, in Table 7, or in Chapter 6.

Plate 68 Nothing can match the neatness of a factory-swaged wire rope terminal.

Table 7

Wire rope cost comparisons

Rope diameter	Stainless steel						Galvanized steel								
	1 × 19 for standing rigging			7 × 19 for running rigging			1 × 19 for standing rigging			7 × 19 for running rigging			7 × 7 Norselay plastic impregnated		
	Breaking load in kg	£ in UK	$ in USA	Breaking load in kg	£ in UK	$ in USA	Breaking load in kg	£ in UK	$ in USA	Breaking load in kg	£ in UK	$ in USA	Breaking load in kg	£ in UK	$ in USA
$\frac{1}{8}$ in 3 mm	760	8	30	630	12	40	700	6	24	500	10	26	650	8	34
$\frac{5}{32}$ in 4 mm	1360	13	50	970	19	55	1300	9	35	800	12	38	1100	10	34
$\frac{3}{16}$ in 5 mm	2110	19	70	1520	25	70	2000	11	45	1110	15	50	1800	12	44
$\frac{1}{4}$ in 6 mm	3040	28	110	2180	37	105	3000	14	60	2100	18	65	2500	15	58
$\frac{9}{32}$ in 7 mm	4150	40	145	2970	45	135	4000	18	72	2700	22	77	3600	19	70
$\frac{5}{16}$ in 8 mm	5420	48	180	3880	55	170	5300	23	90	3300	30	95	4750	24	85

Note: All costs per 10m length excluding sales tax

8
Sails and Canvaswork

Much care is needed to keep one of the most vulnerable parts of a sailing craft – her sails – in good order. They are an important power source, and greatly influence safety. The amateur should get to know all about the subject. Fair weather sailors could make a suit of working sails last more than twelve years, but under deep sea and racing conditions, five years is more likely.

Types of canvas

Except for nylon spinnakers (and expensive Kevlar and Mylar examples), most yacht sails are of polyester synthetic cloth such as Terylene (in Britain) and Dacron (in the USA). Cotton has always been popular for traditional gaff rigged craft. Flax, once used for the heaviest sails on clipper ships and coasting schooners, is rarely seen nowadays. Sailcloth resistant to sunlight degradation is ideal for roller reefing or furling headsails, or the so-called sacrificial panels sewn to the foot and leech of such sails.

Polyester benefits
Synthetic materials are generally smoother and more airtight than natural cloth, giving a superior racing performance, particularly to windward. They do not rot when left wet, and although mildew will form on them, it does not damage the structure. For equal strength, both polyester and nylon weigh less than cotton, so synthetic sails draw better in light

airs and are easier to handle. They do not need stretching when new, and keep their shape better. Drying out before stowage is not essential.

Polyester problems
Compared with cotton, polyester is stiff and uncomfortable to stitch, rather like thick paper. All stitches stand proud above the surface and are thus vulnerable to chafe. Continuous strong sunlight can ruin a regular synthetic sail in little more than two years, both cloth and stitches becoming brittle. Stowing below (or sail coats) must be a feature of sail care in the tropics.

Use of nylon
Working with the thin but strong nylon cloth used for spinnakers is akin to dressmaking (whether machine or hand sewn), except perhaps for the various multi-layered reinforcements. Nylon takes no harm from being creased when stowed, but it tears easily and so needs careful handling. Stick-on tape or repair patches stay on it well, as do sail numbers. Nylon sailbags are popular nowadays.

Cotton sails
When rendered rot-proof and water repellent, cotton is still a possibility for motorsailers and other craft where reaching and running are the preferred points of sailing. These sails need stretching when new, starting with light breezes only, and tensioning each luff (and the foot of a mainsail) gradually over a period of at least twenty hours. Cotton suits the

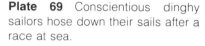

Plate 69 Conscientious dinghy sailors hose down their sails after a race at sea.

impecunious handyman, as all types of repairs are easier and more enjoyable to carry out than similar ones in polyester.

Drying off

Avoid stowing cotton sails wet. When you have no option, dry them as soon as possible afterwards, preferably no later than the following day. Salt encrustation harms both synthetic and cotton sails. The dinghy racing enthusiast hoses down both hull and sails (Plate 69) after a sea race. The cruising enthusiast may not always have a suitable fresh water hose at hand, but hoisting sails on a calm rainy day is sure to help. A thorough bathtub wash for dinghy sails (and a scrub on the lawn for cruiser sails) is always wise before winter storage (see Chapter 12).

Cotton covers

White or green proofed cotton duck material is best obtained from a commercial tent or blind maker nowadays. The most useful weights are 12 oz (400 g) or 15 oz (500 g). Brush-on rot proofers are readily available, and need a maintenance application once a year. On canvas covers which are painted, apply proofer to the inside only. The special paint made to go on canvas is not readily available, but some people have success with whitewall car tyre paint.

Vinyl work

Awning makers usually glue the seams of vinyl-coated nylon material before sewing. This stops leaks and also holds the material in place during stitching. Polyester or nylon thread is now almost universally used for this and for all types of canvaswork. The only drawbacks of vinyl-coated materials are their stiffness in cold weather, and their tendency to sweat inside. Proofed cotton duck is still preferred for boat covers by some folk.

Bending sails

Unless a mainsail is very large, stowage below decks is advisable during long periods at moorings. (Old-time sails were often tanned with cutch to extend their life when constantly exposed.) A well fitted sail coat (slightly open at the bottom to allow air circulation) eliminates the need to unbend a big mainsail or mizzen. With a gaff and mast hoops, unbending is a lengthy process. Bending jibs, stay-sails, trysails and special running sails goes on all the time, so their attachment is made to be as quick as possible.

Modern mainsails

When calm, engage any foot slides (or groove) first. Secure the tack eye next, followed by fixing and adjusting the clew outhaul. Slip in the battens, attach halyard, and engage luff slides, slugs, or groove. Use of a topping lift is not essential until hoisting sail.

Luff grooves

It should be noted that the use of a mast groove to house the mainsail boltrope (instead of track and slides) reduces weight aloft, but is mainly suitable for racing dinghies and small catamarans, having no provision for reefing. On a cruising boat, a luff groove prevents the mainsail from lowering under its own weight. Also, it needs two people to hoist sail – one on the halyard and one feeding the boltrope into the groove. However, luff grooves can be converted to track by using cylindrical slugs (lashed to luff eyelets) to act as slides. Slugs are useful on twin running staysails set on a twin grooved headfoil after removing the regular roller reefing jib.

Battens

The ends of full-length battens need cars running on track, but in-boom roller reefing is possible; junk rig (Plate 70) needs no track. Conventional leech battens (Plate 74) cause a lot of bother. They are on the most active part of the sail and they must always be there when under way. Unless battens are exactly the right length, width and thickness, rapid damage to their pockets could result. When shortening battens, always cut from the stiffer end close to the leech. Regular inspections for fractured stitches and chafed canvas are essential in the vicinity of batten pockets.

Gaff sails

The absence of battens is one of the merits of a gaff sail. Modernization of the rig has been tried, using tracks along mast, boom and gaff. This makes bending simpler, but loses some good characteristics of a traditional loose-footed gaff mainsail, such as instant reefing by tricing up the tack (called *scandalizing*) and rapid lowering with the aid of free running mast hoops. Many gaff sails have hemp boltropes which shrink when wet, so clew and peak outhaul adjustment may be called for.

Girts

Wrongly adjusted outhaul or halyard tensions create wrinkles called *girts*, which are often seen in gaff mainsails. Typical ones are shown in Fig. 71. If they are allowed to form too often, you could find a permanent deformity. The usual fault is a girt from throat to clew (Fig. 71(a)), caused by failure to swig up the peak halyard sufficiently. The creases seen in Fig. 71(b) are usually caused by a slack throat halyard.

Plate 70 As well as being efficient, junk rig is ideal for singlehanded sailing.

Lacings

The usual way to lace a sail or awning to a spar is by marling – a series of half-hitches as shown in Fig. 72(a) and described in the previous chapter. You cannot pass a coil of line through an eyelet, so threading takes a long time; better to locate the middle of the line and work in both directions from the central eyelet, or fit separate loops, as in Fig. 72(b).

Safety lashings

If marling breaks or chafes through, the whole lacing will fail. A reef knot at each eyelet position provides safety, but is difficult to tie with a long cord, and prevents tightening little by little after reeving. Individual lashings are safest, each one a double pass of cord reef-knotted close to the boltrope for neatness. Do not cut the ends off too close: whip or knot them so that the same cords can be undone and replaced many times.

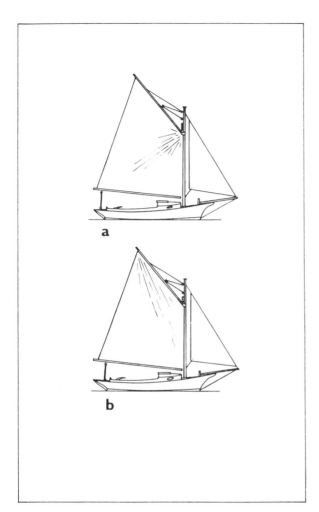

Fig. 71 Gaff mainsail girts must not be allowed to form. **a** peak halyard needs swigging up. **b** peak halyard needs slackening.

Fig. 72 Traditional and quick-loop marling.

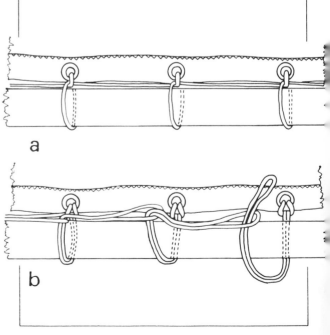

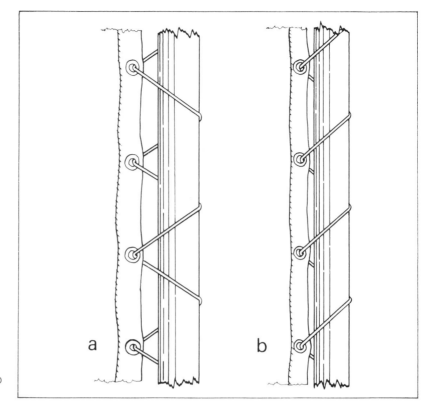

Fig. 73 Two ways of lacing sails to yards and masts.

Gunter lacing

A simple gunter mainsail is laced to the mast to avoid the need for hoops or track. Either of the systems shown in Fig. 73 will do for this, allowing freedom of movement up and down. Unlacing the lowest eyelets is quickly done for roller reefing. The lacing will self-stow neatly enough for jiffy reefing purposes.

Hoop seizings

For roller reefing with mast hoops, the lowest ones are either replaced by lacing, or the hoops are equipped with quick-release cordage seizings. All other hoops need strong, permanent seizings to the luff eyelets or cringles (Fig. 74) using polyester cordage or leather thongs. Make as many passes as the eyes will allow. Make all the frapping turns in the form of half-hitches, in case one or two of them work loose when the sail flogs. If you attach each cord semi-permanently to its luff eye with a bowline or eye splice (and whip the ends neatly) the same cords should survive many sail bending operations, and you will not lose them. Alternatively, knot the middle of each cord to its eyelet, and pass the turns

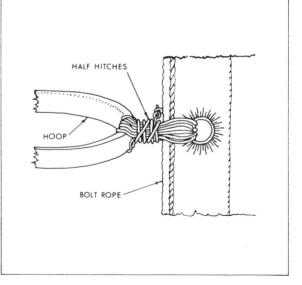

Fig. 74 Mast hoop seizing.

symmetrically left and right, finishing with a reef knot.

Jamming hoops

A gaff mast is best maintained by scraping and oiling in way of the hoops. There is a temptation to use varnish and to leather the hoops to prevent chafe. The friction created causes jamming, especially when lowering sail. The same thing may happen when hoops are slightly too small in diameter. The traditional remedy is to rig a thin line down the hoops (for'ard of the mast), clove-hitched to each hoop, or passed through a small hole with a stopper knot each side. A tug on this should release any jamming hoops when lowering sail.

existing hoops with packing strips between them, as shown in Fig. 75(a). Leave gaps between the strips for the insertion of lashings to clamp the laminations into position. Use ash or hickory strips of the original thickness, and taper down the ends. Steam or boil them for at least ten minutes before bending. Secure the ends (with two copper rivets or seizings) the following day.

On the bench

To avoid having to laminate a hoop on board, fabricate it in two halves (Fig. 75(b)) at home. This

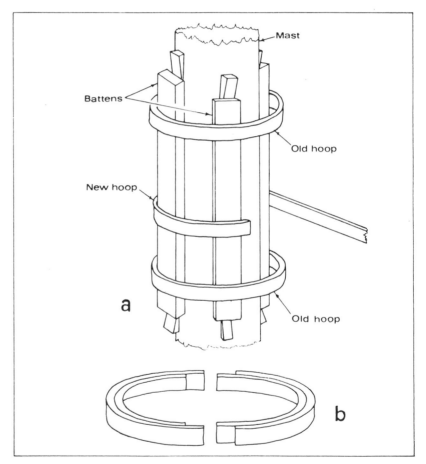

Fig. 75 Two methods of making new mast hoops.

New hoops

A good marine store can still order mast hoops of most diameters. Getting these on involves unstepping the mast, so if one hoop breaks or rots, it pays to renew them all. The masts on some big craft are never unstepped. In such a case, a new hoop must be laminated around the mast. Make a jig from two

comes out just as strong as a traditional one if resin glue is used for both laminations and for the scarf joints when assembling around the mast. Woodscrews will do to clamp these joints. Small blocks tacked to a bench will form a jig, but make these high enough to allow space for clamps to hold the laminations.

138

Slide seizings

On big craft, mast track slides or slugs are sometimes attached to the luff eyes by special shackles. However, seizings of tape, webbing, leather strap, or cordage are less likely to damage a boltrope or its stitching. Tape is sewn to a slide, wound four or five times through cringle and slide, then all is sewn together. For sailing dinghies, waxed polyester twine suffices on slides and hanks – threaded through a big needle to speed up the work. Note that when each slide has a circular thimble (as in Fig. 76) the twine is intended to pass around the outside score (groove) of the thimble, not through the middle.

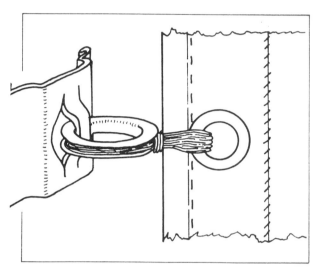

Fig. 76 Seizing for a light-duty slide.

Hanks

When refixing slides or hanks, copy the method previously used, for the sake of uniformity, unless this has proved unsatisfactory. Some plastic hanks and snap hooks are designed to clip on with no seizings. Others fix with set screws. Many piston hanks have twin eyes for two separate seizings to each.

Setting sails

Some experience helps when trying to find which corner of a sail is which, especially at night. If you remember that the boltrope is traditionally sewn to the port side of each sail, and the leech normally has no boltrope, sorting out the corners is possible with eyes closed.

Complications

Except perhaps for a spinnaker which is not encased in a sock, hoisting sails in the dark is feasible, once you have learned which halyard is which. Dinghy sails are normally hoisted before launching, so there is no panic. The same applies to minisails and sailboards where the luff hem slips over the entire mast. Cruiser sail damage is likely if you hoist a mainsail without topping up the boom, or a headsail without first freeing the sheets. Once set, the complications of precise trim commence (particularly with racing sails), involving zippers, cunninghams, ookers, flatteners, leech lines, boom vang (kicking strap), backstay and baby stay controls, barber hauler, whisker pole, jockey pole, boom preventer guy, and telltale streamers. Care reduces maintenance costs.

Tack tackle

Getting a jib luff sufficiently taut and straight is essential for efficiency. Without a powerful winch, this is readily achieved by using a simple tack tackle at deck level, which is taken up after swigging the halyard hand tight. The same arrangement works well on a mainsail, provided the gooseneck has a little up and down movement on a track or bar.

Headsails

Even with a single roller headsail, sheet lead positions need shifting according to the number of rolls. Marking the deck track or pierced toerail (Plate 71) at suitable positions for the snap-shackled turning blocks helps a lot. This may get complicated with multiple forestays and such foredeck sails as bigboy, genoa, ghoster, spinnaker, yankee, cruising chute, and storm or flying jib.

Headfoils

Extruded headfoils permit controlled roller reefing, but bashing by a spinnaker boom set shy can prove costly. Follow makers' instructions on lubrication, or the drum bearing seal could let water in, and the top swivel could freeze and snap. Examine the roller line often – breakage in a gale is serious. Check jib sacrificial panels too. They might need renewing or restitching long before the bulk of the sail. If the jib creases during roll-up, get a sailmaker to sew sausage-shaped padding centrally along the luff. When furled, always clap a tier around all at the clew.

Booms and clubs

Automatic tacking without tending sheets is the joy

Plate 71 Pierced footrails permit the accurate positioning of jib sheet snatch blocks.

of a boomed staysail. One snag: unless the clew outhaul is eased when setting or stowing the sail, a girt will form as shown in Fig. 77, which will ultimately damage the sail. A club is shorter than a boom (Fig. 78) and is not laced along the foot. It should eliminate the girt problem, and also has the advantage of automatically putting extra belly into the sail when squared off (Fig. 79).

Twin boomed staysails make the best rig for prolonged running before the wind. Self-steering from sheets to tiller is readily contrived. The booms tend to be longer than spinnaker poles, so stowage up and down the mast often proves best. Special tack eyebolts nearer the mast are required for best results.

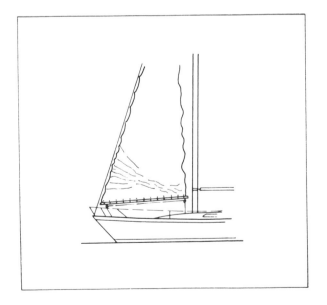

Fig. 77 Boomed staysail cannot be lowered without easing the clew.

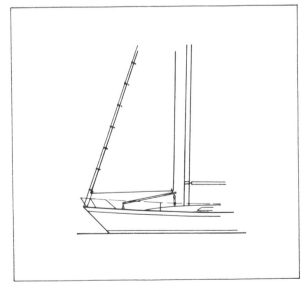

Fig. 78 How a staysail club is rigged.

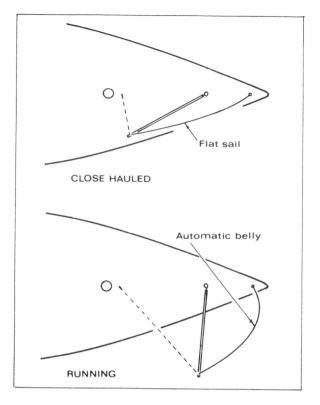

Fig. 79 A club adjusts the sail-set automatically.

(Figure labels: Flat sail; CLOSE HAULED; Automatic belly; RUNNING)

Topsails and trysails

Fair-weather sails are not infrequently the most difficult to set. A gaff topsail with its luff running on a wire jackstay from deck to masthead should be reasonably easy to control. A yard laced along the luff is advantageous, except for the extra weight and the difficulty of stowing it.

Extra fair-weather sails include a trysail between both masts on a ketch, bonnets to add to the bottoms of existing sails, enormous jibs and spinnakers. To tame the latter, a chute, tunnel, or turtle is built into the foredeck of some small racing craft. A downhaul from the belly of the sail through the tunnel ensures foolproof stowage. For a cruising spinnaker, a full-length sock provides instant furling without lowering the sail. Some gadgets can reduce wear and tear markedly.

Vangs

Useful on racing dinghies to flatten the mainsail by bending the boom downwards, the boom vang or kicking strap (Plate 72) is not uncommon on bigger boats, where it prevents Chinese gybes, as well as helping to regulate mainsail set. On a wishbone ketch, a vang from mizzen mast to wishbone end is useful to reduce sail twist, but the idea is rarely applied to a traditional gaff. Slab (jiffy) reefing is supplanting roller gear, primarily to avoid having to release the boom vang while rolling in a strap for it or fitting a claw-ring which could damage the sail when

Plate 72 Much revered by the racing fraternity with bendy booms, boom vangs have improved mainsail set on many cruising sailboats.

rolled. A double-acting screw or hydraulic boom vang eliminates the need for a topping lift.

Furling

Do not lower a boomed sail without having at least one of the tiers (pronounced *tires*, and alternatively called sail stops, furlers, or gaskets) handy, to muzzle the sail before proper stowage. If much tugging is needed to get a sail down, pull on the luff, because the delicate leech could be distorted by such treatment. Furling many a mainsail is simplified by twin topping lifts having lazy jacks hanging from them, looped under the sail. This forms a basket to muzzle the lowered sail, and is also seen with some wishbone booms (Plate 73). Careful handling increases sail life greatly.

Plate 73 Except for sailboards, wishbone booms and gaffs have never attained the popularity they deserve.

No panic

If a mainsail jams completely when partly lowered (creating panic), release the clew, bunch the sail against the mast and frap around it with any halyard tail which is free. Should the same thing happen to a jib, slacken the sheets right off, bunch the sail towards the stay, clap on a tier, and frap around the high parts with a halyard – even the burgee halyard, if nothing else is available.

Stowing

For a quick mainsail stow, roll the canvas as best you can (with battens lying parallel to the boom) and whip on a few tiers. Shockcord furlers having ball and loop (or toggle and loop) ends, rather than steel hooks, are especially useful for this job, as are those secured by Velcro. Without a proper sail coat, it pays to stow a boomed sail down below during long periods at moorings. This is really only practicable on yachts up to about 40 ft (12 m) overall, as hatches are no wider on bigger boats, though their sails are stiffer, heavier and more bulky!

Mainsail reefing

The simplicity of mainsail roller reefing gear (Plate 74) is somewhat marred by the difficulty of using a boom vang and by poor sail setting when reefed, eventually stretching the canvas unfairly. Through-the-mast gear helps prevent the luff from bunching, having more clearance between mast and tack. The infuriating droop to the clew end is often cured by attaching tapered battens along the outboard one-third of the boom's length, or by rolling lots of sailbags into the bunt as reefing proceeds. Roller gear and goosenecks need grease rather than oil – not forgetting an outer boom end swivel fitting.

Slab reefing (Plate 75) is kinder to a sail when properly handled. With modern versions, all pendants (pronounced *pennants* by seamen) are permanently rove and led to the for'ard end of the boom, or back to the cockpit. Old style reef pendants need careful stowage to prevent them getting lost or used as spare rope. In-mast roller reefing is ideal but very expensive, normally requiring a special mast. In-boom reefing cuts cost and weight high up.

Reef points

When replacing a single reef point, reproduce the method previously used. Port and starboard tails are normally a single length of cordage, middled through a sewn eye, with both rope parts stitched through the sail just below the eye (Fig. 80(a)). Sometimes you will find separate tails each side, stitched on with clover-leaf loops as shown in Fig. 80(b).

Lacing eyes

For neatness, especially on slab reefing sails, eyelets are used in place of reef points. Separate lacings are then used to tie down a reef. Few owners bother to use them all, thereby reducing sail life greatly. When punched eyelets fail, replace them with sewn eyes through additional diamond-shaped reinforcing

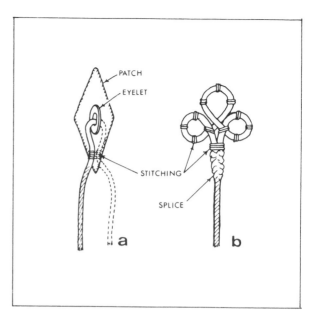

Fig. 80 Two systems of attaching reef points to a sail.

PATCH

EYELET

STITCHING

SPLICE

a

b

Plate 74 The convenience of roller reefing is often marred by poor sail setting and a drooping boom end.

Plate 75 Jiffy reefing looks neat if properly tied. It simplifies the attachment of sheet and vang. (*Photograph by courtesy of Pickthall Picture Library*.)

patches. Such sewn eyes need metal rings plus swaged liners to permit the lacing to run through them with minimum friction.

Earings

Stresses on the luff and leech earings used to pull down reefs are far greater than those on reef points. Cringles (see page 157) enable earings to resist these high stresses. They require wide circular thimble inserts to ensure smooth rendering of the pendants.

Examining and cleaning

If you stow sails dry, prevent them from flogging in high winds or flapping in a calm, avoid using light canvas in heavy weather, keep them clean, free from chafe, and correctly set, a good 'wardrobe' can last twelve years, albeit with a gradually increasing need for repair.

Examination

The 'Stitch-in-Time' proverb works well for sails. Stitching is the main cause of failure, and its thorough examination at laying-up time is essential. Professional repairs need to be put in hand before winter in Britain and most of North America. Examination takes a long time if you scrutinize every seam. Extra attention is needed on boltropes, corner patches, batten pockets and eyes. Mark any defects with vinyl tape. When stitching looks suspicious, slide a sail needle underneath and pull the twine to confirm that there is no breakage.

Sail wear

Small holes in light canvas are easily detected by shining a powerful light through the canvas. Sails which slide into spar grooves can wear along this line. Remember this also applies to certain jibs with roller furling gear. Soiled canvas often indicates a chafe area. Look for wear along the foot of a low-cut jib, and on any jib which overlaps the shrouds. Some wear on the heavily reinforced clew corner may not be too serious, but it needs watching.

Metal parts

Distortion of the circular thimbles lining eyes and cringles (or a broken internal ring) is common at clews, cunningham holes and slab reefing earings. This leads to torn canvas unless renewed immediately, as described later. Put some light oil on piston hanks and snap hooks, then wipe them to avoid soiling smart canvas. A silicone-based grease

is generally beneficial on zippers. If external headboard rivets get slack, they are easily tightened by resting a flat hammer underneath and peening on top with a ball-ended hammer. If a jib luff rope is corroded, it will make a rustling sound when bent to and fro – long before rust stains show outside.

Removing stains

Any efforts to remove dirty marks are best tackled shortly after they occur – and certainly before the sails are given an overall scrub with soap and warm water. Patent cleaning fluids may not always work like magic, but they are normally harmless to the material. Some traditional recipes such as bleach and oxalic acid (salts of lemon) can cause harm if too strong, or left in contact for too long. When in doubt, try a mild cleaner first, then graduate to more powerful chemicals.

Rust marks

A warm 5% aqueous solution of oxalic acid crystals is effective, but try a mild patent cleaner first. A pharmacy will mix oxalic acid for you, but ½ oz (14 g) of crystals dissolved in ½ pt (300 ml) of warm water is about right. The same treatment applies to verdigris stains.

Mildew

Complete obliteration of mildew is difficult, particularly on cotton canvas. Always try dry scrubbing first, using a stiff brush. Household (Scrubbs) ammonia may help, or 10% household bleach, failing this, try the latest product at a marine store.

Grease and oil

Although solvents such as trichlorethylene, toluene, and carbon tetrachloride will dissolve clean oil, they are rarely successful in removing dirty grease stains, sometimes forcing the dirt further into the canvas. Most effective are the hand-cleaning jellies (such as Swarfega or Sta-Lube Formula 2) used by car mechanics. Rub this in thoroughly, leave for one hour, rub on some more, then scrub with warm water and soap.

Paint

The appropriate thinner, perhaps followed by hand cleanser, will usually remove fresh paint or varnish. Once hard, avoid paint stripper, but try cellulose thinner, acetone, or amyl acetate, in that order. Prolonged dosing is often necessary. Remember that the appearance of dyed sailcloth is easily marred by using bleach or other strong chemicals.

Bloodstains

Scrubbing with soap and cold water soon after the occurrence will normally shift bloodstains. Where older, use a biological household detergent with cold water. If necessary, finish the job with mild bleach or oxalic acid.

Failures

Should the above methods fail, the types of sail-makers having facilities for laundering and storing sails of all sizes can usually tackle almost any stain. However, they are certain to tell you that results cannot be guaranteed.

Sewing canvas

You cannot always rely on having an ideal crew, accomplished in all the trades connected with boating. Sewing canvas is an easily acquired skill which is satisfying and, at times, extremely useful. You are unlikely to obtain the speed and precision of the professional, but strength with tolerable neatness is the thing to strive for.

Spacing

When repairing a sail seam with hand stitching, the original holes serve as a guide to spacing, though you may only utilize one hole out of two. Uneven stitches look amateurish, so use a rule and pencil on new work. The only problem then is directing all stitches at the same angle, with the same amount of thread exposed each time. That comes with practice (see later).

Needles

As the cost is so low, it pays to keep a good range of sail needles, with some spares. A proper sail needle (Fig. 81(a)) has a conventional eye, but from there down, the round shank merges into a triangular section, to help part the cloth weave without breaking too many threads.

The following stock will suffice for nearly all boating needs: four no. 19 (the smallest size made); six no. 18; four no. 17; three no. 16; two no. 14; one no. 12; also a packet of household darning needles for nylon and thin Dacron.

Storing needles

Sticking needles into a lump of cork is a tempting way to store them, but the points corrode in time if you do this. Good storage is provided by a flat lozenge can with a little sewing machine oil poured in. Rolling them up in oily rag is also a good method.

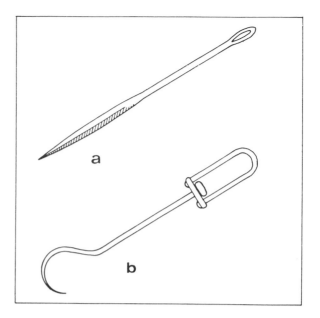

Fig. 81 Sail needle (**a**) and sail hook (**b**).

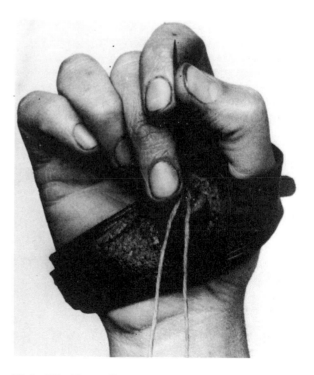

Plate 76 The sailmaker's thimble is mounted near the middle of a leather palm.

A cheap, plastic magnifying glass in your sail repair kit is useful for reading the size numbers stamped on sail needles!

Palms and thimbles

Sailmakers use a palm (Plate 76) instead of a thimble to force needles through thick canvas. This consists of a leather strap around the wrist, with an indented metal disc (to press on the eye end of the needle) in the middle. Special palms are made for left-handed operators. A domestic thimble is also useful for light work.

Other tools

A sail hook (Fig. 81(b)) is cheap and useful, with or without a built-in swivel. With a lanyard attached, this hooks into a finished seam to support stitching work continuing further along (see Plate 77). Some sort of sail rubber is needed to crease folded canvas; the handle end of an old table spoon serves quite well for this. You will need a sharp knife, a pair of scissors, a rule, a pencil, a marline spike, and some pins. An electric soldering iron is useful to seal polyester cloth edges.

Beeswax

Twine sews better and beds down more neatly if waxed. To do this, having threaded the needle, draw the thread three times across a lump of beeswax. Candle wax is usually too hard, but tallow, soap, or Vaseline are possible alternatives. A smear of tallow on the needle assists when many thicknesses of cloth are being stitched.

Punched eyelets

If you become a canvaswork enthusiast, it pays to keep a small stock of brass eyelets. Kits are available for the smaller sizes, including cheap but adequate steel dies and punches to swage the eyelets into place. Of the larger sizes, ½ in (12 mm) bore is the most often used. For the occasional largest ones, buying the eyelets and borrowing the tools is usually not too difficult. The following stages are needed to insert eyelets, illustrated in Fig. 82:

(a) Use a wad punch (or a piece of thin metal tubing with one end sharpened for cutting) to pierce the canvas with a hole just large enough to force the eyelet liner through.

(b) If lacking a punch, make two incisions at right angles. Cut a little off the four tips, but not too much.

(c) Push the eyelet liner upwards through the hole and place the washer on top, trapping the surplus canvas around the cut hole.

(d) With the steel die block underneath, insert the punch tool into the mouth of the liner.

(e) Hammer the punch downwards until the rim of the liner is well and truly riveted over the washer. (This will be the uglier side of the eyelet.)

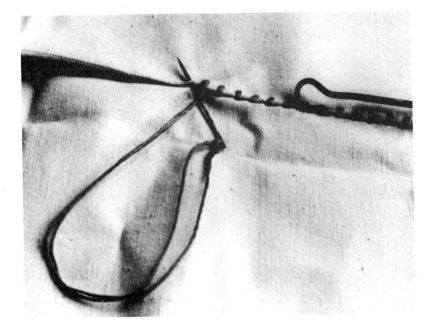

Plate 77 Flat seam stitching in progress.

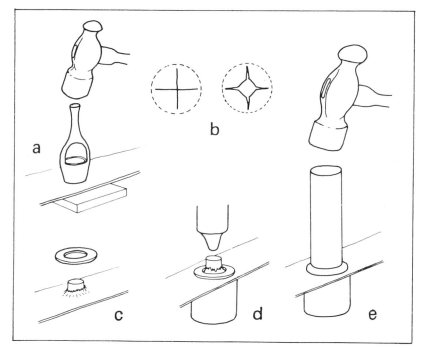

Fig. 82 Punched eyelet procedure. **a** a wad punch makes the hole. **b** optional knife cut hole. **c** eyelet is in two parts. **d** die underneath, punch on top. **e** finishing position.

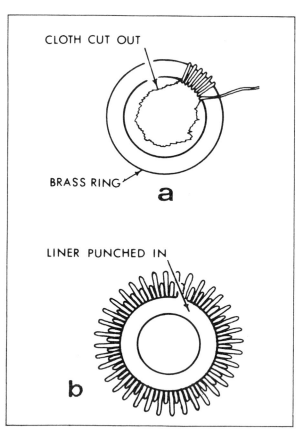

CLOTH CUT OUT

BRASS RING

a

LINER PUNCHED IN

b

Sewn eyes

Brass punched eyelets can tear right out under conditions of heavy load and flogging. The strong eyes needed for sailmaking are made by sewing a metal ring (or grommet) to one side, as shown in Fig. 83(a). Note that, particularly in polyester cloth, the needle punctures the cloth rather than parting the threads, leaving a ring of weakness. To minimize this, use fairly thick twine with the smallest size needle you can thread it through – or stagger the circles, as indicated in Fig. 83(b). A heavy duty sewn eye should have a circular metal turnover thimble inserted. As one end of this should be flared with special tools, it may be better to get a sailmaker to do it.

Round seam

For a single row of stitches along a seam which is normally only visible from one side, the round seam stitch (Fig. 84(a)) is simple and quick. Right-handed workers find it most convenient to stitch from left to right along a seam, pushing the needle upwards and slightly away from the body.

Fig. 83 Making a sewn eye.

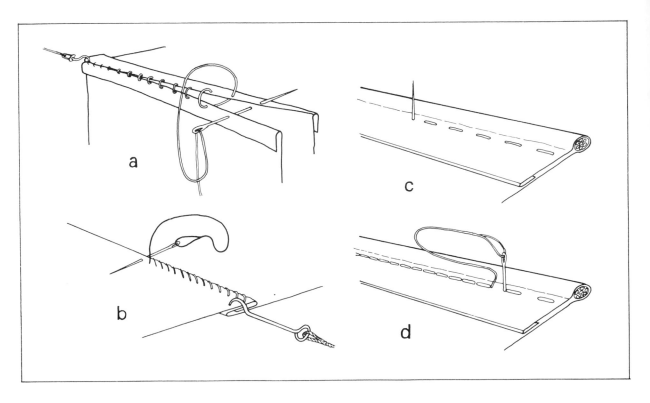

Fig. 84 Hand stitching. **a** round seam stitch. **b** flat seam stitch. **c** single running stitch. **d** double running stitch.

Flat seam

When joining widths of cloth together, the flat seam stitch is used. The same applies for tabling (hemming) the edges of a sail, or the top of a sailbag. The diagram in Fig. 84(b) shows how a flat seam is formed, with two rows of stitching the width of the seam apart. With the raw cut edges folded under, the needle passes through three thicknesses of cloth. With a selvage, there is normally no need to fold under.

Needle angle

Stitches across a round or flat seam obviously have a pitch angle, like a screw thread. Most amateurs sew the simplest way, pushing the needle through at right angles to the seam. This produces stitches straight across the seam on the far side, with all the pitch angle facing you. However, work looks neater if you push the needle through at a slight angle, making the pitch equal on both sides. Right-handed professionals work from right to left, pushing the needle towards them and angled to the left.

Stitch size

With about ten stitches per inch (every 2.5 mm) on fine work and five per inch (every 5 mm) on thick canvas, it pays to practise on scrap cloth before marking out stitch positions. Zigzag machine work does not usually go over the fold. To imitate it by hand means sewing along and back again, entering the needle from front and back each time. Amateurs often prefer to work as in Plate 77.

Heavy work

By bending the canvas slightly when stitching a flat seam, the needle will go in one side, out at the back, then up through the three thicknesses to emerge on the original side. With heavy cloth, stitching is speeded up by suspending the work vertically and having a second operative at the far side, to receive the needle and push it back through.

Turning over

Having completed one row of stitches along a flat seam as seen in Plate 77, turn the work over so that the procedure for the second row is an exact repetition of the first one.

Running stitch

Apart from the round and flat stitches described above, the only other type likely to be encountered is the running stitch, shown in Fig. 84(c). This is used along the tabling of a jib to hold the luff rope in position; also across patches, reinforcements and encased headboards. For the latter, the stitches pass through prepared holes in the board. Running stitches normally progress along the other side, back up through, then along once more. Particularly for headboards, having reached the far end, the process is repeated towards the start, making a continuous line of thread (Fig. 84(d)) both sides.

Threading needles

Try the smallest size of needle that the twine will thread through. Wax the bitter end of twine, then flatten it to pass through the eye. Always use the twine double, but do not tie the ends together. A 7 ft or 2 m single length is about right (a little more if your arms are unusually long), making a loaded double length of about 3 ft 6 in or 1 m. After the first stitch, lay the bitter ends along the seam and sew the next three stitches over them. After re-threading your needle on a long seam, twist old and new ends together, and sew three stitches over them. At the end of a seam, back-sew two stitches and pass the needle under three further stitches before cutting off.

Holding the needle

As illustrated in Plate 76, the needle should be held one-third of its length back from the point, between thumb and first finger, using the middle finger to guide the eye end into the indented metal boss fixed to the palm. Waterproof-type sticking plasters (such as Band-aid) around the points of .contact will prevent soreness to tender fingers.

Machining

Although light work on dinghy sails and spinnakers is possible on a household sewing machine (without the facilities to make zigzag stitches), a proper sailmaker's machine (with long reach and feeding jaws on top as well as underneath the cloth) is superior. In some places these machines are available on hire, and 12-volt ones are made to run off the ship's batteries. If a machine lacks adequate instruction literature, spend a little time learning from the hirers. Domestic sewing machine dealers normally stock bigger needles than those used for dressmaking.

Repairing canvas

The most common types of sail repairs include the darning or patching of tears, re-stitching seams, repairing chafe at clews and headboards, and re-roping. As with all practical work the careful amateur should produce excellent work, though perhaps taking as much as ten times as long as the professional. The most troublesome factor is likely to be obtaining cloth which is exactly the same as that used originally.

Herringbone stitch

For tacking back into position the two sides of a short, straight or L-shaped tear, the herringbone stitch is ideal. Avoid the temptation to bunch the parts together with round seam stitches as this will cause wrinkles and stretch the surrounding canvas unfairly. Sail repair tape is better than that for an emergency job. There are optional styles of herringbone stitch, but the most popular is shown in Fig. 85. Staggering the stitch length (Fig. 85(e)) adds strength, and facilitates turning the right-angled corner of an L-shaped tear. All sewing is done from one side. With an overhand knot at the bitter end of some thick double twine, proceed as follows:

(a) Direct needle through slit and upwards through cloth at far side.
(b) Bring thread right across slit and down through near side.
(c) Bring needle up through slit, on left of previous stitch.
(d) Pass needle over previous thread, down through slit and up through cloth on far side, bringing you back to stage (a).

Tightness

Draw up each stitch only just tight enough to almost close the slit. Over-tightening is sure to cause puckering or wrinkles when the cloth is laid down flat. At the end, reef knot the double twine close to the cloth and trim off.

Darning

A common dressmaker's over-and-under darn is used for sails and covers, to seal burns and other holes up to about ½ in (12 mm) diameter, or tears of similar length. The thread for this should be only a shade thicker than that used for adjacent seams.

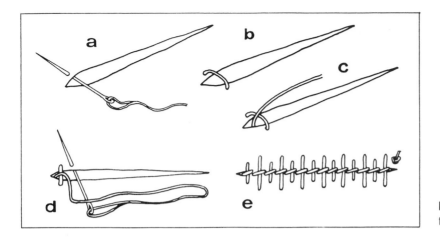

Fig. 85 Repairing a torn sail with the herringbone stitch.

Light patches

Almost any tear is repairable without loss of strength by sewing on a neat patch. For dinghy sails, a domestic sewing machine makes a passable job. Having sewn around the edges, make criss-cross rows of stitches all over to seal the parts together. Self-adhesive repair cloth, perhaps used on both sides, often has a long life, but is easily made permanent by stitiching over. Duct tape 2 in (50 mm) wide is cheap and strong. Hardware stores keep cloth tapes 1½ in (38 mm) wide in white and basic shades, often with tear-off backing.

Creasing

Having found some patch material (identical to the original, if possible), align the weave direction, and

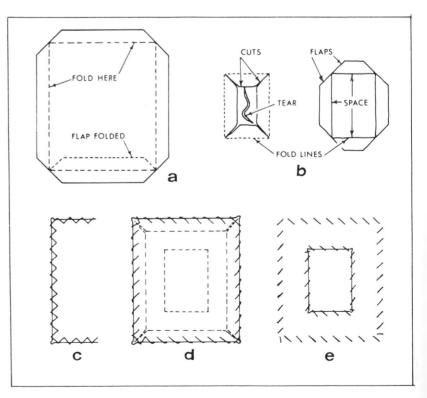

Fig. 86 Patching system for a bad sail tear.

cut off the corners as in Fig. 86(a), enabling the edges to be turned under ready for sewing. Use a sail rubber (see page 146) to crease these folds and keep them in place. Cut around the tear (Fig. 86(b)), enabling that to be folded back under the patch and creased. A domestic steam iron will crease thin cotton nicely, but too much heat is bad for synthetic cloth.

Heat sealing
There is no need to fold edges if you trim off polyester cloth with a hot soldering iron, so it cannot unravel. Such a patch is really neat if machine sewn, so that the zigzags overlap the edges, as shown in Fig. 86(c).

Positioning
Contact adhesive to keep a patch exactly in position simplifies stitching. Double-sided sticky tape works equally well. Pins create unwanted puckers on all except the thinnest materials.

Heavy patches
Hand sewing suits the amateur best for patches on cruiser sails or awnings. Use small, flat seam stitches around the edge first (see Fig. 86(d)), then turn the sail over (Fig. 86(e)) to sew along the inner creases. Running stitches between the two rows should not be necessary on a patch of correct size, especially when adhesive has been used. If a patch is needed close to a boltrope, take the patch over the rope and around the other side of the sail.

Corner patches
If it involves re-roping and re-eyeleting, the repair of chafe on sail corners is difficult for the amateur to accomplish, but stitching a reinforcement piece to each side (avoiding rope and eye) is simple enough. Where there is no roping, unpick the tabling and tuck the new patches underneath before re-stitching. Make one patch slightly larger than the other to keep the flat seam stitches separate each side. For running stitches or machining, with accurate alignment, through-stitching is possible. Rows of running stitches radiating from the eye are customary, in addition to using glue.

Tabling
Narrow through-stitched tape each side will often fix torn tabling. Position this by means of double-sided sticky tape. Hand stitching will be necessary on a leech in way of a batten pocket. Whether roped or unroped, a better method is often to encase the sail edge in wide tape, lapped around as shown in Fig. 87. If hand sewn, you would then use a flat seam stitch along the tape edge, with running stitches close to the rope. Cut out any eyelets buried by new tape and shift the new ones along a bit. Take care to avoid stitching near a leechline or drawstring.

Mylar mend
A sewn patch looks dreadful on a clear Mylar windsurfer sail. Super Glue (cyanoacrylate) can be used to bond on a piece of similar film, preferably backed up with an identical patch on the other side.

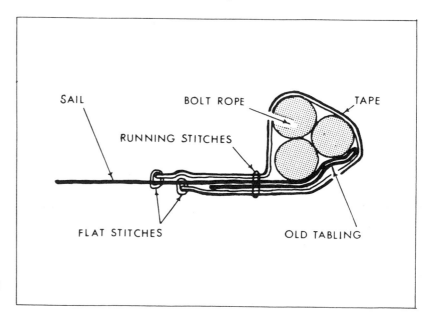

Fig. 87 Exaggerated section of chafed tabling repair.

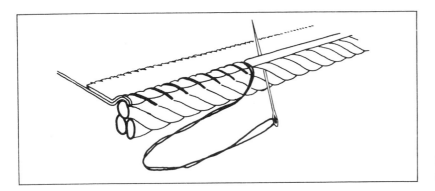

Fig. 88 How a boltrope is sewn to a sail.

Boltropes

Although a boltrope normally lasts the life of a sail, chafe and accidental damage sometimes necessitate splicing in a short length. Galvanized luff ropes on jibs are prone to rust near the tack eye (see page 144). Encasing a boltrope with stitched-on leather or canvas is a useful precaution at points of known chafe.

Setting-up
As observation will show, a sail tabling is sewn over about one-third of the rope circumference, each stitch bedding the canvas down into the spiral groove between rope strands. Stretch the rope horizontally in front of you, with the sail hanging down behind it. Stitch as in Fig. 88, pushing the needle away from you against the lay, and getting between strands rather than through them.

Stretching
When re-roping a long length, stretch both rope and sail evenly, then make pencil match-marks at 6 in (150 mm) intervals across both to ensure correct tension when stitching. Should the rope marks get ahead of the canvas marks, the stitches are too tight. If the reverse happens, gather a little canvas at each stitch. With all twist taken out of the rope, mark a straight pencil line along it and keep the canvas edge to this when stitching.

Tapered tail
Strong, sewn webbing takes the place of roping on spinnakers and some light duty sails. With slug slides, a taped sail will fit a mast with luff groove. The leech is rarely roped on small boat sails – the roping wraps around the head and clew eyes to disappear along the leech in a gradual taper. Shape this as described for tail splicing on page 128: unlay rope, shave down strands, grease them and twist into position. Sew to edge of tabling with round seam stitches of ever decreasing size and pitch.

Inside tabling
Wire luff ropes are housed inside the tabling, with running stitches close alongside to prevent movement. Cordage boltropes are sometimes encased in wide tape folded in half (longways) as shown in Fig. 87. After securing the rope with close stitching, the sail edge is inserted (usually with no additional tabling) prior to through-stitching, preferably using zigzag machined stitches.

Luff wire
The renewal of rusty luff rope has given many an old jib a new lease of life. The bottom end invariably rusts first. Unpicking sufficient tabling to enable a short splice to be made is easy enough. If the whole rope needs renewing, just unpick the running stitches which clamp the wire into the tabling, and pull a 'messenger' cord through as the old wire comes out. If the tabling is too narrow to pull in the eye splice of the new rope, splice it afterwards by gathering up the tabling to make room.

Special finned plastic-coated wire rope is made for jib luffs, which will not slip inside the tabling. For uncoated wire, parcel with vinyl adhesive tape, or use strips of thin sailcloth, marled with twine.

Splices
If short lengths of cordage boltropes are renewed with long splices (see Chapter 7), there is sure to be some loss of strength, but it will more than halve the work of a complete re-roping. Inserting just one strand is sometimes all that is required. Knot and tuck the ends as for a long splice.

Canvas sundries

As well as doing repair work to sails and covers, you can save money further by making the many pieces of canvas equipment found on board a successful cruising boat. Much of this is useful work for winter evenings.

Fenders

Air-filled fenders (fendoffs) of rubbery plastics are expensive things to lose. The old-fashioned canvas types (Plate 78(a)) filled with cork granules, kapok, or foam rubber, work just as well and are interesting items to make. Fenders for cruisers should be cylindrical to roll along the ship's side instead of chafing it. However, pad fenders (Plate 78(b)), which flip over the gunwale when needed, are useful on certain dinghies (see page 221). Cork granules are sometimes obtainable free from wine or fruit stores, while upholsterers generally keep kapok or foam rubber.

End panels

Before cutting out each top and bottom panel, draw a circle in pencil showing the seam line (using a saucepan as a template) and allow about 1 in (25 mm) of spare canvas all around, outside this line. Insert an eyelet in the middle of each disc, gauged to fit the chosen rope (see Fig. 89(a)).

Side panel

Trace a piece of string around the above-mentioned pencilled circle to get the wrap-around length of the side panel. Choose the height as required. Having drawn this rectangle, leave 1 in (25 mm) of spare beyond it on all four sides (see Fig. 89(b)).

Sewing

Having creased the appropriate seam lines, with the work inside out, sew on the top disc, using the round seam stitch described earlier in this chapter. This will produce an exact position for the vertical seam, sewn next (see Fig. 89(c)).

Filling

Align the bottom seam using pins, staples, or sticky tape, altering the creasing positions if necessary to improve the fit. After sewing two-thirds of the way around, turn the fender right-side-out (through the gap), reeve the lanyard, insert the filling material, then sew the gap with round seam stitches applied from the outside, as in Fig. 89(d).

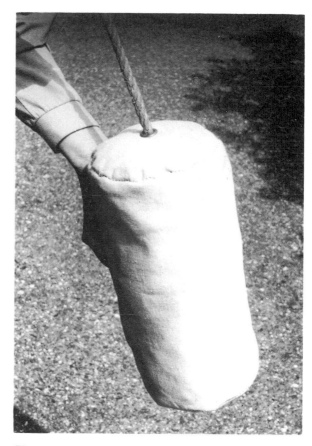

Plate 78 Homemade fenders. **a** cylindrical type with lanyard. **b** pad type for launch or tender.

a

b

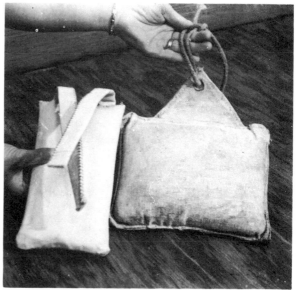

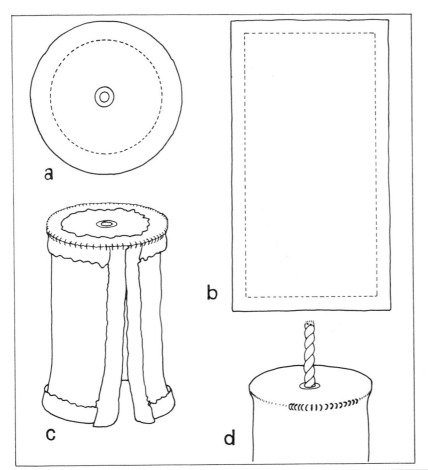

Fig. 89 Four stages in making a canvas fender.

Canvas bucket

The simplest form of bucket has a canvas wall nailed (over a smear of bedding compound) to a circular wooden bottom. A better type for deck washing and for carrying provisions and tools has a canvas bottom similar to that of a fender. Both types have a hem tabled around the rim. The handle is round stitched as shown in Fig. 90(a), then pulled inside out and stitched to the bucket sides. A stiff rim is advantageous, made by sewing a strop of thick rope around the rim, perhaps with a rope handle spliced into this.

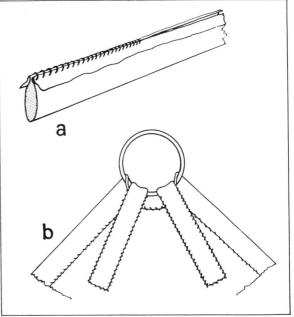

Fig. 90 Stitching applications. **a** bucket handle sewn inside out. **b** strengthening straps on bunk lee-cloth ring.

Carpenter's bag

Long and narrow, but made the same way as an all-canvas bucket, a tool-bag needs to be capacious enough to hold a handsaw (well wrapped in canvas), a hand-drill, and your longest screwdriver. Fit a separate loop handle in the middle of each long side, enabling the mouth to be opened wide when searching for items. A pocket sewn to the inside is most useful for housing small parts.

Internal neatness

Unlike fenders, some items have visible interiors. For extra neatness, the spare canvas along each seam may be trimmed off to within about ¼ in (6 mm) of the stitching. Alternatively, crease these flaps down neatly with a steam iron, or turn the raw edges under and stitch them to the main canvas with fine thread.

Other items

Other canvas sundries made in the same way as fenders and buckets include sailbags, cases for rolled charts, and covers for such things as hatches, skylights, ventilators, funnels, and binnacles. Most of these items have either a drawstring or shockcord sewn into their hems. Snap fasteners are easy to buy, fit and replace, but remember to keep them doped with zip fastener lubricant.

Ambitious jobs

Keen amateurs sometimes tackle big canvaswork jobs such as sails, awnings, dinghy covers, canopies and cockpit covers. Items which include a lot of flat seam stitching and eyeleting include dodgers, bunk flaps, ventilation windsails (see page 83), hammocks, and root berths.

Bunk flaps

Triangular or trapezoidal canvas leecloths are more satisfactory than traditional leeboards for keeping mattress and occupant in place at an angle of heel. The lower edge is best clamped down under a bolted batten, to facilitate removal for annual washing. Eyes at the top (for suspension from the deckhead) need plenty of reinforcement. One good way to prevent disaster is to sew one or more bands of polyester tape through the eye, as shown in Fig. 90(b).

Awnings

A white cotton tropical awning (Plate 79) is translucent and cool. Some flat ones have central drains for collecting rainwater. Spinnaker-nylon flaps noisily in a breeze, even for a small bimini on struts. A launch canopy (Plate 80), often in blue or striped polyester, has scalloped fringes to hide the rolled-up side curtains. Narrow tape creased down the middle makes good piping to finish off scalloped edges.

Windows

Side curtains, or a cockpit tent to fit over the boom, benefit from the fitting of see-through vinyl panels. To fit these without creating permanent wrinkles, sandwich the panel between the uncut cloth and a patch of the same material, the same size and shape as the vinyl. Stitch right through with at least two rows, then cut out the canvas on both sides, carefully using small scissors to avoid damaging the window. It pays to glue all seam surfaces. Corners should be well rounded.

Canvas adhesives

Common contact glue works well to seal and stick seams, patches, and windows, prior to stitching. Similar latex glue is used by shoe repairers, and you may be able to scrounge a little of that. If you aim to use silicone rubber sealing compound, test a sample first, to make sure it does not seep through the canvas and look unsightly.

Dodgers

Polyester sailcloth is the best material for making cockpit dodgers (Plate 18) which lace onto the guardrails. This is a popular place to apply a ship's name, cut from the sheets of self-adhesive or iron-on material made for sail numbers. Folding pram hood or navy top dodgers (Plate 98(a)) are tricky for the average amateur to make, but by no means impossible if you avoid hurry and check the fit after sewing each seam.

Sail coats

With an old one as the pattern, there are few problems in making a sail coat. A new one is tricky to tailor around the mast, but make sure the rest is big enough to fit when the sail is not necessarily stowed to perfection. Leave a gap at the bottom to allow some ventilation, but use waterproof vinyl-coated material in preference to sailcloth, which can leak rain. Use nylon to make a spinnaker sock which (with its own continuous halyard/downhaul) muzzles the sail completely to simplify hoisting and furling.

Plate 79 Cockpit or deck awnings improve living conditions in port under tropical heat or cool wet weather.

Plate 80 An electric launch with scalloped canopy.

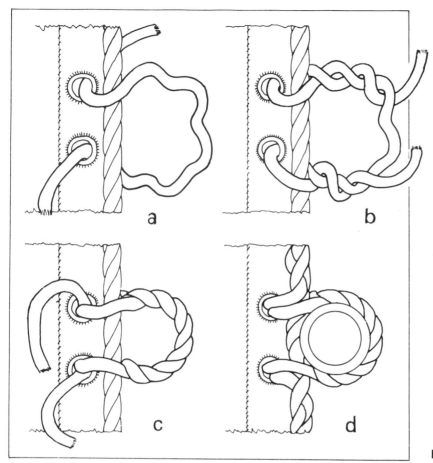

Fig. 91 How a cringle is formed.

Cringles

A proper cringle is an eye outside the boltrope (Fig. 91(d)), held in place by a rope grommet, woven *in situ* through two strong sewn eyes in the tabling of a sail. Particularly in the larger sizes, most amateurs finish up with a loose thimble. Being laid up from a single rope strand, a grommet stretches far more than an eye splice. It may take several attempts to get it right. Even then it often pays to bind around thimble and grommet away from the working section to prevent the thimble ever falling out. This latter idea is useful on any existing cringle which has a loose thimble.

Weaving

Having formed the two eyes, proceed as shown in Fig. 91:

(a) Middle your single rope strand. Poke one end through the upper eye and the other end through the lower eye.

(b) Lay up the free ends towards each other, as for a traditional three-strand grommet (see page 125).

(c) Feed each end again through an eye, and tuck three times against the lay, over-one-under-one.

(d) Stretch the aperture with a large wooden fid and fit the thimble. Details of sewn eyes are given on page 147.

Sail care

When crewing, remember that most sailboat owners have their own pet methods for sail stowage, whether on the boom or in the bag. Spinnakers especially are often bagged with the corners outermost, ready to hitch on.

Fig. 92 Flaked down mainsail stow.

Fig. 93 Fold-and-roll method of boom stowage.

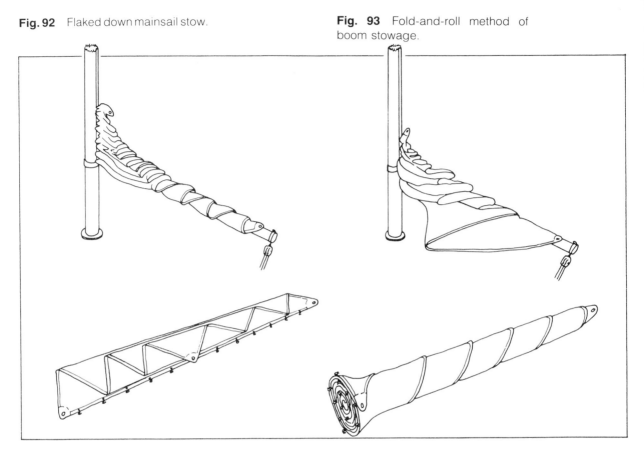

Fig. 94 Jib flaked down parallel to luff.

Fig. 95 Luff rolled ready for length-wise folding.

Boom stowage

Flaking down (Fig. 92) makes the neatest stow with slides left on track. This is really a job for two people, as you need to hoist the sail and lower it in stages as flaking proceeds. To avoid hoisting, draw the leech out (Fig. 93), fold this back to the boom several times, then roll.

Jib folding

Many jibs are too long to fold neatly on board, especially in a good breeze. When you have space, either flake down a jib parallel to the luff (Fig. 94) and roll from head to foot, or wind the luff as in Fig. 95, then roll from luff to clew.

Creases

Some polyester sails crease badly when stuffed at random into a bag. Folding in the above way reduces this greatly, especially if the method of folding is varied occasionally. Creases in lightweight working sails do not often disappear under way, and may have an adverse effect on racing performance. Creases on spinnakers normally do no harm. Any Mylar or Kevlar is best not bagged at all.

Laying-up

Most well-used sails need a soapy fresh water scrub before the winter lay-up period. To do this, spread them on a lawn in preference to a concrete or tarmac yard. Rinse off thoroughly with a hose. The best method of drying is full length suspension (with the head at the bottom) using guy ropes, from a high window or roof. Loose storage across boxes or ropes in a clean loft is better than storage in bags. If there is any likelihood of rodent attacks, leave plenty of newspaper about: they prefer that to sails!

9
Engines and Such

Only the most competent fitters scorn the use of an engine handbook or workshop manual, though there will always be a few owners whose ability is limited to knowing how to start up, control and stop the brute!

To avoid damaging the originals, keep on board photostat copies of maintenance sheets and important pages from lengthy manuals. Illustrated spare parts lists serve a secondary role by helping to show how things fit together – a useful check when assembling a pump, gearbox or toilet. Knowing part numbers saves a lot of bother when ordering spares. Be very wary of using cheap engine parts and filters of uncertain pedigree.

Sterngear

Except in the case of sterndrives, saildrives, hydraulic transmission and water jet propulsion, nearly all inboard marine engines have a sterntube or a shaft log to take the propeller shaft through the hull. As well as bearings, these have a stuffing-box (or patent gland) to prevent the ingress of water.

Lubrication
Most modern external bearings are of the cutless fluted rubber type (Fig. 96) which are water-lubricated – sometimes through small scoops (see Plate 39) at each side, sometimes by bleeding some engine-cooling water into the sterntube. At every opportunity, make sure that the scoops are clear.

The Babbitt-metalled plain bearing mostly used at the internal end is lubricated by means of a stauffer screw-down grease cup (Fig. 97) feeding into the space between the bearing and gland. When a metal external bearing is also used, the greaser fills the space between the two, for the full length of the sterntube. Some craft have a large capacity lubricator, mounted in a convenient place, connected to the sterntube via a length of copper pipe, as in Fig. 98.

Oil seals
Other types of sterntubes have patent seals at each end, the space between being filled with thick oil, fed automatically from a small header tank, well above the boat's waterline. Consult the makers' literature for details of the maintenance and renewal of such seals.

Bearings
With a shaft up to 1½ in (38 mm) diameter, you can see whether the outer bearing is worn by shaking the propeller, perhaps by using a short lever and fulcrum. Metalled bearings at each end are screwed to the sterntube and prevented from loosening by coach screws (lag bolts) on a wooden hull, or through-bolts on a hull of metal, plastics, or ferrocement. With bolts removed, if an assembly will not screw off, apply heat with a blow-torch until it will, but avoid heating adjacent fibreglass or wood. Hand the part over to a marine engineer for re-metalling.

With the shaft withdrawn, a cutless bearing will

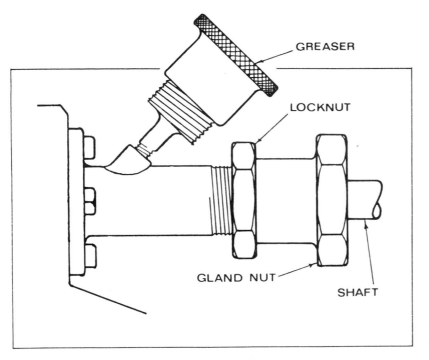

Fig. 97 Screw-down grease cup on sterntube.

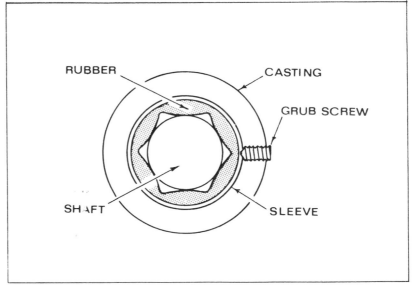

Fig. 96 Section through cutless rubber bearing.

slip out or in readily once the retaining Allen grub screws (see Fig. 96) are removed. Check these screws for slackness as frequently as possible. Cutless bearings can wear out in two years in muddy or sandy waters, so spare ones are useful. Metalled bearings can last twenty years if properly lubricated.

Flexible glands

A P-bracket (Plate 88) or a twin-strut A-bracket often has no sterntube. A wet, soapy cutless bearing will go in without removing the shaft. The inboard bearing is a shaft log, as in Fig. 98. A *flexible* shaft log has a short rubber hose (with pipe clamps) between log and

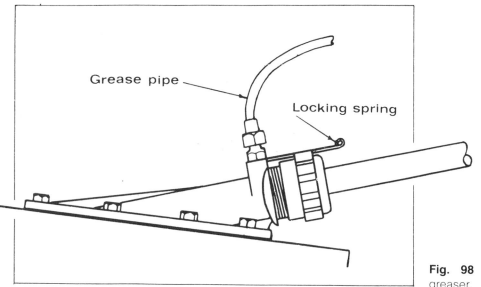

Fig. 98 Shaft log with remote greaser.

stuffing box. Note that the hose is merely an anti-leak gaiter – excess torque is held by two metal lugs on one part which ride freely in notches on the other part. Beware of units made with no fail-safe interlock. Without this, if someone over-tightens the packing (or the bearing runs dry, overheats and *picks up*, the gland will keep twisting until the hose ruptures and lets water in.

Plummer block

To prevent whipping, a long length of propeller shaft is often supported by an intermediate plain bearing called a *plummer* (or *pillow*) block. Under way its greaser needs a half-turn every ten hours. Turn a sterntube greaser every three running hours; just sufficiently to feel some resistance. Keep surplus grease wiped away to prevent it from fouling the bilge. To check plummer block alignment, slacken the mounting bolts. If the block does not shift, but can be slid a little fore and aft, the shimming is normally correct.

Thrust block

Modern gearboxes contain thrust bearings to absorb the fore-and-aft propeller forces. Certain boats with converted vehicle engines, or V-belt transmission, may have a separate thrust bearing mounted somewhere along the propeller shaft. This also acts as a plummer block and has similar greasing requirements.

Universal joints

You will rarely find the discrepancy between propeller shaft line and engine position great enough to need a pair of universal joints. However, resilient couplings (permitting only slight misalignment) are found whenever an engine is flexibly mounted.

Hot bearings

If a bearing feels too hot to touch, grease it and stop the engine. This could be a result of faulty alignment, a bent shaft, a damaged propeller, or a gland packed too tightly. The latter is easily cured by re-packing, but the other faults may well demand the services of a marine engineer. Slack engine mountings could cause similar trouble.

Alignment

With rigid engine mountings, any misalignment is soon detected. Part all coupling flanges (Fig. 99), and check with a short steel rule for concentricity (Fig. 99(a)) and with a feeler gauge around the gap for angularity (Fig. 99(b)). Some boats bend a little when taken out of the water, so always check the alignment while afloat. Flange edges should never be more than 3 thou. (3 mils or 76 microns) askew. Always remember that a heavy coupling on the end of a long, slender shaft can droop slightly under its own weight when unbolted; support it gently before checking the alignment.

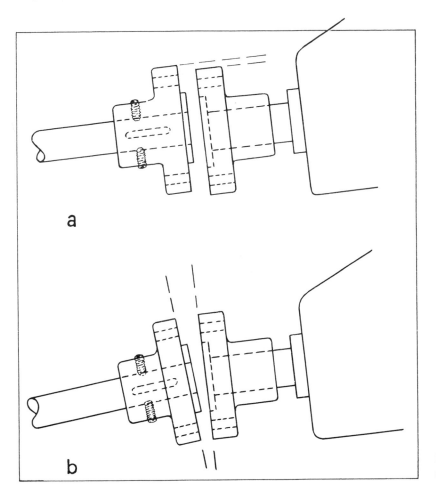

a

b

Fig. 99 Two types of propeller shaft coupling misalignment.

Mounting shims

The fault in Fig. 99(a) could be caused by shrinkage of the engine bearers. Correction means chocking up the engine sufficiently to insert extra shims cut from thin steel plate or sheet. These should be notched to fit around the holding-down bolts and underneath the engine's feet. For the Fig. 99(b) situation you shim up the for'ard mounts more than the aft ones. To align a flexible coupling, borrow (or make if you have a lathe) a so-called dumb-bell (split or all in one) to substitute temporarily for the elastic coupling.

Coupling faults

As they are rarely locked with tab washers, mounting and coupling bolts can work loose during the season, and an occasional check is prudent. As flanges and bolts are normally of steel, keep rust at bay with WD40, or a smear of underwater grease.

Flange removal

To slide out a propeller shaft with the engine in place, you must remove the half-coupling. Clear out the gland packing and draw the shaft astern. To obviate the need to unship them, some rudders have a notch or hole, enabling the shaft to pass through when the rudder is turned, perhaps with the steering gear disconnected. Half-couplings are keyed to a shaft, sometimes held by Allen grub screws (Fig. 99), sometimes with a taper and nut like a propeller.

Shaft

A bent propeller shaft can often be straightened successfully by specialists at less than half the cost of a new one. Most shaft wear occurs at the stern bearing, and is normally repairable economically by brazing and machining. Bad electrolytic action in this vicinity has caused propellers to drop off!

Crevice corrosion is liable to occur on stainless

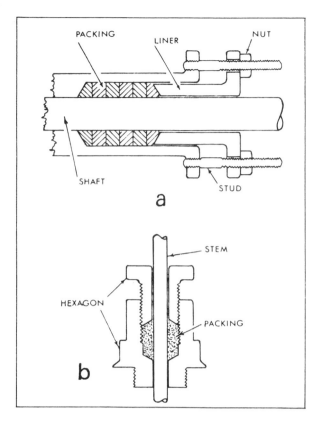

Fig. 100 Propeller shaft and pump rod glands.

steel shafts through cutless rubber bearings where craft lie idle for long periods. Cupro-nickel (Monel) shafts are generally the most durable.

Attachments
Pulleys, sprockets and eccentrics are attached to shafts for driving generators, refrigerator compressors, or pumps, perhaps needing special lubrication. A metal strip pressing on the shaft may be wired to a zinc anode (see Chapter 10), or to a keel bolt to suppress radio interference. A sailing clutch allows a shaft to spin freely when sailing. A shaft lock fixes a two-bladed propeller in line with the sternpost or skeg when sailing, to reduce turbulence.

Vibration

A damaged propeller or a bent shaft are the usual causes of vibration in small craft. If lack of care has led to slack engine mountings, some shims may have fallen out. Vibration often warrants expert diagnosis, as neglect could cause serious damage in time. Having checked all bolts (including the stern-

tube), and checked that the shaft runs true, swapping propellers or getting the original one balanced is usually the next move.

Stuffing-box
Conventional packing rings are pressed down inside the stuffing-box, or gland, by a liner (see Fig. 100(a)) having a flange with two studs and nuts, or a separate cap nut of large diameter, as in Fig. 98. Some pumps have a simpler arrangement (Fig. 100(b)) with nut and liner in one piece, as for a domestic water tap or faucet.

Packing rings
House faucet packing looks like thick string. A continuous length is wound into the gland and cut off before screwing down the nut. For big shafts the

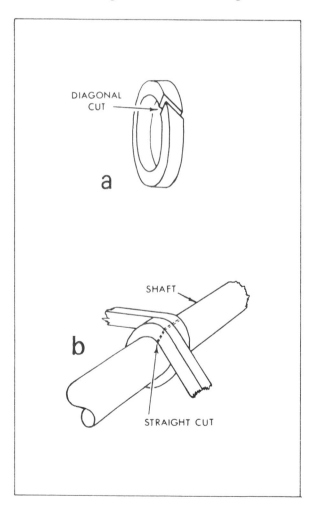

Fig. 101 How to cut packing rings.

packing must be square in section, of exact size, cut into a series of rings (Fig. 101(a)), and pressed into the gland one by one with staggered joints. Ring diameter is easily checked by wrapping each one around the shaft before sliding it into the gland. Diagonal joints as shown in Fig. 101(a) make a sounder job than straight butts. However, butts are easy to cut through both parts at once (Fig. 101(b)) while the packing is wound tightly around the shaft. Make an extra ring in case there is room for this when the others have settled down.

Right materials

Traditional gland packing is stiff, square braided cordage impregnated with tallow, but similar-looking white PTFE (Teflon) is now widely used. The most popular sizes are $\frac{3}{16}$ in (4.5 mm), $\frac{1}{4}$ in (6 mm) and $\frac{5}{16}$ in (7.5 mm). Find the size by poking the shank of a twist drill into the gland, or by measuring the liner thickness with calipers. The small amounts of material normally needed are best obtained from a boatyard workshop, or from a factory using steam boilers.

Raking out

Inserting an extra ring on top of well compacted old packing is only a temporary expedient to stop leakage. Raking out old packing is easy with the shaft removed. Otherwise you need a thin screw-driver, a few old dentist's probes, and a lot of patience. Screw-in extractors are made for packing exceeding the $\frac{1}{4}$ in (6 mm) size.

Steering shaft

Rudder stocks frequently have bearings and glands similar to sterngear. Proper lubrication of this equipment is often neglected. On most small sail-boats, rudder stocks and pivots (gudgeons and pintles) are not intended to be lubricated.

Propellers

The design of boat propellers (occasionally referred to as wheels or screws) is highly specialised. Not even the experts can always strike the right formula, and the performance of many craft could be improved by finding a propeller with the ideal diameter, pitch, blade area, and number of blades. For an assortment of types, see Plate 81. As well as having two, three, four, or five blades, there are high speed, low speed, weedless, folding, and controllable pitch types.

Markings

The dimensions of a propeller are normally stamped on the boss. For instance, in English-speaking countries, LH 17 × 12 signifies left-handed rotation (anticlockwise when looking for'ard), 17 in diameter and 12 in pitch. Metric sizes would be given in millimetres. You can tell the rotation at a glance because, like a screw thread, when viewed from either side, a blade tilts to the left at the bottom (Fig. 102) for left-handed rotation. Most direct drive propellers are left-handed, marine engines normally running that way, the same as car engines. Twin screws may be of opposed rotation and not exactly of the same pitch.

Metal

Although bronze is still widely used for casting propellers, you may encounter plenty made from light alloy or plastics. While renewing a corroded bronze propeller, seek advice from the suppliers about alternative materials, particularly when there has been trouble from electrolysis (see Chapter 10) in the past. Light alloy propellers have proved successful on outboard motors for many decades. The great advantage of bronze lies in the comparative cheapness and ease of repairs.

Blade tips

In rocky or shoal waters, when propeller damage occurs regularly, it pays to keep a spare propeller. Unless made of nylon, superficial blade tip damage is easily repaired *in situ* by filing, and by hammering while a heavy dolly is held the other side. Any good propeller maker will repair more serious damage, such as bent blades or wasting away caused by corrosion. They can also change the pitch slightly, should the engine be overloaded or race freely without producing full power. For slow turning propellers, barnacles and jagged blade tips do not affect performance greatly. For high-speed power-boats, clean and accurate blades are essential for peak performance.

Cavitation

Good bronze rarely corrodes, but it can happen to high-revving propellers as a result of prolonged cavitation. The blades lose contact with the water (especially at the tips) and eroding oxygen bubbles implode at supersonic speed. Many an outboard motor (Plate 85) has a flat cavitation plate above the propeller to reduce this. Even more effective is a Kort nozzle (Plate 81(d)) – a cylindrical shroud surrounding the propeller. Sanding and polishing a

a

c

b

Plate 81 A 3-bladed propeller appears in Plate 39. Folding types are in Plates 82 and 88. Here are some other configurations: **a** 2-bladed. **b** 4-bladed. **c** 5-bladed with Kort nozzle. **d** reversing and fully-feathering unit. (*Picture by courtesy of Watermota Ltd, Newton Abbot, England.*)

d

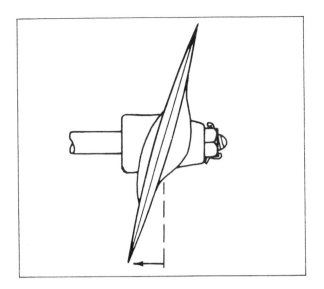

Fig. 102 For left-handed rotation, propeller blade slopes to left at the bottom.

pitted propeller helps to preserve it. See also page 188.

Removal

Some outboard motor propellers are linked to the shaft with a shear pin. Others fit on a well greased splined shaft and should slide off easily once the retaining nut is removed as detailed in the manual. The same applies to many sterndrive and saildrive units. Instead of a shear pin, these types may have a slipping clutch or resilient drive to avoid damage on running aground. Special pullers are made to remove outboard propellers with through-hub exhaust. Most other propellers are keyed onto a taper. Having removed the cotter pin (or locknut) and eased back the retaining nut, a sharp blow on the for'ard face of the boss should free it. A streamlined cap (as in Plate 81(b)) usually has flats for gripping. Some caps form the actual retaining nut.

Hammer blows

A copper or lead hammer works well for small propellers. To avoid bending a shaft thinner than 1 in (25 mm) and damaging the thrust bearing, get a helper to hold a heavy lead dolly against the end of the shaft, and use two hammers, one each side of the propeller boss. When singlehanded, borrow a bearing puller, using a two-jaw for two and four blades and a three-jaw for three blades. Without this, heat from a blow-torch has never been known to fail. When sledges and club hammers are needed on a big propeller, always insert hardwood buffers (or strips of thick copper) between boss and hammer.

Keyway

If the key need not be removed, wrap it with adhesive tape to prevent loss. To withdraw the shaft for'ard, the key must come out of its keyway. A Woodruff type is soon broken free by rocking it with alternate taps on each end (see Fig. 103(a)). A plain key can be obstinate, especially when of rusted steel. Before removal, pop-mark one end, with a corresponding mark on the shaft, to ensure correct

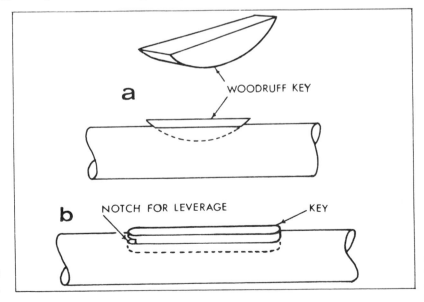

Fig. 103 Two sorts of shaft key are in common use. **a** Woodruff. **b** plain.

replacement. If releasing oil, grips, or hammer and punch fail, file or saw a nick at one end, as in Fig. 103(b), and lever it out with an old screwdriver.

Security

With so many yachts parked ashore (even when in commission) propellers get stolen. A rope cutter or vane steering gear is also at risk. Incidentally, if you fit a cutter, leave some of the clearance seen in Plate 88 between propeller and bearing for thrust movement. Try to chain, lock and wrap all unattended gear.

Propulsion units

Although many boat engine designs follow familiar road vehicle practice, transmission systems are more specialized and varied. Valveless (two-stroke or two-cycle) engines are common afloat, particularly for outboard motors, and you may find a sprinkling of orbital (Wankel) units, gas turbines, steam engines, and electric motors. However, with the aid of these general notes and all the available makers' literature, the amateur should be able to keep any machinery in reliable working order.

Transmission

Outboard motors have the advantage of integral transmission, but this increases their weight, making them difficult to manhandle in the larger sizes, and more vulnerable to theft. Saildrive units (Plate 82) have similar transmission to outboards,

Plate 82 Saildrive or S-drive units have bevel gearing like outboard motors.

but are fitted permanently beneath the hull, and coupled to inboard engines. Outdrive, sterndrive, or inboard/outboard units are similar, but are mounted on a transom stern (Plate 5) with the facility to tilt clear of the water, athwartships or backwards. These devices generally need separate lubrication attention, plus a watch for corrosion and faults with oil seals and neoprene boots, bellows, or gaiters. With hydraulic drive, the propeller unit is connected to the engine unit by two pipes, often of considerable length. Jet propulsion units (Plate 83) have no

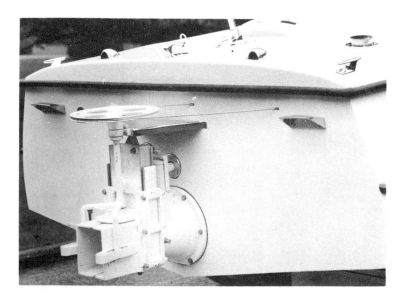

Plate 83 Jet propulsion is ideal in shallow water. It glides over thick weed and cannot injure swimmers.

exposed propellers, and similar equipment is used for bow thrusters on big craft.

Shaft drive

Simple, traditional shaft drive from gearbox to propeller is still used for most inboard installations. Where an engine cannot be in line with the propeller shaft (and especially for electric propulsion) you may find multiple V-belt drive, often resulting in a big speed reduction. Special gearboxes (U-drive or V-drive) are made to put a hairpin bend into a propeller shaft. In such cases, engines are situated well aft, transmitting towards the bow, with the propeller shafts passing underneath them. Note that it may be unwise to permit a propeller to spin when under sail alone, unless a sailing clutch is fitted and used. A good engine manual will clarify this.

Configurations

Whether fuelled by diesel, gas oil, petrol (gasoline), kerosene, bottled gas, or petroil (petrol/lubricating oil mixture), most marine internal combustion engines have their cylinders arranged either in line, in Vee-formation, or horizontally opposed. Many inboards are adaptations of industrial, car, or truck engines, equipped with marine gearboxes, oil cooling, rustproof oil pans, water-cooled exhaust manifolds, and perhaps overhead hand-starting gear. Air-cooled engines eliminate the problems of water circulation, but they tend to be noisy, and effective air ducting is not always easy to install. Because they are nearly half the size for equal power, two-stroke engines of the valveless type are more popular for outboards (and some small inboards) than the prolific four-stroke car engine types with valves. The old, slow-revving and everlasting marine engine (Plate 84) is rarely seen in a yacht nowadays. With crankcase side doors, piston rings and big-end bearings could be renewed without shifting such an engine.

Controls

Simple rod and bell-crank linkages for gear and throttle controls have nowadays mostly been replaced by sophisticated hydraulic, flexible cable and solenoid devices, which are almost impossible to repair at sea. All should be well if makers' maintenance tasks are adhered to, especially with regard to adjustment, lubrication, and inspections for damage along the route. Similar devices are used for wheel steering to rudders and outboard motors, and for trim planes or trim tabs. Other engine controls such

Plate 84 Almost antiques now, old style marine engines were bulky, but easy to overhaul and quiet running.

as choke cable and diesel stop button can generally be operated in some alternative way, should anything fail. Discuss with your crew what to do if the throttle jams wide open, especially with an antiquated installation. Make sure that each control actuates faithfully the requisite movements at the remote end. Note that with a gearbox having an internal hydraulic gear shift mechanism, the engine should never be stopped with the control in either ahead or astern positions. Clutch adjustment is especially critical for some mechanically-operated gearboxes.

Instrumentation

The simplest marine engines have no electrics and no instruments. With modern expensive and sophisticated units, a full range of gauges and telltale lights helps to diagnose problems before they get too serious. In addition to the basic ammeter, oil pressure gauge and coolant thermometer, complete panels often include tachometer, oil level and temperature gauges, battery state indicator, fuel tank gauges, running hours recorder, vacuum gauge, and also telltales for charging failure, oil filter state, heater plugs or choke, low oil warning, and water in the fuel.

Wiring

In low voltage work, tightness and cleanliness of all terminals and contacts is imperative. With so much vibration around, make occasional checks on the connections to instruments, sender units, all engine electrics, and the bonding cables from sacrificial anodes (see Chapter 10). Ensure that wiring looms and stray cables are properly clipped or strapped, and kept well away from heat and chafe.

Ancillaries

With correct installation, basic engines are incredibly reliable. Most of the faults which occur involve ancillary equipment, including controls, electrics, and fuel and water systems. Twin engines each need separate equipment, while the ancillaries on a single screw installation need duplication (or back-up) as far as possible. This is fairly easy to contrive with controls, batteries, charging and fuel filters, but not so simple when it comes to ignition, starting gear and coolant pump. Carrying a small spare outboard motor (with suitable bracket and shaft length) on board is a useful safety precaution for many sailing and power craft under about 30 ft (9 m) in length.

Dipsticks

Sailors trained on car engines need to watch the oil level situation on some marine engines. There could be separate dipsticks for engine, gearbox, reduction gear, injector pump, and turbocharger. As few engine oil pan plugs are accessible for draining the oil, a sump pump will be found on many inboard installations, hand operated, and mounted to one side of the block. Sometimes a separate pump is used, with a pipe to feed through the dipstick aperture. Cleaning the gauze filters in crankcase breathers and fume-extraction systems is all too easily neglected for years on end. Remember that some gearboxes have separate breathers and filters. Some use special hydraulic oil; not automotive oil.

Air filter

With comparatively clean air over the water, marine induction filters tend to get neglected, but salty spray can damage them. Some engines have no filter, but they should then have a flame arrester and a noise-reducing cowl. Any modifications depend upon whether or not an engine was tuned for the slight restriction of a filter. Mesh screens fitted to the inlets and outlets of air-cooled engine cooling ducts generally need scrubbing annually, plus regular checks to ensure that nobody has placed a cushion or other equipment over one of the screens.

Clean fuel

Dirt or water in fuel tanks can be troublesome when stirred up under way. Check filters before departure. Clearing fuel lines and filters at sea is not an enviable job! See page 179 for details of bacterial sludge and wax. Grit and water will damage a diesel injection pump. Airlocks are further hazards, though hopefully short-lived. With a boat in regular use, keeping diesel turned on at the tank helps to avoid airlocks.

Hours run

With no other way of recording engine running time, keep a note of all fuel quantities used. Most owners know the average quantity of fuel their engine burns per hour. Operation manuals often quote maintenance requirements in hours run, and recommend the replacement of certain components in these terms. To keep a jump ahead of trouble, carry any such spare parts on board, especially when cruising in remote areas. An hour meter can be fitted to any engine, the cheaper ones operating by vibration.

Decarbonizing and valve grinding are winter jobs which are best done before the allotted time interval has expired. See Table 8 for typical costs.

Overloading

To produce full power, an engine must be capable of reaching full designed revs. It cannot do this if the propeller pitch is too high. If the pitch is too low, it might race away, again not producing full power. Borrow a proper workshop tachometer to measure full revs direct from the engine, but always check this when the boat is under way; not with the propeller churning still water. Fitting a folding propeller (see Plate 82), or a two-bladed one to clamp vertically in line with the sternpost, skeg, or fairing, will often improve performance under sail.

Table 8

Typical engine maintenance costs, excluding any tax

Type of engine	Change oils and filters, including gearboxes				Treat plugs, contacts, carb. or injectors, check fuel lift pump				Decarbonize head and exhaust. Grind valves				*Rebore or renew liners. Renew bearings, valves, pistons and rings			
	Amateur		Boatyard		Amateur		Boatyard		Amateur		Boatyard		Amateur		Boatyard	
	£	$	£	$	£	$	£	$	£	$	£	$	£	$	£	$
4 hp outboard	5	7	18	36	7	9	38	78	11	19	60	135	95	250	Not economic	
8 hp 2-cyl. gasoline inboard	20	30	40	94	11	19	62	155	20	32	110	280	215	470	575	1100
15 hp 2-cyl. diesel inboard	25	45	75	182	24	52	64	132	31	57	188	460	325	690	780	1550
20 hp 2-cyl. outboard	7	10	24	45	10	17	43	98	18	33	72	198	210	430	360	950
25 hp 4cyl. gasoline inboard	22	32	45	112	17	28	85	208	50	88	270	650	450	960	880	1860
30 hp 4-cyl. diesel inboard	37	59	90	206	50	120	110	244	60	110	325	760	590	1210	920	2300
100 hp 6-cyl. outboard	12	17	42	96	15	35	75	170	50	100	150	370	450	980	960	2200
100 hp 6-cyl. diesel inboard	50	80	130	280	75	180	140	330	90	160	510	1280	970	1900	2000	4800
250 hp 8-cyl. diesel inboard	60	90	180	390	96	200	186	440	150	270	750	1800	1600	3500	3000	7600

*Including removal and replacement of engine where applicable.

Outboard motors

Most reliable if kept in peak condition (and prevented from dropping overboard), outboard motors do a wonderful job propelling a wide range of power and auxiliary craft. As with sterndrives, on fast boats they tend to raise the bow and limit vision ahead. Without trim tabs, you can now clamp planes (hydrofoils) on top of the cavitation plates of these engines to lift the stern. From the noiseless electric outboards and the basic Seagull (which you can strip right down in under an hour) to the 250 hp monsters, they are practical and reliable nowadays.

Fuel

Lubricating oil is mixed with the fuel of most outboard motors. As the proportion is critical (and is not the same for all makes), care is needed when preparing it, or when ordering it ready mixed. The special oil made for this purpose stays in solution well, but it pays to shake the fuel tank before starting, especially after a long spell ashore.

Fuel tank

With gravity feed, turn off the fuel at the tank (also the air valve on top of the tank) and use up all fuel in the carburettor and pipeline when stopping the engine at the end of a day. This prevents oil from thickening in the jets, and eliminates leakage when the engine is unshipped and laid down flat. Make sure that a remote fuel tank cannot slide about, either when stowed or when under way. Also, guard against anyone treading on pressurizing and delivery hoses.

Stowage

In shed or on parent ship, stowing outboards upright minimizes damage, leakage and corrosion. Any sort of covering is advantageous. If left on the stern, try to keep the propeller tilted above water and use a waterproof top cover.

A safety lock is essential these days. Thick steel plates to prevent the clamps from turning (with a shielded lock underneath) will stop a thief's bolt cutters – much better than a chain and padlock. Except by removing the fuel tank, there is often no simple way to immobilize an outboard motor against the activities of drive-away thieves. Removing spark plugs is a good deterrent, provided these are replaced by blanks which need a special tool to loosen them. Through-bolts in addition to the clamps are a wise precaution for semi-permanent installations.

Support

Being simple to fabricate, an outboard motor stand (see Plate 22) is well worth having, for overhauls as well as storage. If not to be run for a long time, drain off all fuel and keep a battery charged. See Chapter 12 for laying-up procedure.

Fouling

Where the raised angle of tilt is insufficient (particularly common with outdrive units), rapid fouling by marine growth can occur, eventually damaging enamel finishes. If not left too long, wiping with a phenol and water solution is effective. Use a scrubbing brush on more obstinate growth, together with a liquid or powder bath cleaner. Chronic cases demand the use of antifouling paint.

Wetting

Dunking a whole motor in water momentarily is not necessarily disastrous. Some have been known to start immediately afterwards, but the safest procedure is to drain all fuel, remove spark plugs, then turn the engine by hand while supporting it upside down and at various other angles of tilt. If possible, rinse off with fresh water. After that, give the engine a long run under load. If there is a flywheel magneto, failure to start may be due to water in that department. Douse with denatured alcohol or carbon tetrachloride (avoid breathing the latter's fumes) and blow out with air. A final spray with car ignition sealer is usually beneficial. Having a safety lanyard on the motor might not prevent accidental dunking, but it could prevent total loss.

Submersion

Turning too sharply has been known to rip an outboard motor off the transom. Whether running or not at the time, prolonged submersion (particularly in sea water) demands immediate stripping down after the rescue. Get rid of salt water by rotating several turns while submerged in fresh water, if there is likely to be any delay before stripping. Hose out water pump and cylinder jackets to get rid of silt or sand. After cleaning and drying, oil the working parts as necessary before re-assembly.

Spares

Modern outboards with transistorized capacitor discharge ignition and surface discharge plugs do not need spare contact breakers, condensers or spark plugs. As well as gasket sets, some motors need shear pins and basic tools – others perhaps also a complete recoil starter or simple cord. The amateur mechanic should not be without a spare parts book and workshop manual.

Trouble

Valveless engines are notoriously bad starters when slightly worn – or when any component is not functioning at peak efficiency. Carburettors cause least trouble; spark plugs (unless of the surface gap type) cause the most trouble, through carbon deposits and fuel wetting. Weak compression is ruinous, caused by piston and main bearing seal leakage. Excess oil in the crankcase can be troublesome, and some inboard two-strokes have crankcase plugs to enable free oil to be drained away. After an idle period, squirting a little oil on top of the pistons often helps compression. Incorrectly set or pitted contacts are anathema to easy starting, so an electronic ignition system has advantages in this respect.

Stoppage

In case the makers' fault-finding chart omits them, three common reasons why an outboard should stop itself after running for perhaps one minute are:

(a)   The water cooling system is defunct;
(b)   the ignition condenser has broken down; or
(c)   the exhaust system is fouled with carbon – a common problem with engines which require oil to be added to the fuel.

Such an engine may start again once cool, but the fault will recur at each attempt.

Decarbonizing

Hard carbon needs scraping from piston top, cylinder head, and ports on most two-strokes after about 200 hours of running. Car engines and diesels commonly run 2000 hours between top overhauls. If you do this work yourself, always keep the necessary gaskets in stock. If the cylinder head is detachable, the job does not take long. With an integral head the cylinder block has to come off. This enables the ports to be cleaned more thoroughly, and broken piston rings to be detected. When using electric drill wire brush attachments for cleaning such a block, a shaft extension will be necessary. Avoid scoring the metal if old screwdrivers are used. Finish off with medium emery tape soaked in light oil, perhaps tacked to a short stick.

Stripping

Complete stripping demands reference to the workshop manual, and sometimes the use of special pullers and presses for removing and replacing flywheel, bearings and crank webs. Make sure that gaskets and likely parts are available before you start. Vetting by an experienced fitter is generally advisable when deciding what parts to replace. He will have a micrometer to measure cylinder bore wear and ovality, and be able to fit new piston rings without breaking them.

Piston rings

Make sure the lands (grooves) are completely free from carbon before fitting new rings. Check ring wear by comparing an old ring with a new one, or by pushing each in turn into the bore a certain distance (using a piston to keep them square) and measuring the gaps with feeler gauges. Ring wear leaves a ridge near the top of each bore and special stepped upper rings should be used unless the ridges can be honed off. Note that some rings are located by pegs to ensure that the gaps do not coincide with the cylinder ports. Borrow suitable piston ring expanders and clamps for assembly, and lubricate bores and pistons beforehand.

Carburettor

Outboards are not noted for their fuel economy, but the simple carburettors used are generally foolproof, without tiny jets that could clog. Some types do contain narrow passages which can become constricted – particularly if water has entered at some time and started corrosion. The adjustment of an idling mixture screw is delicate. It should be set (when the engine is hot) as detailed in the handbook. Float chamber flooding is usually caused by either a punctured float, or a damaged or dirty float valve. Jiggling the tickler (when fitted) will often clear dirt. With a dirty fuel tank, the fuel filter gauze could clog rapidly. Should this occur, rinse out the tank with fresh fuel and carry a spare gauze to avoid the delay of cleaning this should the trouble recur.

Cooling

Water intake holes near the gearbox (Plate 85) are easily blocked by debris and need regular inspection. If water fails to emerge from a circulation telltale pipe when running, stop immediately and check the intake. If there is no fouling, refrain from running the engine until a hose can be squirted through (never from the exhaust outlet end), or the water pump removed for examination.

Plate 85 Five small scoops each side constitute the cooling water intakes on this outboard motor.

Gearbox

Kept filled with the correct oil, even the gearboxes with reverse and clutch facilities give little trouble. Few owners ever bother to drain the oil, but this is an essential annual procedure to check the presence of water (which gives a milky appearance), sludge, and bits of metal. In-season topping up is generally recommended every 25 hours of running time. Follow the instructions, as the oil level plug may need to be replaced before withdrawing the nozzle of the squeezy oil tube from the filling aperture. All the above usually applies also to outdrive and saildrive legs. Dismantling gearboxes is not normally within the amateur's domain.

Flexible cables

Long life and easy maintenance is assured when the makers are thoughtful enough to provide a grease nipple on a cable outer sheath. Use thin graphited cable grease. When the grease emerges at one end, seal this with a binding of vinyl tape and cord, then continue pumping until grease emerges at the other end. With no nipple, half fill a toy balloon from the grease gun, bind this over the cable end (including the disconnected terminal) and squeeze gently.

Cable ends

Some terminal fittings are removable, enabling the inner cable to be withdrawn for greasing. If the cable is buckled, it may not feed back into the sheath, so check the availability of a new one

beforehand. Oil linkages and clevis pins regularly and keep all exposed metal parts greased or sprayed with protective oil.

Swivels

Do not forget to lubricate the tilt tube and steering swivel (either with grease gun or oil-can according to the manual) at least at the start and middle of the season; preferably monthly. Much the same applies to the retracting gear or lift used to withdraw a heavy motor effortlessly from an outboard well built through the boat's bottom, or on a transom bracket.

Valved engines

Most inboard motors are of the four-stroke (four-cycle) road vehicle type, with inlet and exhaust valves. Running periods of more than 1000 hours are commonly achieved between top overhauls, but long periods of idleness cause valves to stick and their seatings to corrode. Otherwise, there is normally good warning of valve leakage, cylinder wear, and bearing failure.

Cylinder wear

Piston slap (rattle), high oil consumption, and fuming from the oil filler cap or crankcase breather are indications of bore or piston ring wear. Valved engines will tolerate quite a lot of cylinder wear, though diesels need good compression for easy

173

starting, especially when not fitted with heater plugs or decompressors. Even with a starter motor, hand starting gear is useful to check the uniformity of compression on each cylinder, and to keep everything free during long periods of idleness. Oil squirted into each cylinder may help compression temporarily, but without a decompressor, more than a trace of oil in diesel engine cylinders could break a piston, due to the high compression ratio.

Bearing wear

Crankshaft main bearings and connecting rod little ends often have a life of 4000 hours, while big-end shells should last 2000 hours. If journals are oval or scored, the crankshaft must be re-ground, and undersize shells fitted. Early renewal is always a good thing, before low oil pressure or knocking indicates serious wear.

Oil pressure

Bearing wear is the usual cause of low oil pressure, but it can be due to an oil pump or relief valve fault, or to a fouled-up sump strainer. One cause of the latter is topping up with detergent oil when a straight mineral oil had previously been used – a point to watch when buying a boat. Note that diesels should be fed with oil which has been specially formulated for that breed.

Oil leaks

Old engines frequently leak oil – hopefully into a proper drip tray rather than into the bilges! Such leakage is not always easy to cure, unless tightening the bolts on oil pan, rocker case, inspection plates and timing case will suffice. Leaky oil seals on crankshaft and gearbox may have to await a major overhaul, but remember to check all dipsticks frequently when there is leakage. Wiping an engine down occasionally saves a lot of mess and obnoxious smells.

Listening rod

It takes an experienced fitter to diagnose the cause of warning noises. Some amateurs have trouble differentiating between diesel knock and a failed big-end, between pinking (pinging) and piston slap, or between loose bearer bolts and slack tappets. A listening rod is most useful to locate strange noises. Any piece of thin metal bar (or a long screwdriver) will do. Place your thumb on one end, press your ear to the thumb nail, and use the other end of the rod like a stethoscope, held on suspected parts of the engine.

Tappets

Hydraulic tappets need no adjustment and can funtion even when worn sufficiently to become noisy. Check adjustable tappets or rockers every 250 hours. To identify a noisy one, poke a strip of 6-mil shim or an old feeler gauge into each gap in turn, while the engine is idling. This will immediately silence the wide one. Follow the workshop manual instructions when adjusting, taking care to note whether the readings are with engine hot or cold. If noise persists, even with slightly reduced gaps, tappets or valve ends have worn irregularly. Fit a new sealing gasket when replacing the rocker case (overhead valve engine) or the tappet covers (side valve or L-head engine) to avert future oil leaks. Engines turn easily by hand with plugs or injectors removed.

Top overhaul

Removing a cylinder head for decarbonizing and valve grinding is simple except on a massive engine, or with an overhead camshaft. With side valves, most of the work must be done on board, but with modern engines you can take the head home (or to a fitter) complete with valves, leaving only the piston tops to clean up on board. Examine the cylinder bores carefully for score marks indicating broken piston rings, and for any slackness of wet or dry liners. Do not forget to drain all cooling water before removing a cylinder head!

Breaking the joint

Old-style marine engines have jacking bolts for breaking the seal once all cylinder head nuts are free. They also serve as lifting eyes to draw the head off its studs. Without such aids, squirt penetrating oil around the studs, dress the side of the head with a lead hammer (or a club hammer hitting a block of hardwood) then turn the engine smartly, hoping that compression will free the joint. Some heads have recesses cast into them (or external lugs) enabling a lever to be inserted for breaking the joint. With a copper/asbestos gasket forming the joint, an old screwdriver makes a good wedge to drive between head and block, but do this gently, shifting the tool along after each blow. A chain hoist on sheer-legs may be needed to raise the head of a big engine.

Cleaning

Of the many fluids capable of cleaning the sticky grime off internal parts (as well as the outside of an engine), kerosene is the least harmful, being kind to the skin and not too readily combustible. Lamp oil, paraffin oil, and domestic boiler fuel oil of 28 seconds viscosity are similar to kerosene. Without a proper cleaning bath (having a pump and filter) you need two trays: one containing relatively clean fluid for the final rinse. Use old tooth brushes, bottle brushes, and paint brushes in the first tank. Have layers of newspaper handy on which parts can drain prior to wiping with clean rag. Note that if spilt, some commercial engine-cleaning fluids can cause serious damage to a fibreglass hull.

Stripping

Overhead rocker gear unbolts in a few minutes, while push-rods draw out in seconds. After cleaning, store the latter in correct sequence, as described later for valves. With a suitable (borrowed or bought) valve lifter, stripping off valve springs is not difficult, especially if you have a magnetic screwdriver to lift out the small collets. With the inlet and exhaust manifolds removed, this is a good opportunity to clear carbon from the valve ports, as well as normal decarbonizing in way of each piston.

Waterways

Wash out any salt in the water jacket, preferably using a high pressure water jet. Hard scale has to be dissolved with a mild acid, such as the hydrochloric or formic acid used to de-fur kettles and central heating boilers.

Core plugs

Disc or cup freeze plugs are peened into turned recesses to seal the core plug holes left by the foundry. If you replace a leaky one (which is not of stainless steel) and find it badly corroded inside, it would be wise to renew them all. This permits a good inspection inside the water jacket. Any fitter can tell you how to tackle this job. Marine water jackets are often cathodically protected against corrosion by removable zinc anodes. If pitted, these should be renewed.

Valves

Unless a valve seating and face can be reground by hand in ten minutes, it pays to get both professionally skimmed. Always replace a burnt or chipped valve. Specialist firms can sometimes renew valve seat inserts which have been reground too many times. Trouble with integral seats usually indicates purchasing a new head, or a good second-hand one. Grind valves briefly with coarse Carborundum paste until (after wiping clean) dull, even faces are produced. Finish with at least two applications of fine paste, wiping clean each time. If you are not conversant with this job, a fitter will explain how to rotate a valve with the suction tool, holding a finger under the stem to lift the valve intermittently.

Guides

Put each valve stem back in its guide to check for wear. Only the slightest sideways movement is permissible. Details of any specially shaped ferrules required for pulling out old valve guides and pressing in new ones (with the aid of a fine-threaded bolt) are normally given in the workshop manual. Such ferrules can be turned on a small lathe if necessary.

Springs

A broken valve spring could be disastrous at sea, so examine each one carefully under a strong lens to check for cracks. As groups, inlet and exhaust springs should be of equal length, and almost equal to new spring lengths if known. New valve stem oil seals or O-rings are always included in top overhaul gasket sets and must be fitted correctly to prevent oil seeping into the cylinders.

Marking

Keep all small parts in boxes, labelled if necessary. Valves must not be mixed up, so store them in numbered holes bored in a block of wood, or punched through a cardboard box. As soon as a cylinder head is removed, plug all apertures against the ingress of dirt and carbon. Injector pipes and suchlike should be taped over at the exposed ends.

Gaskets

Jointing compounds such as *Hermetite* in Britain and *Permatex* in America should only be needed on cylinder head and manifold joints if the metal surfaces are known to be slightly distorted. Some fitters stick a rocker case gasket onto the cover and grease the other face, to enable the cover to be removed for tappet adjustment without breaking the gasket. Special pastes are made for alloy to iron (or steel) joints.

Joint faces

All metal faces must be thoroughly cleaned before assembly. A bearing scraper (or an old wood chisel) will remove bits of gasket harmlessly on cast iron, but beware of scoring light alloy. An excellent finisher is 240-grit silicon carbide abrasive paper dunked in kerosene and wrapped around a cork sanding pad. When cleaning off the cylinder block face, stuff a rag into the bores (with all pistons level) and wipe each bore carefully on completion. Similarly, avoid using sharp tools for decarbonizing: pistons are nearly always of soft alloy.

Major overhaul

When a cylinder head is removed, check the bores for score marks. A noticeable wear lip near the top (see page 172) may be the first indication that a rebore, or new liners, will soon be necessary. Unlike car engines, boat engines cannot be repaired at just any time. Overhauls need to be done out of season and well in advance of trouble. Make adequate notes about all connections when taking an engine out of a boat, including details of any shims under the mountings. Some dismantling of joinerwork is sure to be necessary – perhaps including the wheelhouse roof, or a special panel in the roof provided for this purpose.

Engine stand
A major overhaul at home can be done more quickly and safely if an engine stand (Fig. 5) is made from timber or welded steel to support the engine at a convenient working height, enabling it to be rotated and locked in any position, and preferably adjustable as the centre of gravity shifts. With head, gearbox and starter removed, the remainder of an engine under about 100 hp can, with care, generally be dealt with on a wide bench.

Sump
Having lifted an engine from its bearers, always take this opportunity to clean sludge from the oil pan, also to clean all gauze strainers, and perhaps to remove a big-end bearing cap to check for wear and scoring. Tiny specks of metal in the sump (or in the oil filter bowl) undoubtedly mean a partial break-up of at least one bearing shell. On replacing a pan, stick a new and undamaged gasket to it – making sure all bolt holes coincide – and then smear oil on the exposed gasket surface before offering up. Use a torque wrench to makers' specification, taking care not to over-tighten with a light alloy crankcase.

Big-ends
The steel-backed shells lining most big-end bearings are simple and cheap to replace without needing to withdraw the pistons. They normally have alignment nibs, so you cannot fit them wrongly and obstruct oil passages. You may need to remove an oil gallery pipe from the main bearings before you can get at the big-ends. Badly worn shells are often pitted, scored, and show coppery surfaces where the Babbitt metal has worn through. If the bearing caps are not numbered, pop-mark them before removal. Always oil bearing surfaces before assembly. Use several pipe cleaners bunched together to clean out oil feed holes, especially if the dismantled engine has been standing about for some time uncovered, or if emery cloth has been used near by.

Main bearings
Although crankshaft removal is necessary to expose main bearings completely, some caps are readily taken off to examine those halves of each bearing which wear the most. Crankshaft removal does mean that any renewable oil seal (provided with a full gasket kit) will be renewed. On assembly, you must get the camshaft drive correctly aligned in accordance with the workshop manual. Firms specializing in crankshaft journal grinding often supply the correct new bearing shells to match.

Special tools
If your boat undergoes a winter lay-up period, work need not be rushed, allowing plenty of time to borrow or hire any special tools. These may range from unusually thin or extra large open-ended or socket wrenches, stud extractors and circlip (retainer clip) pliers, to pullers, piston clamps, ring expanders and nut breakers.

Assembly
Although amateur fitters have been known to make expensive mistakes, large sums of money can be saved by merely undertaking the laborious dismantling, cleaning and assembling yourself. Coat all bolts (including spark plug threads) with graphite grease to inhibit corrosion and facilitate future removal. Discard all rusty nuts, bolts and washers. Test or renew any components that are suspect. For instance, as a thermostat has the opening temperature stamped on it, test it in a heated pan of water, with a cookery thermometer inserted.

Finishing
Spraying after assembly is certainly the quickest

way to enamel an inboard engine, but the results look better if certain components such as filler caps, controls, wiring, filters and pumps are masked, and perhaps later coated with contrasting paint. You must use heat resistant paint (see page 64). A smart engine is likely to get better attention than an apparent heap of junk with rust around the top and dirty oil around the bottom! Occasional use of WD40 (or a similar preservative) helps keep corrosion at bay.

Specialists

Even professional fitters call on the services of specialist firms for cylinder reboring, crankshaft regrinding, and repairs to an injector pump, dynamo, alternator, starter, magneto, or turbo-blower. The amateur usually needs to go further and summon help for gearbox work, spark plug and injection nozzle testing, camshaft sprocket setting, final distributor dwell adjustment, and all baffling fault-finding problems.

Running in

It pays to keep the piston speed low at first on any new engine, or one that has received a major overhaul. Unless the makers say differently, do not exceed about one-third of maximum revs for about twenty hours. Short emergency bursts of speed should do no harm after the first ten hours.

Precautions

A gradual build-up of spare parts to carry on board is always a useful goal, whether you are competent to fit them or not, especially for deep sea cruising. Some engine makers market boxed kits of spare parts, but you certainly need at least an assortment of bolts, plus spark plugs, contacts, hoses, pipe clips, injectors, heater plugs, filters, fuel pump repair kit, brushes for dynamo and starter, fuses, and plenty of oil. More parts are, of course, necessary for other engine-room equipment such as charging set, pumps, space heater, evaporator, or exhaust-heat calorifier. Winterization procedures are described in Chapter 12. Approximate present day costs for common engine overhaul work are given in Table 8.

Fuel system

Although good maintenance should ensure that clean fuel keeps flowing, some fuel systems have built-in faults which are potential hazards. When changing boats, it pays to get a marine engineer to

check this over – as well as other aspects of the installation. Even the simple fire precaution of a gauze-covered drip tray beneath a carburettor may have been missed.

Tank materials

For diesel fuel, tanks should be of mild steel (uncoated inside), stainless steel, or fibreglass. Leave such tanks full in winter to avoid moisture forming inside. For petrol or gasoline, brass tanks create gum in pipes and filters: tinned steel or stainless steel tanks prove best. Always empty a brass or copper tank in winter to eliminate gum formation. Flexible tanks (see page 206) are rarely used for fuel.

Tank fittings

Some small gravity tanks have only the basic fittings: an outlet connection and a filler cap with built-in breather. As shown in Fig. 104, superior tanks have the following:

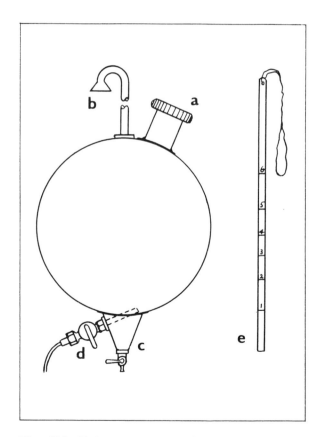

Fig. 104 Fittings on a small fuel tank.

(a) Leakproof screw-on filler cap to prevent spillage by surging.

(b) Breather pipe extended high up, preferably with gauze filter across the downward-facing orifice.

(c) Sump with draincock for getting rid of water and sludge.

(d) An internal pipe in the stopcock, extending above sump level, sometimes with a gauze strainer.

(e) A calibrated dipstick. If not provided, this can be made from dowel wood.

Big tanks

Some of the additional fittings which sprout on big tanks are detailed in Fig. 105, labelled as follows:

(a) Hose connection to deck filler plate. A separate cap just below deck is less likely to let water in.

(b) Vent pipe with swan neck through coaming. (Must have a snorkel-type non-return valve on a deep sea vessel.)

(c) Fuel gauge with vertical transparent tube. Needs an isolating cock at top and bottom to prevent loss of fuel after accidental damage to the tube. A remote electric fuel gauge is generally preferred, or a clock-type gauge on the tank, actuated magnetically by an internal float.

(d) Outlet union to a pumped fuel system. Top mounting eliminates a potential source of leakage.

(e) Leak-off pipe connection from diesel injection pump and nozzles.

(f) Balancing pipe from another tank.

(g) Draincock. Tank fitted with a slight tilt towards this point.

(h) Internal baffles to prevent fuel surging about in a seaway.

There may also be one or more bolt-on inspection panels.

Pipelines

Transparent fuel pipes assist the detection of air bubbles and cannot corrode, but they are vulnerable to chafe and fire damage. Steel pipe is best for diesel fuel, though copper is sometimes used to obviate external corrosion. Make sure that long runs are secured at 12 in (300 mm) intervals with padded clips. Check these annually for tightness.

Pipe vibration

A short length of approved flexible fuel pipe near the

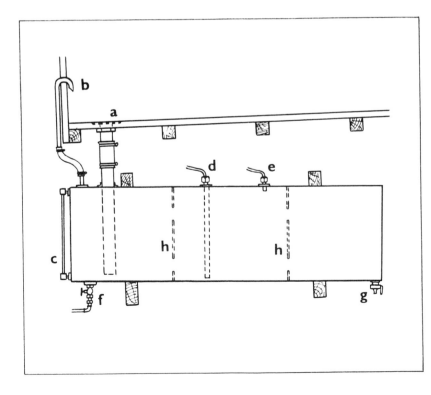

Fig. 105 Typical diesel tank arrangement for a big boat.

engine prevents fatigue failure caused by vibration in the remaining metal pipeline. A large diameter horizontal double coil (Fig. 106) is incorporated in all-metal fuel pipes to reduce such embrittlement. Good practice with copper is to anneal (soften) it every two years, by heating to medium redness all except the bitter ends and unions. An engineering shop will do this on a hearth, and quench it for best results. At home, pass a blowtorch slowly along without quenching. Work in a semi-dark place, to help achieve an even redness, and to avoid overheating to bright orange.

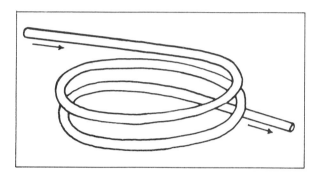

Fig. 106 Horizontal anti-vibration coil in all-metal fuel pipe.

Bugs and gum

Draining all water from the bottom of a diesel tank is difficult. Where water and fuel meet is where bacteria, algae and fungi collect, creating foul filter sludge and darkening the fuel. Tiny doses of an additive like Biobor will stop this. Otherwise, use phenol to clean out empty tanks and pipelines, preferably finishing the latter with a blast of compressed air – see page 212 under *Quick pumping*. For cleaning gasoline gum from pipes and carburettors, acetone works well. Regular diesel forms wax particles in icy weather: you may need special winter fuel or a commercial additive to combat this.

Airlock

With a carburettor, direct its fuel feed into a can while working the lift pump lever (if fitted), or running the engine by feeding the float chamber with a pipette. If the pump will not prime, crank the engine a full turn to shift the cam. Airlocks cause many diesel faults. Handbooks always tell you how to bleed the system. Without pet-cocks or automatic bleeding, slacken each union in turn, following the flow until air-free fuel flows out. Catch the smelly spillage carefully with rag or newspaper. Crack open each nozzle union before cranking the engine, or it might fire. Keep the throttle wide open and the stop control set for running. Do not over-tighten any unions, but check them for leaks once running. Diesel tanks are normally left turned on to avoid airlocks, but should a fuel pipe leak during lay-up, connection as shown in Fig. 105(d) could siphon all the tank's contents into the bilges.

Fuel filter

To discourage air bubbles, the filter should be set low down, the piping rising smoothly from it in both directions. Some bleeding is essential after disturbing a filter. As well as gauze and paper element filters, there are mechanically cleared ones operated by a handle, with sump and drain to remove sludge and water. Duplex filters are used on big diesels, enabling one to be serviced under way while the other is operating. Fuel contamination is not uncommon on boats and this is best detected early by checking filters regularly while in port. The removal of moisture is especially important for diesels.

Changeover valves

For swapping duplex filters and water intakes, bringing separate fuel tanks into use, and switching from starting fuel to main fuel on kerosene engines, changeover valves are used. Make sure you know where they are, and check occasionally for leaks. Such complications are not found on the simple auxiliary motors of most family sailboats.

Injection

Dirty diesel fuel can cause injection pump wear and drooling injectors, indicated by smoky exhaust. However, smoke can also be created by the wrong fuel, engine wear, overloading, or a dirty air cleaner. Few owners carry spare injectors. Any garage undertaking diesel maintenance work will lap the nozzle valves and test the cracking pressure and spray pattern. When using a test rig, care is necessary to keep skin well away from the spray. You can withdraw a nozzle and use the engine as a partial test rig, but remember to slacken the unions on the other nozzles to prevent the engine from firing. In any case, the wise owner will have injectors serviced every 400 hours or so. When replacing, renew the copper gaskets and tighten the nuts evenly. Injection pumps are best serviced every 1500 hours, but be prepared for a big outlay if replacement or major repairs prove necessary.

Detection

A faulty spark plug can often be identified by removing or shorting-out the HT leads one by one while an engine is idling. Much the same idea will often pick out a faulty injector. Slacken the feed pipe unions one at a time and listen for the one that makes no difference to the idling speed, or observe the one that reduces smoke emission. Loss of fuel from injector leak-off pipes is quite common, as vibration slackens unions and flexible piping connections. Another item to check before you go to sea!

Turbocharger

If you have a blown engine, the turbocharger should not be neglected, needing blade and intercooler cleaning every 500 hours or so, while there could be a separate oil system with dipstick and filter to keep an eye on.

Cooling

Direct sea water cooling, with a single engine-driven pump, works well for outboard motors, and is widely used for small inboards (see Fig. 107). However, cylinder and exhaust manifold jackets corrode and can become caked with salt, which causes overheating. Pumping hot, soft water through for some 30 minutes is an effective way to get it out. Do not forget to treat an oil-cooling heat exchanger if fitted. Remove any zinc anodes from jackets before inserting acid, and consult the makers first if the block or head is of light alloy.

Intake filter

Unless an engine has duplicated cooling water intake fittings with changeover valves, the strainer should be housed in a vertical standpipe rising above the waterline. This enables weed and other debris to be cleared from the gauze (Fig. 108) without the need to turn off the supply.

Temperature

Many direct cooled engines never get up to an ideal temperature, causing unnecessary wear. A thermometer lashed to the outlet pipe (and lagged over with rag or tape) will soon show whether the makers' recommended figure (usually round 165°F or 77°C) is being attained. It may be a simple matter of adjusting a by-pass valve, or renewing a thermostat. Some installations have no provision for a by-pass

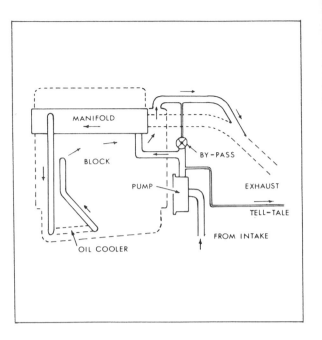

Fig. 107 Direct raw water cooling system.

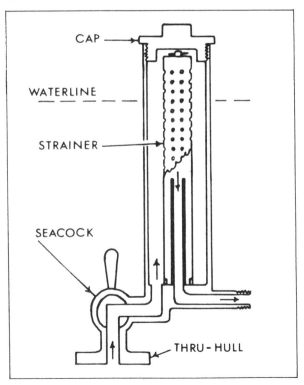

Fig. 108 A proper water intake strainer can be cleared under way.

(see Fig. 107) and modifications are then indicated. Thermostats are fail-safe and more often cause underheating than overheating. Air-cooled engine temperature depends on the weather, unless adjustable baffles are incorporated in the ducting.

Telltale

If spent cooling water is mixed with the exhaust, viewing the outlet to check water flow is not always easy. A small-bore pipe through the topsides (Fig. 107) simplifies the visual check and is an easy modification to carry out.

Emergencies

An added complication is a two-way changeover valve at the intake filter to enable the cooling water pump to be used for draining the bilge. This is useful in leaky old boats (or in an emergency), but trouble could arise if this valve is left in the wrong position. The intake seacock is best turned off when the vessel is unoccupied (the same applies to all seacocks) but you must remember to turn it on before starting up. Should the water pump fail, you may be able to improvise by coupling up an electric bilge pump with short pieces of hose. Even a person on deck pouring water down a hosepipe might suffice in an emergency!

Closed circuit

Keeping the same fresh water circulating around an engine (as in a car) reduces scale formation, allows the use of light alloy castings, and also the use of corrosion inhibiting and antifreeze additives. The simplest form of closed circuit uses a keel cooler (see Figs. 10 and 109) with a small header tank; its pressure cap must seal well. As a keel cooler is vulnerable to damage, important installations use inboard heat exchangers cooled by sea water. Such an arrangement may utilize two pumps.

Routine care

As certain lengths of rubber hose are sure to be used in a cooling system, regular checks for leaks and cracks are advisable. Always carry some spare hose on board and renew any rusty hose clips with stainless steel ones. Vinyl electrical tape (or self-amalgamating tape) is useful for emergency hose repairs. Turn the lubricator on a pump drive shaft or jockey wheel before a run, and wipe away any surplus grease. Keep V-belts tight enough to avoid slipping, and carry spare ones. Over-tightening will cause premature bearing wear. Apart from a fouled intake strainer, stoppage sometimes occurs when a

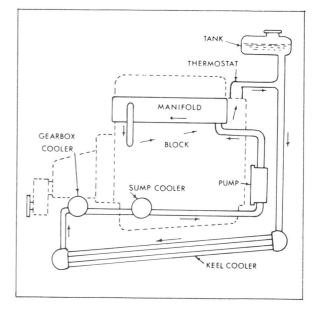

Fig. 109 Fresh water cooling layout with single pump.

plastic bag gets stuck across the opening. A long thin rod (or wooden dowel) makes a handy prodder, if there is no dog-leg as in Fig. 108, or external grille. Laying-up chores are described in Chapter 12.

Exhaust

The slightest exhaust pipe leak could risk the crew's health on a decked boat. Scale, blown gaskets, flaking rust, collapsed muffler baffles, or overheated flexible piping create these conditions. It pays to dismantle the system at about five-yearly intervals to check the condition, depending on materials used and amount of use.

Regular metals

Mild steel is commonly used for diesel exhaust systems; copper for other types. Flexibility is provided by a section of special rubber piping with a wet system, or segmented stainless steel for a dry system. If flanged connections are held by brass bolts, these can work loose with vibration and may need occasional tightening. Any steel bolts need a good coating of graphite grease before assembly.

Red hot

A dry exhaust (usual for an air-cooled engine) needs

thick lagging to reduce radiation and to prevent injury and fire damage. Asbestos tape or rope is often used to lag the short red hot part of a wet system. Lagging restricts the inspection of pipework. It also absorbs moisture, the steam from which looks like exhaust leakage when starting up. Most pre-formed pipe lagging will not stand exhaust heat. Asbestos wool is now considered a health hazard, but mineral wool (with an outer layer of glass cloth sewn into place) has a long life.

Silencing

Water injection reduces noise by cooling the gases, and enables a neoprene muffler to be fitted near the outlet (Fig. 110). Injection bends often corrode and need annual inspection. A coolant thermometer is advantageous to give warning of circulation failure. A waterlock silencer is intended to be fitted at the lowest point in a system and below the waterline. All other types must be as high as possible. Most dry silencers are of the straight-through perforated tube type, packed internally with mineral wool. Proper marine ones need no maintenance until they break up with old age. However, if used with engines requiring oil to be added to the fuel (see page 172), bad carbon fouling can occur after less than 1000 hours.

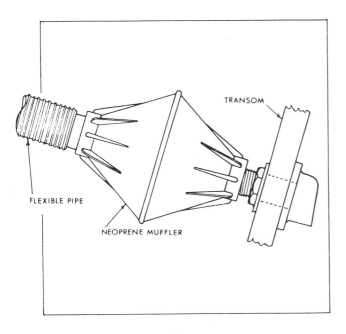

Fig. 110 Neoprene muffler on wet exhaust system.

Back flow

Make sure you do not have a badly designed installation which allows water to splash up the exhaust pipe and into the engine. A swan-neck near the outlet (Fig. 111) works well, but when there is insufficient space for this, you may find a seacock or an external flap valve. Some owners insert a bung of wood or rag. This is a good idea when laid up afloat, but is a nuisance when in commission.

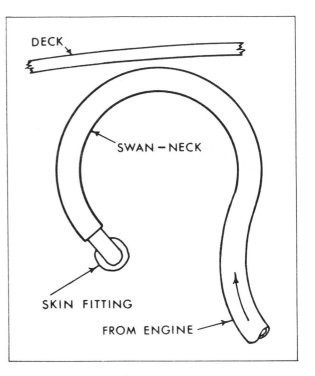

Fig. 111 Swan-neck to prevent water flowing back to engine.

Draining

When antifreezing precautions are necessary, always drain a wet exhaust system. If there is no drain cock at the lowest point and under the silencer, run the engine for several minutes with the water cut off. Discounting frost damage, a damp exhaust system invites corrosion when laid up.

Ignition

The problems of moisture on ignition equipment are

being overcome by modern electronic and capacitor discharge systems, but these cannot be amateur-maintained at minimal cost like the traditional systems. With the latter, spark plugs, condenser, contact breaker and high tension leads must always be in first-class order. An aerosol can of demoisturizing spray is useful, but there are times when you may need to put all the offending parts in a slow oven before getting an engine to start!

HT leads
For neatness, the plug leads of some engines run through a fore-and-aft duct. This can be troublesome when damp, and may have to be scrapped. The best procedure with old leads is to renew them before trouble starts. Use the same type of cable as originally fitted, which is more likely to be copper-cored than carbon-cored. Identifying insulation cracks is not always easy. Early renewal removes all doubt and also ensures that cable ends are made fast properly.

Suppression
Spark plug ignition causes most radio interference trouble, but static from tanks and drive belts (plus signals from fluorescent lights and motors) are likely culprits on boats driven by diesels. Make sure that tanks, fuel filler plates, engines and shafts, are bonded to ground plates (Fig. 10) or through-hulls. If baffled, call in a marine radio expert.

Distributor
Failure to start (or uneven running) is sometimes caused by barely visible cracks in a distributor cap. It pays to keep a spare one. Number the lead sockets to avoid connecting them to the wrong spark plugs – a possible cause of carburettor flare-up on starting. When spraying against moisture, remember to treat the inside of the cap as well as the outside. A contact breaker cam needs a touch of grease. An advance/retard mechanism (and the impulse trip on a magneto) needs a touch of light oil.

Timing
When removing a magneto or distributor for winter lay-up or repair, mark the vernier coupling or dog to ensure correct timing on replacement. When the whole drive shaft has been removed, re-set the sprocket in accordance with the workshop manual, then use a dwell meter to set the contact breaker opening precisely. The injection pump on a diesel must, of course, be timed with the same accuracy.

Firing stroke
If you can decipher the marks on the rim of a (perhaps rusty or painted) flywheel, these may include valve events, contact breaker opening position, top-dead-centre (TDC), plus a reference pointer. The TDC marks refers to no. 1 piston at top of stroke, but remember that this position is reached twice in every cycle on a four-stroke engine. You need the firing stroke for ignition or injection timing – easily identified as both valves are closed, and air is blown forcibly out of the spark plug or injector hole before TDC. No. 1 piston is at the for'ard end of most marine engines.

Starting gear

Small marine engines need brief but rapid rotation for reliable and immediate starting. With a neglected battery, or in cold weather, you may not get enough urge to effect firing without special aids (see later). Big diesels start on compressed air. This is most reliable provided leakage is prevented and the pressure tanks are kept fully charged. Similarly, percussion cartridge starters are foolproof, but rarely found on yachts.

Handle
Nowadays, hand starting gear is mainly used on charter sailboat diesel auxiliary engines to eliminate the need for batteries. Overhead gear is sometimes difficult of access in the confines of small craft and extended shafting (with a bearing through the bulkhead) may well prove a worthwhile modification. Such equipment requires little attention except oil on the bearings and pawls, and graphite grease on the chain. When there is no provision for adjusting the chain tension, renewal is often the best way to eliminate slackness due to wear.

Inertia starters
These include hand-wound flywheels or springs which are clutched in to provide high starting torque, and the *handraulic* type, where fluid is hand-pumped under pressure, then discharged through a rack and pinion mechanism on the crankshaft end. Lubrication is the thing to watch, plus keeping nuts tight and fluid level correct.

Starter motor
On land, an electric starter motor rarely receives attention until it fails. At sea, maintenance is more important. Cleaning and lightly oiling the Bendix

drive prevents jamming, while greasing bearings, cleaning commutator, freeing brushes, cleaning connections, checking solenoid and tightening bolts are not too much of a chore if done every two years.

Aids to starting

Reluctant engines have been around for a long time! Except for cold and damp weather, there are several common faults leading to starting failure, well detailed in most makers' fault-finding charts. With decompressors, excess fuel levers, glow plugs or intake heaters, most marine diesels are well equipped for easy starting. Aerosol cans of ether (for spraying into the air intake as an engine is turned) work well if the air filter is first removed, but excessive use can prove harmful. An impulse magneto has a trigger device to produce fat sparks at slow speed. If you cannot hear the click, it may just need oiling. Although rarely seen nowadays, a Kigass pump acts like an easy-start aerosol, but is a permanently built-in fitting.

Pre-heating

Although modern diesels often utilize electrical heaters for inlet manifold or combustion chambers, cylinder plugs containing chemicals which glow on compression are still used. A faulty electric glow plug (when wired in series) can create starting trouble. On removing such plugs to check whether they glow, be careful to apply the correct voltage, which may be only 2 volts on a 6-cylinder engine. If a faulty plug is shorted out to get started, reduce the heating period as much as possible to prevent overloading the good plugs.

Electrics

Effective batteries are the heart of engine-room electrics, so their maintenance and system of charging must never be neglected. Nowadays, all except the smallest outboard motors have battery starting, often plus complex electrically-operated remote controls, including a tilting device with trim angle indicator, gearshift, choke, telltale lamp for charging failure, and sound alarm for cooling water stoppage. Although marine electrical equipment is designed to resist moisture damage, its reliability is safeguarded by storing in a dry place ashore during a winter lay-up period.

Dynamo

The faithful old d.c. generator has been known to function for 5000 hours without attention. However, the wise owner will strip down a dynamo after not more than 2000 hours to grease or renew bearings, to polish the commutator and to fit new brushes. Testing, rewinding, and skimming commutators are generally jobs for the professionals. Rapid bearing wear could be caused by keeping the drive belt too tight.

Alternator

Although it is the standard generator on car and marine engines today, the alternator has delicate electronic controls. Deep sea yachts carry spare rectifiers and diodes – often a complete unit. Take care not to disconnect any terminals (or change batteries) while charging, or to switch off a diesel before the stop control has brought the engine to a standstill. The cut-outs and regulators intended for charging engine starter batteries are inefficient for dealing with the ship's deep-cycle service batteries. For this you need a so-called smart regulator which cuts down the alternator current only when the batteries are 100% charged. A smart regulator can reduce greatly the hours needed to be run by a noisy charging set.

Controls

Cut-outs and voltage regulators can fail unless kept free from corrosion and moisture. Except for sealed units, all switch contacts, fuses, terminals and circuit breakers need coating with Vaseline or petroleum jelly. Some sprayed inhibitor fluids are insulators and prevent low tension contacts from functioning properly. Always keep panel switches labelled. Borrow a *Dymo* or *Rotex* tool for this if you cannot afford ready-made tablet labels. Make sure you know what everything does and how to start the engine should the solenoid fail, or if the starting key gets lost. Pass this information on to other crew members. Useful data on charging panels and other electrical equipment is given in *Boat Repairs and Conversions*.

Charging set

It is not only luxury yachts that have a generating plant for charging batteries in port when no shore supply is available: portable sets have long been made which find a place on small cruising boats. Beware the air and noise pollution problem with any type of charging set. Makers' maintenance requirements are normally minimal, but try to keep a log of hours run to help avoid neglect.

Plate 86 Electrical power for free.
a windmill type generator. **b** solar
panel.

Free energy
Solar panels and wind-driven generators (Plate 86) will trickle charge your batteries whenever conditions are suitable. Trolling types rotate under water while a boat is sailing, or is anchored in a strong tidal current. Except for problems with weed, they are virtually maintenance-free.

Self-steering
Both motor-operated automatic pilots and wind vane self-steering gears need some lubrication. The latter should be immobilized by removing the vane when not in use, to avoid accidental damage, wear, and theft.

Battery types

Small craft manage with a single car battery for engine starting and for running a few lights. Big craft have multiple banks with spare capacity and changeover devices giving charging priority to the engine starting bank. Batteries made especially for boats are expensive, either lead/calcium sealed units, or with extended vents to prevent spillage under way. Metal cased alkali batteries are almost indestructible, but they are heavier and much more expensive than the common lead/acid variety. Vehicle batteries are fine for engine starting, but the deep-cycle types you really need for lights, pumps, refrigerator and fans are more costly.

Battery care

In soft water areas, many people use household water for topping up batteries. When in doubt, use de-ionized or distilled water, stocked by filling stations and pharmacies. Battery tops must always be kept clean and dry. White corrosion will not form if all terminals are kept tight and liberally smeared with Vaseline. The same applies to all low tension connections.

Battery life

Keeping batteries well away from the heat of an engine helps prevent premature breakdown. Frequent slow discharge to about half capacity, followed by a slow charge, creates the healthiest conditions, as detailed on page 249. The need for frequent topping up is often a sign of pending breakdown. A direct reading battery state indicator is useful. If you use a separate hydrometer, wash it well after use and stow it carefully in a padded box.

Caution

Batteries produce explosive hydrogen, so keep flames and lighted cigarettes away from them. Do not put batteries in an airtight casing, but provide a lid sufficient to prevent tools and other metal objects from falling across the terminals and starting a fire. Acid in the bilges can cause great damage, so a drip tray or box lined with stainless steel, lead, zinc, or PVC is well worth installing. Batten down all batteries to prevent movement, even if the ship should turn turtle!

Electronic experts

Added to compass and chart, a depth sounder is perhaps the most valuable navigational aid for day-sailing. Of the dozen or so additional electronic wonders designed mainly to help racing, safety and landfall accuracy, radar is the one that definitely deserves an expert installation check and adjustment. Other electronics might include RDF, fluxgate compass, VHF or SSB, Decca/Loran/GPS, radar detector, speed/log/wind/VMG, autopilot, chartplotter, fishfinder, Navtex/Weatherfax, gas detector and bilge-water sensor. Some makers of these may also require their agents to vet amateur installations for warranty purposes.

Go carefully

For do-it-yourself wiring, grounding and mounting, keep the following in mind:

● New equipment arrives with full instructions and the correct cable, terminals and couplers for each connection. A unit without these is probably stolen property.

● Good sets can cope with wide voltage fluctuations and surges. Cheaper products may require in-line stabilizers and surge suppressors, plus wiring direct from battery. If polarity is critical, remember that any needle voltmeter will kick backwards unless connected positive to positive.

● As equipment is added, check for compass deviation and interference with other wizardry. A fluxgate compass should not be affected.

● Seek advice from experts when modifications are desired, such as adding twin transducer changeover switches, repeater dials, interfacing the autopilot, a forward-seeking sounder mode, or audible alarms for windshift, low voltage, dangerous depth, weather reports, intruders or bilge-water state.

● On a secondhand boat, make sure you have all relevant manuals, detailing wiring, screening, cable glands, transducer voltage limitations, built-in emergency batteries and desiccators, also correct whip aerial lengths.

● Site separate antennas well away from each other and from the rigging. A backstay (with insulators) makes an inconspicuous aerial for some MF and HF radio equipment.

● Make sure that cockpit, flybridge, or mast-mounted electronics are fully waterproofed.

● Run twin cable to each appliance. Avoid the use of grounded returns as used on cars.

● If in doubt, leave any installation or repair job to an expert.

10
General Mechanics

As well as with engines, you need to be a jump ahead of trouble with all the other mechanical equipment found on modern boats. From factory-worker to accountant, amateur sailors often acquire the knack of smelling trouble in good time.

What to expect

Even on sailing dinghies you find small items of mechanical equipment, including self-bailers, snubbing winches, drop keel and boom vang (kicking strap), winches, shroud and forestay adjusters, trailer and launching trolley, mast step slide and jack, rudder pivots, cam cleats and clutch stoppers.

Sophistication
In addition to the above, bigger craft sport electronics, wiring with cut-outs, fuses and switches, vane or electric self-steering gear, reverse osmosis or evaporator, plumbing, pumps, sheet and halyard winches, telescopic boom vang, space heating and cooling equipment, windlass, rotating log, tracks and slides, adjustable fairleads, runner levers and backstay tensioner. Some swing keels weigh over a ton, with complex hydraulic ram control. You need to remember which equipment requires in-season maintenance, and keep the relevant literature on board.

Corrosion
Mechanical matters are closely tied to the use of metals, many types of which corrode only too easily under salty (or merely damp) conditions. Even stainless steel corrodes under certain marine conditions, and the die-cast and chromium-plated parts used on some modern equipment need protection (such as regular wax polishing) for survival.

Electrolytic action
Water or spray containing any impurity – especially salt – forms a crude battery when covering two or more dissimilar metals (at least up to arm's length apart), causing corrosion. This electrolytic (galvanic) action needs to be carefully watched everywhere on a boat. The severity of the problem depends on proximity, temperature, types of metal, and the degree of salinity.

Galvanic series
In the crude battery, some metals invariably take on the role of cathode, while those forming anodes are the most likely to get eaten away. Table 9 lists most marine metals in sequence from strongest anodic to strongest cathodic.

Severity
Metals near the top of the list corrode most rapidly when forming a battery with metals near the bottom. The closer they appear in the series, the slower the action. The uppermost one corrodes, while the lower one is protected.

Cathodic protection
Making use of the series given in Table 9, underwater protection is readily given to all metals by

Table 9

Galvanic series
for most boat metals

BASE END – ANODIC   Pure zinc
Galvanized steel
Cadmium plate
Pure aluminium
Light alloy
Mild steel
Cast iron
Stainless steel (active)
Babbitt metal
Lead
Manganese bronze
Common brass
Copper
Silicon bronze
Gunmetal
Nickel
Monel
Stainless steel (passive)
Chromium plate
NOBLE END – CATHODIC   Graphite

INCREASING NOBILITY

Plate 87 Only pure sailboats get by without at least one sacrificial anode to protect submerged metal.

fixing one or more sacrificial zinc anodes (Plates 87 and 81(c)) to the hull. These are eaten away in preference to other metals, and are renewed when exhausted. Marine stores sell zincs of various shapes and sizes, including ones to clamp around a propeller shaft or rudder stock (Plate 88), and ones that are dangled overboard (on the end of a wire cable) when a craft is moored up. You will also find anodes in unexpected places, such as in engine water jackets, oil coolers, and heat exchangers.

Continuous circuit
For nearly a century, small squares of zinc have been screwed onto boat hulls to protect important metals. A superior form of zinc is used for today's sacrificial anodes, which does not become shielded by white oxides. They are through-bolted to the hull, with flexible wiring (12-gauge or $6\,mm^2$) bonding to tank fillers, through-hulls and sterngear – also across flexible shaft couplings. Note that magnesium alloy anodes are often used instead of zinc in fresh water. Consult a specialist if you have problems, especially with a metal hull.

Protective paint
Thorough paintwork forms an excellent protection against all types of corrosion, but is not completely reliable. Watch that nobody puts antifouling paint on top of your sacrificial anodes! Remember that scratched paintwork on a light alloy hull could lead to local corrosion more vigorous than with the entire hull surface left bare. It would not be a good idea to moor a bare alloy hull alongside one with copper-based antifouling or copper sheathing.

Stray current
Devastating electrolysis (particularly in metal hulls) sometimes results from leaky electric wiring insulation, or faulty equipment. The best cure for this is to isolate batteries and shore supplies with master switches when a craft is unattended. Minute stray currents in reverse are used to good effect on some big vessels which utilize the so-called *imposed current* cathodic protection system.

Stainless steel
Nothing is perfect, and certain types of stainless steel are not immune to corrosion, as indicated by the active position in the above table. The main cause is known as *crevice corrosion*, which occurs where two pieces of the same metal are riveted together or in close contact. Also, curiously enough, within rubber bearings, or on through-hull fastenings where no oxygen exists.

Blade damage
Except for cavitation (see page 166), bronze propellers rarely corrode if protected by an anode.

Plate 88 A spherical anode clamped around a propeller shaft.

Coating with hard antifouling paint helps further, and also prevents barnacle growth (Plate 81(b)) when a boat sits idle in the water for long periods.

Cover it

A good way to minimize galvanic corrosion to the fastenings of a planked or plywood hull is to sheath it with fibreglass or nylon (see Chapter 5). Above the waterline, metal parts are best protected with paint, varnish, anhydrous lanoline, underwater grease, or car chrome protection lacquer. Regular polishing will keep verdigris off brasswork. This is laborious, but yacht varnish ruins the appearance of bright metal, while clear permanent exterior metal lacquer is difficult to buy in small quantities.

Pumps

Sailing dinghies manage to drain their bilges by means of self-bailers, transom flaps, bungs, scoops, and sponges. Even the smallest keelboats and motor tenders have at least one bilge pump. A twin engined motorsailer could have as many as eighteen pumps of various types on board, including: four on each engine for cooling, fuel and sump pump; one hand and one mechanical bilge pump; two on the heads; three for water supply (fresh hot and cold, plus sea water); perhaps a deck-wash pump, an inflator for the rubber dinghy, and a hydraulic windlass pump.

Repairs

Few pumps ever wear out completely. The few wearing parts involved are normally easy to maintain or renew. The need for expertise arises when trying to fix obsolete pumps (or certain modern imports) for which no spare parts or instruction sheets are available. Some boatyard employees are particularly good at fixing troublesome pumps, but the bill may be higher than the cost of a new pump!

Bilge duties

A hand-operated bilge pump needs to be of ample capacity. Any type will do – semi-rotary, plunger, diaphragm, bucket, or geared centrifugal – but always choose a new one with the facility for cleaning debris from valves in a few seconds. Engine-driven and electric bilge pumps are popular on cruising boats, but such craft need at least two separate systems for dealing with bilge water in an emergency.

Semi-rotaries

Pictured in Plate 89(a), the familiar old semi-rotary pump contains two inlet and outlet flap valves to give a continuous flow. These pumps have a long life if dismantled and greased at laying-up time, but except for re-pinning the valves and re-packing the stuffing-boxes, they are not easy for the amateur to overhaul once bearings and suction faces have worn.

Diaphragms

The mechanism of a diaphragm pump (Plate 89(b)) is on the dry side of the oscillating membrane, eliminating the need for a gland. Some handles are of plastics and can break, but the only spare part you normally need is a replacement diaphragm. Should the diaphragm split (and you have no spare), cover both sides temporarily with pieces cut from an old foul weather suit or a thick plastic food wrapper. Double-acting types still need no gland, for the small amount of rod movement can be absorbed by a flexible gaiter.

Plungers

A brass single-acting plunger pump (Plate 89(c)) lasts a long time, but the valve at the bottom of the

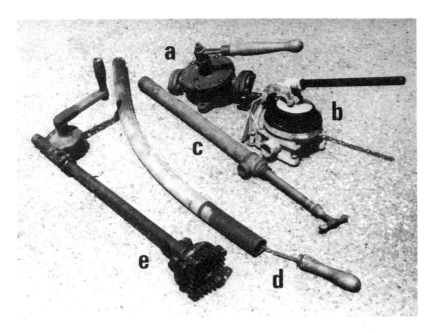

Plate 89 Some portable and fixed bilge pumps. **a** semi-rotary. **b** diaphragm. **c** vertical plunger. **d** flexible plunger. **e** Vortex centrifugal.

barrel (and to a lesser extent the valve inside the plunger) is usually difficult to clear of debris. Double-acting and differential pumps deliver an almost continuous stream. They have solid pistons and look similar to Plate 89(c). To prevent leakage caused by metal-to-metal wear, some plungers have renewable seals of leather, neoprene, or rubber, or packing (like a gland) wound into a central groove.

Bucket types
The ancient bucket pump (set flush into the deck) is not to be despised. With the barrel top open, water flows away over the deck. Most barrels are big enough to allow your hand inside for clearing the bottom clapper. Clearing the plunger valve is easy, as the assembly pulls straight out. Beware of losing it overboard!

A variation on the same principle is the dinghy hose pump seen in Plate 89(d). The 1¼ in (32 mm) bore hose has a rubber valve at the bottom and another in the plunger. The latter is attached to a length of stiff wire rope with a handle at the other end. Water is discharged from the open end, duly held over the gunwale.

Impellers
Power pumps are generally of the centrifugal or vane (Jabsco) type. The Vortex (see Plate 89e) is a geared-up hand bilge pump working on this principle. Having no valves, impeller pumps fail mainly

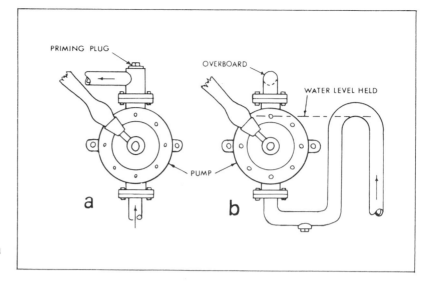

Fig. 112 Priming devices for a worn pump.

because of leaky seals or glands. The average sailor can usually fit the necessary parts from the makers' kit without much trouble. Big axial flow impeller pumps are used for main engine water jet propulsion units (Plate 83) or bow thrusters. Jabsco neoprene impellers can stick when left dry, causing damage when started. The makers recommend filling with glycerine at laying-up time. If the cover plate is removed to obviate freezing in cold climates, glycerine can be brushed in and the pump rotated a few times.

Hydraulics
The vane and swash pumps used for main propulsion or winch drives (also the actuating pumps and rams for controlling drop keel, gearbox, rudder, or trim planes) are best renewed as exchange units when trouble arises. Bleeding, topping-up the fluid, renewing hoses and lubricating linkages, is similar to the maintenance of brakes and power steering on a car.

Strum box
Choked valves are a rarity with an efficient strum box (strainer) at the bottom end of a bilge pump suction pipe. However, too fine a gauze will need constant clearing. Most pump valves will tolerate a certain amount of small debris. A foot valve next to the strum box is not normally essential, but it does keep a column of water in the suction pipe, and assists priming.

Priming
Unless faulty, plunger and diaphragm pumps start to deliver without delay. Centrifugal and impeller pumps prime themselves most reliably when submerged. Semi-rotaries are often fitted with a plug on top (Fig. 112(a)), enabling water to be poured in before starting. A suction pipe swan-neck (Fig. 112(b)) will retain water inside any type of pump and provide instant priming. Short and rapid starting strokes will generally prime a reluctant hand pump more readily than slow, long strokes.

Poppet valves
Some hand- and engine-driven plunger pumps have circular metal valves and seatings. The small amount of grinding-in that such valves normally need is best done with metal polish such as *Brasso* or *Brite Boy*. Standard grinding paste is far too coarse for bronze. Examine each face under a magnifying glass. If too pitted for Brasso, get some 1000-grit Carborundum powder and dab this on after smearing oil or grease onto the face. A damaged valve face must be skimmed on a lathe. A damaged seating usually means having to return the pump to its maker.

Grease
Most pumps without grease or oil points are not intended to be lubricated, but a smear of grease on plunger rods (and on any steel parts which could

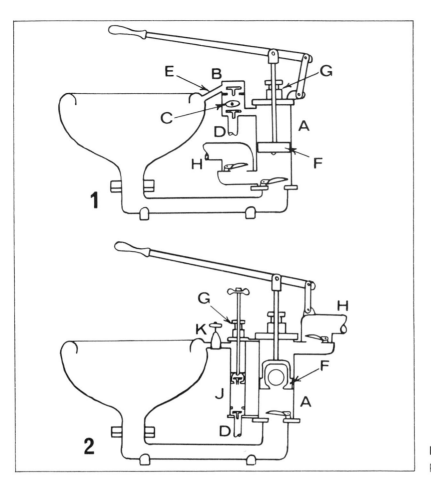

Fig. 113 Two patterns of hand-pumped yacht toilets.

rust) does nothing but good. Watch that the dirt which accumulates on such parts is not likely to soil clothing – especially in the case of heads with plunger pumps.

Toilet treatment

The regulations on waterways and at marinas often prohibit the dumping overboard of crude sewage, enforcing the use of holding tanks, chlorinator/macerator equipment, or chemical heads, instead of traditional direct hand-pumped or electric yacht toilets.

Hand pumping

For over fifty years, the methods outlined in Fig. 113 have been popular for hand-operated toilets. Method 1 uses one double-acting pump A, the lower part of which handles the soil discharge, while the upper part pumps sea water to flush the bowl, via the valve chest B. The cam C is connected to a lever (or pedal) marked ON and OFF. The cam stops the flow of flushing water by raising the top valve and holding the lower one on its seating. Pipe D is the flushing water intake, and pipe E the delivery to the bowl rim. F is the pump plunger, G the gland, and H the soil discharge. Most of the earlier Simpson-Lawrence and Wilcox-Crittenden toilets work on this principle.

Other systems

The popular Baby Blake uses separate single-acting pumps (Fig. 113, method 2). The soil pump A has a bucket-type plunger (Plate 90), the valve within it consisting of a rubber-covered metal ball resting on a bronze seating. As well as the normal flap valve at the base of the pump, an extra valve is fitted in the outlet pipe H to prevent siphoning back in case some paper jams the other valve partly open. Wilcox-

Plate 90 Toilet soil pump plunger stripped down.

Crittenden use a joker valve (see later) for this job, plus a vacuum-breaking valve at the highest part of the discharge pipe. The smaller pump J draws flushing water through suction pipe D, with a stopcock at K for below-waterline installations.

Some models have a flushing pump operated by foot pedal. Other modern toilets utilize a large diaphragm pump (see Fig. 114), including the SL 400 and the Lavac. The latter has a sealed seat and lid to draw in flushing water by vacuum. Electrically-pumped heads often incorporate a macerator unit – a great advantage, even when not required by law. Push-button operation is provided on the PAR model in the USA. Most electric toilets are foot-pedal operated.

In season
Keep everything clean and use a drop of oil on the pivots occasionally. Sea water disinfects, but when chemicals or cleaners are required, use only the types recommended by the makers. Keeping seacocks closed at night and when ashore is a sound habit to acquire.

Lay-up
If you can find time, unship a toilet every four years or so, to check for faulty valves, worn parts, and leaks. Touch up chipped or dirty paintwork before replacing. Drain against frost by disconnecting unions, syringeing out the bowl, and working the

pumps. Some makers supply a lay-up fluid which keeps plunger washers supple and lubricates pump bores.

Unshipping
If steel base bolts have rusted solid, saw the nuts off, using a hacksaw blade in a pad handle for the more awkward ones. Next time, use bronze or stainless steel bolts. Scrape any paint from the backs of union nuts before freeing them. A slight tightening with the wrench before unscrewing helps to prevent damage and to release the thread bond. If not of stainless steel, hose clamps may have to be cut off. A few toilets (such as the Hydra) have nylon-coated light alloy basins, but the majority use vitreous china which needs handling with care. Apply protection against the risk of dropped tools.

Spare parts
You may find obsolete models on old yachts, but otherwise spare parts are easy to obtain. Improvising or substituting parts from other makes will overcome some problems on old models, perhaps with the exception of the leather or rubber cup washers for pump plungers. These are difficult to make satisfactorily, and failure to get them could lead to the scrapping of an otherwise good old toilet.

Overhauls
Some makers will carry out complete overhauls, including the reboring of pumps. Get a quotation

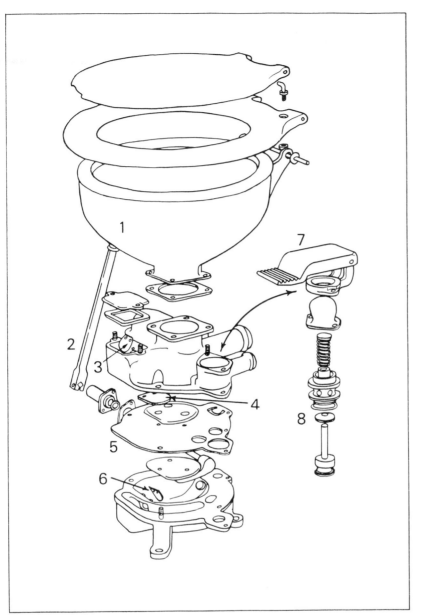

Fig. 114 Exploded view of toilet with single diaphragm pump.
Key 1 Pan; 2 Pumping lever; 3 Soil discharge valve; 4 Soil inlet valve; 5 Pump diaphragm; 6 Flushing inlet valve; 7 Control pedal; 8 Control valve.

first, as a new toilet may prove a better investment. However, unless you can install this yourself, the inevitable modifications to pipework could prove expensive. Start repairs early in the off-season to allow plenty of time for ordering or making any necessary parts. Try to test everything on shore (by connecting to a water tank), to make sure there are no problems.

Pump faults

The maintenance of plunger or diaphragm toilet pumps is similar to the procedure for bilge pumps (see page 189). Worn plunger washers (see Plate 90) and leaky or stiff valves are the most likely causes of moody pumps. The plunger itself normally comes apart to enable new cup washers to be fitted.

Plunger rod

Pump action will never be smooth if the rod is worn. If the gland is tightened to prevent leakage at mid-stroke, the rod may jam in the gland towards each end. By cutting accurate threads at the ends, most replacement rods can be formed from standard brass bar without the use of a lathe. Such jobs become increasingly difficult as metric measurements take over from the inch in Britain.

Pivots

Lever-operated pumps (as in Fig. 113) often have three pivot points which become sloppy with wear if not oiled regularly. Fitting new clevis pins or bolts does not take long, but if the bearing holes are worn oval, the clever handyman can ream these and fit bushes or oversize pins. Do not delay this. Once started, wear increases rapidly.

Flap valves

Generally noiseless and free from jamming, soil pump flap valves (Plate 91) are easy to repair. They are either made from sheet rubber with a small weight screwed on top, or the weight incorporates metal hinges, with a disc of rubber underneath to form the seal. Double pinned hinges with a short link between are sometimes used to enable the clapper to lift bodily when passing an obstruction.

Ball types

About the same size as a table tennis ball (Plate 92), the spherical weight used in some soil pumps is either of brass working on a renewable rubber seating, or of rubber covered lead working on a metal seating. Similar valves using smaller stainless steel balls are used on some flushing pumps.

Joker valves

Like a rubber bag, open to full bore at one end and with a slit across the other end, a joker valve (or reed valve) is a simple and reliable form of non-return valve used on some marine toilets. No maintenance is possible, and as the cost of a replacement is modest, it pays to keep some spare ones in stock.

Instructions

Landlubbers rarely know how to operate the heads. Suitable instructions (home-made, if not supplied by the makers) stuck to the bulkhead save a lot of embarrassment and reduce the likelihood of break-down. As well as explaining the controls, instructions should stress the need for ample flushing, should warn against the use of harmful disinfectants or

Plate 91 Flap valve at base of soil pump.

Plate 92 Soil valve consisting of a bronze ball on a rubber seating.

cleaners and against using the toilet to dispose of oil and galley waste, or forcing the pumps when the seacocks are turned off.

Holding tank

Where regulations demand it, any pumped toilet can be directed via a two-way valve to discharge into a holding tank while in port. The introduction of a macerator between the two improves the efficiency. All necessary equipment is particularly easy to obtain in America. Flexible or rigid tanks are available, ranging in size from 40 to 120 litres. A holding tank is completely sealed except for an overboard vent pipe and a discharge connection which is hand- or power-pumped via a changeover valve, to allow emptying at sea or to an onshore sewage installation. Keep the vent well away from its fresh water counterpart! Gauge the contents by viewing rigid translucent polyethylene or feeling flexible hypalon. See pages 206–209 for further details of tanks.

Deodorizer

Especially in the USA, marine hardware stores keep Permanent Toilet Deodorant. One litre is flushed into the empty tank to deal with every 80 litres of full capacity.

Macerator

Toilet discharge cannot be reduced to an innocent liquid without strong chemicals or an electric macerator. Some electric heads (with foot-operated switch) have a macerator attached. A chlorinator feeding to the macerator disinfects and deodorizes the effluent automatically, provided its fluid tank is kept filled. Unless subject to a motor failure, a macerator (like a household food waste disposer) should enjoy a trouble-free and maintenance-free life.

Skin fittings

To fit an intake or overboard discharge pipe (above or below the waterline) you need a through-hull fitting. This may be like a large hollow bolt with backnut, or flanged to receive four or more through-bolts (see page 180). The traditional bronze ones remain as popular as the cheaper plastic varieties, especially for moulding into fibreglass hulls.

Fracturing

On steel hulls, skin fittings are often welded directly to the plating, and vigilance is necessary to ensure that no corrosion occurs at these points. Cheap brass fittings can become weak in sea water, and then break off unexpectedly. The same applies to through-hull bolts, so it pays to drive one out every five years for examination. Some fittings protrude a long way inboard, and are vulnerable to damage if people tread on them, or if a heavy object (such as a spare anchor) falls on them. Most skin fittings are attached to pipework, but similar devices are used to house retractable speed/log impellers or pitot tubes.

Pads

Most yacht hulls need a reinforcing pad of hardwood or marine plywood on the inside, to prevent local stresses (and consequent leaks) where a skin fitting passes through. This is especially important on thin hulls. With fibreglass, a glassed-in plywood pad is not so sound as a solid fibreglass blister, as water may get into the wood via the bored hole and cause expansion or rot. When renewing a skin fitting, make sure that you have an adequate pad, and that its concealed face is properly bedded in mastic to prevent rot.

Vigilance

Because of timber shrinkage, nuts may need tightening, especially on newish craft. Never let a fitting rotate to break its seal through the hull. Hold the threaded body with a pipe wrench (preferably over thin packing of copper or lead) while tightening a backnut. Be suspicious of discoloration due to seepage or electrolysis. Make sure all nuts are tight before bashing a skin fitting with a mallet to test for brittleness, otherwise you could break the seal.

External attention

Blistered paint around the outside of a skin fitting usually means corrosion, though it could be due to overheating around an engine exhaust pipe. The latter situation needs action if the exhaust system is a dry one. With a wet exhaust, the trouble probably occurred through a one-time temporary water circulation failure. Consult a marine engineer concerning the insulation of a dry exhaust skin fitting. Inlet strainers with bars or holes sometimes get choked with barnacles and often need removing for effective clearance. Paint the insides of open pipes below the waterline with antifouling to check marine growth.

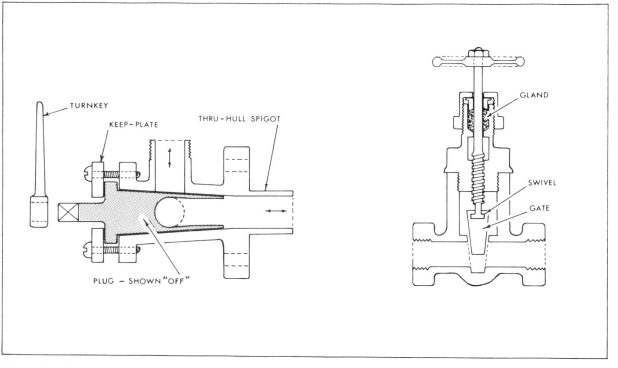

Fig. 115 Seacock with tapered plug core.

Fig. 116 Inside a gate valve, with gate half open.

Seacocks

The full-flow barrel-type seacock (Fig. 115) is preferred for toilet soil outlets, engine exhausts and cockpit drains. Instead of the tapered barrel, some modern seacocks have a stainless steel sphere, bored centrally to provide full-flow opening. Fitted with nylon or neoprene seatings, these valves have a long, maintenance-free life. Gunmetal or bronze gate valves (Fig. 116) are commonly used on all other pipework. Even brass domestic ones are (unwisely) used on many skin fittings above the waterline, such as sink waste outlets.

Barrel stripping
It only takes five minutes to strip down the average toilet seacock. The parts are shown in Fig. 115. On some American cocks, a thrust plate is fitted at the back of the barrel, as on most small fuel tank cocks. Grind in the tapered barrel with nothing coarser than metal polish. Buff the keep plate and its seating with a power mop. Smear all surfaces lightly with underwater grease. Some seacocks have greasers built in.

Broken screws
A small propane torch helps to ease obstinate screws or nuts. Even an electric soldering iron held on the head for several minutes might work. If a seacock keep plate screw shears off during removal, it should be possible to drill and re-tap for a new screw without unshipping the whole valve. Although similar in appearance, different threads are used in different countries. For instance, no. 12, with 24 threads per inch on an American seacock, is equivalent to ¼ in Whitworth in Britain and 6 mm isometric in France. If you cannot borrow the correct tap, you may have to use screws a size larger and get the appropriate tap to suit them.

Gate stripping
The stem thread and the body thread (see Fig. 116) can fight each other and cause damage when dismantling a gate valve, so make sure both parts are free to move all the time. The gate is tapered to shut firmly when right down. Should it leak, a new valve is the best solution. The only maintenance requirements are underwater grease on the stem, its thread, and the gate swivel, plus gland tightening

and re-packing when necessary. Globe valves intended for steam work can be ground in, and some have renewable seatings. They look similar to gate valves, cost about three times as much, and have internal constrictions.

Accessibility

Some seacocks are so difficult to reach that they never get turned off or properly maintained. If a gate valve is involved, shifting its position is usually simple by introducing one or more elbows of various angles, perhaps coupled with a short straight pipe. Clip the seacock to a chock if there is any risk of damage from heavy footsteps.

Modifications

Skin fittings are not often wrongly sited, but alterations are called for when an engine-cooling water intake sucks air with the boat heeling, or when a toilet flushes foul water because its skin fittings are located too close together. To avoid having to seal the hull, some owners cap off an old fitting but leave it in place for possible future use.

Being close to the waterline, galley sinks and self-draining cockpits sometimes receive back-flow at an angle of heel. The cockpit problem is usually cured by simply fitting flaps of sheet rubber across the

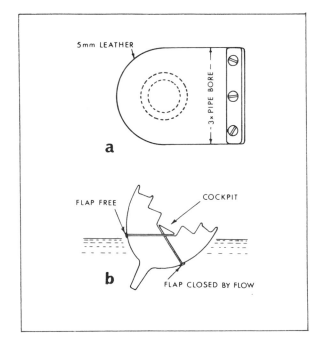

Fig. 117 Methods for preventing back-flow in cockpit drains.

outlets, as in Fig. 117(a), or crossing the pipes as in Fig. 117(b), or both. The sink problem is usually better solved by adding a plumber's non-return valve inside the hull.

Identification

Labels on cocks are normally only needed when you get three or more close together on a distribution manifold, such as where one seacock serves a deck-wash supply, galley pump, engine cooling, desalinator inlet and bilge discharge. However, ON/OFF labels are handy on some full-flow seacocks partly hidden from view.

Plumbing repairs

In addition to domestic galvanized, copper, stainless steel and plastic pipework and fittings, your boat may have various types of flexible hose, plus the special range of metal tubing and unions used on engines. The practical owner of a big boat is sure to become an accomplished plumber with the amount of alteration and renewal which normally goes on aboard such craft!

Copper tubing

With a hired or borrowed lever-operated bending machine, domestic copper tubing is easily shaped, so that joining mid-way is only necessary when long lengths cannot be fed under or behind obstructions. A hand-turned pipe cutter is smoother and quicker than a hacksaw for trimming ends, and no swarf gets inside the pipe. Domestic stainless steel pipe is used in the same way as copper, and uses similar fittings.

Brass fittings

Plumbers like the quickness of compression fittings (Plate 93(a)), though the capillary or solder types (Plate 93(b)) are cheaper and neater. To fit the former, slip the nut over the pipe, feed on the olive (sealing ring) as in Plate 94, then screw up the nut with a wrench while holding firmly the body of the fitting, and making sure the pipe end stays fully inserted. When breaking such a joint and reconnecting, clean the olive and smear it with jointing paste to avert leakage.

Soldering

The secret of success with solder (pronounced *sodder* by engineers) is to clean the outside of the pipe and the inside of the fitting body (including the outer

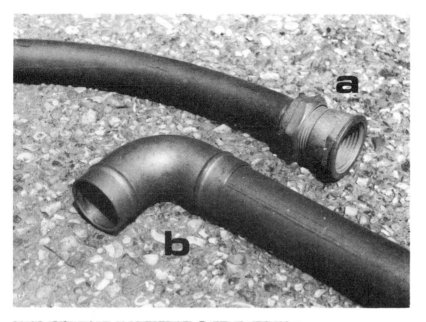

Plate 93 a compression fitting attached to copper pipe. b capillary fitting soldered to copper pipe.

Plate 94 Showing the soft brass ring which seals a compression fitting.

Soft pipe

Annealed copper pipe up to ½ in (12 mm) outside diameter is available in coils from auto factors. Special compression or flare fittings are sold for this pipe. If you prefer solder fittings, always braze these on for engine work, or use silver solder such as Easyflo. Domestic copper pipe is always measured by inside diameter, for inch sizes and outside for metric. The popular ½ in (15 mm) and ¾ in (22 mm) sizes are sold in annealed coils which may be formed to all except the tightest bends by pulling it around a timber post with bare hands. Domestic lead pipe is easy to bend, but is considered a health hazard. It requires wiped solder joints which are best avoided by the amateur.

Flexible connections

Copper engine-cooling water pipes are usually connected by short rubber hoses, as on a car heater or radiator. Such hoses are best renewed every five years — more often if they feel hard or show cracks when bent ruthlessly. Car hoses with ready-made bends are useful in tight corners.

Hose clamps

Only stainless steel hose clamps (Jubilee clips) should be used on boat work. Plated ones soon rust (especially when situated in the bilges) and eventually need to be cut off with a hacksaw. If you must use these, grease them lightly and oil the threads before fitting, then cover over with electrical tape (or

edge) with fine sandpaper or steel wool. Never use emery cloth or tape. Wipe clean, apply flux to these parts, engage the pipe fully, then heat the fitting (straight away) until the solder runs freely out of the joint. If the solder is not built into the fitting, apply pure solder wire, not cored solder.

impregnated pipe-wrap) after tightening. Clamps may need taking-up half a turn every couple of years. Flexible drivers are available to get into tight spots. It pays to fit clamps in pairs to avoid leakage, especially on pressurized systems. A slight flare formed on the end of soft copper piping prevents a hose from coming adrift unexpectedly. Rubber adhesive in addition to clamps makes a sound job, but hose renewal is then much more difficult.

All hose

Plumbing entirely in rubber or plastic hose is common practice for cold water supplies on small boats, but most hose imparts a foul taste to water. Only reinforced rubber, ABS, or nylon piping is suitable for hot water. On big craft with complicated plumbing, hoses can be sources of failure due to kinking, chafe and heat distortion, but they do have the advantage of easy coding.

Identity coding

Make hot water supplies in red rubber hose (or white nylon), cold water in blue, sea water in green, and waste pipes in black. Dabs of paint on metal pipes serve the same purpose. No piping for water should ever be transparent: the action of light allows

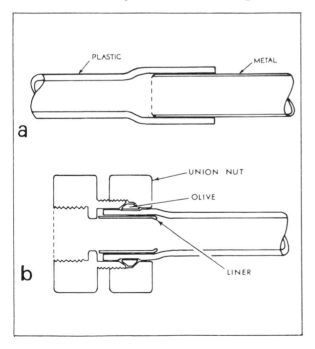

Fig. 118 Metal-to-plastic pipe joints. **a** low pressure. **b** high pressure.

green slime to form inside. Some plastic hose becomes so brittle in cold weather that freezing water can fracture it. All the required unions, tees and reducers to go with standard sizes of hose are stocked by good marine hardware stores in brass or plastics.

Polythene

Cheap polyethylene (polythene) tubing is fine for cold water, but must be *food grade* for drinking use. Fittings or standard copper pipe may be pushed into the end if the pipe is first heated with boiling water, and no clips are necessary for low pressure work (Fig. 118(a)) if the fit is correct. For high pressure work, compression fittings with olives are used, but a copper ferrule (Fig. 118(b)) must be pushed into the bore of the polythene before each compression fitting is tightened. Any garage will fit the unions used on plastic fuel piping. To improvise should one of these leak, cut off the external crimped ferrule with a hacksaw, shorten the pipe, and use a hose clamp to secure the union spigot.

Internal spring

Before heating a polythene pipe to make a sharp bend, you must insert a plumber's spring to prevent buckling. Springs for all sizes of pipe are usually easy to hire or borrow. They have an eye at one end for attaching a lanyard or wire to facilitate withdrawal where bends are remote from the pipe ends. Springs are always used for bending lead pipe neatly. An external spring is sometimes used when bending soft copper pipe without a bending machine. Simple jigs are sold for bending copper fuel pipe up to ⅜ in (9 mm) outside diameter. Failing that, melt rosin or lead into the bore, make the bend, then heat sufficiently to run out the filling.

Rigid plastics

A popular trend in domestic cold water plumbing is the use of stiff PVC (or similar) piping with glue-on, push-on or compression fittings of the same material. For hot water work, be careful to buy a brand which is guaranteed for that duty. Suitable adapters are made for coupling to copper or steel plumbing. Alteration or repair means cutting out (with a hacksaw) a sufficient length. With a coupler each end, the new section may then be bent slightly to spring it into place. These are cheap and light materials that anyone can install. They will not corrode or cause galvanic action, and are especially useful for waste pipes.

Pump suctions

Rigid plastics will serve for bilge pump and other suction pipes equally as well as metal. Soft plastics and rubber hose can collapse without warning under vacuum unless armoured with an integral wire or plastic spiral. Even a small leak will prevent a pump from priming. Electrical tape will often seal a leak well enough to get you home. Cutting a perished hose and inserting a short length of metal pipe makes a good jury repair. If there is a wire spiral inside, pull out a few turns, cut the wire, then push the spiral back in, allowing the metal pipe to be inserted and secured with hose clips.

Steel pipe

Mainly used nowadays for exhaust systems and diesel fuel pipes, black or galvanized steel water pipe requires more know-how and special tools to install it than any of the above methods. When altering or repairing, amateurs tend to insert new piping of copper or plastics, but the rigidity of steel is advantageous where long, unsupported runs are necessary, and where stopcocks and branch pipes would otherwise need support brackets. Plastic pipe is, of course, a big fire risk when carrying liquid fuel or gas.

Bending

Elbows of various angles are normally fitted to change direction on steel pipework. However, small amounts of curvature (such as to follow the contours of a boat's hull) are easily applied to the popular ½ in (12 mm) and ¾ in (18 mm) sizes if two people pull the pipe around a wooden post. Working alone, the same thing can be done by holding the pipe in a strong vice, or pushing it through a convenient hole in a timber balk. Larger steel pipes need local heating with an oxygen torch before bending.

Fabrications

Not all craft have stainless steel pulpits and guardrail stanchions. Galvanized water pipe has always been used for this purpose on many of the older (and usually larger) yachts, as well as on commercial craft. You may also find galvanized pipe used for mast supports below decks, for pipecot frames, grabrails, and root berth spars.

Threading

Once the ends of a steel pipe are threaded, screwing on any standard fitting is simple. A plumber will cut the threads for you, but if you have a large number to do, it pays to hire a pipe vice and the appropriate

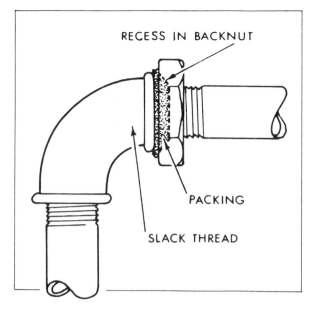

Fig. 119 Backnut to stop slack joint from leaking.

stocks and dies. A smear of cutting compound (or a squirt of engine oil) helps to produce a clean thread, as does attention to the clearance of swarf. A new die works far better than an old worn one. British threads are parallel like a bolt; American threads are mostly tapered.

Malleable fittings

As well as elbows, easy bends, junctions, and reducers (and adapters from steel to copper or steel to plastics), the range of steel pipe fittings includes connectors and unions to enable any section to be dismantled readily in the future.

Jointing

Threads used to be sealed with a smear of jointing paste and a few turns of hemp. Nowadays, thin white Teflon or PTFE tape is wound on to the male thread before screwing up. Liquid PTFE (such as Loctite PST) is superior for use on rough or tight threads, where tape might be damaged. On hot exhaust piping, graphite jointing compound works well. If a slack thread creates leakage, fit a backnut (as shown in Fig. 119) with some turns of asbestos string smeared with graphite paste, squashed between the nut and the fitting.

Routine cleaning

Most plumbing receives little maintenance until it fails. Hot water causes the most trouble, especially with small bore pipes, where scale from lime or salt may eventually cause a blockage. After dismantling, clear as much scale as possible using tools of wire, flexible curtain rod, dowel wood and pull-throughs, followed by repeated soakings with one of the fluids sold for descaling kettles or central heating systems. Hand pumps, taps, or faucets, need cleaning, descaling, re-washering, greasing and gland adjusting as necessary. Waste pipes need to be kept clear and sweet, while a shower rose is sure to need dunking in descaling fluid at least once a year to keep the tiny holes running free.

Gas work

The convenience of bottled gas on small craft is appreciated by most owners, but there is potential danger, as any leakage accumulates in the bilges, waiting to explode. Lighter-than-air gas (such as CNG in the USA) is slowly becoming available for boat use. Although copper branch piping of ¼ in (6 mm) outside diameter is normally used to feed each appliance, make sure that the main pipe from the tank is big enough. You may need ⅜ in (9 mm) on a long run, when several appliances are likely to be used at one time. Blow *dry* compressed air through a new pipe, to remove particles which could block the tiny jets used in most gas burners.

Clipping

Keep piping away from the bilges to prevent corrosion and damage. Always clip copper piping to the hull at intervals of not less than 2 ft (600 mm), using small, self-tapping screws into hollow fibreglass sections if there is no convenient wooden batten. Clips or straps are easy to make from 20-gauge copper sheet. Electrical clips are better than nothing, but should be of plastics to avert corrosion.

Propane hose

Even the special rubber hose made for gas is not considered safe on a boat. Short lengths of approved flexible braided pipe (fitted with a union at each end) must be used next to a gimbal-swung stove, but a long rubber hose may just have to be used for a gas-heated smoothing iron, or portable space heater. Make sure there is a stop valve at the bulkhead before the start of any such hose.

Escaping

The standard way to check gas leakage at a joint is to smear on a strong soap solution and watch for bubbles. With a slow leak, it could take a minute or two for this to happen. Special jointing compound is available from gas equipment stockists, and this should be used on all surfaces when assembling compression fittings, or attaching hoses to copper piping or brass spigots. In this latter case, it pays to fit twin hose clamps for extra security. Proper cone unions have been known to leak – even the main gas bottle union when fully tightened – largely due to damage or grit. A smear of the gas joint paste will usually cure slight union leakage. See page 205 for safety measures.

Bilge contamination

Ideally, all gas burners on a boat should have flame failure cut-off valves (with reset buttons) to save dangerous accumulations of heavy gas in the bilges should a flame blow out unobserved. There is a particular danger with items like refrigerators and water heaters which light automatically from a pilot jet. Extractor fans need sealed motors for gas leak safety. Gas detectors are expensive, but could prevent total loss of the ship and her contents. Always turn on a detector when arriving on board and before anybody strikes a match, starts an engine, or turns on an electric bilge pump. Remember that gas detectors can be triggered by other fumes, including smoke, burnt food, gasoline and alcohol. Submersion in bilge water could damage the sensor unit.

Clearing bilges

When leakage has occurred, clearing gas completely from the bilges is a formidable task. The standard way is to seal off all openings in the cabin sole (especially around the edges and underneath berths and settees) using mats and rag, then rig a windsail (see page 83) through the forehatch attached to a length of 6 in (150 mm) flexible duct down into the fore peak bilge, with a similar outlet duct right aft. With watertight bulkheads in the way, separate clearance of each section is essential, allowing about three days of ventilation for each part. A less popular method consists of flooding the bilges up to sole level via a seacock (or by siphoning from overboard), then arranging maximum ventilation through the boat for as long as possible. Never use a vacuum cleaner or exhausting fan which might cause an explosion due to sparking in its motor. Natural dispersal of undisturbed gas tends to occur after about six weeks.

Heating and cooking

Except for the small bulkhead-mounted charcoal stoves with 1 in (25 mm) diameter flue, solid fuel stoves and ranges – often with back boilers for central heating and hot water supply – are normally only found on certain larger and older yachts which are used all year round in the cooler climates. Away from marinas, electrical power on small craft is best conserved for lighting and engine starting, so bottled gas is popular for supplying piped hot water, while diesel, kerosene or alcohol (methanol) is considered safer for cooking. Electrically-controlled automatic diesel-fired units are almost universally used on big boats for water heating, cooking, and space heating by radiators or ducted warm air. Efficient and smart stoves for every purpose (and burning every type of fuel) are readily available in Britain and America. Every stove must be securely bolted in place. Cooking appliances need plenty of space if mounted to swivel athwartships; they also need fiddles (sea rails) around the hob.

Water heating

A calorifier tank heated by engine cooling water will supply ample hot water on power boats – for as long as 24 hours after shutdown – provided the tank is large enough, and well lagged. A battery charging set engine may add further heat, but a gas or diesel fired water heater will still be necessary at times. A calorifier needs little maintenance if fresh, soft water is used. Most other water heaters need periodical cleaning and you must keep the appropriate instruction sheets.

Scale

In hard water areas a softener (de-ionizer) or scale inhibitor is ideal on the feed to all water heaters. Scale inhibitors need no maintenance, but they contain balanced magnets which emit a slight magnetic field, so site well away from any compass.

Running water

With pipes of large enough bore, a header tank on deck (filled from the main tanks by a hand or power pump) will ensure you have hot and cold running water with a minimum of mechanical problems. A few boats use compressed air to pressurize a main water tank. Most big craft use automatic electric pumps, some activated by the pressure drop when water is drawn at any point; some activated by electrical contacts on each tap or faucet. Adjustable constrictor valves may be fitted to the cold supply to showers and similar equipment, where you need both hot and cold running in unison and at the same speed. A complicated small bore radiator system is certain to need a circulating pump at the water heater or calorifier. If you want hot or cold running sea water in addition to fresh, a separate automatic pumping unit is required to handle it.

Solid fuel

Smokeless solid fuel made from coal and sold in convenient paper bags is clean to handle and creates almost no soot. Ordinary coal or logs are cheaper, but can be troublesome to stow on board. Compressed sawdust or straw impregnated logs are widely used in the USA. Each one will burn for an hour. The paper wrapping, covered in a layer of wax, starts the first log burning at the application of a lighted match.

Lighting up

If you have a propane or butane poker, lighting any form of solid fuel is simple. Otherwise, wax fire lighters, or paper and chopped pinewood sticks will do. To light a fire with no other aids but newspaper, roll whole sheets with your fingers to form tubes no bigger than ⅝ in (16 mm) in diameter. Cut the tubes into 6 in (150 mm) lengths and stop from unrolling with Scotch tape or twine. Thirty of these should start most types of small coal.

Scorching

Solid fuel stoves cannot be turned off instantly, and they are heavy. Secure mounting is essential, also some sort of guardrailing, and adequate heat insulation between stove and bulkhead. On older boats the latter was usually arranged by mounting an asbestos-cement panel about 1 in (25 mm) away from the bulkhead, using bolts and spacer tubes. Two panels of 20-gauge stainless steel with mineral wool between looks better and cannot crack. A hot water supply jacket around the flue will need additional staying from the bulkhead because of its weight. Keep anything that will burn well away from the stove. Empty the ash pan frequently, damping the contents to both cool them and prevent dust flying.

Flue

Whatever type of fuel you adopt for a stove, having an efficient and clean flue is important to health and to reduce humidity. All stove makers can supply suitable equipment. The portable cowl and stack above deck (called a *Charlie Noble* by seamen) must be of correct design to exclude rain and spray while also increasing the draft. Note that atmospheric sensing devices are available, which raise the alarm (or turn off a gas stove) if poisonous fumes or smoke should build up in a badly ventilated cabin.

Chores

By following the instructions on the can, repairing broken fire-brick linings is easy to do with furnace cement. Similar cement is used to set replacement lining bricks. A cast iron outside surface needs rubbing with liquid black lead (graphite) to prevent rust. Spillage stains on stove enamelling are best treated with oven cleaner prior to washing, preferably when a stove is cold. Tackle bright metal parts with chrome cleaner or brass polish as often as possible.

Kerosene

Wick lamps and stoves have been used successfully on boats since before living memory. Their safe and noiseless operation, fuel economy and low first cost, are marred only by the need for wick trimming and the tendency to smell. The same type of lamp oil (stove oil) is used in pressure stoves working on the Primus principle (see Plate 95). Maintenance needs are minimal, but considerable preheating is necessary to get them started, and tank pressure demands occasional pumping when in use. Mantle lamps working on the same principle give an intense white light.

Wick care

An oil lamp only needs filling, wick trimming and glass cleaning to keep it in good order. A fuel fill normally lasts about 12 hours, while wick trimming and glass cleaning comes around every 48 hours or so. When trimming is due, a lamp smells and smokes when turned up sufficiently to produce proper light. Trim the wick straight across with a sharp pair of scissors so that all the carbon is removed.

Wick stoves

The big asbestos blue-flame wicks used for stoves are circular, and are trimmed every 100 hours or so by means of the special tool provided. Such burners have small air holes and gauzes which must be kept clear, and also a mica window (to view the flame), which needs wiping carefully to avoid breakage. Some circular wicks have a travel of only about 1 in (25 mm), so keep a spare one on board. Avoid running low on fuel, which leads to a burnt wick and

a bad smell. Once dried out (or when fitting a new wick), leave for at least one hour for soakage.

Primus principle

Whatever the make, most pressure kerosene stoves use the Primus system with vaporizer tubes built into the burner head. After preheating with a shot of alcohol held in a tray under the burner, the vaporized fuel hisses out of a jet to ignite with a blue flame. A clamp-on asbestos wick igniter is used on some stoves. Insufficient preheating causes a flare-up, or yellow flame. It pays to keep a low tank pressure for a few minutes (or to throttle down the jet if a regulator control is provided) until a steady flame is established.

Primus care

If cleaning all burner air holes and renewing the jet will not cure a faulty burner, the vaporizer is probably carboned up: a new burner head is not too expensive. Keep the air pump leather plunger supple with a monthly smear of Vaseline.

Other fuels

Pure gasoline (SBP in Britain and white gas in the USA) is used on some appliances similar to those above, so make sure you are using the correct fuel. Alcohol pressure and gravity feed stoves are widely used in the USA and need virtually no maintenance. European methylated spirit needs some 1% pure water added to burn like methanol (denatured alcohol). Meta fuel in tablet form burns like alcohol but is smelly and costly. As already mentioned, diesel fuel is popular for the larger boat stoves and ranges, as the same fuel is used for the main engines.

Gas burners

Catalytic space heaters convert bottled gas into heat without a flame, and have proved successful for over twenty years. However, as with all combustion, they push a lot of moisture into the atmosphere if not vented. Most other gas appliances use a burner with a small metering jet for the gas, and apertures to admit the correct quantity of air. Stripping burners for cleaning is rarely necessary more often than once in three years; some people wait until a weak or uneven flame indicates trouble. Makers' maintenance instructions are always useful. Unshipping parts can be annoying during the season.

Adjustments

Over the years, appliances can get out of adjustment,

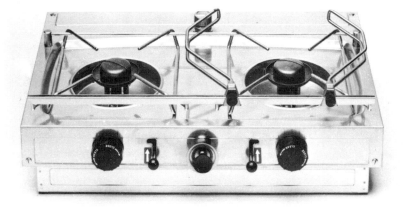

Plate 95 Modern kerosene stove showing the jet regulating and cleaning controls (outermost), the quick-start levers, and the pressurizing pump. (*Picture by courtesy of Optimus Ltd, Rushden, England and Bridgport, Ct, USA.*)

perhaps due to a change from butane to propane, or by a variation in pipeline pressure caused by renewal of the regulator – the reducing valve attached to the cylinder. To put matters right, you may need to replace the burner jet with a larger or smaller one, or to vary the size of the air gap. The amateur cannot be expected to know what a properly balanced flame (or pilot burner) should look like, so professional help is sometimes expedient. Built-in igniters on stoves (and especially on ovens) are convenient, but one more thing to go wrong. A wax taper lit by a match will reach any burner, while domestic lighting guns (spark emitting, piezo, or glow-plug types) are useful.

Gas safety

Modern appliances have a flame failure cut-out device with reset button to be operated when lighting. This is essential with pilot jet burners on refrigerators and water heaters. Turn off the supply occasionally, then on again after a pause, to make sure the cut-out is still operative. Crew training ensures safety. Make sure that everybody lights burners without letting any gas escape, prevents flames from blowing out unnoticed, keeps the isolating valve turned off when an appliance is not in use, and shuts off at the cylinder (or trips a master solenoid valve near the regulator) whenever the boat is unoccupied. Inspect piping and fittings regularly as mentioned on page 202, and save up for a gas detector if you lack this wonderful safety measure.

Bottle handling

All cylinders (including spare ones) must be stowed either in a top-entry locker which is vented overboard, or on deck. Always have the correct wrench to tackle the big regulator-to-cylinder union, and remember that the thread is often left-handed (sometimes indicated by nicks across the nut corners).

Weighing a cylinder is the only way to determine its contents when there is no built-in gauge. The tare (empty weight) is stamped on, together with the liquid petroleum gas weight when full. A spring balance or bathroom scales will suffice. Having tandem cylinders coupled together (with an automatic or manually operated changeover valve) saves a lot of bother. Failing this, a small reserve cylinder will tide you over until reaching the next stockist. Note that a dangerous piping explosion could occur if a gas bottle should topple over when in use.

Mantles

Gas cabin lamps produce a pleasing and powerful light economically and silently. Bumping them causes the mantles to shatter, so always carry spares. Other than glass cleaning, the maintenance chore most likely to arise is a choked jet. A strand of electrical wire thin enough to enter the hole bends too easily to shift an obstruction. Soaking a jet in paint thinner or boiling water, followed by a blast of air, will usually do the trick.

Refrigerator

A new era of economical solid state electric refrigerators is coming in, but most craft at present which do not have a conventional electric or gas unit employ a top-loading insulated ice-box using dockside ice or freezer packs. The drain must never lead to the bilges, but into a tub, covered to stop warm air entering. Any ice-box or refrigerator smells musty if left out of use with the door closed. Wash out occasionally with bicarbonate of soda solution. If a hinged door is left open when out of use, lash or wedge this to prevent it from banging about due to the wash from other boats. There is no problem on powerboats using a shore electricity supply when in port and having a shaft-driven unit for use under way, but the battery drain needs to be carefully watched on most sailboats.

Turning off

A gas refrigerator running continuously is a possible safety risk if not in perfect order. Turn it off when taking fuel on board, or when the boat is rolling badly in a seaway. All types need adequate space and air circulation over the condenser. Defrosting is not a problem unless you are living aboard for long periods. Try to empty ice trays before turning off a refrigerator, even for a day or two.

Ranges

All the same systems found in space heaters are available for operating cooking stoves. Generally, solid fuel types have flues and are rigidly mounted, while gas types and some oil ones have no venting, and are mounted in gimbals to keep tolerably level in a seaway. Gimbals are always on the move and need frequent oiling. As well as fiddles or sea rails around the hob, all cookers really also need adjustable bars or springy cables to hold saucepans and kettle steady.

Water tanks

Some of the information given for fuel tanks in Chapter 9 applies also to fresh water and holding tanks. Impeccable anchorage is especially necessary to keep such heavy weights in place should a total or near capsize ever occur. Tank water is often unpalatable unless boiled, so it pays to keep a breaker or two of really fresh water on board at all times for drinking purposes. With a sump and drainplug for dealing with sludge and condensation, plus proper filtering, fuel tanks rarely need to be cleaned out, but large rigid water tanks need bolt-on cover plates for internal access.

Construction

You may find tanks built into the hull skin of plywood, fibreglass, steel, light alloy and ferrocement boats. Some of these materials are also used for removable water tanks. Flexible ones of plastics or reinforced synthetic rubber are made in a variety of shapes and sizes to house in the bilges like buoyancy bags. Most of these do not have internal baffles, creating funny noises at times! Galvanized steel water tanks are popular and generally the cheapest, though many owners prefer to pay more and go for stainless steel. Remember to give any new tank a test under slight pressure before installation on board.

Inspection

For a bilge tank, the rubber gasket under a bolted top inspection plate only has to seal against splashing. Vertical plates on sponson tanks must not leak a drop, so the gasket is best renewed whenever a panel is disturbed. Boatyards, plumbers and builder's emporiums stock suitable rubber. Without a wad punch (see Fig. 82) to make the holes, file a sharp edge on one end of a short piece of thin walled steel tube and press this through in the vice, with a block of wood the other side. Alternatively, drill the holes while clamping the rubber between two offcuts of ⅜ in (9 mm) plywood, after having marked out one of these as the template.

Many fibreglass tanks have no inspection panel. If the water is to be used for drinking purposes, you had better know what is going on inside. Installing such panels is a useful winter exercise for the handyman (see later). A tank with internal baffles may need more than one inspection panel to enable all parts to be cleaned. Whether round or square, ports need to be at least 8 in (200 mm) across.

Cleaning

It often takes ten years to get rid of the foul taste of water from a fibreglass tank. Cleaning out with vinegar or dilute acetic acid improves matters, especially if the fluid is sloshed around for several days, having taken a tank ashore. When domestic bleach or formalin is used for tank cleaning, ensure perfect rinsing. Avoid phenol, for it could then take months to lose the foul taste. Generally, a scrub with fresh water or brine is adequate. Many marine stores keep harmless additives for sterilizing whole plumbing systems. This is best done three times a year.

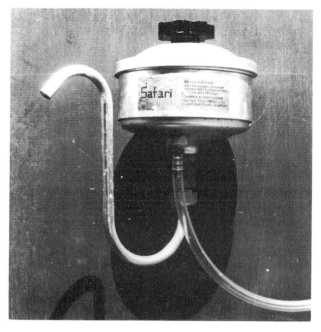

Plate 96 Bulkhead mounted water purifier with renewable filter and activator.

Drinking water

Purifying tablets to rid suspect water of germs are a useful item to keep on board, even when in home waters. Small bulkhead-mounted purifying units (Plate 96) may be plumbed in over any sink where drinking water needs to be drawn from a tank. Always use tablets in a tank which was left partly filled during the lay-up period.

Unwelcome flora

Any container for drinking water should be opaque. Even a small amount of light will cause green slime to grow on the inside. The best way to remove this from portable breakers is to put a small quantity of sand and water (plus a little salt) inside and shake it about, rinsing well afterwards.

Renewals

Galvanized steel tanks are the ones most likely to need renewing on an old boat. Once the inside starts to rust, a tank will continue to serve for washing water, possibly for another five years. However, it pays to postpone renewal by internal painting, as some tanks are very difficult to unship, and a new replica is not likely to be cheap.

Internal painting

You need a special paint for the inside of a tank, such as *Tantectol* by International Paint. Epoxy pitch is normally too stiff to spread to all corners, especially if the tank has baffles. After preparing the surface as described on page 34, follow the paint makers' instructions implicitly. All loose rust must be removed using wire brushes and abrasive paper, followed by a vacuum cleaner and tackrag. The traditional way to deal with small removable tanks without inspection panels is to drop a fathom of ¼ in (6 mm) chain inside and shake vigorously. A compressed air lance helps to get rid of the final dust. With a small quantity of paint poured in, such a tank is rotated slowly until all surfaces are covered and then stood upside down to drain. Any extra thick paint is best allowed to congeal at the top. Two coats of any tank paint are better than one, eliminating all unseen 'holidays' and pin holes.

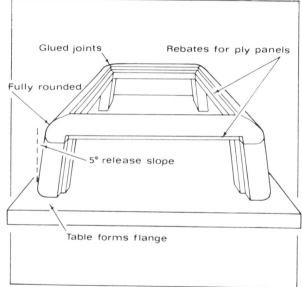

Fig. 120 Making a male plug for one half of a glassfibre tank.

Making tanks

Many hobbyists are capable of welding up a steel tank. If zinc spraying is easier to get done locally than hot dip galvanizing, make the whole top to bolt on, so the metallizers can spray inside. Most amateurs prefer to make glass fibre tanks. Use a male mould (Fig. 120) for each half of the tank, so the inside will be glossy. Form flanges to bolt or bond the two parts securely together. See *Complete*

Amateur Boat Building for further details of fibre-glass work, including the addition of strengthening ribs.

Baffles

As well as lessening the extra load (and annoying noise) caused by surging water, internal baffles also add useful strength to a flimsy tank. They need to be strong, but with waterways left underneath or through them. When making a fibreglass tank with glossy interior, you can tooth the baffles through slots in the tank walls, to be glassed over on the outside after assembly.

Cover bolts

For steel tanks, welding standard bolts (with hexagon heads inside) around the cover plate aperture is no problem. If studs (bolts with no heads) are used, care is needed to set them square to the plate. With fibreglass, some brazing or welding is necessary to equip bolts or studs with lugs or T-heads (see Fig. 121) for glassing in securely. Alternatively, glass to the inside a complete metal bezel with nuts welded on to receive set screws through the cover plate.

Old bolts

When cleaning out a tank, fit new bolts or nuts (as the case may be) if the old ones are corroded. Otherwise, clear the threads with a die nut or tap, as any tightness could cause something to shear off next time. When clearing threads, make sure that no swarf drops inside the tank.

Deck fillers

If any tank is connected direct to a deck filler plate (Plate 97), make sure that the leather washer or O-ring is in good condition, to avoid contamination. Much better to have a large deck plate covering a separate cap on the end of the filler pipe. There could be disastrous consequences if deck plates are not clearly marked with words like FUEL and WATER! Ensure that the pronged or square turnkey is always kept in a safe place, with an adequate lanyard to minimize loss overboard. Keeping a spare turnkey is a wise precaution.

Venting

Tanks with airtight filler caps need vent pipes as described on page 178. A little spillage from an over-full water tank rarely matters, and a vented cap below deck will let in enough air to prevent a vacuum forming as the water is used. A vent hole larger than ⅛ in (3 mm) needs a gauze cover to

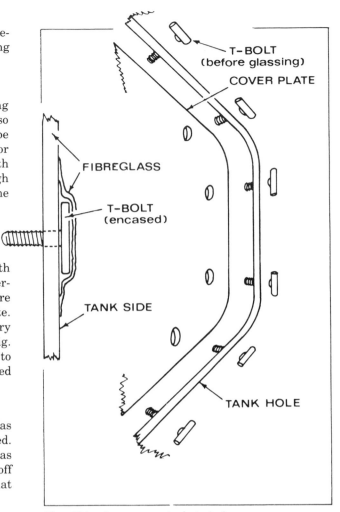

Fig. 121 Arrangement of studs for tank cover plate.

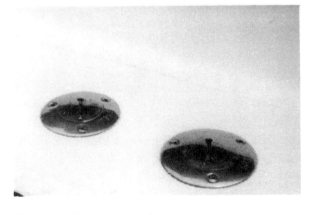

Plate 97 Fuel and water filler plates close together need clear labels cast into the metal.

exclude bugs. Remember to keep hole and gauze clear of dirt.

Fixing

Ensure that all tanks are well bolted into place. Nuts, steel straps, wooden stringers, or wire ropes and turnbuckles could have been omitted at some time when a tank was unshipped. For the estuary or gunkholing sailor, a shaped bilge tank is unlikely to come adrift, but cabin sole bearers are not strong enough to keep a half-ton tank in place should the mast top ever go under water. Flexible tanks can change shape and roll about if not securely battened down. Even on a new boat you could find problems in this department.

Gauging contents

Some methods of gauging tank contents are mentioned on page 178. Sophisticated pneumatic gauges can be fitted through a tiny hole near the bottoms of tanks. Up to ten tanks can be referred to one dial on a console with appropriate selection switches.

Be safe

The practical sailor cannot be expected to foresee failures with electronic navigation aids or a smart charger. Most mechanical troubles can be anticipated. A little care will reveal whether vibration has loosened bolts on tank or engine mountings, pipe clips or propeller shaft couplings. Turn off the gas and all seacocks when leaving a boat, but remember especially to open the cooling water intake before starting an engine. A Jabsco type pump must not be run dry.

Thunderbolts

With most yachts docked for 90% of the time, lightning conductors are grounded ashore and coupled to the rigging in the tropics. Failing that, a weighted cable hanging overboard is better than nothing. A proper job gives wonderful satisfaction when thunderbolts get too close for comfort. Remember, your compass may misbehave after a strike (or near strike), especially with a steel hull.

Mast conductor

A tall metal mast will protect any hull provided its heel is grounded via a copper rod to a minimum 1 sq ft (0.1 m²) copper plate outside near the keel. Connecting direct to a metal hull is normal – or via a keel bolt to an exposed (not encapsulated) iron or lead ballast keel. Use 8-gauge battery/starter cable as a minimum (or bare $\frac{5}{32}$ in (4 mm) rod), always routed with the gentlest of bends. Even a shorter mizzen mast is best grounded also. Keep connections tight and free from corrosion.

Extraneous

Any big metal part within about 6 ft (2 m) of the above route is best also grounded. Include any engine even if well outside this range. The cathode protection bonding from zinc anodes is no help in dissipating thunderbolts.

Mast of wood

Few wooden masts get treated with protection more elaborate than bonding the masthead shroud chainplates to deep through-hull fittings. To do it properly you need a masthead spike at least 1 ft (300 mm) above any antenna or Windex. Coupling this to a rod all down the mast is far better than relying on shroud tang contacts. A masthead spike is, in fact, a wise practice on a metal mast.

Crew

During an electric storm, keep everyone down below if possible and well away from any wiring or metal fittings.

Isolation

Pulling all cables from electronic equipment on modern yachts would be impracticable. You need surge suppressors at each item (in accordance with makers' instructions) and lightning arresters on antennas. With a shore powerline, that also needs surge protection. Some damage to electronics and wiring is sure to occur in the event of a direct strike.

No sails

A powerboat with token masts is not so vulnerable, but to make sure, have a bonded spike at least half the boat's length above the lower deck. This is usually easy to arrange with a flybridge. Two equal masts can be 25% lower than the above.

11
Dinghies and Trailers

To get away from the stresses of modern life, many a man will buy himself a powerboat with two noisy diesels, capable of whisking him from port to port in the shortest time possible, and he might moor where the blaring of radios is only interrupted by the noise and fumes from battery charging sets!

In similar fashion, when choosing a dinghy to act as tender to the parent vessel, he will probably choose a rubber boat which is a pig to row, needing a noisy outboard motor to get anywhere.

Practicability often needs to be weighed against ease of stowage on board.

Tender choice

Few modern yachtsmen have experienced the joys of rowing a well-proportioned clinker (lapstrake) dinghy, but such a boat will not stow easily on a car roof and really needs davits (pronounced *dayvits* by seamen) to assist lifting on board. Remember that having a tender that will sail can add greatly to the enjoyment of a cruise, especially when children are present. The only problem is that water can splash up through the daggerboard case when the tender is well loaded. A cover is usually easy to devise, held down with the same shockcord used to keep the board down.

Towing
The deck stowage of a rigid dinghy is almost impossible on any yacht smaller than about 22 ft (7 m). Tender size changes little in relation to parent

vessel size, yet the smaller yacht which is least able to cope with the additional drag is often forced to tow her dinghy. As well as using the painter, a secondary towrope (often left slack) is advisable (see page 225). Whether short or long scope is used depends on the prevailing conditions. Some tenders ride better with 56 lb (25 kg) of ballast in the stern. An overall cover is ideal to prevent waterlogging on a long passage.

Stowage
Popular stowage methods are illustrated in Plate 98. If your transom is high enough to hoist a dinghy well clear of rogue seas, stern davits (Plate 98(c)) not only simplify launching and recovery, but also eliminate obstructions to deckwork and sunbathing space. However, they are not really compatible with wind vane self-steering gear. Other stowage methods include either-way-up on the foredeck or cabin top; fore-and-aft, athwartships, or diagonally on the after deck; and leaning against the guardrails (or cabin trunk) along one side deck.

Hoisting
Lifting a heavy dinghy on board is difficult, even when using a halyard to take the strain. Some people improvise a davit by utilizing the main boom, gaff, staysail boom, or whisker pole. At a pinch, the job can be done singlehanded.

Inflatables
With their advantages of light weight and all-round fendering, air-filled rubber dinghies are also con-

a

b

Plate 98 Some common positions for tenders stowed on board. **a** on cabin top. **b** athwartships on foredeck. **c** in stern davits. **d** over aft cabin. **e** between mast and samson post. **f** rubber boat partially deflated.

c

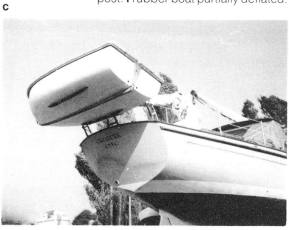

d

e

f

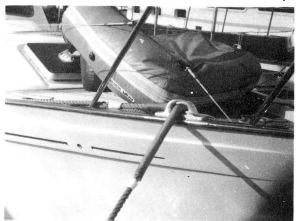

venient to stow (below decks or above) when deflated. However, pumping up is such a daunting task using hand or foot bellows that many owners tow them or resort to partial deflation for deck stowage, as in Plate 98(f). Liferafts are a special form of inflatable rubber boat, opening when the painter is tugged after launching. A hydrostatic release operates if a yacht should sink – provided any anti-theft device was unlocked beforehand. Cheap inflatables may last only three years, but good quality ones should last at least ten years, unless often used from a shingle beach. Semi-inflatables (having a fibreglass bottom with rubber sides) are heavy but perform well.

Quick pumping

To avoid exhausting exercise many owners nowadays keep an electric or engine-driven air compressor on board to speed up inflation. An electric compressor stowed in the car is useful for dock-side use. Alternatively, keep a scuba diving cylinder in the car, equipped with a pressure-reducing valve as used with oxyacetylene welding equipment.

Collapsibles

Since the end of the last century, folding boats (Plate 99) of various designs have been available. Typical ones have plywood sides and bottom joined together with canvas. Many sail or awning makers will normally repair the canvas parts whenever wear or damage necessitates this. The wooden parts need regular painting or varnishing as for a plywood dinghy, or a fibreglass one with wooden seats and trim.

Plate 99 This folding dinghy has plywood topsides with stretched canvas V-bottom and transom.

Sectionals

Different types of sectional plywood dinghies come and go in the boating industry. Most sectionals appear in two varieties. One type has a demountable double bulkhead which unclips to enable the bow half of the boat to nest inside the stern half. In the other type, half-shells are clipped together on a rubber gasket running centrally through keel, stem and transom. Any removable transom can often make deck stowage easier.

Heavy tenders

Although a proper inboard engined yacht's tender may not be more than 10 ft (3 m) in length, davits are necessary to handle the considerable weight. The same thing applies if you wish to carry any but the smallest class of racing dinghy. Stowing the mast is generally a problem with such a boat – up and down the parent ship's mainmast is often the only place. A sailing tender (Plate 100) should have gunter or lugsail rig (or a jointed mast) so that all her spars will stow inside her.

Plate 100 With a lugsail rig, all spars will stow inside the boat.

Sea sled

Another type of tender needing davits is the sea sled, which is like a catamaran with the two hulls fused together (Plate 101). These tow well at speed and will often take a powerful outboard motor safely. They have a high loading capacity and are less likely than other types to turn turtle when some landlubber steps on the gunwale!

Power

There is a temptation by newcomers to fit oversized outboard motors to ordinary rowing boats. This can be dangerous for the inexperienced and can also damage the transom. A 1½ hp motor should be adequate to propel a tender up to 10 ft (3 m) in length, while a 3 hp motor can cope with up to 14 ft (4.5 m). Such motors are easy to lift on and off. They give a dry ride with good economy and minimal noise, while children will come to no harm when allowed to take joyrides. Shipping and unshipping any outboard motor is a risky business when a dinghy is tied up alongside. Always fit a lanyard to prevent loss overboard and try to keep a second person in the bows to improve the equilibrium.

Material

Remember that a dinghy of single skin fibreglass or metal can sink without trace unless equipped with full buoyancy. Although easy to maintain, many of these (like inflatables) do not row anything like as well as traditional wooden dinghies. There is always some element of compromise. Chine or flat-bottomed plywood dinghies are normally cheaper than any other type, but some are not particularly robust; neither are the next cheapest dinghies, which are cast in thick, lightweight rigid foam plastics, forming their own buoyancy. However, they have little or no wood trim and the outside is sprayed with a coating which requires no maintenance except for the occasional wash with sponge and fresh, cold water.

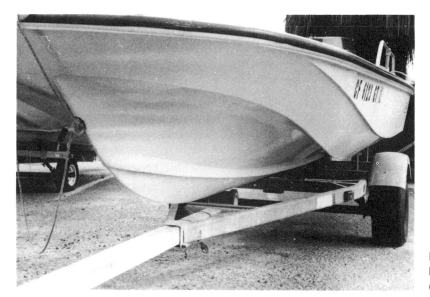

Plate 101 Sea sleds or cathedral hulls combine high speed with excellent stability.

Racing

Each class of racing dinghy has its band of enthusiasts, who know exactly what they want. If you are undecided on such a matter, join an active sailing club and gain experience and knowledge from other members before deciding. Generally, a second-hand boat is the best first choice. After a lot of fun tuning her and experimenting with new fittings and perhaps a change of sails, you might well be able to sell at a profit and search for a more competitive boat, perhaps in a different class.

Minor repairs

Especially with racing dinghies, the scars left by minor damage should be repaired as part of annual maintenance. With a little care, you can normally camouflage these completely so that the boat's value is not reduced. The lost time and hassle involved with insurance claims and boatyards can often be avoided. Major repair works to dinghies are treated in *Boat Repairs and Conversions*, including holes through fibreglass, light alloy and plywood hulls.

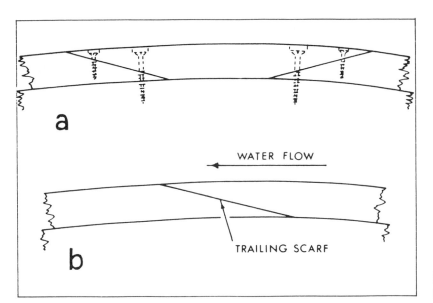

WATER FLOW

TRAILING SCARF

Fig. 122 Gunwale beading or rub-rail repairs.

Here, we are mainly concerned with such handyman jobs as repairing the wooden trim on hulls of plywood, fibreglass, and metal.

Long beadings

External half-round rub-rails are normally easy to repair. Where screwed on and varnished, remove the whole section up to the nearest joint. Good marine hardware stores (and some boatyards) stock the popular sizes. If not of the original species, a little artful staining before varnishing should produce a good match.

Short beadings

Short lengths are readily scarfed into painted beadings (see Fig. 122(a)) without marring the appearance. You may need to steam or shape a short piece to fit the curvature. Sometimes struts from a wall are useful when screws, Spanish windlass, or wedges will not exert sufficient pressure.

Glued beadings

Where mouldings are pinned and glued to the planking, chisel around the pins and remove them with pincers before chiselling away the bulk of the moulding. Finish off with a Surform plane which will not be damaged if the odd brass pin is encountered.

Laminations

Wide, overhanging gunwales are generally lamin-

ated from several strips glued together. Most damage only affects the outer two strips, so do not scarf in replacement timber to a greater depth than is necessary. Similarly, the repair shown in Fig. 122(a) need not be taken down to the full thickness of the moulding.

Scarfs

Joints in exposed mouldings are less likely to split in a collision if cut pointing aft, as shown in Fig. 122(b). Short repairs are simpler if one scarf is cut the other way, as in Fig. 122(a). Make male and female templates in cardboard before shaping the new piece. Whittle away at the new piece until the template fits before offering it up on the boat. Good scarfs are almost invisible when glued, though mistakes are easily concealed with the correct stopping. If hideous, change from varnish to paint!

Plastic wood

On a wooden boat with painted finish, car body filler, or one of the excellent plastic wood type fillers (such as Mendex or Woodtex) which plane down like wood after hardening, can be used to build up almost any depth of indentation damage. To prevent this ever coming adrift, first bore a few shallow holes or drive a few pins or screws which become embedded in the putty. The same system works well for score marks and bruises on other parts, such as stem, planking, transom and keel. Needless to say, matching old varnish is always difficult. Great improvements are possible by mixing a little paint of similar shade and applying this with a small brush before varnishing as described in Chapter 4.

Rudder
Together with daggerboards, drop keels, and the like, sailing dinghy rudders soon get chipped around the edges. Most of this damage is easily repaired on the above lines, using wood filler, fibreglass, or plastic metal, whichever is compatible with the original material. Care in preparing sound and clean surfaces ensures good adhesion.

Obsolescence
Replacement boards, rudders, tillers, gudgeons and pintles can be bought for most modern racing dinghies. This could form an insurance claim. For an obsolete class of dinghy the breakage could create an interesting project for the handyman. If fittings are not repairable by welding or brazing, it may mean having to fit new ones of completely different type.

Keel bands
Dinghies of wood and fibreglass often have keel and stem protection in the form of half-round or half-oval metal (sometimes called *cope*) secured with wood screws, self-tapping screws, or small bolts. The method of renewing this is similar to that for mast track as described in Chapter 6, including the problems of loose screws. Good chandlery stores stock the popular sizes. Curvature around the forefoot must be formed before drilling the screw holes: otherwise kinking is inevitable. Rounding the ends and tapering down is best started with a coarse file and finished with a fine file. Always bore and countersink screw holes on a bench, centralizing each one with a pop mark. This is difficult to do on the

boat. Offer up each strip first to make sure the holes are aligned away from all original screw positions. Fill the old screw holes with stopping or glued plugs. Paint or varnish any hidden parts which are of wood.

Slot rubbers
The above banding is generally used to clamp the rubber flaps which prevent turbulence where a drop keel or daggerboard comes through the keel. Use only the reinforced rubber sold for this job. Instead of using two strips meeting in the middle, a good way to avoid puckering is to use a single width of rubber and slit this after fitting, using a sharp trimming knife. Punch the holes carefully and make them a little larger than the keel band fastenings, to obviate stretching the rubber.

Glued clinker
Some dinghies, mainly racing types, have glued clinker plywood planking with no seam fastenings or internal ribs. Should a seam spring apart, clean out dirt and old glue using a hacksaw blade followed by an old table knife, then by feeler gauges. Bore for small screws to act as clamps. Mix up some epoxy or resorcinol glue and press this into the seam with a stripping knife (as shown in Fig. 6(a)) until it oozes out the other side. Insert the screws and wipe off surplus glue. Hide the screws with stopping and touch-up paint.

Camouflage
When many seams have failed in the usual area at the bottom of the hull amidships, it often pays to add strength with long hardwood tread plates (Fig. 123) inside the boat. These have the added advantage of allowing much longer screws through the lands.

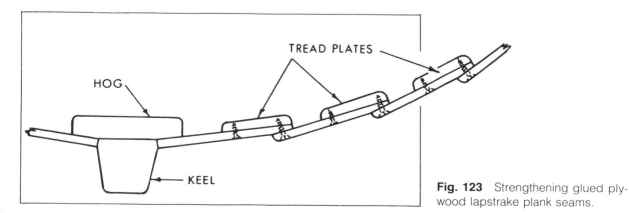

Fig. 123 Strengthening glued plywood lapstrake plank seams.

Fibreglass

Compared with a big yacht, keeping the topsides of a fibreglass dinghy highly polished is no great chore, particularly when a power mop is available. Special restorers stocked by chandleries help to get rid of those chalked-out patches especially prevalent on red and blue topsides. For big yachts, the process can prove expensive and time-consuming. The popular fibreglass cutting compounds and wax polishes may be all you need. Make sure any restorer includes full instructions. As mentioned on page 49, never use a polish containing silicones if the hull is ever likely to be painted. While polishing, inspect for gelcoat cracks. If these radiate from a spot, keep an eye on them.

Reinforcement

If cracks extend right through the skin, always add some reinforcing matt and resin to the inside (see later) before filling the external gel coat cracks. If extensive damage occurs (especially when subject to an insurance claim), sending the boat to the makers or other approved professionals is usually expedient.

Resin filler

To seal fine gel coat cracks, clean these by wiping over with acetone and rag, followed by dry rag. Brush on some matching gel coat resin. Spread a sheet of polythene on top (clingfilm may wrinkle) and squeegee with a smooth plastic strip. Leave the polythene in place, for most gel coat resins will not harden properly in the presence of air. Next day remove the covering, flat down with fine wet paper, and polish the surface.

Bad cracks

When tapping the surface with your knuckle, a dull sound indicates that the gel coat has parted from the matrix. In this case, chip away the loose gel coat with a scraper or old wood chisel and fill flush with epoxy putty. Sand this down after hardening and paint on some pigmented gel coat resin, covering it as described above.

Coloration

However carefully you add pigments to clear resin, even following the supplier's instructions to the letter, matching any surface other than white is almost impossible. For the successful repair of large or conspicuous areas, it will probably be necessary to paint at least the whole side concerned. The best fibreglass repair kits always include instructions covering all aspects of their use.

Through break

The thin shell of the dinghy pictured in Plate 102 had fractured completely along the keel and at the turn of the bilge. Although the inside appearance could never be quite the same, repairs were rapidly carried out by reaming out the cracks cleanly with a hacksaw blade, then laying up three thicknesses of glass cloth inside the boat. When cured, the hull was turned over and the cracks made good with resin putty and pigmented resin.

Overlaps

Although such a job is simple, you must take care to sand or grind away the old interior surface ruthlessly to ensure a good bond. If the sides of the crack do not align, use struts or thick adhesive tape to correct this. In any case tape over the outside to prevent resin from seeping through. Make the first layer of cloth run at least 1 in (25 mm) beyond the crack at each side. Make the second layer overlap a further inch all around, and increase the size of the third layer by a similar amount, as shown in Fig. 124.

Foam core

Rowboats and sailboards with glossy inside and outside skins filled between with rigid polyurethane foam are easy to repair if a visible patch does not matter (see Fig. 125). If the core is damaged, cut it out, pour in some fresh (with the hull suitably tilted), saw it off flush after expansion, then build up the skin with mat and surfacing tissue. Stagger all overlaps by at least 1 in (25 mm). The ingenious handyman will be able to make an invisible repair by forming a rabbet around the skin opening before foaming and final glassing.

Polyethylene

Beware of types of craft similar to the above, whose skins are of polyethylene or polythene. A special heat gun fed with rod of the same material is needed to weld on a patch, or to seal a crack. An amateur would need a lot of practice to do this properly. Effective cements and pastes are made for repairing ABS, PVC and suchlike plastics. Professional advice is really needed to identify some of these materials, let alone to repair them satisfactorily.

Punctures

Amateur repairs to punctures through light alloy hulls are easily and successfully undertaken by

a

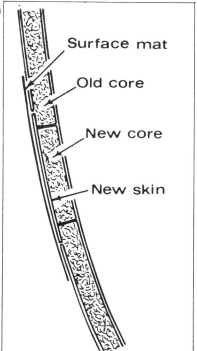

Fig. 124 Repairing severe split in fibreglass hull.

Plate 102 The most common fibre-glass dinghy repair. **a** laying up patches over the cracks. **b** flushing the outside with resin filler.

Fig. 125 Core damage repair on double skin plastic dinghy.

b

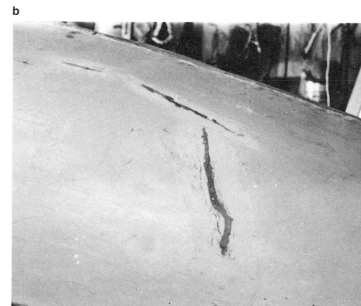

using fibreglass, provided a polished metal finish is replaced by paintwork. A two- or three-layer patch (as described above) on the inside, plus resin putty filling outside, is normally adequate. Note that ordinary polyester resin does not adhere reliably to metal, and epoxy resin is better. In any case, always scuff the metal ruthlessly – preferably with a coarse abrasive disc.

Riveting

Serious light alloy damage is normally a job for the original makers, but the handyman can get by with a doubling plate riveted to the inside. Make this the same thickness as the hull skin. Radius the corners neatly and use a double row of staggered countersunk rivets all around, with further single rows across the plate if necessary. Grind the rivet heads flush on the outside and make good with resin putty. Bed everything in mastic, especially below the waterline.

Glued tingles

Surprisingly successful repairs to holes and cracks no wider than $\frac{3}{16}$ in (4 mm) in metal dinghies can be undertaken with *tingles*. These are single patches of canvas stuck on (and doped with) epoxy glue, both inside and outside the hull, then painted over. A quick repair to a hole under ½ in (12 mm) in diameter is possible by using a saucepan mender. This consists of a small through-bolt sandwiching a pair of rubber washers each side of the hull skin, covered by metal washers under head and nut. Standard hardware store fittings will do for a steel hull, but for light alloy you need to make the washers and bolt from compatible metal, to avoid galvanic action.

Tacked tingles

Small holes and leaky bolt heads on wooden craft are traditionally repaired with tingles. These are made as in Fig. 126, comprising a canvas patch set in thick paint or mastic, covered by a copper plate held with closely spaced copper tacks around the edge. Cut the plate first (from 24-gauge (0.6 mm) sheet copper) and pierce the tack holes using a sharp spike and hammer. Mark its position on the hull, apply filler to seal the leak, cut the canvas a little smaller than the copper, then soak this with paint, stick it to the hull, and tack the copper into place. Unless it looks unsightly, such a tingle may be left in place indefinitely.

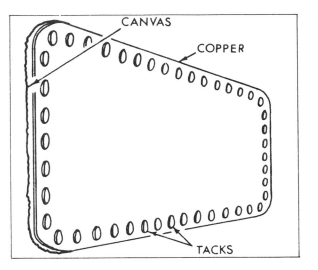

Fig. 126 Components of a tingle to cover planked hull damage.

Rubber

Pin-holes in the fabric of a rubber boat are easy to repair with one of the kits which most makers supply. To avoid failures on reinforced seams or big splits, stitch across first as in Fig. 85. This also stops a lot of glue seeping through on to the opposite wall. After degreasing, fine sanding is essential before sticking on a patch. One can buy plastic clamps to screw over a split – one strip inside, one outside. For porous old boats there are rejuvenation kits with a liquid sealer to pour into each compartment, plus external paint. A serious tear is normally the subject of an insurance claim, but the makers of inflatables may refuse to work on a boat that is more than about five years old (except to renew towing eyes, oar sockets, or outboard motor mountings) when the fabric is still far from the write-off stage.

Wet and dry

For dealing with wet suit damage, most chandleries stock repair kits with good instructions. In fact, you can fabricate a whole suit from a kit of parts. Metal zippers need careful rinsing in fresh water to delay corrosion and stop salt encrustation and the outside of the teeth should be lubricated with candle or beeswax. The less-well-off dread having to renew torn foul weather clothing. When buying new, aim for the makers who can supply repair patches for outside and inside, and are willing to renew zippers.

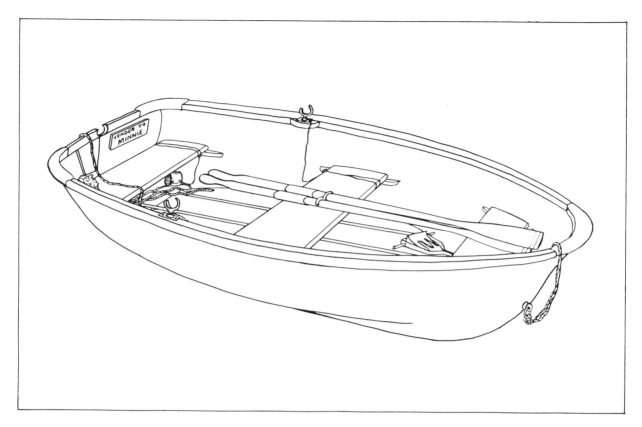

Fig. 127 A tender needs good fendering, a sculling notch, a name-plate, buoyancy, painters fore and aft, locking for the oars, lanyards on the rowlocks, an anchor, bailer and swab.

Improvements

Although a new racing dinghy is supposed to be complete and competitive, it may still be necessary to equip her with a towrope, anchor, paddle, bailer, and compass, while the experienced helmsman may wish to experiment with bottom paint, sail alterations, rigging adjusters, and such items as a turtle, chute, or basket for housing the spinnaker.

Painters
Few yachts' tenders are properly equipped as in Fig. 127. First, you need an eyebolt in the transom as well as in the stem to take painters fore and aft when securing her alongside the parent vessel. You may be able to rig an after painter around the stern thwart, but many dinghies have a buoyancy tank beneath the thwart with nowhere to make a rope fast. You also need a sculling notch, buoyancy, name-board, bailer, thief-proof oar security, anchor, swab, good fendering and perhaps a spare bung on a lanyard. A motor tender needs oars, just as a sailing dinghy needs a paddle.

Shipshape
Unless rowlocks (oarlocks or crutches) are of the captive variety, make sure they have proper lanyards rove onto them (see later). Some transoms need a reinforcing chock to receive an outboard motor, obviating damage from the clamps and from vibration and thrust. Without adequate buoyancy, a fibreglass or light alloy dinghy will sink if flooded. Grabrails like bilge keels (see Plate 98(e)), are a wise safety precaution in case of capsize and to prevent hull damage when beaching; also to locate the webbing gripes used to secure a dinghy on deck, as seen in Plate 98(a). A wheel built into the forefoot or stern facilitates handling on shore, especially when singlehanded – see later.

Plate 103 Rope fendering needs to be well stretched to avoid drooping between wire ties.

Protection

Rowing (and even racing) dinghies without rubber fendering are a menace and cause untold damage to other craft. This should extend over the top of the gunwale, stemhead, and transom quarters, as well as around the topsides. The same applies to runabouts and launches.

All-around-rope

A workboat-type coir rope fender is cheap and easy to fit. To stretch this, secure at the transom with the rope straight, then yank it out over the gunwale as shown in Plate 103. For a superior job which avoids grit getting into the rope, sew canvas over it before fitting. A smaller rope on top of the gunwale is necessary to ensure complete protection. Raising the rowlock sockets may be necessary. To terminate the big rope at the transom more neatly than seen in Plate 103, cut off square and whip. Bend up two small sheet brass straps to screw or bolt over the rope, tight enough to become slightly embedded into the lay. This method creates no obstruction to the use of an outboard motor.

Wire ties

Separate ties of 16-gauge copper wire sunk into the lay at about 6 in (150 mm) intervals are normally used to fix the rope in place. This works on most types of hull. Bend each tie into a U-shape and push the ends into two pre-drilled holes, then twist the

parts together inside the hull. If the sharp ends cannot be hidden under the gunwale, wrap them with vinyl tape.

Twisting hints

There is a knack to twisting wire parts neatly together (see Fig. 128). Cross the parts at right angles, give two twists with finger and thumb then, using heavy pliers, tighten these turns (pulling towards you at the same time) and continue twisting to make six turns. Make sure that the turns are even (avoiding the situation where one strand remains straight while the other winds around it) and be careful not to break the wire. With wire cutters, nick half-way through each wire close to the last turn, then make a seventh twist. By rocking the untwisted ends with your fingers, they should break off cleanly at the nicks, leaving a neat finish.

Using hose

Extruded white rubber fendering is expensive. Scrap 3 in (75 mm) bore canvas fire hose filled with granulated cork (or small cubes of upholstery foam) makes an effective alternative. It need not be in one continuous length. Sew across one end, forming a fixing flap, perhaps with eyelet, then make a funnel from cardboard and staples to simplify filling. If the hose is too large, sew along it to form a tab (see Fig. 129(a)) and use this to fix it to the boat. Otherwise, webbing straps at 14 in (350 mm) intervals work best, and enable the fender to be mounted above

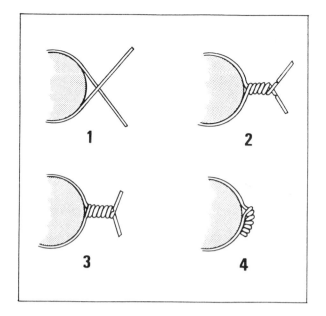

Fig. 128 Twisted wire will not cause injury if nicked before the final turn.

gunwale level (Fig. 129(b)). Such fendering is fairly easy to take off for painting, varnishing, or cleaning the hull. Inflatable fendering of large diameter is now becoming available – ideal, but not cheap.

Fibreglass fixing

Stainless steel self-tapping screws drive well into thin fibreglass provided the correct size pilot hole is bored. If their points would be exposed, use small bolts with cap nuts to prevent injury. Always fit generous washers where screw or bolt heads come against canvas or rubber. An outboard motor can shake nuts loose, so glue the threads with Loctite fluid. When shopping for brass or stainless steel fastenings, take a small magnet with you: plated mild steel can look identical to the real thing, but must never be used on a boat.

Fender pads

Particularly for a motor tender or launch with inadequate all-around fendering, home-made pad fenders (Plate 78(b)) are superb. The padded straps are screwed beneath the gunwale inside, allowing stowage under way as in Fig. 130(a). When coming

Fig. 130 Pad fenders need just a flick of the wrist to place outboard.

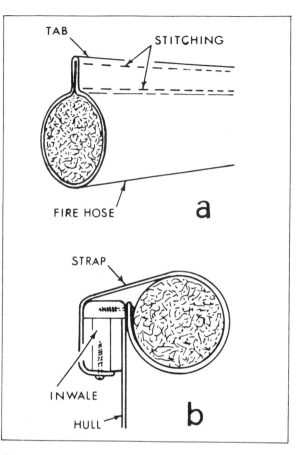

Fig. 129 Two ways to mount fendering made from stuffed fire hose.

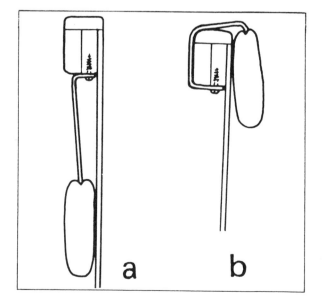

alongside, flip as many as necessary over the gunwale to position themselves automatically ready for action, as in Fig. 130(b). For instructions about making these, see page 153.

Buoyancy

Nearly all racing dinghies have built-in buoyancy as required by the class rules. It pays to equip even wooden rowboats and motor tenders with as much buoyancy as possible to improve safety and subsequent recovery should they go adrift.

Air bags
Supplying inflatable buoyancy bags (or making them to the shape you require) is a regular chandlery service. Finding adequate fixing points inside a modern dinghy is not easy, but bags must be well secured. On wood, plastics, or metal hulls, bond hardwood chocks inside the boat with epoxy adhesive. Make sure that surface preparation is perfect and that the chocks are shaped to fit any curvature. Standard eye straps can then be attached to receive the buoyancy bag lashings.

Permanent buoyancy
Air tanks beneath the thwarts look neat and are not too difficult to install, but take care not to obstruct foot-space for a comfortable rowing position. This is certain to necessitate two separate boxes under the stern bench with a space in the middle. Often the best location is port and starboard just below thwart level, running as nearly as possible the full length of the boat.

Rigid boxes
The cheapest and quickest way to build in buoyancy is to use expanded polyurethane blocks, boxed in with painted or varnished plywood. Fibreglass panels should be laid up on formers of wood, metal, or glass (covered with cellophane for easy release) and then shaped to bond into the hull. For extra rigidity, make foam sandwich panels – Airex or balsa cores covered each side with thin fibreglass. The super-handyman can rivet tanks of sheet metal into a light alloy hull, duly sealed with mastic, but plywood is easier to handle for the majority.

Poured foam
Unless hollow compartments are to be used as lockers with watertight doors, it pays to fill them with poured foam plastics. Having added the catalyst, a measured amount of the liquid is poured in

through a prepared hole at the top. After a brief time interval, this expands to fill the compartment. Any surplus which exudes through the aperture (and other unexpected cracks) may be cut away after hardening.

Pressure test
Hollow tanks are sure to leak at some time, and drainage bungs should be provided. Boxes housing blocks of lightweight plastics also need weep holes at the bottom. To locate a leak, pressurize the tank with air, and watch for bubbles when soapy water is brushed along all the seams. To supply pressure, make up a cork bung with a piece of metal tube pushed through it. Get an old truck inner tube with no valve. Blow it up by mouth using a length of rubber pipe. Couple this pipe to the inserted bung and squeeze the inner tube. Higher pressure than this is not normally necessary or advisable.

Rowing and sculling

The useful expedient of propelling a dinghy by means of a single oar (supported by a notch at the top of the transom stern) is rarely practised nowadays. Modern boats of fibreglass, light alloy, or rubber have insufficient grip on the water, except when heavily loaded, for effective sculling. The method is certainly useful when you lose an oar, or when ferrying a big pile of gear in the dinghy precludes rowing with oars.

Wrist action
Big, straight-keeled dinghies scull best. For maximum speed, stand up and clap both hands on the oar. The knack is soon acquired. Sweep the oar from side to side keeping the blade at an angle of about 45° (see Fig. 131), angled in the direction which keeps the blade submerged. Without changing your grip, rock your wrist (or wrists) through 90° at the end of each stroke, as gracefully and effortlessly as possible. Naturally enough, a light boat with little submersion will yaw at each stroke, while the oar blade remains almost static!

Transom notch
The inexperienced sculler needs a fairly deep notch (see Fig. 127) to keep the oar from jumping out unexpectedly. Normally, the notch need be no deeper than the oar diameter. As oar leathering is rarely in the right place for sculling, it pays to line the notch with leather (see page 101) and dope this

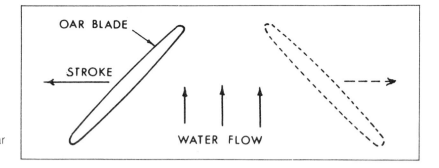

Fig. 131 When sculling, the oar works like a propeller blade.

occasionally with leather oil. Any conventional crutch, rowlock or oarlock (with its socket mounted on a chock bolted inside the transom) acts better than a notch on big dinghies, and when the sculler is standing up. However, a notch is also useful to guide the rope when recovering a kedge anchor.

Rowlocks

The devices for supporting oars range from simple pairs of upright wooden pegs (tholepins), through removable rowlocks of various shapes (see Fig. 132), to foldaway types and hollow plastic ones that will float. Beginners might appreciate the boating-lake system with oars permanently attached by special swivels. Normally, pins or crutches that cannot be unshipped are a curse, marking topsides and creating snarl-ups with painters and other lines. The stream-lined moulded rubber crutches on inflatable dinghies snarl ropes to a lesser extent, but if the oars are a tight fit in these, apply soap or Vaseline to prevent the oars from creeping inboard as you row.

Horn shapes

The best rowlock has one horn longer than the other, as in Fig. 132(a). This is not designed to prevent the oar from jumping out, but to turn the rowlock into line as soon as the oar touches the long horn. With equal horns (Fig. 132(b)) you will need one hand to

rotate the crutch while the other drops the oar into it. Such loss of time can be important in an emergency. The pattern in Fig. 132(c) is good for sculling, and in the larger sizes for sailing craft which use a pair of long sweeps instead of an auxiliary motor.

The Yuloh

For prolonged manual propulsion, the yuloh (of Chinese origin) is the most effortless device known. Although similar to sculling, there are three advantages. First, the single shaft (up to 33 ft (10 m) long) stays put without being held, having a cord from handle end to deck and a pivot at the stern. Secondly, the blade reverses its angle automatically by means of flexibility in the outboard half of the shaft. Thirdly, anyone can operate it, for the handle is merely pushed and pulled gently athwartships.

Lanyards

Ordinary rowlocks are sure to get stolen or lost overboard unless equipped with lanyards. Do not buy rowlocks with no groove or hole just below the horns to receive this. The small hole at the bottom of the shaft is there to enable a spare pair of rowlocks to be wired together and hung from a nail on the shed wall. A short safety lanyard with a weight attached can be made fast to the small hole at the

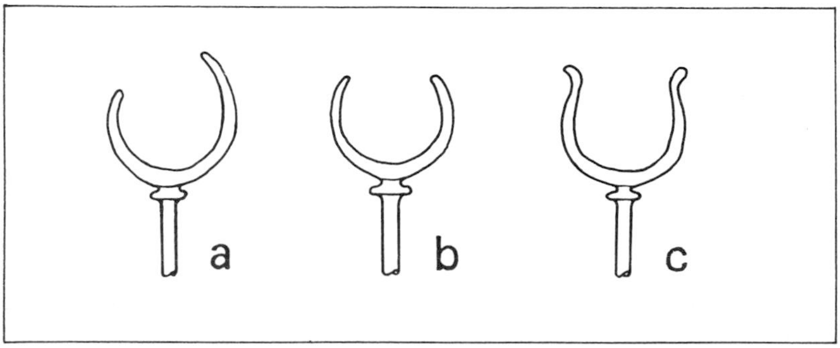

Fig. 132 Three common patterns of rowlock.

tip, but sooner or later the knot will jam in the gunwale socket and you will need two hands to ship the rowlock. A lanyard spliced to the neck groove is much better. At the other end, make an eye splice large enough to pass the rowlock through. Allow adequate cord length for the lanyard to be noosed around the nearest thwart, as in Fig. 127.

Interference

For a brief spell ashore, unship the rowlocks and wind one lanyard around the oars to minimize interference from children. For a longer spell ashore, take the other rowlock with you. Still better, have a ramshorn oar lock (Fig. 127) and take both rowlocks away. If you frequent a place where meddling is rife, fit a chain painter. Provide an enlarged link at the bitter end equipped with a decent padlock.

Oars

Details of oar lengths and how to make them are given in *Complete Amateur Boat Building*. Dinghy oars are usually of silver spruce, while sweeps up to 10 ft (3 m) long are generally of ash or hickory. Plastics have not so far proved any better or cheaper. Most jointed oars for rubber dinghies have a metal spigot and socket in the middle. This needs wiping and lightly smearing with Vaseline once a month to prevent it from jamming. Leave such oars assembled whenever possible to exclude dirt.

Racing oars

Note that although the spoon-bladed oars used by rowing clubs are more efficient than sea oars (blades identical both sides), the latter are essential for yachting, as on a dark night there is no need to worry about the blade orientation. Also, sea oars rarely have *buttons* (stops) to align the oar against the rowlock, thus preventing the leathering from wearing in one spot, and allowing rowing from one thwart either singlehanded or by two people.

Sleeves

Some modern oars have a moulded plastic sleeve instead of leather, usually with a button incorporated. Sleeves sometimes work loose and require a couple of small countersunk screws near the outboard end, using carefully drilled holes to prevent cracking the sleeve.

Leathering

Renewing oar leathers is a fascinating job for the handyman. Chrome leather a full ⅛ in (3 mm) thick is ideal (see page 102). Make them about 1 in (25 mm) longer than the old leathers to cover the original tack holes. If the old leathers were in the wrong place for your boat; now is the time to centralize them.

Skiving

When measuring the leather to wrap around an oar, allow at least ⅜ in (9 mm) overlap for the joint. Flush joints in leather are made by skiving – similar to joining two pieces of wood by scarfing – see Fig. 133(a). A skiving knife (like a stiff palette knife, with the tip sharpened into a slightly curved blade) is ideal for this. You can make one out of a piece of heavy duty machine hacksaw blade (see page 27). Lay the leather flat on a piece of board and skive away to make a bevel along the edge of the leather, pushing the knife away from you and tapering down almost to a feather edge. Notice from Fig. 133(a) that the overlapping edge of the joint is skived on the inside (rough) surface of the leather, whereas the underneath part of the joint is **skived on the outside** (smooth) leather surface. Check the length around the oar and determine whether both oars are the same diameter. Skive off a little more if necessary: too short is better than too long. Finally, skive from the inside of the hide along the ends of each piece (Fig. 133(b)) to produce the neat tapered finish shown in Fig. 133(d).

Softening

If necessary, apply two coats of varnish to the wood which will be covered by the leather. Submerge the leather in water over night to soften it. Use five or six tacks through the underneath skive to align the seam as in Fig. 133(c). Position this in line with the oar blade so that the seam will never bear fully against the rowlock.

Close tacks

Bands of tape or ribbon help to stretch the leather around the oar. It pays to scratch marks on the seam overlap to prevent driving any of the final tacks on top of the hidden ones. Flat-headed cut copper tacks ⅜ in (9 mm) long, set ½ in (12 mm) apart, suffice for both seam and ends, when using leather of normal thickness. The hide will shrink on tightly when dry and that is the time to apply a few coats of neatsfoot oil. Apply more of this occasionally over a period of time; it will increase the life of the leather greatly.

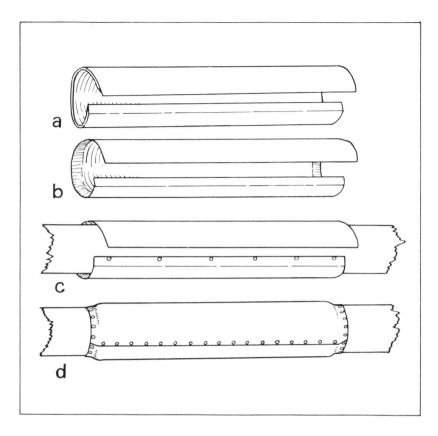

Fig. 133 Fixing leather to an oar.

Adding buttons

As mentioned above, buttons are helpful for children and other people learning to row. Six helical turns of standard ¾ in (18 mm) leather strap will usually build up an adequate button diameter. Keep driving occasional copper nails of increasing length as you wind, and glue between each turn with latex adhesive, as used by shoe repairers. You will need to drill pilot holes, as nails will not drive easily through thick leather. Skive underneath the bitter end to make it lie flat.

Towing a tender

As mentioned previously, a tender is best stowed on deck when a yacht is on passage. Ironically, inflatable dinghies which tow with little effort are the easiest to hoist aboard. A heavy dinghy can snatch the tow line in rough weather, the situation worsening if she becomes waterlogged by spray.

Surging

To discourage a tender from surging forward and hitting the parent vessel, some enthusiasts make a rigid tubular towbar with a universal joint at each end. Heavy-duty spinnaker boom end fittings suffice to make quick-release attachments. The painter should be used as a safety rope. Some people tow a bucket over the dinghy's stern to act as a drogue, and lessen surging.

Yawing

Any sort of tender keeps on station more readily if twin towropes are used, one made fast to the port quarter and one to starboard of the yacht. If she rides better with one rope, leave the other one slack as a safety measure. To guard against eye-bolt failure, secure one rope around the for'ard thwart. Make sure that neither rope can chafe anywhere. To stop an inflatable from yawing or blowing over, bring her bow right up to the taffrail.

Logline

Certain precautions may be necessary to prevent a towed dinghy from fouling the line of a taffrail log spinner. Well-found yachts have two log recorder sockets for this reason, one on each quarter. If you use the windward socket, the dinghy will normally drift slightly to leeward and keep out of the way of the logline, while the yacht's leeway will also assist.

Swamping

If shut manually on arrival, a self-bailer stops swamping, but an overall cover is better. Bailing alongside while under way is dangerous. With all open boats (and cockpits too), make sure that sole boards and floatable gear is always well secured. Should a boat sink when moored, such gear could disappear for ever.

Running maintenance

If annual fitting-out is thorough, a dinghy, sailboard, or runabout should need little in-season maintenance except for cleaning and careful storage when out of use. As with big boats, speedy touching up of paint and varnish keeps a dinghy smart, and may save a much bigger workload at the season's end.

Hosing

All seagoing dinghies benefit from a regular hose down with fresh water, drying off completely with a sponge or wash leather on completion. Unless there is heavy rain at the time, this should always be done to a sailing dinghy after racing (see Plate 69), starting with the hoisted sail. A hose jet is not only quick, but reaches all interstices better than bucket and sponge treatment. Removing saltiness helps minimize absorption of moisture by a wooden hull, which can add considerably to a dinghy's weight.

Washing

Unless the cruising owner is based at a marina, his tender will have to be taken ashore for washing. The method is similar for a rigid dinghy, inflatable, or collapsible boat.

Remove bottom boards (Plate 104) and all loose gear, then up-end her (Plate 105) against a pile, or with helping hands behind her. Dash several buckets of water into the bilges, scrub out with a soft haired brush, then douse again. Lay her upside-down to scrub the bottom, turn right way up, then wash topsides and transom to remove any mud or grit accumulated during the previous operations.

On shore

Windage on the mast of a sailing dinghy left ashore can blow her over unless she is stabilized with padded squats or car tyres. A small tender is best

Plate 104 Removing dinghy bottom boards prior to bilge cleaning.

turned over and supported slightly above ground. An unpainted light alloy boat can corrode if left in contact with damp ground or grass.

Airing

Leave dinghies ashore tilted (with the stern bungs open) so that water can drain away. Self-bailers might get damaged if left lowered. With a waterproof cover rigged, leave buoyancy tank inspection covers open to ventilate inside. The varnish may peel from a plywood deck having a buoyancy tank beneath it which is constantly damp.

Covering

If the boom is used as a ridge pole under the cover, pack a sponge or some rag under it at any point where it rests on deck or coaming. A good way to stop rainwater from ponding is to bend a halyard to the eyelet in a special tag sewn to the cover (Plate

Plate 105 The quickest way to clean out a tender when no hosepipe is available.

Plate 106 Main halyard used to stretch a sailing dinghy cover. This avoids rainwater ponding as seen in Plate 17.

106). On a rowboat or tender you need three springy wooden bows (or light alloy tubes) to hump an overall cover upwards. Special sockets are made to secure the ends of bow slats.

Bottom
Antifouling paint is not required on dinghies which are normally kept on dry land. Without such protection, a dinghy left afloat (or at a tidal landing stage) will grow weed and barnacles if not brought ashore occasionally for a scrub. Use hard racing antifouling paint where applicable, as this will not rub off so easily when the boat is hauled up a beach. Your racing dinghy may have a minimum friction graphite-painted bottom which needs monthly flatting with very fine wet abrasive paper.

Performance
A perfect bottom finish is essential for high performance boats. Experts have their own pet maintenance procedures, including matt graphite and wax polished matt or glossy varnish. The enthusiast who intends to win races must also keep an eye on rigging adjustments, toe or hiking straps, faults in fittings, washing sails and sheets, and removing any roughness on the tips of drop keel and rudder. When a sailing dinghy is on shore, leaving halyards to rattle against the mast, and burgee (or wind vane) to oscillate night and day not only causes unnecessary deterioration, but is also a source of noise pollution.

Hazards
Especially when winter (frostbite) sailing is undertaken, constant safety checks on rigging, rudder, buoyancy and loose gear are essential. Small leaks in PVC buoyancy bags are easy to seal with repair kits unless they occur right on a welded seam. In such cases, returning to the makers, or the purchase of a new bag is expedient. Make sure that equipment such as anchor, paddle, and bailing scoop are made fast, to minimize theft risks and loss during a capsize.

Deep sea
Intrepid voyagers have made long passages in suitably equipped sailing dinghies, such as Frank Dye, whose exploits in his 16 ft (5 m) Wayfarer (often accompanied by his wife) included trips from England to Norway and Iceland. A lot of experience is necessary before trying this, and the craft must be prepared with great precision. Extra-strong through-bolted rudder fittings are essential, and there must be no wear at the drop keel pivot. Certain stores and gear must be kept dry as well as secure and out of the way. Except in an ideal climate, you need a snug over-boom tent to rig at night.

Winter work

With the exception of true or simulated clinker planking, dinghy hull surface preparation, painting, or varnishing, can follow the instructions given in Chapters 3 and 4. Clinker (lapstrake) should be treated plank by plank instead of in panels. If the inside has steamed timbers, good work becomes laborious. Unless planked with plywood, clinker boats should be stored in a cool place and not allowed to dry out too much. Winter is generally the best time to deal with repair jobs.

Laying-up
If such a boat must be laid up out of doors, turn the hull upside down on chocks and sheet her over, preferably using canvas that can breathe. Once painting and varnishing is completed and the hull turned right-way-up, keep her hosed down during warm dry weather to prevent the seams from opening. Do not leave water in the bilges when there is any risk of frost.

Best months
Planking shrinkage is best avoided on any traditional wooden craft when on shore. This will not occur in most parts of Europe and North America between the months of November and April. Outside this period, hosing down will be advisable, but remember that a large quantity of water in the bilges could damage the fastenings and caulking of an old hull. Wooden open boats are sometimes seen submerged in shallow water or partly filled to hasten the process of taking up the seams. This does no harm provided the water is bailed out before the boat sits on the bottom in tidal waters.

Lapstrake interiors
Power tools are of little value when sanding or stripping the inside of a traditional clinker or lapstrake boat. Discoloration around copper rivets, and previous neglect, make it advisable to change from varnish to paint on some old boats. It may be possible to leave thwarts (gunwale capping, transom and other parts) as varnishwork for a few more years if this will improve the boat's appearance.

Special tools

An old hacksaw blade is handy for scraping dirt from the numerous tapered slots behind the steamed timbers when stripping, but for a quick annual refit, a small bottle brush dipped in paint thinner is adequate. A range of flat and triangular scrapers of varying sizes will be needed to tackle the numerous small panels without damaging adjacent parts.

Sweeping out

A vacuum cleaner saves hours of work when clearing out the debris. If there is no power outlet handy, buy or borrow a 12-volt model, or a converter to enable a domestic cleaner to be operated from a car battery.

Lapstrake outside

Painting the exterior of a clinker hull is in many ways simpler than for a smooth carvel surface. The division into narrow panels makes sanding or scraping less tiring and enables paint or varnish to be laid off more neatly with only one drying edge to watch. Run-marks from the plank seams are minimized if the hull is upside-down. When painting the inside, start at the hog (keel), sitting inside the boat to do most of it (and under any decking), then stand outside leaning over the gunwales to reach the remainder. Watch continuously for runmarks from the lands and alongside the ribs.

Cleaning rubber

With age, the rubber used for fendering tends to powder at the surface. This makes it easy to clean with a detergent scrub, while paint marks are easily scraped off. Hypalon, polyurethane-coated nylon, and similar rubber-like fabrics used for inflatables look smart after a good scrub, but removing stains is often impossible without damaging the surface. Small paint splashes should be left until rock hard, when they may fall off if pushed with the back of a knife. If paint thinner is used straight away, wash off with soapy water as soon as possible afterwards. Good marine hardware stores keep special paint for rubber.

Liferaft in winter

Unless a liferaft has been used, few owners bother to follow makers' instructions and have them serviced every year. On extended cruises this may be impossible. Rather than neglect such an important item, get the necessary details from the maker, so that you can inflate the raft with a hand pump to check for leaks, weigh the pressure cylinder, check the stores and equipment, apply French chalk, and re-pack everything in the correct manner. However, going for three years without a professional check-up is an invitation to disaster. In general, inflatable boats are best stored partially inflated when not in use.

Trailers and trolleys

Many racing dinghy enthusiasts keep a road trailer. Even those who never need to trail their boat behind a car need a simple launching trolley that will not get damaged by repeated dunking in water.

Heavy towing

For economical winter lay-up at home, some owners of cruising boats up to about 29 ft (9 m) in length keep a heavy duty four-wheeled road trailer (Plate 107), though it may need the hire of a stouter vehicle than the family car to tow it. In between these and the dinghy size comes the trailer/sailer equipment, with rocking break-back or rolling piggy-back launching cradle arrangement. The strong integral winch must be capable of pulling the boat off as well as on without needing to submerge the wheels of either trailer or car, (see Plate 108).

Night time

Towing at night with an overhanging load is particularly dangerous, so make sure that your trailer is equipped with efficient tail, brake, licence and turn signal lights, plus all necessary reflectors, including a hazard sign to hang at the end of the mast or other overhang. These items are sensible (and usually legal) requirements, even in daylight. For a night trip it pays to be prepared for trouble by carrying the usual roadside hazard signs and flashing lights.

Simple trolley

As you can observe at any yacht club dinghy pen, a launching trolley is easy to fabricate at home from wood, steel tube and bar. Marine stores often stock suitable wheels. Those wheels with plain bearings running on bar axles need frequent oiling to prevent squeaks and undue wear. Solid rubber wheels with no bearing sleeve will not last long unless the axles are of brass or stainless steel. To convert mild steel stub axles, it may be possible to cover them with short lengths of copper water pipe or chromium plated brass towel rail, bonded with epoxy resin.

Plate 107 Trailing a heavy boat requires four road wheels.

Plate 108 This trailer-sailer is being launched from a breakback trailer. (*Picture by courtesy of Newbridge Boats Ltd, Bridport, England.*)

Wide wheels

Small, solid trolley wheels are ideal for launching on a boat ramp, but for a shingle beach you need rubber tread with an overall diameter at least 12 in (300 mm). On soft sand or mud you need extra wide pneumatics of large diameter. Failing this, double wheels on single axles work well, or wooden slat rollers, as seen in Plate 109.

Supports

Road trailers have adjustable bilge and keel supports, perhaps incorporating rollers to facilitate single-handed loading, aided by a small winch. The supports on a trolley are often shaped to match one boat and can soon deteriorate due to repeated submersion. Annual renewal of support coverings could be necessary if sheet rubber (which perishes and tears) has been used, or old carpet, which gets charged with grit. One of the best coverings is old 3 in (75 mm) canvas fire hose. Slit this lengthways to form a sheet 9 in (220 mm) wide.

Spare wheel

Except on short journeys, it pays to carry a complete spare road trailer wheel, plus a jack and a wheel nut (lug) wrench. A blow-out may go unnoticed for some distance, and cause considerable damage. Ordering replacements of correct size could involve long delays. Stow the wheel in your car to prevent theft from an unattended trailer.

Inflation

A foot pump to deal with slow leaks is worth carrying. Even better would be a small 12-volt compressor, perhaps one of those spark plug hole adaptors with sufficient length of airline, or a scuba diving bottle with suitable pressure reducing valve.

Greasing

Light road trailer wheel hubs have a grease nipple between the two ball races which needs little-and-often pumping with the grease gun. If the trailer is submerged for launching, grease before and after the event, always using underwater grease. Keep the ball coupling socket well greased, not forgetting its locking mechanism. Note that special clamps are made to lock across road wheels and coupling to deter thieves from hitching up on a dark night.

Plate 109 Homemade slatted roller trolley for launching over soft sand.

Brakes

The wheel bearings of larger trailers with brakes are often sealed like those on a car, without nipples. It pays to dismantle these and pack the bearings with fresh grease every two or three years. Keep all wheel nuts and studs well coated with graphite grease. Overrun brakes, over a certain weight limit, are mandatory in most countries. Also, exposed outboard or sterndrive propellers are considered a dangerous load, so cover them with stout canvas bags, duly lashed on.

Steelwork

If you get some matching paint with a new trailer, you can keep it looking like new for at least ten years. All the steelwork should be galvanized, so be careful not to scratch this when stripping old paint. Painting by brush is quite good enough for a trailer, though the original may have been sprayed on. Steel tubes and box sections often corrode more inside than out. Used regularly, the various anti-rust products intended for cars work fine. Saturating with automotive oil is cheap and effective, but somewhat messy. Filling with foaming polyurethane (see page 222) suits new trailers.

Springs

Although most modern dinghy trailers have bonded rubber or torsion bar springing, older types utilize coil or leaf springs, which often rust badly. You must remove such springs for effective cleaning and painting. If you intend to keep the trailer for several years, it will pay to send coil springs away for shot-blasting and zinc spraying. Leaf springs are best kept smeared with underwater grease and protected by canvas gaiters secured at their ends with stainless steel hose clips. However, springs with rubber inserts between the leaves should be painted instead of greased.

Slack bolts

Dreadful things can happen on the road if parts of a trailer come adrift, so do not rely entirely on an annual check for slack bolts and wear. Fitting locknuts or doping the threads with Loctite should cure the problem of parts which persistently loosen. Bolts or nuts with badly worn threads must be renewed. Never use strong-arm tactics on obstinate stud nuts. Penetrating oil may need a day or two to act, but heat from a small blow-torch normally provides instant relief. If you are not mechanically minded, get a motor fitter to check and adjust overrun brakes. Make sure you have a safety chain between car and trailer to guard against a coupling failure.

Roof stowage

Dinghies under about 60 lb (27 kg) in weight are easily carried upside-down on a car roof rack. Up to 120 lb (54 kg) is possible on a big car, if a special roll-on-roll-off frame is provided. Sailboards, canoes and demountable catamarans are good subjects for

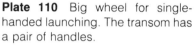
Plate 110 Big wheel for single-handed launching. The transom has a pair of handles.

car roofs, provided help is always available when shifting them. Roof racks incorporating rollers (especially at the rear end) make single-handed loading and unloading feasible.

Single wheel
Some dinghies have a solid rubber wheel built into a skeg under the transom, greatly facilitating single-handed launching. The idea works far better when a large diameter wheel is mounted on brackets under the stem, as in Plate 110. Handles on the transom then give excellent control when one person needs to move the boat. A wheelbarrow wheel with quick-release demountable bracket made by the handyman ensures that performance will not be upset when rowing or if towed behind a yacht. Although not quite so convenient, a pair of wheels can be clamped to the top of the transom and the boat turned upside-down for wheeling.

Launching rollers
Two or three large-diameter inflatable rubber rollers under the keel simplify beach launching greatly. They can even be utilized as buoyancy bags if secured inside a dinghy after launching! Such rollers need to be about 3 ft (1 m) in length and at least 8 in (200 mm) in diameter.

12
Berthing, Mooring and Laying-up

Books about boat handling and seamanship are readily available at bookshops and libraries. This chapter treats the subject of berthing, mooring and laying-up from the maintenance viewpoint: how to keep a boat safely when left unoccupied or on shore, without boatyard assistance. But for books, it would take the newcomer many years to acquire the longshore know-how of the older hands.

Berthing

Apart from using a boat's own anchor, or hauling out, there are six basic methods of berthing or mooring, with many variations possible.

(1) Swinging to a permanently anchored buoy or chain.
(2) Keeping steady between two buoys, or piles.
(3) With shore lines astern and the bow secured to a buoy, or by the boat's anchor and cable.
(4) At a marina slip or floating pontoon.
(5) Alongside another boat.
(6) At a quay, wall, or stage mooring.

Swinging
With secure ground tackle, a swinging mooring (Plate 6) is normally safe, clean, and easy to pick up. You either bring the buoy on board with its rope followed by the rising chain, or the buoy remains afloat and has an attached strop which is brought on board. The best swinging moorings keep a boat in deep water at all times. Many craft are driven onto the mud at low tide in creeks when the wind is in a certain direction. Half-tide moorings are frequently used nowadays when space is so limited.

Chain-make-off
To make fast reliably, take a couple of round turns to check surging, then take a bight of chain under the standing part (see Fig. 134) and loop it over the post, finishing with another two round turns. In some places it may be advisable to clap a padlock across the links. Fit anti-chafe packing if there is no proper roller fairlead and rig a bow fender (Plate 111) to prevent the chain from scraping the topsides during wind-against-tide conditions.

Buoy ring
When mooring to a massive buoy with no strop, make fast initially with a temporary rope through the ring on the buoy, but shackle the ship's anchor chain to the ring (or bring the end back on board for handy slipping later) if staying for any length of time. When mooring between two buoys, you may have to use rope aft, but always rig a secondary line for additional security.

Grab-it hook
A special type of boathook is made to simplify the above operations. It has a large snap hook at the business end with a rope attached to it. As soon as this touches the ring, your boat is moored, and the boathook handle can then be detached by twisting it.

233

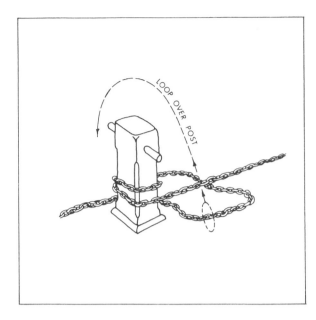

Fig. 134 To belay a chain, pass a bight under the standing part and loop it over the post.

Plate 112 Sliding ring on pile keeps mooring lines taut as tide level fluctuates.

Plate 111 Bow fenders save damage from anchor cables as well as in bow-to-pontoon mooring situations.

Between piles

Fore-and-aft moorings between piles are frequently encountered. Striking a buoy when approaching normally causes no harm but great care is necessary when getting close enough to a pile for a line to be passed. In blustery conditions the tender is often useful when getting a rope across to the after pile.

Kites

In tidal water, each line must be made fast to a device which slides up and down the pile. One arrangement consists of a square wooden frame called a *kite* which is slipped over each pile and floats on the water. In another system, there is a vertical steel bar fixed to each side of each pile, upon

Plate 113 Mediterranean stern-to mooring simplifies rigging the gang-plank.

which slides a big steel ring, suspended by a rope to prevent it from dropping out of reach (see Plate 112).

Bow direction

You will normally find all boats facing the same way at fore-and-aft moorings; usually stemming the ebb tide in a river or creek. Do not let this jeopardize your method of approach – once moored, turning the boat end-for-end is simple if you wait for slack tide conditions.

Stern-to

In many European ports, yachts are obliged to moor as in Plate 113, at right angles to a quay or pontoon. Stern-to simplifies rigging a gangplank, but getting into position unaided in a gale of wind is far from easy, even when a buoyed mooring or pile is provided for the bow line. You need plenty of fenders and you may have to drop the anchor (with tripping line attached) under foot while a long warp is rowed ashore.

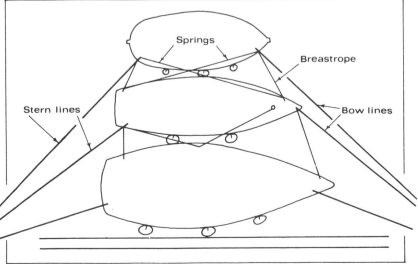

Fig. 135 Customary system of lines for crowded moorings in tidal waters.

Marina slip

Although similar to the above, entering a marina finger berth is easier, as you normally go in bow first, and there is a pontoon or catwalk alongside each boat, obviating the need for a gangplank. A pair of lines radiating from the bow to the main jetty, with a similar pair at the stern leading to piles, keep the boat steady and free from abrasion. Such berths are supposed to be supervised, but you need to ensure that all lines are covered with hosepipe or similar anti-chafe gear through chocks or fairleads and around mooring bollards.

Alongside

A gentle, well-fended approach is essential when tying up alongside another boat. Get the bow made fast quickly and if necessary put someone on board the other boat to receive the stern line. Again, turn her around at leisure if the safest approach must be made in a contrary direction. You must be prepared to provide all necessary fenders and lines. Where several craft are on a *trot* (rafted together), any new arrival must add separate warps to the piles, buoys, jetty, or wharf, and rig springs (see Fig. 135) as well as breast ropes to the adjacent boat.

Fenders

Ugly rubrails alongside can chop off your fenders in a swell. Stout shockcord lanyards help. To prevent a fender from riding upwards, rig a line from its bottom eye right under the hull, up to the opposite toerail. See also page 15. Slip on fender-boots to ward off dock scum. Hang canvas aprons to stop fenders from scratching your topsides.

Quay wall

Fending off from a quay with conventional vertical piling is successful only if a long spar or plank is hung outside the fenders, as seen in Fig. 136. Few boats carry fender boards, but suitable ones are sometimes kept available on the quay. In tideless waters, booming off is possible. A whisker pole for'ard, and perhaps a pair of oars lashed end-to-end aft, secured with rope snotters (Fig. 137), will sometimes suffice. Mooring whips are even better. Like huge springy fishing rods, they lean over the water at 45° with light lines from their tips to the boat.

Shore lines

At a tidal quay, you need very long bow and stern

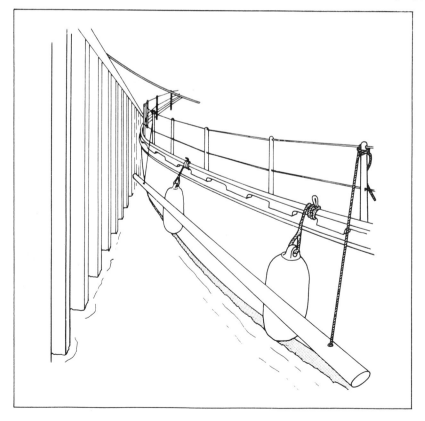

Fig. 136 Fenders will not lie against a piled wharf without using a plank or spar.

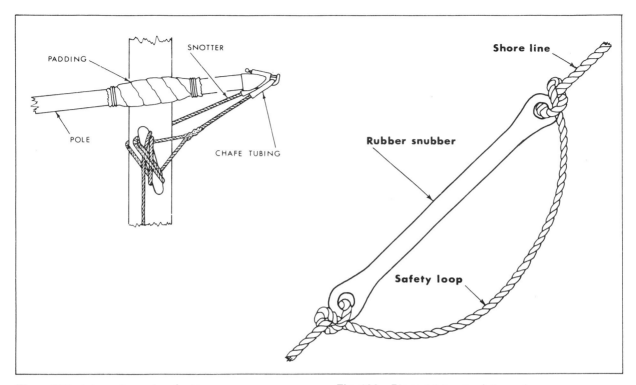

Fig. 137 Inboard end of improvised pole to hold a boat away from a rough bank.

Fig. 138 Rigged this way, failure of a rubber snubber will not cause disaster.

lines to obviate the need for adjustment as the boat rises and falls. A heavy weight (an *angel*) suspended from the middle of each line (as in Fig. 46) helps to prevent drifting away from the quay at high water. On the short lines used in marinas and stern-to berths, snubbers are of great benefit. One of these should be coupled near the landward end of each line to provide elasticity. There are rubber ones (Fig. 138) and steel spring types, as in Plate 114. Note that each line must loop around a snubber, as seen in Fig. 138, so that the line will remain intact if the snubber should break. When moored alongside, keep breast ropes slack and springs fairly tight, not forgetting due allowance for shrinkage when wet if hemp rope is used.

Listing

To prevent a deep-keeled boat from falling outwards as the tide drops, a few fathoms of anchor chain, some filled water breakers or sandbags and, for bigger craft a row of ballast pigs, will usually list her adequately towards a quay or scrubbing piles.

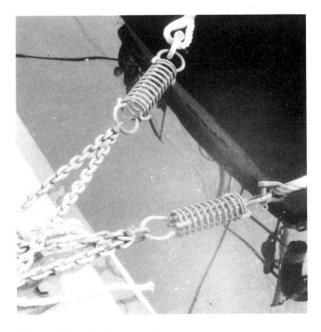

Plate 114 Spring snubbers use fail-safe compression springs.

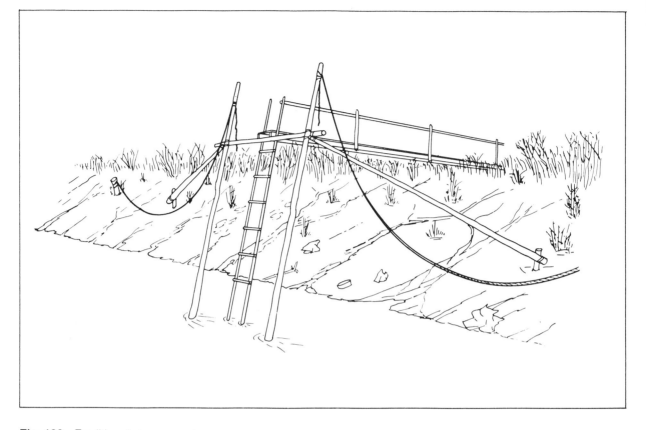

Fig. 139 Traditional stage mooring with shore lines ready to take on board.

Beware of the wash from passing powerboats which can cause an incorrect list at the critical moment. Remember, your boat could carry a permanent list which may affect the amount of ballasting required. With someone always on hand, a halyard leading from mast to shore can be adjusted to give the right amount of heel before she touches. With a small tidal range, this device can be automated by suspending a weight from the catenary, provided nobody tampers with it.

Stage mooring
Along tidal and non-tidal rivers and creeks you see these* made from sawn timber, fir poles, or old scaffolding tube, of various designs and dimensions. A typical stage mooring is shown in Fig. 139. When erecting one, care is necessary to ensure that the boat is kept well out into the stream, while the poles and catwalk are sufficiently high to ensure safety under exceptional high water levels. With long

enough fore-and-aft lines, no adjustment is necessary. Make these fast to stakes (or other forms of anchorage) around mid-tide height, and in such a manner that meddling is avoided. For additional safety, rig a wire hawser from stake to stake (or preferably to separate anchorages near by) and clap flexible wire breast ropes to this with wire rope clips. If each breast line ends with a thimbled eye, it can be belayed on board with a padlock. Lead the ropes through plastic hose to avoid chafe. (See later in this chapter for details of how to erect a simple stage.)

Swinging arms
Where a creek bed is too soft to support a stage, swinging arms are sometimes used. These are hinged at bank top (or further down) as in Fig. 140, and made fast to special stanchions above deck at each end of the boat. Similar shore lines to those for a stage mooring then keep the boat on station. Floats on the arms help to keep them free of mud

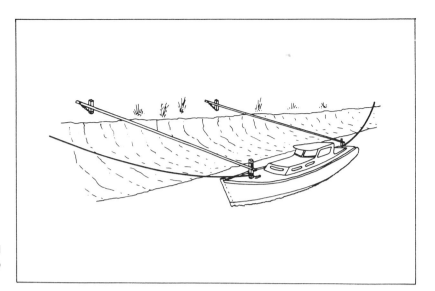

Fig. 140 Swinging arms work well in a tidal creek and help to keep intruders at bay.

when the mooring is unoccupied. A few links of chain make good onshore hinges, allowing for plenty of lateral movement. Like a deep water mooring, you normally need a dinghy to gain access to a boat on swinging arms. This helps to keep vandals at bay.

Running chain

At some locations a running mooring is most satisfactory, especially for dayboats, shoal-draft cruisers and small powerboats. From a block attached to a heavy anchor or driven pile, perhaps as much as 200 ft (60 m) offshore, an endless chain is rove, locked to a stake above high water mark. A bridle is shackled to the chain at one point. Having stepped ashore from the boat, the bridle is made fast to her, and by pulling on the ground chain the craft is moved out into deep water. The same system with rope (Plate 115) is used at sheltered locations.

Hypotenuse

The hypotenuse mooring shown in Fig. 141 is even simpler. The boat comes ashore with the ground chain or rope at point A, but she is transferred to deep water when full scope is made fast at point B.

Plate 115 In vandal-ridden locations, running moorings can be of chain with onshore locks.

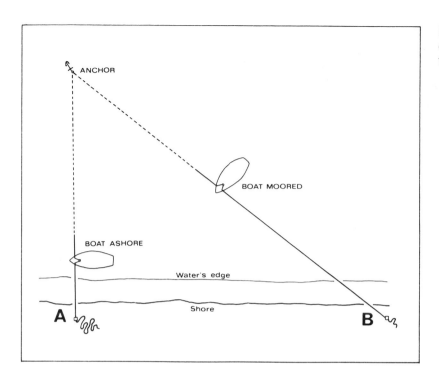

Fig. 141 In certain waters, nothing could be simpler than the hypotenuse mooring.

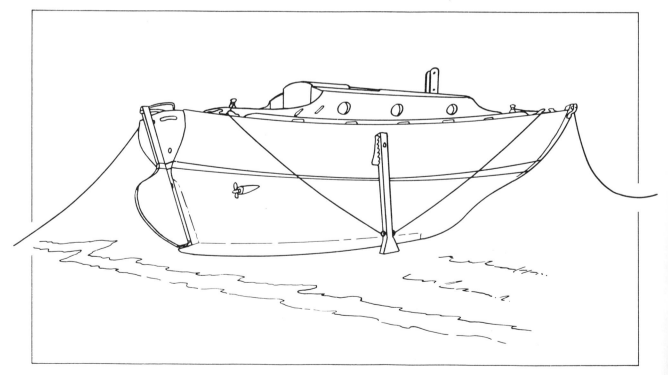

Fig. 142 Legs need guys to stop them from collapsing if the boat yaws.

On the beach

Other types of mooring are in use, such as sitting on a beach (or perhaps on soft mud) in a port which dries out. Most shoal-draft yachts will lie happily in this situation. Deep draft vessels should be equipped with legs (see Fig. 142) to keep them upright, then moored all fours, or with a heavy chain cable at bow and stern.

Legs

Once you have the topside bolt holes (with internal chocks) fitted, making a pair of legs is simple. Telescopic light alloy legs simplify the stowage problem and are adjustable for length. However, making legs of square timber (with padded curved chocks attached to conform to the shape of the topsides) suits the average handyman better. They should splay outwards slightly from the vertical, have adequate swelling at the heel to resist sinking in, and provision for rigging the essential fore-and-aft guy ropes seen in Fig. 142. The length should be 2 in (50 mm) to 3 in (75 mm) shorter than the full keel depth. On legs, some fin-and-skeg hulls can tilt or slew. Damage could also occur if a leg sinks like the bilge keel in Plate 116.

Laying a mooring

Although the yachting scene is so commercialized nowadays, there are still locations where it is possible to get permission to lay a mooring, but this usually means forgoing the amenities of fresh water, electricity and handy shopping.

Ground chain

To limit the turning circle, and to prevent fouling neighbouring installations, most swinging moorings have a very heavy ground chain laid at right angles to the tidal flow (or to the prevailing wind in static water), secured at each end to a sinker or anchor. The boat is made fast to a bridle chain, ideally shackled to the mid-point of the ground chain. Use short link (or stud link) chain of ½ in (12 mm) diameter for boats under 16 ft (5 m) in length; ⅝ in (16 mm) up to 22 ft (7 m); ¾ in (18 mm) up to 29 ft (9 m); 1 in (25 mm) up to 36 ft (11 m); 1¼ in (32 mm) up to 49 ft (15 m); and 1½ in (38 mm) up to 62 ft (19 m). With these sizes, only the middle few fathoms should ever shift across the bed when under load.

Bridle

The length of bridle chain is usually about double the depth at high water and the link diameter should be the same as that of the boat's anchor chain down to low water level, with a size larger from there down to the ground chain. Use a longer bridle if you are lucky enough not to have near neighbours and can keep clear of shallow water.

Swivel

To keep twists out of bridle chain, buy a heavy duty galvanized swivel to shackle between the light and heavy sections. Inspect this every three months to make sure that it will still turn. Some owners fit a second swivel just outboard of the boat's stem, to be on the safe side. In sandy waters, a swivel which is constantly submerged can wear quite rapidly.

Anchors

Special anchors are available for securing the ends of a ground chain, but many owners improvise by burning one fluke off a traditional anchor (Plate 117), or by bending one fluke to touch the shank (Plate 118), thus preventing damage or fouling. Typical anchor weights to match the ground chain sizes listed above (in pounds, with kilogram equivalents shown in brackets) are: 40 (18); 60 (27); 100 (45); 160 (72); 220 (100); 300 (135). If CQR (plow) anchors are used, and the bed is known to be suitable for these, the above figures may be halved.

Sinkers

Concrete block sinkers, or old engines, are sometimes used at the ends of mooring chains. They need to be at least three times the weight of an anchor and are thus difficult to get into position. Even if dug in, the tide may scour around them, reducing their holding power.

Mud anchors

For light moorings on mud, circular concrete slabs with concave bottoms are popular. They hold in place by suction. Steel mud anchors (shaped like

Plate 117 Cutting one fluke off an old anchor for a mooring ground chain.

mushrooms with long stems) work well, while screw anchors are even better in positions which dry out. Shaped like enormous corkscrews, these are wound into the mud capstan-style by two strong men heaving a wooden pole inserted through the top eye.

Deadman

Provided a deep trench can be excavated at low tide in which to bury it, a *deadman* made from a length of old steel girder (with the chain shackled around its middle) makes a most effective anchorage, with

Plate 118 Fisherman anchor with one fluke bent down to avert fouling or damage on a mooring.

nothing protruding above the bed. The same principle is often used for securing mudberth mooring lines on mud flats and saltings. In this case, an old balk of timber or a chunk of tree trunk about 10 in (250 mm) in diameter and perhaps 5 ft (1.5 m) long, is commonly used. A long chain from this comes to the surface via a sloping trench and the mooring line is attached to that. Always backfill by treading the excavated material in thin layers.

Corrosion

In some waters, rusty second-hand chain can have a life of at least ten years, but it pays to have all underwater parts examined by a scuba diver every two years. Alternatively, use new, tested galvanized chain and lift the whole lot for inspection every ten years. The chain on a mooring which dries out may rust more rapidly than underwater parts, but regular inspection is then simpler. Fitting sacrificial anodes is said to increase mooring chain life. Zinc cubes cast around short lengths of chain are available.

Shackles

Screwed shackle pins must be moused with thick plain galvanized wire and the threads smeared with graphite grease before assembly. Avoid these if possible and use proper chain shackles with oval pins which fit fully into the chain links. Use two of these shackles back-to-back when joining two lengths of chain together. Connecting links (Fig. 45) are best for joining chains of equal size.

Stretching

The best way to lay a deep water mooring is to hire a powerful workboat, preferably with flush deck and derrick. With the chain flaked down on deck (and the bridle buoy rigged) lower the first anchor on a bight of rope so that it lies correctly. Slip the rope. Then motor in the desired direction, paying out chain slowly, until the chain is fully stretched. Having slung the second anchor on a bight of rope, motor on further while paying out the rope, then let the anchor settle and slip the rope.

Winter buoy

When a swinging mooring is out of use in winter it pays to fit a large steel buoy on a length of flexible wire rope and stow the summer buoy and rope at home. The bridle chain and swivel can also be removed to keep them in good condition. If you need to moor up to a steel buoy, keep it away from the hull by rigging a bull-rope from the buoy to the end

of a horizontal spinnaker pole firmly guyed. This is simpler when you have a bowsprit!

Lost buoy

Without a diver, it usually takes an hour or so to pick up a bridle chain should the buoy go adrift. This is a two-man job, one rowing while the other trails a grapnel (Plate 62) on a nylon line. To assist this, you should have shore transits to pinpoint the true mooring position; this also helps to confirm whether or not the ground chain has dragged after a bad storm.

Buried chain

On a sandy bed, a bridle can become deeply buried in winter. Under these conditions, some owners prefer to lift the whole mooring at laying-up time and re-lay it in the spring.

Local custom

Following local practice is always advisable when installing a mooring. For instance, three anchors are sometimes used instead of two, and the frequency of lifting chain for examination varies according to local conditions of corrosion and abrasion.

Simple stage

In its simplest form, a stage mooring consists of an almost vertical ladder held away from the bank by a catwalk and a pair of diagonal struts. This is fine provided the mooring ropes remain taut under all conditions. In tidal waters, if one line slackens, one end of the boat could slew onto the bank slope, allowing her to fill on the next tide. To obviate this, erect posts either side of the ladder (as shown in Fig. 139), sited about half the boat's length apart.

Stage pile

For a durable job, do not drive the vertical posts and ladder into the mud. Instead, drive short piles of long-lasting hardwood into the bed, protruding sufficiently above low water mark to enable each post to be bolted on. If a two-man post driving tool is used (instead of a sledge hammer or maul) you will need to use longer piles and cut them off to length after driving.

Rubbing

Any craft lying at a stage mooring needs full length rubber fendering or a rub-rail surmounted by a metal band. Failing this, heavy-duty rubber can be nailed to the vertical riding posts. Floating kites (duly padded) work fine at some locations.

Leaving her afloat

Due to high costs and scarce facilities, many big boats are doomed to stay afloat permanently, except for bottom treatments. If boat pox has started (see page 65), wintering ashore is doubly beneficial. For liveaboards, minimal rolling when moored is desirable. Home-made *flopper stoppers* work well – like vertical sea anchors each side, suspended from short athwartships booms. Big open-topped ballasted boxes with flap valves in the bottom are easy to make.

Drying wood

To ensure maximum life, all wooden craft fare best if allowed to dry out during a European or North American winter. If the planking seams show signs of opening up, this nearly always means that the boat was hauled out too early or launched too late. As mentioned previously, wooden dinghies and launches are best hosed down daily if they must be left out in hot weather.

Mudberth

Although inconvenient for maintenance work, laying up in a mudberth (Plate 27) is normally safe and is good for boats of most materials. You need four radiating wire ropes or nylon lines to make her settle into the same depression (or *wallow*) every tide. Before choosing a good high tide to move her in, it may be advisable to dig a trench in the mud to house, at least, the keel and part of the bilges. It takes a long time for a boat to create her own wallow, depending on the hardness of the mud.

Dry below

Unless properly vented, an oil or gas heater will increase condensation. Moist heat increases wood rot. A dehumidifier is ideal – mounted high enough to drain into a sink or holding tank. If freezing is a problem, arrange thermostats to switch from dehumidifier to heater. Luckily, relative humidity is usually low in freezing weather.

Insurance cover

Few boatyards carry insurance cover for laid-up vessels, so your annual premiums may be no higher for laying up afloat. Read the small print – insurance cover ashore may stipulate removal of all electronic equipment, navigational instruments and propane cylinders. Perhaps even the draining of fuel tanks.

Severe weather

Winter storms often cause havoc to boats lying afloat and it pays to use steel wire mooring lines with good anti-chafe precautions. Floating ice acts like a saw. In some locations, timber packing along the waterline is necessary, especially at bow and stern. Static surface ice is not necessarily harmful and can usually be kept at bay by installing a *bubbler*. This consists of an air compressor feeding a perforated weighted hose sunk below the boat. The rising air bubbles prevent surface ice forming.

Hauling out

As mentioned above, dry land is the best place for small craft during cold winters. An added advantage is simplified access for fitting out, when most of us have all too little time for such chores. For those with sufficient space (and agreeable folk next door) backyard storage is ideal.

Cranes

Hiring a transporter or mobile crane poses no difficulty in most districts nowadays. Boatyards generally know the best people to hire. Mobile cranes come equipped with strong nylon webbing slings, so there is no need to worry about hull protection. Most quayside cranes have only wire rope slings (see Plate 119), so when employing one of these you may need some old mattresses, and also wooden stretchers (with a notch at each end) of the correct length to hold the ropes apart and prevent them from crushing your gunwales. Keep a scale drawing of your boat's profile to help a crane operator.

Slipways

Large boatyards often have a marine railway launching ramp (Plate 5) with steel cradle, several powerful electric winches, and perhaps a turntable at the top. Small yards have greased ways with timber cradles. Each cradle consists of two planks to ride on the greased ways, and a grid of balks across these to support a boat's keel. Vertical legs braced to the balks are used to keep the boat upright. To haul out, the cradle is moved to the bottom of the ways at low tide and is weighted with iron ballast called *kentledge* to prevent it floating. At high tide the boat is moved over the cradle and winched out. Once in position, the boat is jacked up onto chocks and the cradle is dismantled.

Plate 119 When craning a narrow-beam yacht, stretchers between the strop legs are not necessary.

Raising

Craft under about 25 ft (8 m) in length may be lifted (one end at a time) by means of a long lever, little by little, enabling chocks to be slipped under the keel. For larger craft, a hydraulic jack is used in the same manner. A lever is usually about 9 ft (3 m) long, of tough sound hardwood about 3 in × 3 in (75 mm × 75 mm) at the business end, preferably tapering to a round section at the handle. Sometimes a length of thick steel tube with an outside diameter of about 2 in (50 mm) is used.

Wedges

Large timber wedges are useful when packing of exact thickness is not available. An ideal size of wedge is about 12 in (300 mm) long, 4 in (100 mm) wide, tapering from 1 in (25 mm) at one end to about ⅛ in (3 mm) at the other end. Wedges are best used in pairs (called folding wedges, as in Fig. 143) producing a flat top, and capable of exerting considerable pressure when driven towards each other with two heavy hammers.

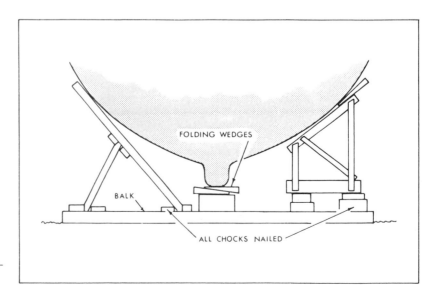

Fig. 143 Bilge squats may be improvised in various manners.

Fulcrum

A lever can only work properly when the fulcrum is in the correct spot. This requires big chocks at ground level, but always surmounted by a narrow strip of hardwood to allow the lever to rock. Keeping the fulcrum close to the keel for maximum leverage, it may be impossible to gain more than about 1½ in (38 mm) of lift at each setting. Unless the lever is kept almost horizontal, a smooth keel can slip off the end, so it pays to keep to small lifts. A team of two people is ideal for the operation.

A jack is much quicker as it requires no fulcrum.

Squats

As a boat is raised, she must be kept dead upright by means of constantly adjusted *squats* (Fig. 143) under the bilges. If she has substantial rub-rails, suitable legs may be wedged beneath these. Deep bilge keels are ideal for placing squats under. With a short keel and long overhangs, strut each end against pitching as you work on deck. Remember, after heavy rain, squats and struts can shift. Earthquake zones are another hazard!

Striking over

Once ashore, a yacht of almost any size can be moved considerable distances on wooden (or steel tube) rollers into a shed or other location for laying-up. The amateur may need to undertake some work of this nature in his own backyard. Moving a boat sideways on land is called *striking over*. Small craft weighing less than about 2 tons can be inched along by means of a crowbar or lever under the keel, while the keel slides on two athwartships balks. A jack will do the same job if angled in the direction you want to go.

Snatch blocks

To speed up the process of striking over, boatyards sometimes use greased planks under the keel and slide a boat sideways rapidly using the winch rope. A system of anchor points around the yard enables snatch blocks (turning blocks) to be positioned so that the main slipway winch will exert a pull in any desired direction. Sometimes a tractor-mounted winch is used. Without such facilities, a three-fold rope purchase will do, with a party of friends mustered to pull on the fall. Yacht blocks are of little use for this type of work – you need well-oiled, commercial steel blocks with large diameter sheaves and a 1 in (25 mm) diameter rope which is easy to catch hold of. Remember to keep a supply of beer or other suitable lubricant with which to reward your willing helpers!

Rollers

The amateur can strike over by using rollers and short planks. Rollers of scrap thick-walled steel tube with outside diameter about 3 in (75 mm) are ideal. You need two sets of rollers, arranged as in Fig. 144. The upper plank needs cleats nailed either side of the keel to prevent slipping. Pass the spare rollers and planks around as the boat moves along. Permanent squats nailed to the upper plank save the

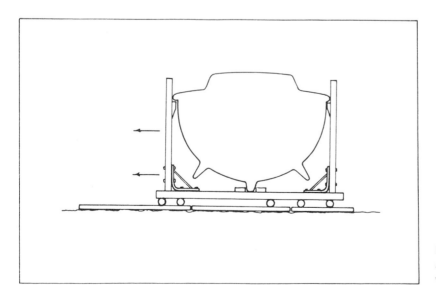

Fig. 144 Using steel tube rollers and planks to strike a boat sideways.

bother of holding the hull upright at all times.

Damage

Some old vessels are too frail to be moved about in a jerky fashion on land, especially if ballast is stowed in the bilges. Some boatyards might not worry about this but the careful owner of an antique should empty water tanks, and unship ballast, anchor and chain, (and, of course, sensitive electronic equipment) before hauling out.

Scrubbing

With the facility of a high-pressure water jetting plant (see Plate 120), bad fouling below the waterline (including much of the paint) may be blown off a sizeable hull in little more than one hour. The traditional method, even with a range of short and long-handled scrubbing brushes, takes at least four times as long. The work is less laborious if done immediately after hauling out.

Important rinse

Always finish bottom cleaning with a fresh water rinse – either from a hosepipe or by dousing, using buckets. Fresh water dries off twice as quickly as brine – and any time-saver is invaluable when painting between tides (see Plate 40). For the end of season scrub, a fresh water rinse will obviate the sweating which occurs in humid weather when traces of salt are left on the surface.

Gloves

Antifouling paint is loaded with poisonous chemicals and is not a good thing to have on your hands before eating sandwiches! Wearing gloves when scrubbing keeps the worst at bay, and helps to prevent the open wounds so easily caused by barnacle scratches. Even more detrimental to health is the dust created when dry sanding, or the smoke from burning off below the waterline. Use a paint-sprayer's nose filter, and change the pad frequently.

Barnacles

Offcuts of ⅜ in (9 mm) plywood (held as shown in Fig. 18) will remove wet barnacles almost as quickly as a steel scraper, while doing less harm to the hull. Pieces of batten, dowel wood and an old broom handle, help to reach the awkward places behind bilge keels, between rudder and sternpost, and inside waste pipe fittings. Do not scrape barnacles from a depth sounder transducer: pinch the tops off with pliers, then dissolve the remainder by repeatedly brushing on dilute spirits of salts (hydrochloric acid), or kettle fur remover (formic acid).

Boat pox

If many blisters are found on FRP (see page 251), urgent action (typically by authorized Interspray yards) may be expedient. Full treatment might cost £2800 or $5000 for a 30 ft (9 m) yacht, so do-it-yourself treatment pays if you find, say, no more than forty blisters on the bottom of this size of hull – see page 29. But it could get worse unless epoxy sealed before

Plate 120 A high pressure water jet makes short work of bottom scrubbing.

too long. Some boats are epoxied from new, even when the latest anti-pox layup resins have been used.

Bilges

There is often a delay before transferring a boat from the slipway to the shed or open yard. This is a good time to wash out the bilges, as the boat's trim will lead water rapidly to the pump well or drain plug. Various brands of bilge cleaning fluid are available from marine stores. Scrub this onto every part accessible beneath the sole boards, or under thwarts and lockers, then hose down with fresh water, working aft. Oily places beneath engines or fuel tanks may need two or three applications of bilge cleaner, rinsing after each one. Use a siphon-starter and a garden hose (but not the flat sort) to siphon bilge water to the slipway. Finish off with a syringe and sponge.

Spars and rigging

Modern materials are so durable that even if alloy spars with stainless steel rigging are unshipped at all in winter, the whole lot is frequently dumped on a rack until required again.

Undressing

The traditional system of stripping spars of all removable gear is still the best way to prevent anodized surface blemishes, to minimize theft and to ensure that every part is properly examined. The internal halyards (or in-boom reef pendants) are withdrawn with a string *messenger* attached. Failing this, when fitting out, lean the spar over and drop through a cord with a *mouse* (such as a big shackle pin) tied on. With a mast left stepped, to renew a halyard, bind a messenger to the rope tail and streamline it with Scotch tape. Yank on the wire. If the tail splice jams, cut off the wire thimble and reverse direction. A broken halyard usually means use of the bosun's chair, or getting alongside a high quay.

Internal wiring

Except for delicate windvane and anemometer mast-head equipment, radio antenna, or flux-gate master compass, most electrical parts (including wiring, spreader lights and navigation lights) are normally left in place. However, if you have a problem in this department, deal with it now. A likely instance is one or more internal cables which rattle inside a metal mast. Without internal halyards, glue foam rings along a cable, then draw it in with the mast base removed. Or, before any halyards go in, blob epoxy along the cable. With the mast level the cable will stick.

Labelling

Only on a simple sailing dinghy can you hope to remember where each rope, block or rigging screw belongs, so labels save a lot of hassle. As most parts need to be washed in soapy water and then rinsed before storing, waterproof labels are essential. Without a machine to print on self-adhesive strips, use the tie-on labels made for gardeners, plus waterproof ink.

Dirt

When dry, skeins of cordage can be hung over a pole, high in a shed roof. A sheet of polythene loosely draped over them will keep dirt and dust away. Covering coils of wire rope is important to prevent dirt from rubbing off onto sails next season. Spars need a wash after undressing, but unless kept well wrapped after that, a further brief wash is sure to be necessary before next season. There is no better way to examine a spar for defects than when washing and wiping it.

Notebook

Few defects are likely to be rectified instantly, and so notes detailing the whereabouts of broken strands of wire, damaged servings, worn clevis pins, bent shackles, chafed cordage, wobbly sheaves and similar items are essential. A stiff-covered notebook is far less likely to be mislaid than numerous scraps of paper. If you intend to keep your boat for many years, permanent notes covering the length and sizes of all ropes and wires are sure to prove their worth in the future.

Spar storage

Delicate jib headfoils are usually left on their stay and supported by the mast on its rack with suitable packing. Some foils will dismantle easily by following makers' instructions. Racing masts can buckle under their own weight if hoisted centrally and jerked. When accurately lined up, wall brackets make ideal mast supports. Rotate wooden masts monthly if lying on only two brackets, or a permanent set could result.

Oxidizing

Old spars of light alloy which were never anodized

(or where this has worn away) readily grow a patchy white patina in winter, which feels rough to the touch. Rubbing with a pad of fine bronze wool dunked in warm water and detergent usually brings the finish up like new. Coating with car wax will lessen re-oxidization, while a spray with WD40 or something similar will save a lot of time in the spring. Wash off this preservative with paint thinner before waxing.

Wood treatment

When spars are never unshipped, keeping varnished wood in good shape is laborious and sometimes dangerous. Keeping bare wood doped with teak oil or Deks Olje is much easier and looks almost equally smart. For varnishing procedure, see Chapter 4. Preferably, do the donkey work on a stored spar at laying-up time and give it one coat of varnish. Cover with loose polythene sheeting and give the final coat a few weeks before going into commission. Old wooden spars are often best painted. This lessens the work load considerably.

Checks

When putting spars into storage, examination for defects is simple. Be especially alert for cracks, buckled fittings, loose fastenings, corrosion and worn sheaves. If you have a roller reefing jib, the headfoil spar will have several pinned joints along its length, which might come adrift.

Winterization

In a cold winter climate, extra attention at laying-up time is necessary to avoid deterioration. Take off all loose and movable parts, drain water from tanks and plumbing systems, winterize engines and other mechanical equipment, clean all compartments below decks, and rig a winter cover when necessary. Extra precautions when laid-up afloat were mentioned earlier in this chapter.

Early start

Clearing all gear from a cruising yacht takes a long time; the wise owner will have started this with non-essential items some weeks beforehand. Try to avoid the temptation to leave aboard such items as spare ropes, cans of food, water breakers, dinnerware and cutlery. Some of these may be left for winter use on board, but otherwise everything should go. By taking away any parts which can be varnished or painted at home (such as locker doors, hatch covers

and washboards) valuable hours will be saved and the quality of the work is sure to be the best possible.

Water traps

Draining all water to eliminate frost damage is far from simple on a big boat. Long pipe runs need to be disconnected and blown through to force most of the water out. As mentioned in Chapter 10, pumps and toilet pans retain water, as do some waste pipes and a few unexpected places linked with engines. Remember that removing the cover-plates is often the only way to drain water from Jabsco and most semi-rotary pumps.

Engines

Engine instruction books give full lay-up details – often more suitable for several years than a few months. However, do not forget to drain water from a diesel fuel filter in case of frost. Certain hints are included in Chapter 9. The memory can play tricks, so write down everything you do. A charging set engine also needs lay-up treatment.

Minimum

In a moderate winter, sea water will not freeze so when lying afloat, little harm will accrue if an engine is just sprayed externally with WD40, turned over about four rotations every week, and run for at least ten minutes every month. An inhibitor/anti-freeze must be added to a fresh water cooling system unless completely drained.

Electrics

To minimize future breakdowns, store all electrical equipment associated with an engine in a dry place at home. It pays to label disconnected wires and leads – a small fold of masking tape will suffice, just bearing a code number which corresponds to a master list in your notebook. If you can achieve a proper seal, cocooning each part in a plastic bag containing a silica gel desiccator is the best alternative. Remember to include switch panels as well as the more obvious things such as starter, generator, magneto and distributor.

Discharge

If kept fully charged, batteries should not easily freeze, but do not top them up in icy weather. They are better ashore and can then be kept in ideal condition by a slow discharge and recharge every two weeks. For a 12 volt 60 amp-hour battery, run a 40 watt bulb for 6 hours (12 hours for 120 amp-hours). Never let the bulb lose full brightness.

Piping

The treatment for tanks and pipes was described in Chapter 9, and clearing water from pipes earlier in this chapter. If copper fuel pipes are taken ashore for annealing, the ends of any disconnected components left on board should be taped over.

Induction

Diesel pipes and pumps may be left in place and full of fuel if sprayed externally with corrosion preventative. Carburettors are best stripped and cleaned prior to storage at home. Seal the induction holes with a piece of oily rag, and do likewise when sparkplugs and injection nozzles are taken away.

Exhaust

Cooling water passes out through most exhaust systems and any lurking water should be drained away before it freezes or causes corrosion. If you run the engine briefly to dry out the exhaust, disconnect the water injection pipe first and beware of overheating a flexible pipe section. Bung the outlet securely, after inserting a pack of silica gel. This will also help to keep the cylinder head and valves dry. For preference, disconnect the manifold joint: plug a manifold and exhaust pipe separately.

Engine oil

Engine makers' recommendations vary with regard to winter oil procedure. As the oil pan is not readily removable, the prevention of sludge formation is important. The full treatment generally includes full warm-up, draining, renewal of filter, filling with flushing oil, running engine, draining again, filling with special winter inhibiting oil, running engine, and replacing with standard oil at the start of the season. As previously mentioned, rotating an engine weekly prevents valves and rings from sticking – but remember to take out any plugs of oily rag in the cylinder head apertures. Some makers also recommend flushing gearboxes and reduction gears.

Drives

If you have an antiquated boat which could flex while hauled out, slacken the propeller shaft coupling and check the alignment when back in the water. In some places, careful owners remove propellers and shafts to prevent them from being stolen. Though all steel parts may be sprayed with preservative oil, it pays to grease hand-starting gear chains and sprockets (and all the bearings) at

laying-up time. Always keep dust off such parts by covering them with rag or plastic sheeting.

Outboard lay-up

Outboard motors need a good wash with fresh water, inside the cooling system as well as outside. Some engines have a flushing plug for hose attachment on the leg. Without this, remove the propeller and run briefly with the leg submerged in a tank of fresh water, followed by thorough draining. Ear-muff type flushers are available for connecting a hosepipe to side intakes – also handy for test running. On outdrives, examine the bellows carefully for leaks.

Completion

To complete your outboard lay-up, lubricate the swivel, tilt bearings and clamp screws. Drain the gearbox and replenish. If the propeller is located on a spline, remove cotter pin and nut, pull off the propeller and thrust washer, wipe and grease the spline, then put everything back again.

Outside

Rub the whole of the casing with car wax and polish it. With the flywheel cowl off, clean the exposed parts and spray with WD40. If there is a sacrificial zinc anode beneath the horizontal cavitation plate over the propeller (Plate 85) do not wax this. If it shows bad corrosion, fit a new one. Store your outboard motor in a dry place. Give the flywheel four complete turns by hand every month, or even more frequently. If there is a battery, care for this as already described.

Hull chores

Just as a dinghy needs a good internal scrub at the end of a season, cabin craft of all constructions deserve at least a wipe over all below-deck surfaces with one of the modern 'magic' household wall and floor cleaning fluids, rinsing off according to the makers' instructions.

Lockers

When such work has been neglected, scouring powders could be necessary to revive some paintwork. Inside food lockers, add household disinfectant to the rinsing water. Locker doors (including an icebox) must be left open during the lay-up period.

Niceties

It would be nice to believe that owners launder all woven covers and curtains annually, but if such items must be left on board, spray them with Clearmold or the like to prevent mildew.

More notes

The ever-useful notebook comes into play below decks. As for other parts of the ship, keep separate pages for work that owner and crew can tackle, and jobs for the boatyard. If instructions to deal with the latter are postponed until fitting-out time, you will not be popular with the yard manager! The fussy, non-practical owner with little leisure time is certain to need professional help for tasks such as tight-fitting doors, sole boards and drawers; a bubble in the compass; repairs to radio and cooking stove; adding a metal tray inside the anchor cable locker, or lining the engine compartment with sound-deadening material.

Survey

With safety always to the fore in boatwork, it pays to have a survey taken roughly every five years, while she is hauled out ashore with loose gear removed. If the keel bolts cannot be X-rayed, withdrawing two of them for examination is always a good idea. Remember that bilge keel bolts are almost equally important. Further details of survey work are given in *Boat Repairs and Conversions*.

Blisters

The vigilant amateur should be able to spot under-water osmosis blisters on fibreglass in the early stages without professional help. The slightest surface imperfection needs examination. Except for loose paint, if piercing more than one hump produces a bead of fluid (often smelling and tasting of styrene) your boat is susceptible to ever-increasing osmosis damage, and should be epoxy-treated (see page 247) immediately.

Rudder

Wear in the rudder stock, gudgeons and pintles is not always visible until the rudder is unshipped. The cures are similar on boats of fibreglass, metal, wood, or ferrocement. Temporary repairs to stop rattling noises at night can often be made with epoxy resin or tufnol sleeving, but the matter is so important that it pays to have new parts made or the existing parts built-up to original size by specialists. A survey should reveal the need for repairs to sheathing, keelband and corroded zinc anodes.

Steering

All the time it works, steering gear is rarely given a thought. With an autopilot included, lubrication needs can be complex. Do not forget to oil or grease the sheaves and stub tiller slider on, say, a 20-footer; the worm gears on Edson steering; the rudder stock bearings, chain drives and quadrant on a 30-footer, or the bevel boxes, torque tube or tie rod swivel ends and yokes on a 40-footer.

Tarpaulins

Varnishwork suffers worse deterioration (especially on horizontal surfaces) during a few weeks of winter frost than under several months of summer sun and rain. Sheeting over as in Plate 121 is therefore essential for most yachts laid up in the open or in a shed with a leaky roof.

In shed

In a dry shed, dust covers save a lot of tedious cleaning work before launching, as other enthusiasts are certain to raise clouds of dust with power tools or spray painting equipment. Isolated roof leaks are best dealt with by suspending small tarpaulin sheets high up, sloped to funnel any drips away from your boat.

Cloth

Traditional cotton duck canvas is better than most modern tarpaulin materials as it can breathe slightly, its weight helps to keep it steady in a breeze, and condensation does not form inside it. Some plastics become very stiff in cold weather. The type reinforced with nylon mesh is cheap and serviceable. The most useful sort is translucent. The heavy grade PVC-coated nylon or Dacron woven fabric used for boom and hatch covers is more durable than cotton, but also more expensive. Windows of transparent film in such sheeting facilitate work below during bad weather.

Shape

Although standard rectangular sheets (Plate 122) may suffice, a fitted cover as in Plate 121 is easier to handle and adds to a boat's value. About 30 ft (9 m) is the longest practicable size, so use two or more sections for a big craft. Use athwartship joints with plenty of overlap, laced inside and out. Such joints are handy for opening up in fine weather. A special laced access hatch is worth its weight in gold if no join is conveniently positioned for this purpose.

Plate 121 Properly fitted tarpaulins minimize thefts as well as winter storm damage.

Measurements

When a fitted cover is to be made, erect the framework first, then take an athwartship measurement at every strut, or at intervals of not less than 6 ft 6 in (2 m). Do not forget the overall length and the locations of any windows or hatches.

Framework

Many sailboats utilize the mainmast as a ridge pole, or strongback. This does not do the mast any good, and a plank on edge (preferably rockered fore and aft, as in Plate 123) works best, especially if made in several sections fixed together with cleats and woodscrews. This simplifies erection and storage. Planking about ¾ in × 3 in (18 mm × 75 mm) will do up to about 25 ft (8 m) in length. Up to 39 ft (12 m), use 1 in × 4 in (25 mm × 100 mm) and on up to 70 ft (22 m), use 1 in × 6 in (25 mm × 150 mm). A plastic drainpipe ridge is fine – even better with tees to attach struts of thin tube.

Struts

Light but numerous struts from ridge to gunwale enable a tarpaulin to be kept taut and free from rainwater ponding. A V-notch at each bottom end will lodge over most cappings, footrails, or pierced

Plate 122 Makeshift tarpaulins can cause more harm than good unless constantly tended.

Plate 123 Successful winter covering is impossible without a well constructed framework.

alloy girders, but make sure such notches are lined with leather (see page 101), and tightened if necessary with the rubber wedges sold by hardware stores to prevent sash windows from rattling. If your guardrails cannot be unshipped, lash the struts to the top of each stanchion. Round off all timber edges generously and tie foam padding over any suspicious chafe point, such as the tabernacle.

Circulation

A ridgepole must overhang the hull at each end and the tarpaulin extend also to form ventilation openings. Some ingenious owners screw a bottomless plastic bucket beneath the ridgepole at each end and lash the cover around this to form a reliable duct. A fitted cover may have additional vents built into it, like those on a big tent. Plastic snap-on vents are made to add to any tarpaulin.

Lashings

To avoid numerous cords right under the keel, fit a guest warp around the hull close to the waterline. To save the need for passing any lines under the keel before entering a mudberth, a few small grooved chocks are sometimes screwed to the planking of a big wooden boat to support the guest warp. Once this warp is in position, any number of light lashings may be fixed to it from the tarpaulin edge. Eyelets must be exceptionally well reinforced. Shockcord

lanyards permit elasticity which will often prevent a cover from tearing around the eyelets. Excellent snap-on plastic eyelets are available for instant fitting to any type of cloth or film. These make useful emergency replacements when riveted eyelets break away. Slack or broken lanyards lead to havoc in a gale, so overhaul all ropes occasionally during the winter.

Spring commissioning

Numerous items detailed through the text of this book will be brought into play at fitting-out time, as that is when the majority of maintenance work is undertaken. In the tropics, fitting-out often goes on intermittently throughout the year, but in cold winters, fitting-out should start as soon as a boat is laid up. Job lists are invaluable. Striking off each completed item gives great satisfaction. At any time, a glance at the notes should tell whether you are heading for a mad rush shortly before launching!

Limber holes

Cleaning bilges has already been mentioned. It may take several months for these regions to dry out completely – especially with a wooden hull – so if bilge painting is due (see page 63), it should not be started too early. The limber holes (waterways) beneath frames and bulkheads may be fitted with small chain or knotted cords to free them of debris readily. Remember to unreeve these before any bilge painting is started.

Soft wood

This is a good opportunity to check for rot in wooden frames, for rust problems in steel, and for galvanic action where copper fastenings pass through steel floors. If major repairs are not warranted, deal with spongy wood by saturating it with a marine preservative made for treating wet rot.

Fungicide

A few small holes help when saturating partly concealed places with preservative. The fluid may be fed into timber in any position by using a wick. Cut this from any oil lamp wick and push it into the hole, then dangle the other end of the wick into a jar of preservative suspended close by.

Pigs

Not all yachts have their ballast fitted outside the keel. Some older types have it all stowed inside the bilges in the form of iron, lead, or concrete pigs, weighing up to 100 lb (45 kg) each. If you need to get extra pigs cast, use lead, for preference, and have a 1 in (25 mm) diameter hole cored through the middle (to take a rope for lifting purposes) if a piece weighs more than about 50 lb (25 kg).

Ballast stowage

Some pigs may be specially shaped. To ensure correct distribution it pays to number each piece with chalk and make a diagram of the layout before unshipping. Internal ballast must never shift under way. If this has been overlooked in the past, add it to the list. Stout battens screwed or bolted to the frames (and to brackets made fast to keel bolts) are generally needed. With fibreglass, special brackets or pads usually need bonding to the hull. No ballast should rest directly against a boat's skin or planking: wooden strips called *dunnage* should be used to distribute the load, and also between pigs to prevent any movement.

Storing gear

Most boatyards have a certain amount of undercover storage for their clients' boats, plus separate covered racks for masts and spars. Some clubs and yards have individually locked cabins for storing such items as mattresses, sails and ropes (see also pages 113 and 158). After washing covers and drying all

parts thoroughly, mattresses and cushions should be stood up on edge with packing beneath, all loosely covered by polythene film. Storing inflatable boats and outboard motors is described on pages 229 and 171.

At home

Much time will be saved in the spring if all movable parts on board are unshipped and taken home for overhaul or cleaning. Certainly, such items as anemometer, vane steering gear, extractor fans and all electronic equipment are safer at home. Unship all dry batteries, for even the metal-cased variety can ooze corroding chemicals when old.

Polishing

Any acid will clean the surface of dirty brass (or light alloy and chrome), but a safer expedient is to use *Amway* Metal Cleaner, which is generally available world-wide. Failing this, domestic ammonia mixed with salt does a fair job. Repeated rubbing with household brass polish on frequent changes of rag (or even better, kitchen paper) completes the process. Doping cloth tape and pulling this vigorously to and fro is ideal for the inner surfaces of door handles and cleats. Starting with fine emery tape or bronze wool may be necessary on badly pitted verdigris. If such fittings are taken home, finishing on a power buffing mop (duly coated using a stick of polishing composition) saves much hassle. Remove old lacquer with varnish stripper. For cleaning windows and portlights use Glass Plus or Ajax Window Cleaner, but do read the instructions beforehand (see also page 16).

Watchful eye

On deck, you will need to check that all fittings are tight, plunger holes in jib-sheet fairlead track clear, that a taffrail log mounting bracket is not fouled with fresh varnish and that all scuppers and cockpit drainage waterways are free from debris. Make sure you have adequate anchorages and jackstays for safety harness clips. Give all locks and hinges a drop of oil.

Desiccator

To keep the internal humidity low, many pieces of electronic equipment contain a perforated capsule of silica gel which is removed via a screwed plug at the back of the casing. When the crystals look pink, they are saturated with moisture and should be kept in a warm oven until they turn blue.

Inventory

Few owners bother to keep an inventory list of all items of loose gear, but it can have several uses, including an impressive appearance should you ever wish to sell your boat. An inventory is essential if you intend to charter at any time.

Place for everything
A list is of greater value if it itemizes the contents of each locker or drawer. This is a big help at fitting-out time and ensures that nobody stows beer cans or engine tools near to the compass, with consequent erratic deviation!

All aboard
It is a wise procedure to make three copies of your list – one to keep on board, one at home, and a rough one to tick off when items are brought aboard in the spring. When something goes missing, you will at least know that it was not left on shore.

Ideal list
The inventory in Table 10 is typical for a medium-sized cruising boat. An inventory becomes even more useful if a small plan of the accommodation is included, with the various compartments and locations numbered on both plan and list. In practice, you should leave enough space after each line to allow additions to be made as time goes on.

Safety at sea

Especially on the open sea, a certain amount of danger awaits the ill-prepared sailor. Many of the preceding chapters include notes on safety where applicable. For those who are not inherently safety conscious, the following items should not be overlooked.

Jackets
Children are rarely seen devoid of personal buoyancy aids nowadays, when on or near potentially dangerous water. Club racing rules have helped to make this standard practice for everybody, but remember to stow a few spare jackets on board a cruising boat in case guests arrive without them. Inflatable ones must be tested every year for leaks and other faults. Some will need an occasional bath to get rid of hygroscopic salt. Good jackets are costly, so stow them carefully to avoid damage.

Lifebuoys
Although ring and horseshoe buoys need little maintenance except cleaning, they must have suitable quick release mountings on deck. If the safety lights attached to them are dry-battery operated, test these frequently and renew the cells every year. With one of the lifebuoys, have a whistle and a separate float carrying a 6 ft (or 2 m) man-overboard pole. The pole needs reflective banding and a flag on top. Note that modern lightweight ring buoys will blow down-wind rapidly, so they really need to have a drogue attached. In some waters, all emergency gear needs to be equipped with shark repellent.

Flares
Remember that Very pistols and projector flares are classed as firearms and need careful stowage under lock and key. A firework display is the best opportunity to practise using flares and to test old ones prior to immediate replacement. On a night passage, clip a white flare within reach of the helmsman in case of trouble during a potential collision situation.

Beacon
Should you ever find yourself marooned far from land in a liferaft or open boat, the most useful life-saver is a radio locator distress beacon (EPIRB). This emits a continuous distress call on the emergency frequency. Some of these will float, and contain batteries with a shelf life of ten years.

Emergency pack
For deep sea cruising in safety, it pays to stow some gear and rations near the cockpit in readiness for the dreaded abandon-ship occasion, to augment liferaft equipment, or in case the tender must be used instead. You need at least survival food, sickness and vitamin pills, a flashlight, water for two weeks, some fishing gear, wire, twine and rope, a knife, can opener, bailer, money, compass, water distiller, first aid kit, blankets, towel, some flares, a radar reflector, drogue, some sort of mirror for signalling, and if possible an EPIRB.

Harnesses
As wetness and coldness can lead to inefficiency and sickness, keep a supply of foul-weather clothing and neck-towels on board in case they are needed by guests. Similarly, keep a supply of safety harnesses. Examine the stitching and lanyards on these regularly, and make sure that the snap hooks work freely and have not been strained or bent.

Table 10

Typical inventory for 30ft (9m) motorsailer

(not equipped with GPS, radar, Loran or VHF)

Compartment	Location	Inventory items
Forepeak	Sail rack	5 sails in bags
	Chain locker	30 fathoms (55m) chain
	Port bin	Sea anchor; boom awning; foul weather clothing and lifejackets; weed scrubber
	S'board bin	Black ball and cone (folded); emergency navigation lamps; spare blocks, winch and windlass handles; handybilly tackle
	On hooks	Shrimp net; spare rope; spare lifebuoy; bow fender; 2 wind scoops
	Lashed to bulkhead	2 water breakers; kedge anchor; 1 pair legs; spare oars; extinguisher
Fore cabin	On berths	2 mattresses with covers; 4 blankets in 2 bags; 2 sleeping bags; 2 cushions with covers
	Port aft drawer	Taffrail log, spare rotator and line; 3 towels
	S'board aft drawer	Fishing tackle; flashlight; all spare batteries (3 types); spare bulbs (9 types); 3 boxes of parts for radio and sounder; 20 fuses
	For'ard drawers	Keep empty for clothing
	Under sole	18 cans of beer; 6 bottles of Perrier water
	Fixtures	1 mirror; 2 portlight shades; 2 coat hooks; emergency wick lamp with smoke bell over
Hanging lockers	Port side	1 deck mop; 1 scrubber; 1 squeegee; dusting pan with brush; 1 galvanized bucket; 1 plastic bucket; 1 storm suit; 4 coat/hat hooks; 2 sets fishing rods; 4 coat hangers in covers for shore clothes
	S'board side	Spare dinghy anchor with nylon line; dinghy bilge pump; 2 fenders; anchor buoy with tripping line; 4 coat/hat hooks; 6 coat hangers in silent stowage pockets
Heads	Cabinet	2 packs toilet paper; nail brush; sponge; toothpaste; shampoo; soap; seawater soap; Kleenex; 2 towels
	On bulkheads	Sanitary bin; magazine rack; deodorizer in holder; 1 mirror; 1 coat hook; 2 towel rings; toilet paper holder; brush and disinfectant in rack; emergency wick lamp in gimbals; 2 portlight shades

Table 10

Compartment	Location	Inventory items
Galley	Drawer	4 each of: big knives and forks, dessert spoons, teaspoons, egg spoons. 6 small knives; 2 serving spoons; carving knife and fork; bread knife; fruit knife; cook's knife; potato peeler; fish slice; wooden spoon; can opener; corkscrew; bottle opener; scissors; matches
	Shaped racks	4 large plates; 6 small plates; 4 bowls; 6 mugs; 6 tumblers
	Behind stove	3 saucepans; frying pan; kettle; pressure cooker
	Behind sink	Simmering mat; toaster; cheese board; milk jug; cream jug; coffee pot; tea pot; thermos flask; bread board; detergent; sink cleanser; soap dish; soap; dish mop; scourer; swab
	Ice box	Empty except when cruising
	Top cabinet	Jars of sugar, coffee, tea, salt, pepper, mustard, butter, jam, marmalade; standard packs of honey, cooking oil, pickles, cocoa, dried milk; 2 sandwich boxes; cruet
	Bottom cabinet	Boxes for salad, cheeses, spare butter, fruit, vegetables, longlife milk, bread, cake, crackers, cereals, cookies; dehydrated and canned foods
	Sink locker	Trash bucket; 2 trays; old newspaper; disinfectant; spare soap and detergent; plastic bowl; 1 spare roll cleaning paper
	Fixtures	Emergency wick lamp; cleaning paper roll holder; 2 dish and hand towel drying rails; 1 set curtains; 1 fire extinguisher; water purifier; water heater; 1 portlight shade
Main cabin	Port settee/berth	1 mattress with cover; 2 cushions with covers; 2 sleeping bags and 2 blankets (stowed in berth foot sponson)
	Lazarette under	Signalling lamp; paint cans; spare foghorn; 2 fenders; canvas bucket; 3 cockpit seat cushions; box of flares; 6 mosquito screens
	Drawer under	Keep empty for clothing
	Shelf over	Books; medicine box; first aid manual; burgee on staff; flashlight; shackle key; marline spike; duster; ashtray; box of cleaning equipment (metal polish, furniture wax, window fluid, etc.)
	S'board berth	1 mattress with cover; 1 cushion with cover
	Lazarette under	Bosun's chair; leadline; radar reflector; courtesy flags; emergency rations; spare rowlocks; duffle bag of spare clothing

Table 10

Compartment	Location	Inventory items
	Drawer under	Keep empty
	Cave locker over	2 hanks codline; 1 roll PVC tape; sail repair kit; fire extinguisher; alarm clock; playing cards
	Locked cabinet	All liquor and wines; 6 whisky glasses; 6 wine glasses; extra flares; main and hand-bearing compasses; ship's documents; money
	Locker under steps	Engine toolbox; 2 spare V-belts; oilcan (thick oil); oilcan (light oil); box of engine spares; box of packing and spares for pumps; bosun's toolbox; rags; greases; battery water; spare log impeller, skeg and housing; bosun's storebox with shackles, slides, hanks, wire rope grips, thimbles, hose clamps, split pins, screws and bolts, marline, seizing wire, shockcord, jack knife, whipping twine; 1 small funnel; 1 medium funnel; 1 can engine oil; fender inflator
	Fixtures	Table; stove; 3 coat hooks; clock; aneroid barometer; 2 emergency wick lamps in gimbals with smoke bells; 4 sets window drapes
Wet locker	On hooks	2 sets foul-weather gear; 3 safety harnesses; 2 deck filler plate keys; 1 horseshoe life ring
	Lashed to bulkhead	Boarding ladder; 1 pair thigh boots; 2 cans diesel; 1 can kerosene
	Fixtures	6 coat/hat hooks
Navigation	Berth cave locker	Radio/DF set; barograph; books (including almanacs, tidal atlases and pilots); deviation card; ship's log; note pad; engine manual
	Behind radio	Rolled charts; sextant; deck watch
	Under table top	Charts stowed flat
	On aft bulkhead	Code flags in rack; racks for binoculars, DF attachment, hand-bearing compass; chart light
	On fore bulkhead	Emergency oil lamp; speed/distance recorder; depth sounder; handy rack for logbook and pad; racks for 2 thermos flasks, 2 mugs, 1 sandwich box
	Shelf	Ashtray; parallel rule; eraser; pencils; chart magnifier; course plotter; dividers; roll-up tape rule
Cockpit	On bulkhead	Compass mount; fire extinguisher; ashtray; racks for winch handles, binoculars, 4 mugs, sunglasses, sheath knife, marline spike, shackle key
	Port seat locker	Kedge line; 3 fenders; 1 large fuel funnel; sponge; swab; 1 bucket; ensign flag with pole; cockpit cover and ridge pole

Table 10

Compartment	Location	Inventory items
	S'board seat locker	1 can diesel; 1 water breaker; 1 can lamp oil; inflatable boat pump; 4 mooring lines; anchor windlass handle
	Port cave	Burgee; flares; foghorn; heaving line; 2 fenders; spare deck shoes and seaboots; 2 sheet winch handles
	S'board cave	4 small cushions; diving gear; 1 lifejacket; 1 safety harness; dustpan and brush; swab; leadline; towel
On deck	Port aft lazarette	2 butane cylinders in service, with regulators and changeover valve
	S'board lazarette	1 spare gas cylinder; 2 connectors for foreign cylinders; 2 nylon hawsers for towing
	After deck	1 life ring in holder, with light; man-overboard pole and dan buoy in brackets along backstay; liferaft in casing; liferaft bracket
	Cabin top	1 pair oars, 1 boathook, 1 deck mop lashed to grabrail; 1 life ring on chocks
	Fore deck	Bower anchor; gripes for tender; forehatch cover; whisker pole

Fire

Fibreglass will burn. If only for insurance purposes, all cabin boats need fire extinguishers, positioned strategically for a hasty retreat. Halon (a heavy gas) is best for engine compartments, but will tackle any class of fire. Manual operation (with heat-sensing alarms) is often better than automatic triggering. For quick repairs at sea, you need to know where a fire started. Dry chemical extinguishers are much cheaper, but very messy. Water types are bulky and not recommended for electrical or fuel fires. A gauge gives the state of readiness with Halon (and for the propelling gas in some dry chemical types) but others rely on weighing or annual reloading. A fire blanket is essential in the galley.

Gas hazard

If, in spite of the precautions detailed in Chapter 10, you accidentally release bottled gas or gasoline into the bilges, running the engine or any electrical equipment could spark off an explosion. After spillage, the procedures detailed on page 202 must be carried out before the boat is used again.

Sinking

Cruising boats have been known to sink for various unforeseen reasons. Always be prepared with an efficient routine in case the worst should happen. Some fibreglass cruisers have a complete inner lining shell, so with the loss of some locker space, it may be possible to introduce sufficient self-foaming buoyancy between the two skins to render the yacht unsinkable, as described for dinghies on page 222.

Be seen

Never venture deep-sea without having a radar reflector aloft. Hoisting at the onset of fog or nightfall is not good enough: high-speed craft do not necessarily have alert look-outs. Make sure an octahedral type measures 18 in (450 mm) across and is correctly oriented (see Plate 57) as though sitting on top of a pyramid. The cylinder type (Plate 58) is more expensive but is unlikely to get dented or harm sails and running rigging. Effective ball and cone signal shapes need to be at least 15 in (400 mm) across.

Charts

If your boat happens to be equipped with radar, do not neglect charts and basic navigation gear. Electrical circuits can fail. Chart correction is a useful winter job, though most yachtsmen have this done professionally. The average owner with limited leisure time needs few charts and would be unwise to economize by neglecting correction and occasional renewal.

Fog

For prolonged use in fog, an electric or pressurized-canister siren cannot always be relied upon. For such emergencies, a crude mouthpiece foghorn or klaxon is handy. Like aerosols, canisters are liable to lose pressure after storing for several years, and they can also freeze when in use. If you use this type, keep spare canisters and test them occasionally.

Drogues

Although drogues are standard equipment on liferafts, ship's lifeboats and deep sea cruising yachts, well-manned ocean racers hate to lose speed, relying on expert helming to avoid broaching and pitch-poling. Research (by US Coast Guard and others) has proved that a series of tiny drogues along a single line works better than the traditional type sketched in Fig. 22. Also, a heavy weight is necessary to keep a sea anchor a long way below the surface. Keep a constant watch on chafe whenever you stream a drogue.

Portlights

Big windows can break when a yacht gets caught out in foul weather. Sometimes a Plexiglass or Perspex (acrylic) pane bends enough to spring out of its rabbet. Storm shutters are ugly, but if you make these of transparent Lexan or Makrolon (polycarbonate) they can remain rigged for all deep sea work.

Scratched panes

Lexan will not craze like acrylic and is unlikely to go frosted after repeated cleaning. Scratch damage is removable only after patient buffing with metal polish. Leaks around a window may be cured temporarily with silicone sealant outside, but re-setting frame or pane in mastic is best.

Decklights

Deep prism or Fresnel decklights throw twice as much light below as plain glass and are almost unbreakable. On FRP boats a decklight is often incorporated into a low sprayproof ventilator which is easy to renew. If your opening portlights have gaskets of perished rubber, get a length of square neoprene or vinyl of correct size from your chandlery and stick this in with contact adhesive – butt-joint at the top. Failing this, get the biggest size of O-ring cord that fits in the groove, butt-joint into perfect rings with Super Glue (cyanoacrylate) and stick in with six spots of the same glue.

Index